P9-CNG-241

THE CHRISTIAN FAITH

*Nor do I seek to understand, in order that
I may believe, but I believe, in order that
I may understand. — For he who does not
believe, does not experience, and he who does
not experience, does not understand.*

—Anselm, Proslogion, 1; de fide Trin., 2.

THE
CHRISTIAN FAITH

English Translation of the Second German Edition

FRIEDRICH SCHLEIERMACHER

VOLUME II

Edited by

H. R. MACKINTOSH
and J. S. STEWART

HARPER TORCHBOOKS
The Cloister Library
HARPER & ROW, PUBLISHERS, NEW YORK AND EVANSTON

THE CHRISTIAN FAITH

Volume II

Printed in the United States of America

The English translation of this Second German edition, edited by H. R. MacKintosh and J. S. Stewart, was originally published as one volume in 1928, with second and third printings in 1948 and 1956, by T. & T. Clark, Edinburgh, and is here reprinted by arrangement.

First HARPER TORCHBOOK edition published 1963 by
Harper & Row, Publishers, Incorporated
New York and Evanston

CONTENTS

SECOND ASPECT OF THE ANTITHESIS:
EXPLICATION OF THE CONSCIOUSNESS OF GRACE
INTRODUCTION

§ 86. *The more distinctly conscious we become that the misery involved in our natural state cannot be removed either by the recognition that sin is inevitable, or by the assumption that it is decreasing of itself, the higher becomes the value we place upon Redemption.*

1. Unmistakable evidences of the consciousness of this insufficiency are to be found in almost all other religions, from the lowest to the highest. They all prescribe either sacrifices and purifications, or mortifications and penances, or both. Manifestly these are all devices for getting rid temporarily of the misery caused by sin, in the different forms which it assumes in different religions. By the degree in which this is actually effected, the more believing man is distinguished from the less believing. For, with the exception of those sacrifices which have no relation at all to evil, all sacrifices and purifications—unless we are to suppose that they come simply from an utterly confused superstition—are based upon the conviction that both the admissions referred to in the proposition need to be accompanied by an acknowledgment in the form of an act, it may be only a symbolical act, in order to get rid of the misery. But in a teleological religion this is not permissible. Such a religion sets down as a fact the ineffectiveness of the God-consciousness itself, and so finds here only a contradiction from which no effect can proceed; all that can be done is to admit the state of sin.[1] Mortifications and arbitrary exercises are less symbolical, and have in a greater degree a real content; their purpose everywhere doubtless is to exhibit power over the flesh by means of actions the demand for which does not arise of itself in the ordinary course of life; to supplement, that is, in some way the imperfect manifestation of this power in the demands which life makes of itself. This would be superfluous if the inevitableness of sin itself sufficiently gave peace of mind. Moreover, the wildest superstition

[1] That this is the sense of Heb. 10¹⁻³ is not open to doubt.

reveals itself wherever these exercises are not so treated as to correspond to the given situation.   But since in the life of any society demands are evolved every moment which it is our duty to fulfil, these arbitrary supplementary activities, by taking up time, inevitably prevent the full performance of duty.   Thus through the very activities which are supposed to get rid of the misery, new misery is created.

But, even quite apart from the question whether performances of both kinds are not usually designed rather to avert punishment than to remove guilt, their futility as means to peace of mind is obvious.   Hence every unsatisfied longing which still remains in spite of them is the expression of an inclination towards Christianity; it indicates the likelihood that a Redeemer, in whom is offered not the shadow but the reality, will be accepted.

2. Let us now consider the religious consciousness of the Christian.   It is composed of the consciousness of sin which we have expounded above, and the consciousness of grace which we have still to expound but which we assume to be familiar.   In it, too, we find both elements.   First, the recognition that sin is inevitable for us, in so far at least as that it is not in our power at any particular moment to be sinless.   But no less, the assumption that it is growing less, since this is essentially involved in the consciousness that the strength of our God-consciousness is growing greater. But in spite of this connexion these two elements belong not to the consciousness of grace, or that by which the misery is taken away, but on the contrary to the consciousness of sin, or to the misery itself.   For to be conscious that the disappearance of sin is a thing of the future is the same thing as to have it still actually present ; and, more completely still, the consciousness of its inevitableness is also that of its power over us.   Both therefore indicate our need of redemption, and so cannot carry in themselves the removal of the misery—that would require that it should be established and provable in some special way that the consciousness of sin can be taken away by means of itself.

Let us suppose, on the other hand, that the misery has been removed from some other side ; and add, further, that even the consciousness that sin must inevitably remain while it is gradually disappearing does not hinder the removal of the misery : just on that account the worth of the removal is the greater.   But this can be rightly recognized only if we consider both elements in the natural condition of man as he shares in the corporate life of sin.

In this condition the opinion that sin, because inevitable, does not involve guilt or deserve punishment cannot be derived from the God-consciousness ; rather would this have first to be destroyed, that is, the consciousness that God is holy and righteous would have to be rooted out—which would be a new guilt.　Just as little can we deduce the absence of guilt and of liability to punishment by asserting that the future already exists in the present, the disappearance of sin in its continuance.　For if we are to go beyond the present content of our self-consciousness, we are just as much entitled, indeed we are equally constrained, to say that our present consciousness will be continued in our future consciousness, and with it the misery.　So we are bound to maintain that all such statements as that God forgives sin because it is inevitable, if only it is decreasing, can never establish that removal of the misery of which they would persuade us.　They always come back to a forgiveness of sin, arbitrarily, by ourselves ; and, at best, they are a recourse to the divine compassion,[1] but without first positing redemption, and so also without reconciling compassion with righteousness.　For even if we admit that in the natural state there does occur an increase in the strength of the God-consciousness, even if it is only in so far as it co-operates in the effort after civil righteousness :[2] it must result from this that the more sin decreases the sharper becomes the feeling for right and wrong.　Consequently no increasing satisfaction arises—which is the only thing which could legitimately offer any guarantee for the removal of the misery.　And here it is to be observed that those who think to remove the misery in this way, without redemption, are least in agreement on the question whether human life on the whole is developing towards a greater perfection (so that brutality, where it has once been overcome, does not return), or whether the race is destined, partially, by whatever revolutions it may be, to be continually thrown back, to begin its career all over again.

3. If, nevertheless, such presentations of the forgiveness of sins secure acceptance as Christian, what is specifically Christian must have been long since, and in many quarters, displaced, before conceptions so little Christian could creep in ; or it must have been supposed that the effectiveness of redemption begins only after the misery has already been removed.　But this is the less arguable inasmuch as peace of mind presupposes a decrease of sin, and consequently an increase of activity pleasing to God.　So that to exhibit

[1] Cf. § 85, 2.　　　　　　　　　　　　[2] Cf. § 70, 2 and 3.

this, and to evoke it, would then be no part of the Redeemer's work. Yet it is possible, on the other hand, that even a truly Christian piety may have come to regard this matter in so unchristian an aspect only because it wished to oppose false conceptions of the way in which the misery is removed by redemption, by setting forth another explanation, which at least makes room for the fact that the activity of the God-consciousness, out of which the decrease of sin arises, is determined by the Redeemer. Coming nearest to this false peace, and therefore attributing the lowest imaginable value to redemption, is the view that an increasing activity of the God-consciousness is possible without any special divine help, developing simply out of the natural state of man ; but that, in spite of the inevitableness of sin, sinners would have no right to be at peace regarding the sin still remaining without a special divine assurance about it—so that in essence the Redeemer is represented only as the herald of this divine promise. It does not need to be stated how little historical justification there is for this view in the Christian Church ; it need only be remarked how little reason can be advanced for the demand that we should believe in one who does no more than announce forgiveness, and how difficult it is to understand why such an assurance should have been given only after so long a time and in such a way. From this lowest value on, the felt content of redemption grows the greater, the greater the share attributed to the Redeemer in the cessation of the misery as well as in the rise of what approximates state of blessedness.

§ 87. *We are conscious of all approximations to the state of blessedness which occur in the Christian life as being grounded in a new divinely-effected corporate life, which works in opposition to the corporate life of sin and the misery which develops in it.*

1. This proposition is not to be regarded as a complete statement of specifically Christian piety, since in it no mention is made of the fact that every approximation to the state of blessedness essentially includes a relation to Christ. But it does undeniably express the content of the consciousness of divine grace, as it stands in antithesis to the consciousness of sin. For approximation to the condition of blessedness is the real opposite of the misery, and this approximation is accepted as divine grace in the same sense and degree in which the corporate life in which such elements of experience become ours is posited as due to divine agency.

Consequently all further exposition of what is specifically Christian can easily be attached to this proposition. The relation between approximation to blessedness and removal of misery may, it is true, be presented in a twofold way. First, it may be held that not the slightest approximation to blessedness can occur so long as there is even the slightest misery present, which is as much as to say, so long as sin, and with it evil (or *vice versa*), still occurs in the sphere of human life. This is the view of those who choose to regard the world, even under the influence of redemption, as nothing but a vale of woe ; fortunately they never work out their view consistently. This view, according to which (if we take it strictly) all the effects of redemption can be developed only beyond this present life, will not be advocated here, as is at once clear from the wording of the proposition, in which the beginning of blessedness is attributed to the new corporate life simply in virtue of its opposition to the corporate life of sin—the latter still persisting in the sphere of its activity. But further, that conception does not express the truth of the Christian consciousness as it has been witnessed to from the beginning.[1] Rather, there is always in the God-consciousness, whatever its strength, a blessedness corresponding to that strength ; and even in its beginnings this blessedness removes the misery, though, of course, this can arise again with sin, but only to be again removed.[2] So that we can completely equate the two aspects, and say that the same condition is the removal of misery (when we regard man in his relation to the corporate life of sin), and the beginning of blessedness (so far as he belongs to the new corporate life).

2. In indicating only in a quite general way the place of these approximations in the Christian life we wish to begin with to forestall all one-sided conceptions, which suggest that such approximations can only occur in the form of particular activities or states, and that they are confined, say, to the moments of devotional meditation or ascetic practices. On the contrary, there is an element of blessedness in moments of meditation only when they pass over into thought or act, and in ascetic practices only in so far as they are not properly, or at least not exclusively, ascetic, but are in some way connected with our ordinary vocational activity. The element of blessedness exists just as much in moments of activity proper and of thought proper, though in the former only in so far as they do not proceed from such motives as have their roots altogether

[1] John 1[16], 1 John 3[14, 21], Phil. 4[4].   [2] Cf. § 74, 1.

in the world-consciousness or in such as satisfy mere civil righteousness ; and similarly, it is not present in the latter in so far as they
merely develop the world-consciousness : but in both only in so far
as they have their ground in the God-consciousness, newly awakened
to life.   Without this the religious man cannot experience a growing
blessedness.

3. If now anyone maintains that our proposition, taken by itself,
really applies equally well to all forms of faith, provided only they
involve a fellowship, this is true only in so far as thereby there is
laid upon them the duty of proving that their corporate life is due
to divine agency.   But this by no means assumes that there is a
difference between the growing blessedness which then began to develop in the Christian fellowship and that which proceeded directly
from Christ Himself.   We shall come immediately to the point that
to regard our corporate life as divinely-created, and to derive it
from Christ as a divinely-given One, are the same thing ; just so, at
that time, to believe that Jesus was the Christ, and to believe that
the Kingdom of God (that is, the new corporate life which was to be
created by God) had come, were the same thing.   Consequently, all
developing blessedness had its ground in this corporate life.   Just as
little can one regard it as an approximation to the Roman Catholic
point of view, that this change in the personal state should be
ascribed directly to the common or corporate life.   We cannot as yet
bring out here its real antagonism to the Roman Catholic view ;
that must wait until we come to describe more closely, on the one
hand, the process in detail ; on the other, the nature of the community.   And so the proposition as such is one which applies equally
to the most various conceptions of Christianity.   Two things only
it excludes.   First, the idea that one can share in the redemption
and be made blessed through Christ outside the corporate life which
He instituted, as if a Christian could dispense with the latter and
be with Christ, as it were, alone.   This separatism disregards the
fact that what owes its origin to divine agency can nevertheless
be received only as it appears in history, and also can continue to
function only as a historical entity.   We can therefore only describe
it as fanatical ; it can, in self-consistency, only arise sporadically,
and so must also continually disappear again.   It destroys the
essence of Christianity by postulating an activity of Christ which is
not mediated in time and space ; and at the same time it so isolates
itself that what has been achieved in it can have no continuing
influence.   The second thing excluded is the supposition that,

without the introduction of any new factor, and within the corporate life of sin itself, the better individuals could attain to such an approximation to blessedness as would remove the misery. If this idea be taken strictly, then either another purpose must be assumed for the appearance of Christ, quite apart from the blessedness of man (in which case this would, at any rate, not be a religious purpose) ; or it would have no specific purpose at all (in which case it would be wrong to name anything after Christ). From our standpoint, the only verdict of the Christian consciousness on this supposition must be that it is based upon an inadequate consciousness of sin. For if sin be posited as corporate act and corporate guilt, then, not only is every activity of the individual involved in the production and renewal of sin, however strong an opposition to individual sins it may include, but also every combination even of the relatively best individuals remains only an organization within the corporate life of sin itself. On the other hand, if the supposition is not to be taken strictly, then it may be Christian in the measure in which it regards Christ as a new factor in the situation, and the corporate life as one formed out of the corporate life of sin.

§ 88. *In this corporate life which goes back to the influence of Jesus, redemption is effected by Him through the communication of His sinless perfection.*

1. At the present time it cannot be maintained that this way of understanding redemption is the only one which is current in the Protestant Church. And we by no means wish to refuse to recognize as Protestant Christians those who do not accept the idea of such a communication, provided only that they trace every approximation to blessedness back to Christ, and seek to find it in a fellowship which makes it a principle that, for redemption, nothing need be sought beyond His influence, and also that nothing in that influence is to be neglected. We, however, hold to this conception as the original one, taken over from the primitive Church into our Church, and at the same time as that which most definitely excludes all sneaking complacence, and alone consorts with the stricter interpretation of the corporate life of sinfulness, as may be clearly seen from what immediately precedes. The two things hang together in the closest way. The less specific and absolute perfection we ascribe to the Founder of the new corporate life, while at the same time expecting nothing new that goes beyond Him, the easier must it seem to us to overcome what demanded of Him no greater equipment.

And the less importance we attach to what proceeds from the natural state of man, the less occasion there is to postulate anything specifically different in Him who inaugurates the better state. For the development of the one view—and this is all that is required of a system of doctrine, for that the view should become more generally accepted can be only the result of its presentation—does not require that the other should be refuted, but only that the relation which exists between them should be clearly set forth again at its most significant points. Just as little can there be any question here of proofs in the proper sense. Not, of course, because Protestant theology, as an undertaking within the Protestant Church, itself presupposes the Protestant faith, but because no single modification of it is capable of proof ; it is simply a statement with regard to the stronger or weaker impression which one fact makes in comparison with another. Examples of such differences occur everywhere in the field of history, and always so that it is possible for everyone to be firmly convinced that his impression is the right one, while yet no one can prove its rightness.

2. We set aside, then, all thought of proof. Even of proof from Scripture—not only because of the ambiguity of most of its statements, but because in that way we could prove only the assertion that this is the original form of the Christian faith. Even so, what we must not omit here remains difficult enough ; and that is, to unfold the way in which this faith originated, along with its content. That is, we must show, without recourse to compulsion by means of miracle or prophecy (which is a thing alien to faith), how the conviction could arise, both originally and now, that Jesus possessed a sinless perfection, and that there is a communication of this perfection in the fellowship founded by Him. For it is obvious that in the certainty regarding these two points (and certainty about the one involves a related and parallel certainty about the other), there is removal of the misery and growing blessedness. First, then, our proposition is by no means to be understood as asserting that at a time when the consciousness of sin was powerfully aroused, both as a personal and as a corporate consciousness, in many minds, it was only necessary that an exceptional moral excellence should be adequately manifested in a public life, for the sinless perfection longed for as the only possible help to be attributed to such an individual—a view which might be expressed by saying that it was faith that made Jesus the Redeemer. For in such faith the arbitrary decision of the believer would have become

more marked on every transference of it, since it would not have been supported by the original impression made by His person ; and consequently the certainty would have become less. Gradually the thought would more and more have gained ground that another might come, to whom that conception might be transferred with better right.   So that in this way there could only arise a decreasing faith in Jesus, and thus an increasing unbelief.   And the only remedy for this would be, that the immediate impression made by the community should be such that sinless perfection could be claimed for it, and then, for its sake, for its founder also. It would not be enough even, that the pure and perfect potency of the God-consciousness should have been actually present in Jesus, but faith in it nevertheless only the work of that longing, eager for satisfaction.   For even so He would have been made Redeemer by believers.[1]   On the contrary, our proposition depends upon the assumption that the very recognition of that perfection was its own work, so that it is just as possible that in some persons the full consciousness of sin and the longing which goes with it are first aroused by means of that recognition,[2] as that in others they are already present.   It is only in this way, too, that we can regard the founding of the new corporate life as something more than a special act, without which that exceptional peculiarity could still have existed in Jesus.   Rather, just as the latter could have been manifested only in act, so the former is its essential work.

If, however, the faith of the later generations, and consequently of our own, is to be the same as the original one and not a different faith—and in the latter case, not only would the unity of the Christian Church be imperilled, but also all references to the original testimonies of the faith—then it must still be possible to have the same experiences ;   and the recognition of the sinless perfection in Jesus Christ, definitely constraining us to the new corporate life, must in the same way be still His work.   But there is given to us, instead of His personal influence, only that of His fellowship, in so far as even the picture of Him which is found in the Bible also originated in the community and is perpetuated in it.   Our proposition, therefore, depends upon the assumption that this influence of the fellowship in producing a like faith is none other than the influence of the personal perfection of Jesus Himself.[3]

3. It is no less difficult to expound the second part of our

---

[1] Contrary to the claim of Christ, John 15[16].
[2] Cf. § 14, 2.   [3] Cf. § 14, 1.

proposition, namely, that in the corporate life founded by Christ
there is a communication of His sinless perfection ; while we attribute this to no single individual in the fellowship except Christ.
For, since those who companied with Christ are no longer with us,
and we cannot concede to any group of individuals, however well
they may have been selected to complement each other, the right
to lay down dogmas, that is, rules of faith or life, with any claim
whatsoever to infallibility or enduring validity ; since, on the
contrary, our historical interpretation is based upon the view that
the influence of distinguished individuals upon the mass is to be
thought of as declining : where and of what sort are we to suppose
this communication to be ?   If we regard the mass as a whole,
it manifestly shares so largely in the general sinfulness, and this at
certain times so saliently and in such specially heightened measure,
that it is doubtful whether there is less of this sinfulness at any one
point rather than another, and whether it might not therefore have
been better for the shaping of human affairs if Christianity had not
become such a widely spread historical force.   Against these objections, brought forward with much plausibility by its opponents,
faith alone can prevail ; it must consequently assume that all this
represents only the non-existence of the new corporate life, and
so the existence of the sinful life in which the new really exists but
only in hidden fashion.   Thus our proposition depends upon the
assumption that in the Christian fellowship, outwardly so constituted, there is still that communication of the absolutely potent
God-consciousness in Christ as a thing which is inward, and yet,
since faith can rest upon nothing except an impression received,
capable of being experienced.   This experience is made up of two
elements, one of which belongs to the personal consciousness, the
other to the common consciousness. The former is that the individual
even to-day receives from the picture of Christ, which exists in the
community as at once a corporate act and a corporate possession,
the impression of the sinless perfection of Jesus, which becomes for
him at the same time the perfect consciousness of sin and the removal
of the misery.   And this is already in itself a communication of
that perfection.   The second element is that in all those aberrations of the Christian Church, however much they may resemble
the sinful corporate life, there is still a tendency issuing from that
perfection ; a tendency which in every manifestation—nay, constantly even in the setting up of the concepts of truth and goodness
—falls more or less a prey to non-existence, but which in its deepest

inwardness, or as an impulse, corresponds to its origin, and consequently, in spite of all reactions, will also increasingly make
itself manifest.   And this impulse given by His historical life, an
impulse which, regarded from within, is perfectly pure, is, just like
the first element, a true and effective communication of the perfection of Christ.

4. In the corporate life of sinfulness sin propagates itself naturally, so that an unhindered potency of the God-consciousness in
Jesus cannot be understood simply as a product of that life.   This
God-consciousness, manifesting itself in this potency, can have
come into existence only outside the sinful corporate life.   And
since the whole human race is included in this sinful corporate life,
we must believe that this God-consciousness had a supernatural
origin, though only in the sense which has been postulated above.[1]
So, too, in relation to the Redeemer Himself, the new corporate life
is no miracle, but simply the supernatural becoming natural, since
every exceptional force attracts mass to itself and holds it fast.
But in relation to the corporate life of sinfulness, which hitherto had
included everything and dominated every formation, the new is
something that has come into being supernaturally.   The same is true
of the passage of every individual from the old corporate life into
the new.   In relation to the new creation itself such a passage is
not supernatural ; such effects follow as of course from its nature.
But it is something which has come about supernaturally, so far as
its relation to the earlier life of this individual is concerned.

To sum up : in this whole matter we posit, on the one side, an
initial divine activity which is supernatural, but at the same time
a vital human receptivity in virtue of which alone that supernatural
can become a natural fact of history.   This is the link which connects
the corporate life before the appearance of the Redeemer with that
which exists in the fellowship with the Redeemer, so as adequately to
bring out the identity of human nature in both.   And so, in this
whole context, the appearance of the Redeemer in the midst of this
natural development is no longer a supernatural emergence of a
new stage of development, but simply one conditioned by that
which precedes—though certainly its connexion with the former
is to be found only in the unity of the divine thought.

§ 89. *In the sense in which it can be said that sin is not ordained by*
    God and does not exist for Him,[2] *the term Redemption would*

[1] Cf. § 13, 1.   [2] Cf. § 81.

not be suitable for this new communication of a powerful
God-consciousness. And so from that point of view the
appearance of Christ and the institution of this new corporate
life would have to be regarded as the completion, only now
accomplished, of the creation of human nature.

1. It requires no further explanation, that the conception of redemption is related in the closest way to the consciousness of sin, and that when it is used as an expression for the complete work of Christ, there is included along with the removal of the misery, which alone is properly described as redemption, a growing blessedness as well. For that reason alone the expression is inadequate, and an unsuitable one in this respect, that a word is used for the whole (the imparting of blessedness) which properly applies only to the beginning of it. But there is no objection to its use if this is understood. For it is certain that in our Christian consciousness the divine grace as such is always thought of in connexion with sin ; while sin itself is always conceived of as including our inability to do what our God-consciousness requires us to strive after. So nothing in the divine grace is overlooked if it is described as the removal of sin, in so far as sin is that inability. But if the expression is to be used not only for the effect, but also for the purpose, of the appearance of Christ, in so far as that appearance is ordained of God, then, since we cannot separate it from its connexion with sin and the consciousness of sin, this is only possible in so far as we can regard the consciousness of sin as ordained of God. How far this is possible has already [1] been explained, but it now becomes clearer —God has ordained that the earlier insuperable impotence of the God-consciousness shall become for us, as our own act, the consciousness of sin, in order to intensify that longing without which even the endowment possessed by Jesus would have met with no living faculty for the reception of what He communicates. But, on the other hand, that God is not the creator of sin is, not only strictly true, but also the definite teaching of the Church. The ground for this assertion is best expressed in the formula that evil cannot be a creative thought of God. It follows that the term redemption is not so suitable to describe the divine decree as it is to describe the effect of the decree, for the Almighty cannot ordain one thing for the sake of another which He has not ordained. From this standpoint, which is also that of the Church, no better expression

[1] Cf. § 80.

apparently can be found for the divine decree than a Biblical one which at the same time indicates the effect as a whole.   As everything which has been brought into human life through Christ is presented as a new creation,[1] so Christ Himself is the Second Adam, the beginner and originator of this more perfect human life, or the completion of the creation of man.   This at the same time indicates in the most definite way that it was impossible to attain to this higher life out of the natural order which had its beginning in Adam.

2. That this formula is exactly equivalent in meaning to the first, and attributes to Jesus, as the One in whom the human creation is perfected, the same peculiar dignity and character as does the other when it is fully understood, need not be set forth at length. For this Second Adam is altogether like all those who are descended from the first, only that from the outset He has an absolutely potent God-consciousness.   With this He enters the existing historical order of human nature, in virtue of a creative divine causality.   It follows that, according to the law of this order, His higher perfection must work in a stimulating and communicative way upon the nature which is like His own, in the first place to bring to perfection the consciousness of sinfulness by contrast with itself, and then also to remove the misery, by assimilation to itself.   Now this Second Adam, though He does not belong to the former order, but in relation to it has come into being supernaturally, is yet placed in the historical order, and that too as an individual man.   So in His whole activity He stands under the law of historical development, and that activity is brought to perfection through gradual expansion, from the point at which He appears, over the whole.

That in this way the creation of man is, as it were, divided into two stages has analogies enough in history,[2] and also it has always been asserted of the material creation whenever the distinction has been made between a first and a second creation.   At the same time this formula serves as a corrective to the confusions which arise only too easily from improper use of the others.   How easily the view recurs which was already attacked by Paul,[3] that sin is wholesome, if it is true that it was on account of sin that Christ had to be sent, and so the imparting of blessedness depends upon sin !   Moreover, when considered more closely, this formula is a more precise and direct expression of our Christian self-consciousness than the first.   For to begin with, certainly the most exact term for the

---

[1] 2 Cor. 5[17].   [2] Here too, belongs what has been said above, § 13, 1.
[3] Rom. 6[1].

condition outside fellowship with Christ is consciousness of sin and of need of redemption, inasmuch as and so far as this too is ordained by God. But in fellowship with Christ everything which belongs to a sinfulness no longer productive, is also, just for that reason, no longer in the same sense a consciousness of sin, because it is no longer a being fleshly-minded, but simply an incapacity for what has only just come to be ; and the consciousness of the Redeemer is the consciousness of One who makes us strong.[1]

3. But in the case of this expression also the demand certainly cannot be set aside that here again the conception of creation must be referred back to that of preservation. Not only is the man Jesus called the Second Adam, which can only mean the second Created One, but also all those born again are called the new creation, and thus that is represented as a creation which, quite correctly, we describe as originally a preservation, that is, as a preservation of the ever-prevailing power of Christ for redemption and blessing : but conversely, the appearance of Christ Himself is to be regarded as a preservation, that is, as a preservation of the receptivity, implanted in human nature from the beginning and perpetually developing further, which enables it to take into itself such an absolute potency of the God-consciousness. For although at the first creation of the human race only the imperfect state of human nature was manifested, yet eternally the appearance of the Redeemer was already involved in that. So that, in whatever sense its fulfilment has to be conceived, the unity of the divine decree comes out with equal clearness whether we say that God ordained sin for men relatively to redemption, or that He put human nature under the law of earthly existence in the sense that, just as the sensuous self-consciousness developed first in each individual, while the God-consciousness came only later, and up to a point gradually took possession of the sensuous self-consciousness and subjugated it, so too the God-consciousness in the race to begin with was inadequate and impotent, and only later broke forth in perfection in Christ, from whom it continually extends its authority, and proves its power to bring peace and blessedness to men.

Further, from this standpoint the relation of Christ to those who lived before His appearance, or who are separated by distance from the corporate life inspired by Him—always an important question for Christian thought—becomes clearer. If the first stage in creation is ordained by God only in view of the second, obviously the

[1] Phil. 4[13].

same must be true of everything that forms part of the same natural order with it. Accordingly, in the ordaining view of God everything which belongs to the first period of the world must have a share in the relation to the Redeemer. At the same time it appears the more natural that this otherwise hidden relation should become specially evident at particular points, which is just the assumption that prompts a search for types and prophecies.

§ 90. *The propositions which work out, according to the three points of view given in § 30, the content of the consciousness of grace here presented, also complete the system of Christian doctrine within the limits here prescribed for it.*

1. In elaborating, in what follows, this content, we shall hold to these three forms. In itself, there is no objection to the first and original one, and it is obvious that with a method of procedure which is in any degree correct nothing of any significance in Christian doctrine can escape our notice. But it is difficult to see how we are to distinguish between the first, or the direct description of the gracious state of the redeemed, and the second, or the description of what has come into the world through redemption. For this last is simply the corporate life founded by Christ and its relation to that part of the world of men which finds itself excluded therefrom. The gracious state of the redeemed, again, is simply their activity just in this corporate life and the way in which they are affected by the opposition which still exists to it ; so that the two spheres seem to be exactly the same. Connected with this is the fact that here it is less clear that the description of the state must come first. For, on the one hand, it is only out of this new corporate life that the communication of the divine grace comes to each individual, and so it seems necessary that this should be recognized first. Yet, on the other hand, the corporate life is made up of the redeemed as such, and it seems impossible to understand if we have not first considered the peculiar quality of these. None the less both difficulties disappear at once when we come to look into the matter more closely. It is true that the corporate life consists solely of redeemed individuals, but it has its significance for the world only through its organization. Considered as an organization it belongs to the second form of presentation. The state of the individuals as such, on the other hand, as contrasted with their state in the corporate life of sinfulness, is to be worked out rather from the first standpoint. And if in doing so we must in a certain

sense presuppose acquaintance with the corporate life, yet it is not a dogmatic knowledge of it.   Nor indeed can it be maintained that such acquaintance is really presupposed, since that state of grace was called into being, along with the corporate life, or indeed before it, by the first proclamation of the Gospel.   Thus both methods of presentation are possible, and can be kept apart, even though mutual relations between them are inevitable.

2. Finally, as regards the divine attributes which are to be dealt with in the last section, it would be a very strong objection to the propriety of our whole disposition of the subject if, after we had completed the argument, there still remained divine attributes which represent a factor in our Christian self-consciousness, yet can be definitely distinguished from those with which we have been dealing. So for the present we refuse to admit this, and on the contrary regard it as a good sign that we have reduced the large number of indefinite terms denoting attributes to a smaller number of clear formulæ, and also have definitely excluded all that is merely speculative. The event must show whether we have really done this.   But here we have not only to supply what before was lacking, but also, as we have remarked above,[1] to give their full content (since we are only now for the first time moving in the sphere of the potent God-consciousness) to all those manifestations of the feeling of absolute dependence which could only be indefinitely described in the first part.   For in Christianity it is only relatively to the Kingdom of God that we are conscious of the divine omnipotence and eternity, as well as of the attributes which depend upon them.   It is another question whether in fact the whole doctrine of God which answers to the Christian faith can be dealt with simply by an enumeration of the divine attributes, and whether we ought not rather in addition to set forth the significance of the divine decrees.   But this question arises only if we take cognizance of other treatments of Christian doctrine.   For a proposition indicative of a divine decree is not as such an expression of the immediate self-consciousness.   But if we can bring rightly and completely into consciousness what has come into the world through redemption, then we shall thereby have given the content of the divine decrees also.

[1] § 29, 1 and p. 272.

FIRST SECTION

THE STATE OF THE CHRISTIAN AS CONSCIOUS OF THE DIVINE GRACE

§ 91. *We have fellowship with God* [1] *only in a living fellowship with the Redeemer, such that in it His absolutely sinless perfection and blessedness represent a free spontaneous activity, while the recipient's need of redemption represents a free assimilative receptivity.*

1. This is the basic consciousness that each Christian has of his own state of grace, even where the most dissimilar views of Christianity prevail. The consciousness of one who in no degree relates the potency of the God-consciousness which he finds in himself to Jesus is not Christian at all; while, if he does so relate it, but without in any degree recognizing the contrast noted in our proposition, then, since he finds in himself, not merely no sin, but not even imperfection, and is altogether spontaneous and independent in his activity, he must have left the state of grace behind him, and have himself become a Christ. If, on the other hand, a man relates his state, as touching fellowship with God, to Jesus, but without finding in himself any living receptivity for Him, then he certainly believes in Christ in so far as he assumes Him to possess a saving influence, but as yet he does not find himself a recipient of grace, for he cannot have experienced any change through Christ. For there can be no change in a living being without his own activity; hence, without such activity—that is, in a purely passive way—no influence exerted by another can really be received. Or again, if a man's own activity were one of opposition, if it were simply resistance, then the grace would necessarily have been imparted against his will, that is, by compulsion, and so would not be blessedness. Thus all real vital fellowship with Christ, in which He is in any sense taken as Redeemer, depends on the fact that living receptivity for His influence is *already* present, and *continues* to be present. And this holds true equally for every moment and

[1] Cf. § 63.

degree ; for, once arrived at the limit, the connexion would necessarily break off of itself.

But it cannot be denied that our proposition leaves plenty of scope for the most various interpretations of this relationship, provided they all keep within the limits laid down. One man may regard the relationship as absolutely the same at all moments, so that all the influences already felt in no way alter its character ; another may believe that in the recipient of grace there gradually arises a co-operative self-activity, so that the new Ego considered in its self-identity is a self-active entity and more and more develops itself in that character, and only the person as such, considered as the subject of change, is the seat of pure receptivity ; for which reason he is conscious of the potency of the God-consciousness as something constantly his own, though of course derived from Christ. Indeed, if we go back to the distinction between the personal self-consciousness and the common consciousness and accept our proposition as expressing the common Christian consciousness, but add that every adult Christian can and ought to be conscious of himself personally as free and self-active in the Kingdom of God, while at the same time he has only become such within the corporate life whose consciousness is rightly defined in our proposition—this view also would lie within the limits stated. But, of course, these views are not all equally current in the Church.

2. If then a statement such as we have given is equally valid for all elements, however widely they may differ, within the corporate life founded by Christ, it indicates only one possible division of our subject-matter. We must first explain how in virtue of this consciousness we conceive the Redeemer, next how we conceive the redeemed. The order fixes itself, for whatever in the state of the Christian contrasts with his former state in the fellowship of sinfulness can only be explained by the influence of the Redeemer. Hence the content of this section falls into two divisions. To the first belong all propositions concerning Christ which are immediate expressions of our Christian self-consciousness. If any teaching concerning Christ is given in other treatments of Protestant doctrine, but not here, that omission is not an arbitrary judgment on our part but sure internal evidence that such teaching is lacking in purely dogmatic content, and for that reason possessed only of a subordinate explanatory or subsidiary value (for if it *could* have come in under our plan, it would assuredly by our method

have found a place for itself).   The second division must contain all propositions which directly describe the relation of grace to sinfulness in the human soul, and this as mediated by the entrance of the Redeemer.   This division was, above,[1] marked off from the second section ; accordingly, we must include here everything by means of which the individual obtains and takes a share in the Christian fellowship—only, however, so far as it is regarded as his personal quality or mode of action.

[1] § 90, 1.

§ 92. *The peculiar activity and the exclusive dignity of the Redeemer imply each other, and are inseparably one in the self-consciousness of believers.*

1. Whether we prefer to call Christ the Redeemer, or to regard Him as the one in Whom the creation of human nature, which up to this point had existed only in a provisional state, was perfected, each of these points of view means only that we ascribe to Him a peculiar activity, and that in connexion with a peculiar spiritual content of His person.   For if His influence is only of the same kind as that of others, even if it is ever so much more complete and inclusive, then its result also, that is, the salvation of mankind, would be a work common to Him and the others, although His share might be the greater ; and there would be, not one Redeemer over against the redeemed, but many, of whom one would only be the First among those like Him.   Nor would the human creation then be completed through Him, but through all of those redeemers together, who, in so far as their work implies in them a peculiar quality of nature, are all alike distinguished from the rest of mankind.   It would be just the same, if His activity were indeed peculiar to Himself, but this less in virtue of an inner quality belonging to Him than of a peculiar position in which He had been put.   The second form of expression, that the human creation had been completed in Him, would then be altogether without content, since it would be more natural to suppose that there are many like Him, only they did not happen to occupy the same position.   In that case He would not even be properly Redeemer, even though it could be said that mankind had been redeemed through His act or His suffering, as the case might be.   For the result, namely, salvation, could not be something communicated from Him (since He had nothing peculiar to Himself) ; it could only have been occasioned or released by Him.

Just as little could the approximation to the condition of blessedness be traced to Him, if He had indeed had an exclusive dignity, but had remained passive in it, and had exercised no influence corresponding to it. For (apart from the fact that it is incomprehensible how His contemporaries, and we after them, should ever have come to attribute such an influence to Him, especially when the manner of His appearance was what it was), supposing that the blessedness could have been communicated merely through men's observing this dignity, although there were united with it no influence acting on others, then in the observers there must have been something more than receptivity; His appearance would have to be regarded rather as merely the occasion for this idea, spontaneously produced by themselves.

2. Thus the approximation to blessedness, out of the state of misery, cannot be explained as a fact mediated through Jesus, by reference to either of these elements without the other. It follows, therefore, that they must be most intimately related and mutually determined. So that it is vain to attribute to the Redeemer a higher dignity than the activity at the same time ascribed to Him demands, since nothing is explained by this surplus of dignity. It is equally vain to attribute to Him a greater activity than follows naturally from the dignity which one is ready to allow to Him, since whatever results from this surplus of activity cannot be traced to Him in the same sense as the rest. Therefore every doctrine of Christ is inconsistent, in which this equality (of dignity and activity) is not essential, whether it seeks to disguise the detraction from the dignity by praising in Him great but really alien activities, or, conversely, seeks to compensate for the lesser influence which it allows Him by highly exalting Him, yet in a fashion which leads to no result.

3. If we hold fast to this rule, we could treat the whole doctrine of Christ either as that of His activity, for then the dignity must naturally follow from that, or as that of His dignity, for the activity must then result of itself. This is indicated by the two general formulæ above. For that the creation of human nature has been completed in His person is in and by itself only a description of His dignity, greater or less, according as the difference between the condition before and after is regarded as greater or less; but the activity follows of itself, if indeed the creation is to continue to exist. Again, that He is the Redeemer similarly describes His activity, but the dignity follows of itself to just the same degree. Nevertheless, it is not advisable to choose one of these methods of treatment to the exclusion of the other; this would involve at once both giving up the (traditional) language of the Church, and making a

comparison between our statements and other treatments of doctrine more difficult. Some of the churchly formulæ deal with the activity of Christ ; others are concerned with His dignity ; hence the strongest assurance that the two classes agree is to be found in the fact that the subject should be treated separately from both standpoints. The more what is peculiar in each of them is related to the other, the more probable it is that the propositions which are laid down reproduce with purity an original self-consciousness. The common measure of both, namely, the extent to which activity and dignity are embraced in one presentation, is to be found in the first place in the presentation of the result in individual lives, and next in the presentation of the Church, which must be just as complete a revelation of the dignity of the Redeemer as the world is a complete revelation of the attributes of God.

This division falls accordingly into two doctrines—that of the Person of Christ, and that of His Work. These two are quite different so far as the individual propositions are concerned, but their total content is the same ; from each point of view the content both of the second division and of the second section may be regarded as that which came to pass through Christ.

First Doctrine : The Person of Christ

§ 93. *If the spontaneity of the new corporate life is original in the Redeemer and proceeds from Him alone, then as an historical individual He must have been at the same time ideal* (i.e. *the ideal must have become completely historical in Him*), *and each historical moment of His experience must at the same time have borne within it the ideal.*

1. If the peculiar dignity of the Redeemer can be measured only by His total activity as resting upon that dignity, while this activity can be seen in its completeness only in the corporate life He founded ; if, further, on the one hand, all other religious communities are destined to pass over into this one, so that all religious life existing apart from this is imperfect, whereas in this there is perfection ; if, on the other hand, this life itself, at all times and even in its highest development, has no other relation to the Redeemer than that which has been indicated above,[1] so that it can be all that it is only in virtue of its susceptibility to His influence : then the dignity of the Redeemer must be thought of in such a way that He is capable of achieving this. But inasmuch as His activity, so far as we can relate it directly and exclusively to His person, is to be considered in the first place in His public life, but in this life there are no conspicuous isolated acts which definitely stood out in separation from the rest of it, the true manifestation of His dignity, which is identical with His activity in the founding of a community, lies not in isolated moments, but in the whole course of His life. These are the two truths which, in our proposition, are not simply laid down but are also fully and at every point related to each other.

2. Now, if we live in the Christian fellowship, with the conviction which is common to all Christians, that no more perfect form of the God-consciousness lies in front of the human race, and that any new form would simply be a retrograde step ; and, further, that every increase in the activity of the God-consciousness within the Christian fellowship proceeds, not from any newly-added power,

[1] § 91.

but always and only from an ever-active susceptibility to His influence, clearly every given state of this corporate life must remain no more than an approximation to that which exists in the Redeemer Himself ; and just this is what we understand by His ideal dignity.   But this corporate life is not concerned with the multifarious relationships of human life—as though Christ must have been ideal for all knowledge or all art and skill which have been developed in human society—but only with the capacity of the God-consciousness to give the impulse to all life's experiences and to determine them.   Hence we do not make the ideality of the Redeemer cover more than this.   To this, it is true, it might still be objected that, since the potency of the God-consciousness in the corporate life itself remains always imperfect at best, we must certainly attribute an *exemplary* (*vorbildliche*) dignity to the Redeemer, but *ideality* (*Urbildlichkeit*) (which, properly, asserts the existence of the concept itself), that is, absolute perfection, is not necessarily to be attributed to Him, not even according to the principle laid down above, for it is not necessary to explain the result, which always remains imperfect.   Rather, it might be argued, this is the fundamental exaggeration into which believers fall when they regard Christ in the mirror of their own imperfection ; and this exaggeration continually perpetuates itself in the same manner, since believers in all ages read into Jesus whatever they are able to conceive as ideal in this sphere.   But in this connexion there are two things to be observed.   First, that on this view (if clearly realized) there must be developed at least a wish—for the absolutely perfect is always at least an object of aspiration—the more the individual subordinates his personal consciousness to the consciousness of kind, even a hope, that some day the human race, if only in its noblest and best, will pass beyond Christ and leave Him behind.   But this clearly marks the end of Christian faith, which on the contrary knows no other way to a pure conception of the ideal than an ever-deepening understanding of Christ.   If, on the other hand, this consequence is not consciously realized, or is definitely rejected, then this limitation of the ideal to the merely exemplary can only be a misunderstood rule of prudence, the apparent ground for which will reveal itself later.   Second, we must reflect, on the one hand, that as soon as we grant the possibility of a continued progress in the potency of the God-consciousness, while denying that its perfection exists anywhere, we can also no longer maintain

that the creation of man has been or will be completed, since undoubtedly in progress thus continual perfection remains always
only a bare possibility. And this would be to assert less of man
than of other creatures—for it may be said of all more limited kinds
of being that their concept is perfectly realized in the totality of
individuals, which complete each other. But this cannot hold of a
species which develops itself freely, if the perfection of an essential
vital function be posited in the concept but actually found in no
individual ; for perfection cannot be obtained by adding together
things that are imperfect. And, on the other hand, it is to be considered how difficult it would necessarily be to indicate a difference
between a true ideal and such an example in which there at the
same time resides the power to produce every possible advance in
the totality. For productivity belongs only to the concept of the
ideal and not to that of the exemplary. We must conclude, then,
that ideality is the only appropriate expression for the exclusive
personal dignity of Christ.

With regard to the above statement, however, that the thought
either of desire or of ability to go beyond Christ marks the end of
the Christian faith, here, too, it is not easy to distinguish, among
the various conceptions of it which leave room for the perfecti-
bility of Christianity, between those which, although they do not
seem so, nevertheless are still Christian, and those which are not, yet
wish to pass as such. Everyone recognizes that there is a great
difference between two classes. There are those who say it is not
only possible but our duty to go beyond much of what Christ
taught His disciples, because He Himself (since human thought is
impossible without words) was seriously hindered by the imperfection of language from giving real expression to the innermost
content of His spiritual being in clearly defined thoughts ; and the
same, it may be held, is true in another sense of His actions also, in
which the relations by which they were determined, and therefore
imperfection, are always reflected. This, however, does not prevent
us from attributing to Him absolute ideality in His inner being, in
the sense that that inner being may always transcend its manifestation, and what is manifested be only an ever more perfect presentation of it. But there is another class : those who are of
opinion that Christ is no more even in His inner being than could
be manifested of it, while the fellowship of doctrine and life which
takes its origin from Christ, with the testimonies to Him which it
preserves, has in virtue of special divine guidance so fortunate an

organization that both doctrine and life can easily be re-modelled in accordance with any more perfect ideal which later generations might conceive, without the fellowship needing to lose its historical identity, so that the necessity of founding new religious fellowships has been for all time done away.   A single step more, and even the first presuppositions of the Christian faith will be removed ; and that step may quite consistently be taken.   For if Christ was so much under the constraint of what was necessarily involved in His appearance in history, then both He Himself, and His whole achievement as well, must be capable of being explained simply by what was historically given Him.   That is, Christianity in its entirety can be explained by Judaism at the stage of development which it had then reached—the stage at which it was possible for a man like Jesus to be born of it.   Accordingly, Christianity was nothing but a new development of Judaism, though a development saturated with foreign philosophies then current, and Jesus was nothing but a more or less original and revolutionary reformer of the Jewish law.

3. But however certain it may be that the source of such a corporate life, continually advancing in the power of its God-consciousness, can lie only in the ideal, it is not on that account any easier to understand just how the ideal can have been revealed and manifested in a truly historically-conditioned individual.   Even generally considered, we are compelled to keep the two ideas separate, and, whether we are speaking of works of art or of the forms of nature, we regard each separate one only as a complement of the rest and as requiring completion by them.   But if sin is posited as a corporate act of the human race, what possibility then remains that an ideal individual could have developed out of this corporate life ?   The way of escape, which suggests that the ideal might be produced by human thought and transferred more or less arbitrarily to Jesus, is already cut off.   In that case Christianity would be founded upon an imperfect ideal ; it would therefore have to give up its claim to take up into itself all forms of faith and to develop out of itself more and more perfection and blessedness.   But if our aim is to make room in human nature before Christ, and apart from Him, for the power of producing within itself a pure and perfect ideal—then human nature, since there is a natural connexion between reason and will, cannot have been in a condition of universal sinfulness.   Hence, if the man Jesus was really ideal, or if the ideal became historical and actual in Him—the one expression means the same as the other—in

order to establish a new corporate life within the old and out of it, then certainly He must have entered into the corporate life of sinfulness, but He cannot have come out of it, but must be recognized in it as a miraculous fact (*eine wunderbare Erscheinung*), and yet (in harmony with the analogies established above)[1] only in the meaning of the word ' miracle ' which has here once for all been determined. His peculiar spiritual content, that is, cannot be explained by the content of the human environment to which He belonged, but only by the universal source of spiritual life in virtue of a creative divine act in which, as an absolute maximum, the conception of man as the subject of the God-consciousness comes to completion. But since we can never properly understand the beginnings of life, full justice is done to the demand for the perfect historicity of this perfect ideal, if, from then on, He developed in the same way as all others, so that from birth on His powers gradually unfolded, and, from the zero point of His appearance onwards, were developed to completeness in the order natural to the human race. This applies also to His God-consciousness, with which we are here specially concerned ; which certainly, in the case of others as little as in His, is infused by education—the germ of it is found originally in all—but which in Him too, as in all, had to develop gradually in human fashion into a really manifest consciousness, and antecedently was only present as a germ, although in a certain sense always present as an active power. So even during this period of development, after it had actually become a consciousness, it could exert its influence over the sensuous self-consciousness only in the measure in which the various functions of the latter had already emerged, and thus, even regarded from this side, it appeared as itself something that was only gradually unfolding to its full extent. If we make the mistake of thinking that, on account of His ideal nature, we must deny this and assume that from the very beginnings of His life He carried the God-consciousness as such within Himself—then from the very outset He must have been conscious of Himself as an Ego ; indeed (the deduction is very simple), He must have been master of language from the first, at least so far as its more abstract part is concerned, and before He ever spoke ; thus His whole earliest childhood must have been mere appearance. This excludes the thought of a true human life and quite definitely adopts the error of Docetism ; and on these terms we should have to separate in time that in which Christ is like all men from what in Him is ideal, allotting to the former the whole

[1] § 13, 1.

period of development up to the beginning of mature manhood, and only then allowing the ideal to come in over and above. But this latter is then inconceivable without an absolute miracle. Nay more, sin too would then, at that earlier stage, be at least possible in Him, and therefore also certainly actually present, even if only in the faintest degree ; and thus Jesus would be Redeemer and redeemed in one person—with all the further consequences of that.

The pure historicity of the person of the Redeemer, however, involves also this fact, that He could develop only in a certain similarity with His surroundings, that is, in general after the manner of His people. For since mind and understanding drew their nourishment solely from this surrounding world, and His free self-activity too had in this world its determined place, even His God-consciousness, however original its higher powers, could only express or communicate itself in ideas which He had appropriated from this sphere, and in actions which as to their possibility were predetermined in it.[1] If we wished to deny this dependence of development upon surroundings, we should logically have to assume an empirical omniscience in Christ, in virtue of which all human forms of thought, as well as languages, would have been equally familiar to Him, so that He would have lived in whatever is true and right in each of these just as much as in that of His native land. We should also have to add the same omniscience relatively to the various human relationships and their management. And this, too, would mean the loss of true humanity.

4. Further, whatever is involved in the ideality of the contents of His personal spiritual life must also be compatible with this purely human conception of His historical existence. Thus, in the first place, His development must be thought of as wholly free from everything which we have to conceive as conflict. For it is not possible that, where an inner conflict has ever at any time taken place, the traces of it should ever disappear completely. Just as little could the ideal have been recognized as present where even the slightest traces of this conflict betrayed themselves. The power with which the God-consciousness, so far as it was developed at each particular moment, determined that moment could never have been in doubt, or disturbed by the memory of an earlier conflict. Nor could He ever have found Himself in a condition through which a conflict could have been

---

[1] It will doubtless be generally recognized that this is implied in the statement in Gal. 4[4], that Christ was made under the law.

occasioned in the future, that is, there could have been in Him, even from the beginning, no inequality in the relation of the various functions of sensuous human nature to the God-consciousness. Thus at every moment even of His period of development He must have been free from everything by which the rise of sin in the individual is conditioned.[1] Two things, further, are quite well possible together : first, that all powers, both the lower ones which were to be mastered and the controlling higher ones, emerged only in gradual development, so that the latter were able to dominate the former only in the measure of their development ; and, secondly, that the domination itself was nevertheless at each moment complete in the sense that nothing was ever able to find a place in the sense-nature which did not instantly take its place as an instrument of the spirit, so that no impression was taken up merely sensuously into the innermost consciousness and elaborated apart from God-consciousness into an element of life, nor did any action, that can really be regarded as such, and as a real whole, ever proceed solely from the sense-nature and not from the God-consciousness. What we could lay down above [2] only as a possibility, namely, a sinless development of a human individual life, must have become actual in the person of the Redeemer in virtue of this undisturbed identity of the relationship, so that we can represent the growth of His personality from earliest childhood on to the fulness of manhood as a continuous transition from the condition of purest innocence to one of purely spiritual fulness of power, which is far removed from anything which we call virtue. For in the condition of innocence there is an activity of the God-consciousness, but only an indirect one, which, though still latently, restrains every movement in the sense-experience which must develop into opposition. The nearest approximation to this, which not seldom occurs in our experience, we usually call ' a happy childlike nature.' The adult fulness of power, on the other hand, although its growth is gradual and the result of practice, is distinguished from virtue in this respect, that it is not the result of a conflict, inasmuch as it does not need to be worked out either through error or through sin, nor even through an inclination to either. And this purity must on no account be regarded as a consequence of outward protection, but must have its ground in the Man Himself, that is, in the higher God-consciousness implanted in Him originally. Otherwise, since such outward protection depends upon the actions of others, the ideal in Him

Cf. §§ 67–69.   [2] § 68, 1.

would be produced rather than productive, and He Himself would be just as much the first from the totality redeemed, as afterwards Himself the Redeemer.

Secondly, so far as what is conditioned by race in His person is concerned, Christ could hardly be a complete man if His personality were not determined by this factor ; but such determination in no way concerns the real principle of His life but only the organism. Racial peculiarity is in no way the type of His self-activity ; it is only the type of His receptivity for the self-activity of the spirit ; nor can it have been like a repelling or exclusive principle in Him, but must have been united with the freest and most unclouded appreciation of everything human, and with the recognition of the identity of nature and also of spirit in all human forms ; also it must have been without any effort to extend what in Him was racial beyond its appointed limits. And it is only when we have guarded ourselves thus that we can say that the racial too in Him is ideally determined, both in itself and in its relation to the whole of human nature.

5. Here we can only call attention in passing and by anticipation to the influence which this conception of the ideality of the Redeemer in the perfectly natural historicity of His career exercises on all the Christian doctrines current in the Church, all of which must be formulated differently if that conception more or less is given up. To begin with, the fact that all doctrines and precepts developed in the Christian Church have universal authority only through their being traced back to Christ, has no other ground than His perfect ideality in everything connected with the power of the God-consciousness. In so far as this is set aside, there must be conceded a possibility of doctrines and precepts arising in the sphere of piety which go beyond the utterances of Christ. Similarly, the preaching of the written word, in so far as it contains only glorification of Christ, and the sacrament of the altar, can be regarded as permanent institutions in the Christian Church only if we premise that the whole development and maintenance of Christian piety must always proceed from vital fellowship with Christ. Nor could Christ be presented as a universal example unless His relation to all original differences in individuals were uniform—for otherwise He would necessarily be more of an example for some than for others. This only becomes possible through His ideality. But just as little could He be a universal example, unless every moment of His life were

ideal.   Otherwise it would be necessary first to distinguish the ideal from the non-ideal, which could only be done according to an external law, which (it follows) would be superior to Him.   That law would come in, unless (as His ideality implies) what is racially determined in Him had been limited ; otherwise we should have to consent to adopt into the Christian norm of life all that is simply Jewish in His life.   Moreover, these points, cardinal for the Christian fellowship, are not doctrines which became current only through later developments ; they are the original doctrines of His disciples, closely bound up with the way in which they applied to Jesus the idea of the Messiah, and such as are easily brought into connexion with His own utterances, so far as these are accessible to us.

§ 94. *The Redeemer, then, is like all men in virtue of the identity of human nature, but distinguished from them all by the constant potency of His God-consciousness, which was a veritable existence of God in Him.*

1. That the Redeemer should be entirely free from all sinfulness is no objection at all to the complete identity of human nature in Him and others, for we have already [1] laid down that sin is so little an essential part of the being of man that we can never regard it as anything else than a disturbance of nature.   It follows that the possibility of a sinless development is in itself not incongruous with the idea of human nature ; indeed, this possibility is involved, and recognized, in the consciousness of sin as guilt, as that is universally understood.   This likeness, however, is to be understood in such a general sense that even the first man before the first sin stood no nearer the Redeemer, and was like Him in no higher sense, than all other men.   For if even in the life of the first man we must assume a time when sin had not yet appeared, yet every first appearance of sin leads back to a sinful preparation.[2]   But the Redeemer too shared in the same vicissitudes of life, without which we can hardly imagine the entrance of sin at a definite moment even in Adam, for they are essential to human nature.   Furthermore, the first man was originally free from all the contagious influences of a sinful society, while the Redeemer had to enter into the corporate life when it had already advanced far in deterioration, so that it would hardly be possible to attribute His sinlessness to external protection—which we certainly must somehow admit in the case of the first man, if we would not involve ourselves in contradictions.

[1] § 68, above.   [2] Cf. § 72.

Of the Redeemer, on the contrary, we must hold that the ground of His sinlessness was not external to Himself, but that it was a sinlessness essentially grounded in Himself, if He was to take away, through what He was in Himself, the sinfulness of the corporate life. Therefore, so far as sin is concerned, Christ differs no less from the first man than from all others.

The identity of human nature further involves this, that the manner in which Christ differs from all others also has its place in this identity. This would not be the case if it were not involved in human nature that individuals, so far as the measure of the different functions is concerned, are originally different from each other, so that to every separate corporate life (regarded in space as well as in time) there belong those who are more and less gifted ; and we only arrive at the truth of life when we thus correlate those who differ from each other. In the same way, therefore, all those who in any respect give character to an age or a district are bound up with those over whom (as being defective in that particular respect) they extend an educative influence, even as Christ is bound up with those whom His preponderatingly powerful God-consciousness links to the corporate life thus indicated. The greater the difference, and the more specific the activity, the more must these also have established themselves against the hindering influences of a worthless environment, and they can be understood only by reference to this self-differentiating quality of human nature,[1] not by reference to the group in which they stand ; although by divine right they belong to it, as the Redeemer does to the whole race.

2. But in admitting that what is peculiar in the Redeemer's kind of activity belongs to a general aspect of human nature, we by no means wish to reduce this activity, and the personal dignity by which it is conditioned, to the same measure as that of others. The simple fact that faith in Christ postulates a relation on His part to the whole race, while everything analogous is valid only for definite individual times and places, is sufficient to prove this. For no one has yet succeeded, in any sphere of science or art, and no one will ever succeed, in establishing himself as head, universally animating and sufficient for the whole human race.

For this peculiar dignity of Christ, however, in the sense in which we have already referred back the ideality of His person to this spiritual function of the God-consciousness implanted in the self-consciousness, the terms of our proposition alone are adequate ; for

[1] Cf. § 13.

to ascribe to Christ an absolutely powerful God-consciousness, and to attribute to Him an existence of God in Him, are exactly the same thing. The expression, ' the existence of God in anyone,' can only express the relation of the omnipresence of God to this one. Now since God's existence can only be apprehended as pure activity, while every individualized existence is merely an intermingling of activity and passivity—the activity being always found apportioned to this passivity in every other individualized existence—there is, so far, no existence of God in any individual thing, but only an existence of God in the world. And only if the passive conditions are not purely passive, but mediated through vital receptivity, and this receptivity confronts the totality of finite existence (so far, i.e., as we can say of the individual as a living creature that, in virtue of the universal reciprocity, it in itself represents the world), could we suppose an existence of God in it. Hence this clearly does not hold of what is individualized as an unconscious thing ; for since an unconscious thing brings no living receptivity to meet all the forces of consciousness it cannot represent these forces in itself. But just as little and for the same reason can what is conscious but not intelligent represent them, so that it is only in the rational individual that an existence of God can be admitted. How far this is also true similarly and without distinction if we regard reason as functioning in objective consciousness lies outside our investigation. But so far as the rational self-consciousness is concerned, it is certain that the God-consciousness which (along with the self-consciousness) belongs to human nature originally, before the Redeemer and apart from all connexion with Him, cannot fittingly be called an existence of God in us, not only because it was not a pure God-consciousness (either in polytheism or even in Jewish monotheism, which was everywhere tinctured with materialistic conceptions, whether cruder or finer), but also because, such as it was, it did not assert itself as activity, but in these religions was always dominated by the sensuous self-consciousness. If, then, it was able neither to portray God purely and with real adequacy in thought, nor yet to exhibit itself as pure activity, it cannot be represented as an existence of God in us. But just as the unconscious forces of nature and non-rational life become a revelation of God to us only so far as we bring that conception with us, so also that darkened and imperfect God-consciousness by itself is not an existence of God in human nature, but only in so far as we bring Christ with us in thought and relate it to Him. So

that originally it is found nowhere but in Him, and He is the only
' other ' in which there is an existence of God in the proper sense,
so far, that is, as we posit the God-consciousness in His self-consciousness as continually and exclusively determining every moment,
and consequently also this perfect indwelling of the Supreme
Being as His peculiar being and His inmost self.   Indeed, working
backwards we must now say, if it is only through Him that the human
God-consciousness becomes an existence of God in human nature,
and only through the rational nature that the totality of finite powers
can become an existence of God in the world, that in truth He alone
mediates all existence of God in the world and all revelation of God
through the world, in so far as He bears within Himself the whole
new creation which contains and develops the potency of the God-
consciousness.

3. But if as a person of this kind He needs to have the whole
human development in common with us, so that even this existence
of God must in Him have had a development in time, and as the
most spiritual element in His personality could only emerge into
manifestation after the lower functions ; yet He cannot have entered
life as one for whom the foundations of sin had already been laid
before His being began to be manifested.   We have envisaged this
earlier establishment of sin for all of us,[1] without entering upon
natural-scientific investigations into the origin of the individual
life, and the coming together in us (if we may use the phrase) of
soul and body, but simply by holding to the general facts of experience ; so here, too, we seek to combine with these facts only the
relatively supernatural, which we have already admitted in general
for the entrance of the Redeemer into the world.

The origin of every human life may be regarded in a twofold
manner, as issuing from the narrow circle of descent and society
to which it immediately belongs, and as a fact of human nature in
general.   The more definitely the weaknesses of that narrow circle
repeat themselves in an individual, the more valid becomes the
first point of view.   The more the individual by the kind and degree
of his gifts transcends that circle, and the more he exhibits what is
new within it, the more we are thrown back upon the other explanation.   This means that the beginning of Jesus' life cannot in any
way be explained by the first factor, but only and exclusively by
the second ; so that from the beginning He must have been free from
every influence from earlier generations which disseminated sin

[1] Cf. § 69.

and disturbed the inner God-consciousness, and He can only be understood as an original act of human nature, *i.e.* as an act of human nature as not affected by sin. The beginning of His life was also a new implanting of the God-consciousness which creates receptivity in human nature ; hence this content and that manner of origin are in such a close relation that they mutually condition and explain each other. That new implanting came to be through the beginning of His life, and therefore that beginning must have transcended every detrimental influence of His immediate circle ; and because it was such an original and sin-free act of nature, a filling of His nature with God-consciousness became possible as its result. So that upon this relation too the fullest light is thrown if we regard the beginning of the life of Jesus as the completed creation of human nature. The appearance of the first man constituted at the same time the physical life of the human race ; the appearance of the Second Adam constituted for this nature a new spiritual life, which communicates and develops itself by spiritual fecundation. And as in the former its originality (which is the condition of the appearance of human nature) and its having emerged from creative divine activity are the same thing, so also in the Redeemer both are the same—His spiritual originality, set free from every prejudicial influence of natural descent, and that existence of God in Him which also proves itself creative. If the impartation of the Spirit to human nature which was made in the first Adam was insufficient, in that the spirit remained sunk in sensuousness and barely glanced forth clearly at moments as a presentiment of something better, and if the work of creation has only been completed through the second and equally original impartation to the Second Adam, yet both events go back to one undivided eternal divine decree and form, even in a higher sense, only one and the same natural system, though one unattainable by us.

§ 95. *The ecclesiastical formulæ concerning the Person of Christ need to be subjected to continual criticism.*

1. The ecclesiastical formulæ are, on the one hand, products of controversy, in that, although the original consciousness was the same in all, yet the thought expressive of it took different forms with different thinkers, according as they linked their presentation of what was new to one or another of the existing conceptions. In this way it was possible for Jewish or heathen elements or pre-

suppositions to creep in, even though it were unconsciously, and to evoke corrective opposition. Even the later development of the original formulæ partly took the same road, in order to guard against misunderstandings which might arise from rhetorical or poetic expressions in doctrinal language ; partly it proceeded with that over-subtlety which was later brought to perfection in Scholasticism, and which, utterly disregarding the true interests of Dogmatic, propounded difficult questions simply for the sake of definitions. The result inevitably was that Dogmatic was over-loaded with a multitude of definitions, which have absolutely no other relation to the immediate Christian self-consciousness than that indicated by the history of controversy. The realization of this has produced in some minds a distaste for everything which had a controversial origin ; they will only admit such expressions as lie outside all controversy and obviate in advance, wherever possible, all future controversy ; they are in the keenest antagonism to the tendency of others, who want to retain everything now existing just as it has come to be. So that without a process of elimination and compromise neither adjustment nor progress is possible.

2. For this unavoidable critical process, two rules (in view of the opposing parties) must be adopted. The rule for the one party is this : a thing no longer really exists, but becomes mere matter of history, when it can exercise no further activity owing to the situation to which it properly belonged being no longer present. The rule for the other party is this : if we go back to formulæ which are simple, but just on account of their simplicity are too indefinite for didactic purposes, we gain a merely apparent satisfaction, which lasts only until the disagreement which has remained hidden under the identity of the formula breaks out somewhere or other. The task of the critical process is to hold the ecclesiastical formulæ to strict agreement with the foregoing analysis of our Christian self-consciousness, in order, partly, to judge how far they agree with it at least in essentials, partly (with regard to individual points), to inquire how much of the current form of expression is to be retained, and how much, on the other hand, had better be given up, either because it is an imperfect solution of the problem or because it is an addition not in itself essential, and harmful because the occasion of persistent misunderstandings.

§ 96. *First Theorem.—In Jesus Christ divine nature and human nature were combined into one person.*

Augsb. Conf., Art. 3 : That the two natures, divine and human, inseparably united in one person are One Christ.—*Conf. Angl.* ii. (p. 127 [1]) : ita ut duae naturae divina et humana integre atque perfecte in unitate personae fuerint inseparabiliter coniunctae, ex quibus est unus Christus, etc.— *Expos. simpl.* xi. : Agnoscimus ergo in uno atque eodem domino nostro duas naturas divinam et humanam, et has dicimus conjunctas et unitas esse . . . in una persona, ita ut unum Christum . . . veneremur . . . juxta divinam naturam patri juxta humanam vero nobis hominibus consubstantialem. —*Conf. Gallic.* xv. p. 116 : Credimus in una eademque persona, quae est Jesus Christus, vere et inseparabiliter duas illas naturas sic esse conjunctas ut etiam sint unitae.—*Conf. Helv.* xi. p. 96 : Hic Christus . . . cum . . . totum hominem anima et corpore constantem assumsisset, in una individuaque persona duas sed impermixtas naturas—frater noster factus est.—*Sol. decl.* viii. : Credimus iam in una illa indivisa persona Christi duas esse distinctas naturas divinam videlicet quae ab aeterno est, et humanam quae in tempore assumta est in unitatem personae filii Dei.—*Symb. Nic.* : Ἰησοῦν Χριστὸν, τὸν ἐκ τοῦ πατρὸς γεννηθέντα πρὸ πάντων τῶν αἰώνων . . . θεὸν ἀληθινόν . . . τὸν δι' ἡμᾶς . . . κατελθόντα . . . καὶ σαρκωθέντα, etc. *Symb. Quic.* 28, 29 : . . . Quia dominus noster Jesus Christus dei filius Deus pariter et homo est. Deus est ex substantia patris ante secula genitus, homo ex substantia matris in seculo natus.

1. Although only a few of the credal passages quoted here indicate the object of this presentation of the unique personality of the Redeemer, yet it is unmistakable that the tendency is the same as in the propositions so far laid down, namely, to describe Christ in such a way (*frater, consubstantialis nobis*) that in the new corporate life a vital fellowship between us and Him shall be possible, and, at the same time, that the existence of God in Him shall be expressed in the clearest possible way ; from which it follows at once that the most unconditional adoration and brotherly comradeship are united in our relation to Him. With this we are in complete agreement. Yet, on the other hand, there is almost nothing in the execution of this aim against which protest must not be raised, whether we regard the scientific character of the expression or its suitability for ecclesiastical use.

With regard to the first : to begin with, we must warn the reader against the very confusing description of the subject that results when the expression ' Jesus Christ ' is used, to indicate not only the subject of the union of the two natures (at which point the first

---

[1] The page-numbers for the Reformed Confessions refer to the *Augusti Corpus* etc.

four passages properly stop), but also the divine nature of the Redeemer from all eternity before its union with the human nature ; so that this union no longer appears as an element that goes to constitute the person, Jesus Christ, but rather as an act of this person Himself.   This confusion has, most glaringly, passed over from the two passages drawn from the ancient creeds into the Helvetic Confession.[1] But the New Testament knows nothing of this usage ; even the expression ' Son of God ' it uses (when it speaks independently) only of the subject of this union,[2] and not of the divine element in it before the union.   So our proposition has held to what is correct.   The expression ' Jesus Christ ' itself only became a single proper name originally through misuse (though this happened very early), since properly Christ is only the description of the real dignity added to the proper name ; but even in the combination it is obvious that the historical and the ideal are both comprised.   But far worse than this ambiguous description of the subject is this (which cannot possibly be justified on any strictly scientific investigation), that the expression ' nature ' is used indifferently for the divine and the human.   Any other expression that was used indifferently of both would lead one to suspect that such a formula was bound to become the source of many confusions.   For how can divine and human be thus brought together under any single conception, as if they could both be more exact determinations, co-ordinated to each other, of one and the same universal ?   Indeed, even divine spirit and human spirit could not without confusion be brought together in this way.   But the word ' nature ' is particularly ill-adapted for such a common use, even if we leave Latin and Greek etymology completely out of account and simply take our stand on our own use of the word.   For in one sense we actually oppose God and nature to one another, and hence in this sense cannot attribute a nature to God.   Nature in this sense is for us the summary of all finite existence, or, as in the opposition of nature and history, the summary of all that is corporeal, and that goes back to what is elementary, in its various and discrete phenomena, in which all that we so describe is mutually conditioned.   Over against this divided and conditioned we set God as the unconditioned and the absolutely simple.   But just for this reason we

---

[1] The *Belgic Confession*, too, shares in the same confusion, x. p. 176 : Necesse itaque eum qui Deus sermo filius et Jesus Christus nominatur jam tum extitisse cum ab ipso omnia crearentur.

[2] No one, we may suppose, will cite John 1[18] or 17[5] as instances against this assertion.

cannot attribute a nature to God in the other sense.   For always, whether we use the word generally, as when we speak of animal and vegetable nature, or of an individual, as when we say that a person has a noble or an ignoble nature, always we use it solely of a limited existence, standing in opposition to something else, an existence in which active and passive are bound up together, and which is revealed in a variety of appearances, in the latter case of individuals, in the former of vital factors.   And upon closer consideration it is hardly to be denied that this expression, if we go back to the original Greek word,[1] bears in itself traces of heathen influence, though possibly of unconscious influence.   For in polytheism, which represents the Godhead as no less split up and divided than finite existence appears to us, the word 'nature' has certainly the same meaning in the expression *divine nature* as it has elsewhere.   The fact ought to have been a warning, that the heathen sages themselves had already risen above this imperfect representation of God, and said of Him that He was to be thought of as beyond all existence and being.

It is no better with the relation which is here set forth between nature and person.   For in utter contradiction to the use elsewhere, according to which the same nature belongs to many individuals or persons, here one person is to share in two quite different natures. Now if ' person ' indicates a constant unity of life, but ' nature ' a sum of ways of action or laws, according to which conditions of life vary and are included within a fixed range, how can the unity of life coexist with the duality of natures, unless the one gives way to the other, if the one exhibits a larger and the other a narrower range, or unless they melt into each other, both systems of ways of action and laws really becoming one in the one life ?—if indeed we are speaking of a person, *i.e.* of an Ego which is the same in all the consecutive moments of its existence.   The attempt to make clear this unity along with the duality naturally but seldom results. in anything else than a demonstration of the possibility of a formula made up by combining indications out of which it is impossible to construct a figure.   On the other hand, as soon as the same writer avoids this formula of two natures, he not seldom says something which one can follow, and of which the figure can

---

[1] φύσις.   This censure seems also to fall on a writing which is merely deutero-canonical, for in 2 Pet. 1⁴ the expression is found, θείας ·φύσεως κοινωνοί.   But the immediate context of itself shows that these words cannot be taken so precisely as must be done in the case we are dealing with, where an important dogmatic definition is in question.

be drawn (*nachzeichnen*).[1]   Hence all the results of the endeavour to
achieve a living presentation of the unity of the divine and the
human in Christ, ever since it was tied down to this expression,
have always vacillated between the opposite errors of mixing the
two natures to form a third which would be neither of them, neither
divine nor human, or of keeping the two natures separate, but either
neglecting the unity of the person in order to separate the two
natures more distinctly, or, in order to keep firm hold of the unity
of the person, disturbing the necessary balance, and making one
nature less important than the other and limited by it.   The same
thing comes out even in the vacillation between the expressions
' connexion ' and ' union '—in the latter there is a tendency to
wipe out the difference of the natures, while the former makes the
unity of the person doubtful.   The utter fruitlessness of this way of
presenting the matter becomes particularly clear in the treatment
of the question whether Christ as one person formed out of two
natures had also two wills according to the number of the natures,
or only one according to the number of the person.   For if Christ
had only one will, then the divine nature is incomplete if this is a
human will ; and the human nature, if it is a divine will.   But
if Christ has two wills, then the unity of the person is no more than
apparent, even if we try to conserve it by saying that the two wills
always will the same thing.   For what this results in is only agreement, not unity ; and, in fact, to answer the problem thus is to
return to the division of Christ.   And one or the other will is always
simply a superfluous accompaniment of the other, whether it be
the divine will that accompanies the human or *vice versa*.   And
manifestly, as we are accustomed to take reason and will together
the same question may be raised with regard to the reason ; then
all that has just been said repeats itself, since each nature is incomplete without the reason that belongs to it, and a unity of the
person is as little compatible with such a twofold reason as with a
twofold will ; and it is equally unthinkable that a divine reason,
which as omniscient sees everything at once, should think the same
as a human reason, which only knows separate things one after the
other and as a result of the other, and that a human will, which
always strives only for separate ends and one for the sake of the

[1] Cf. Joann. Damasc. iii. 19 : ἀλλ' οὐκ ἀνάγκη τὰς ἀλλήλαις ἐνωθείσας φύσεις καθ'
ὑπόστασιν ἑκάστην ἰδίαν κεκτῆσθαι ὑπόστασιν. δύνανται γὰρ εἰς μίαν συνδραμοῦσαι
ὑπόστασιν μήτε ἀνυπόστατοι εἶναι μήτε ἰδιάζουσαν ἑκάστη ἔχειν ὑπόστασιν, ἀλλὰ μίαν
καὶ τὴν αὐτὴν ἀμφότεραι,—and iii. 2 : λόγος σαρκὶ ἐψυχωμένῃ καὶ ἐν αὐτῷ τὸ εἶναι
λαχούσῃ ἐνωθεὶς καθ' ὑπόστασιν.

other, should will the same as a divine will, whose object can be nothing but the whole world in the totality of its development.

Finally, for the scientific perfection of dogmatic terminology it is also necessary that related doctrines should be capable of easy comprehension in their relations to each other ; if so, the way in which this formula is related to the formulæ of the doctrine of the Trinity is no great recommendation of it. There the expression 'unity of nature' alongside of the trinity of Persons has been avoided, and 'unity of essence' used instead. But, however praiseworthy this may be, since the term 'essence' is certainly much more appropriate to the Godhead than the term 'nature,' yet the question inevitably arises what the relation is between what in Christ we call His divine nature and that unity of essence which is common to all three Persons of the Trinity, and whether each of the three Persons, outside their participation in the Divine Essence, has also a nature of its own as well, or whether this is a peculiarity of the Second Person. No satisfactory answer to this is to be found either here or in the doctrine of the Trinity. But the matter becomes still more confused through the introduction in the Dogmatic of the whole Western Church of another usage of the word 'Person,' according to which, in the one case, we have three Persons in one Essence and in the other one Person out of two natures. If now we carry over into the doctrine of the Trinity the explanations which are usually given of the word 'Person' in the doctrine of Christ—and there is sufficient reason for this, since it is asserted that Christ did not become a Person only through the union of the two natures, but the Son of God only took up human nature into His Person— then the three Persons must have an independent anterior existence in themselves ; and if each Person is also a nature,[1] we come almost inevitably to three divine natures for the three divine Persons in the one Divine Essence. If, on the other hand, the same word 'Person' means something different in the one doctrine from what it means in the other, so that in the Person of Christ we have still another Person in the other sense of the word, the confusion is just as great.

2. It lies in the nature of the case, that after this formula had once secured recognition as the foundation for all other definitions regarding the Person of Christ, an involved and artificial mode of procedure was inevitable if terms so indefensible were to be kept as innocuous as possible. The almost inevitable consequence was

[1] The formulæ here are taken from Reinhard, *Dogmatik*, § 92, p. 347.

that, as this foundation itself contains an apparent contradiction, the whole development was bound to resolve itself into a disproof of this reproach couched in a series of negative terms—terms which no more express or reproduce the actual content of our immediate impression than they contain a knowledge of Christ in the form of intuition—that is, of objective consciousness (though indeed it would be less of a recommendation to us than to others if they *could* do this last).   Accordingly we are compelled to put a very low estimate upon the value of this theory for ecclesiastical use.   It cannot give any guidance in the proper preaching of Christ, for it takes a purely negative form ;   at most it might serve homiletical diction as a test of whether in the glorification or the vivid presentation of Christ elements may not have been introduced which transgress the pre-scribed limits.   But even in this connexion the definitions of the Schools have long since become a dead letter in which no one any longer can find refuge.   For the devotional phraseology even of the most orthodox teachers, in so far as they are not content simply to hand on the letter of tradition but aim at edification and confirma-tion in a living faith, is so remote from the terminology of the schools that it would hardly be possible to find any current terms to bridge the gulf.   No less unfruitful does this development appear when we regard the divergent opinions which prevail among us, some of them docetic in character, since they identify the Redeemer so closely with God that the truth of His humanity is obscured ; some of them Ebionite, inasmuch as they leave no room for any essential distinc-tion between Christ and an exceptional man.   They are utterly unsuitable for use in determining in either direction the boundary between what is Christian but appears unchristian, whether owing to its own *gaucherie* or to the misrepresentation of opponents, and what has ceased to be Christian altogether, because it is naturalistic or fanatical.

3. It must be remembered, further, that in the original construc-tion of Protestant theology nothing was done for this article—the old formulæ were simply repeated.   For although the question was at once taken up again on one particular side in the contro-versies between the two Protestant parties, this could not lead to a complete new revision, since the matter arose only *à propos* of another point in dispute ; nor did what on this occasion was actually estab-lished secure symbolical recognition anywhere within the sphere of the Augsburg Confession.   And so, if Dogmatics are to be ever more completely purged of scholasticism, the task remains of construct-

ing a scientific statement of this particular doctrine also, in which
the impression of the peculiar dignity of the Redeemer that we have
obtained from the testimonies borne to Him shall not be reflected
merely in negative formulæ, and which at the same time (at least
as much as with other dogmatic definitions) shall approximate to
what can be presented to Christian congregations in religious teaching.   We hope that above [1] we have laid the foundation for such a
revision, which attempts so to define the mutual relations of the
divine and the human in the Redeemer, that both the expressions,
divine nature and the duality of natures in the same Person (which,
to say the least, are exceedingly inconvenient) shall be altogether
avoided. For if the distinction between the Redeemer and us
others is established in such a way that, instead of being obscured
and powerless as in us, the God-consciousness in Him was absolutely
clear and determined each moment, to the exclusion of all else, so
that it must be regarded as a continual living presence, and withal a
real existence of God in Him, then, in virtue of this difference, there
is in Him everything that we need, and, in virtue of His likeness to
us, limited only by His utter sinlessness, this is all in Him in such a
way that we can lay hold of it.   That is to say, the existence of God
in the Redeemer is posited as the innermost fundamental power
within Him, from which every activity proceeds and which holds
every element together ; everything human (in Him) forms only
the organism for this fundamental power, and is related to it as the
system which both receives and represents it, just as in us all other
powers are related to the intelligence.[2]   If this form of expression
is very different from that of the language of the Schools as used
hitherto, yet it rests equally upon the Pauline phrase ' God was in
Christ ' and the Johannine ' the Word became flesh ' ; for ' Word ' is
the activity of God expressed in the form of consciousness, and
' flesh ' is a general expression for the organic. In so far as all
human activity of the Redeemer depends, as a connected whole,
upon this existence of God in Him and represents it, the expression
(that in the Redeemer God became man) is justified as true exclusively of Him ; and similarly every moment of His existence, so far
as it can be isolated, presents just such a new incarnation and
incarnatedness of God, because always and everywhere all that is
human in Him springs out of that divine.   And it would be difficult

[1] § 94.
[2] Precisely as in the *Symbol. Quic.* 25 : Nam sicut anima rationalis et
caro unus est homo, ita et Deus et homo unus est Christus.

for anyone to prove that there is anything docetic or Ebionite in this description. It could be called Ebionite only by one who feels that he must insist upon an empirical emergence of divine properties if he is to recognize a superhuman element in the Redeemer ; and the only thing that could be regarded as docetic is that in the Redeemer the God-consciousness is not imperfect. But neither objection would find any support even in the letter of the accepted ecclesiastical doctrine. Hence even in dealing with the ecclesiastical propositions now to follow, our criticism must be related to the form of statement just given, in order at each point to show how far the intention of these propositions agrees in meaning with our form of statement, and how far the unsuitability and difficulty of those formulæ has, on the one hand, prevented the exposition from answering fully to the intention, and on the other has given scope for subtle inanities.

§ 97. *Second Theorem.—In the uniting of the divine nature with the human, the divine alone was active or self-imparting, and the human alone passive or in process of being assumed ; but during the state of union every activity was a common activity of both natures.*

1. If we take an objective view of the task of presenting Christ clearly as such a unity of both natures, it is natural and indeed inevitable that we should separate from one another the act of union and the state of union. For the former was only the beginning of the Person of Christ as it came to manifestation in the world, and accordingly must be expressed by a reference to the previous non-existence of that Person ; while the latter, as the specific existence of the Person, must be described by a formula which is equally appropriate to all moments of it. But for our task the description of the first beginning, since we are not directly affected by it, seems a work of supererogation. This accordingly is better omitted : such exercises are always of doubtful value. Thus the inclusion of this theorem calls for special justification. But, in the first place, it is quite in order to refer back to its beginnings such a difference as that between Christ and all other men, because it does make a difference if it is recognized as original ; and, again, the expression must be quite differently phrased if the difference is a later accession and hence only a subsequent condition of a person originally entirely like ourselves. And since if we reproduce the impression made

upon us we cannot but deny the latter suggestion, the necessity
arises of presenting the first moment also as continuous with every
later one. And so both the theorems set forth above, while they
definitely insist on the distinction between beginning and further
career, must be understood only as they merge in each other. For,
on the one hand, the beginning of the Person is at the same time
the beginning of its activity ; on the other, every moment so far as
it can be isolated and considered in itself is a new coming into being
of this specific personality. And as every activity of Christ must
exemplify the same relation as that which marks the act of union
(which, indeed, is only a union for such activities), that is, that the
impulse springs from the divine nature ; so also conversely the act
of union must exemplify the same relation as that through which
every activity of Christ exists (since every activity is only an individual manifestation of this union)—that is, that both natures
work together into one. By this canon alone must both the
formulæ presented in our theorem be judged and applied, as
well as all others which appear elsewhere and are derived from
them.

2. There are manifold objections to the expression by which it
is sought to describe more nearly the active participation of the
divine nature in that act of union—namely, that in it the divine
nature has assumed the human into the unity of its Person.[1] Not
only on account of the expression ' divine nature,' but, in the first
place, because it makes the personality of Christ altogether dependent upon the personality of the second Person in the Divine
Essence. For since the Sabellians denied this, but yet believed no
less than orthodox Christians in the union of the divine with the
human in Christ, it seems an injustice to all who may perhaps
approximate to the Sabellian view to attach the expression for
this belief to the orthodox Trinitarian doctrine : especially as the
original faith-constituting impression made upon the disciples, even
as they grasped it in thought and reproduced it, was not connected
with any knowledge of a Trinity. But the worst is, that the
human nature in this way can only become a Person in the sense
in which this is true of a Person in the Trinity, so that we are confronted with the dilemma, that either the three Persons must, like
human persons, be individuals existing independently by themselves,

---

[1] Reinhard's phrasing is particularly infelicitous (*Dogm.* § 91) : Qui (filius
Dei) cum natura *quadam* humana quam sibi adiunxerit unam efficiat
personam.

or Christ as man was not such an independent individual—an assertion which gives us a completely docetic picture of Him. It is, therefore, much safer (as it is also analogous to the origin and development of faith) to establish the doctrine of Christ independently of that doctrine of the Trinity. It is true that even our first proposition might still be regarded as docetic—as if, that is to say, the truth of the human nature in Christ were already lost when we say that in the origin of the Person of Christ the human nature was altogether passive, since obviously in the origin of every other human person it takes an active part, in that its body-forming power shapes itself into a new unity of human existence in the completeness of all vital functions. But if we call to our help the canon set forth above, according to which the act of the union also must have been once a common activity of both—of the self-imparting Divine Essence,[1] and of the human nature appointed to be assumed by it—then the position is that the human nature certainly cannot have been active in being assumed by the divine, in such a way that (to put it so) the being of God in Christ was developed out of the human nature, or even in such a way that there was in the human nature a capacity to draw down the divine to itself ; only the possibility was innate in it (and must have remained in it intact even during the dominion of sin) of being assumed into such a union with the divine, but this possibility is far from being either capacity or activity. On the other hand, in accordance with our canon we must add that the human nature can have been assumed by the divine only as engaged in a person-forming activity, since the divine activity is not person-forming in the way of generation. In speaking, therefore, of the origin of the specific personality of Christ, that is, of the implanting of the divine in the human nature, it must be said that in this the latter was only receptive and could only take a passive part, since no person-forming activity of human nature apart from any activity of the divine nature could ever have produced anything but an ordinary human person. But in so far as Christ none the less was also a perfectly human person, the forma-tion of this person also must have been an act of the human nature ; and so the whole process must have been a common act of the two natures. This is recognized by all dogmatic theologians who, rejecting the opinion that the body of Christ was completely formed

[1] In the proposition itself, even after expressing unqualified disapproval of the term ' divine nature,' I allowed it to stand, purely for convenience' sake. But here in the detailed discussion that consideration is irrelevant, and hence I have reverted to the simplest term.

in a single moment,[1] or that in essentials it came down from heaven
with the divine,[2] reckon the gradual formation of the organism
from the first beginnings of life onwards as part of the truth of the
human nature of Christ. But during this development the human
nature was not altogether passive ; hence there was also a physical
activity of this nature at the first beginnings of life *alongside of* its
merely passive attitude relatively to the divine activity.

On the other hand, doubts of an altogether opposite kind might
be raised against a special divine activity in the origin of the Person
of Christ, namely, that this activity must either have occurred in
time (which conflicts with the first canon, that God must remain
outside every temporal medium), or it would not have been a special
and immediate activity (in which case the already admitted supernatural quality would again be endangered).   So we see how either
of two errors could be chosen even by those of genuinely Christian
temper.   In order to avoid entangling the Eternal in temporality,
one may decide to make it a condition in presenting the peculiar
dignity of Christ that it must be possible to regard Him like any
other person as a product of the human nature.   And in order
at the same time to leave room all the more assuredly for an immediate divine activity, one might propose the view that even the
humanity of Christ did not begin at any particular time—an interpretation which necessarily borders on docetism and threatens the
true historicity of Christ no less than the opposite view does His
ideality.   But vacillation between these two views will be altogether avoided if it be admitted that the uniting divine activity
is also an eternal activity, but that, as in God there is no distinction
between resolve and activity, this eternal activity means for us
simply a divine decree, identical as such with the decree to create
man and included therein ; but the aspect of this decree which is
turned towards us as activity, or its manifestation in the actual
beginning of the life of the Redeemer, through which that eternal
decree realized itself, as at a single point of space so also at a moment
of time, is temporal.   So that the temporality has reference purely
to the person-forming activity of the human nature, during which

---

[1] Joann. Damasc. iii. 2 : καὶ τότε ἐπεσκίασεν ἐπ' αὐτὴν ἡ τοῦ θεοῦ . . . ἐνυπόσ-
τατος σοφία καὶ δύναμις, ὁ υἱὸς τοῦ θεοῦ . . . καὶ συνέπηξεν ἑαυτῷ . . . σάρκα
ἐψυχωμένην . . . οὐ ταῖς κατὰ μικρὸν προσθήκαις ἀπαρτιζομένου τοῦ σχήματος, ἀλλ'
ὑφ' ἓν τελειωθέντος. On the other point, see Athanas., *ad Epict.* (ed. Patav.),
i. p. 731 : πόθεν δὲ πάλιν ἡρεύξαντό τινες ἴσην ἀσέβειαν . . . ὥστε εἰπεῖν, μὴ νεώτερον
εἶναι τὸ σῶμα τῆς τοῦ λόγου θεότητος ἀλλὰ συναΐδιον αὐτῷ διὰ παντὸς γεγενῆσθαι,
ἐπειδὴ ἐκ τῆς οὐσίας τῆς σοφίας συνέστη.

[2] See Gerhard, *loc.* iii. p. 421.

it was taken up into the union ; and we can with equal justice say
that Christ even as a human person was ever coming to be simultaneously with the world itself.[1]

The presentation of this act of union and of the relation of the
two natures in the union involves two other formulæ, one asserting
the *impersonality* of the human nature in Christ before its union
with the divine ; the other affirming His *supernatural conception*.

With regard to the first of these, the statement that the human
nature of Christ in itself is *impersonal*, or that it has no subsistence
of its own, but subsists only through the divine, is, in this scholastic
dress, very clumsy and obscure.   It is not an easily solved problem,
to think of something as the human nature of Christ and yet as
impersonal, since the nature in which we all share can only be
called the nature of an individual in so far as it has become personal
in him.   But if we go into the idea, there must arise the new difficulty, how, in view of this impersonality, the human nature in
Christ can fail to be more imperfect in Him than in us all ?   But
this confusion disappears when the matter is rightly conceived.
The term ' human nature ' can properly mean only this life-form
as a unity, as in essence it is person-forming and has its existence
in the changing course of personal life.   Hence the origin of each
individual of our species is to be regarded as an act which human
nature as a living force brings about by itself.   The meaning is
this—that since by this act there could be given to a person at the
start only the germ of the imperfect and obscure God-consciousness,
not the absolutely powerful God-consciousness itself, while in the
Person of Christ this last must have been included in the development right from the very beginnings of life, therefore without the
accession of the uniting divine activity the Person of Christ would
not have come into being.   But the expression remains an unfortunate one, that the human nature of Christ would have been
impersonal—all that it means is that the human nature would not
have become this personality of Christ, but that that divine influence
upon the human nature is at one and the same time the incarnation
of God in human consciousness and the formation of the human
nature into the personality of Christ.   In the same way, the ex-

---

[1] Of the two terms employed by the Greek Fathers for this act of union,
ἐνσάρκωσις is much to be preferred to ἐνσωμάτωσις.   The latter in part admits
of the idea that the λόγος was implanted in a body already complete, in part
the idea that the λόγος was only allied to a body, but Himself took the
place of the soul.   Neither idea is present in ἐνσάρκωσις.   Hence, where the
subject is handled properly, this term and the corresponding ' incarnatio ' are
much more common than ' corporatio ' and ἐνσωμάτωσις.

pression ' this human nature would have remained impersonal '
(which likewise is only apparently negative) merely indicates the
permanency of that same divine influence and of whatever follows
from it in the Person of Christ. But the formula was shaped with
special reference to those who hold that the Word was united with
the Person of Jesus only long after His Person had reached maturity
—and who therefore assume a personality for His human nature
apart from this union.

It is involved in this formula that in the origin of the Person of
Christ a supernatural activity was operative. The second formula
agrees with it, in that it adds to this yet another *supernatural*
element—namely, the complete exclusion of the male activity *in the
conception of Christ.* For this is a second element : the being of
God in Christ cannot possibly be explained by the fact that no male
activity had any share in His conception. This position must
be considered from a twofold point of view : first, with reference to
the available New Testament testimonies on the subject ; next, with
reference to its dogmatic value. Those stories [1] are never again
referred to in the further course of the history of Christ ; nor does
any apostolic passage appeal to them. They conflict with the two
genealogies of Christ, which go back to Joseph in a simple and
straightforward way without taking any account of these stories.
So far as John is concerned, they conflict not only with his silence
concerning the fact itself, but also with the way in which he relates,
without any corrective remark, that Jesus was called the son of
Joseph by His countrymen and acquaintances.[2] The same sort of
thing is also found in both Matthew and Luke.[3] Anyone who
takes the stories of a Virgin Birth as literally exact has of course one
miracle more to stand for ; but probably no one will wish to maintain that such acceptance of them introduces into our faith an
element at variance with its true nature—though certainly those
who delight in parallels between these birth-narratives and the
various Jewish and heathen legends of the supernatural conception
of distinguished men go as far as they can in that direction. On
the other hand, others have doubts about basing a doctrine, in these
circumstances, solely upon these stories, and even, it may be, about
setting it up as an indispensable part of the creed. They rather
find themselves constrained to conclude from the available evidence
that among the original followers of Christ no great value was

[1] Matt. 1[18-25] and Luke 1[31-34].
[2] John 6[42].   [3] Matt. 13[55], Luke 4[22].

attached to this circumstance, nor was there any quite fixed and
generally recognized tradition on the subject. And if they do so,
we are bound to grant them that it is quite possible to believe in
Christ as Redeemer without believing in His supernatural conception
in this sense.

So far as the second point of view is concerned—that of the
dogmatic value of this belief—first, not only are the passages in the
ancient creeds [1] so expressed that they betray virtually no trace of
a dogmatic purpose, but the same is true also of the modern creeds
borrowed from them.[2] The additions made in the latter to the
expressions sometimes adopted from the old creeds, sometimes presupposed as accepted,[3] have at most here and there a slight dogmatic
colouring, either with reference to original sin or to the implanting
of the divine in human nature—the only points on account of which
the fact can have importance for the Christian faith. A closer
consideration will show, however, that it is without any real bearing
upon either question. For we have already claimed that the
Person of Christ is supernatural, in our sense of the term, in both
these relations ; and thus, although this was not definitely expressed, it has been indicated that no adequate explanation of His
origin can be found in an act of the person-forming power of human
nature, mediated through a double-sided sexual activity. For, as
has been said above,[4] the sinfulness of every individual has its root
in the previous generation. It follows that the Redeemer could not
come into being through natural procreation, since He must not
Himself belong to the corporate life of sinfulness. The same is true
also with regard to the other point. For the reproductive power of
the species cannot be adequate to produce an individual through
whom something is to be introduced, for the first time, into the
species, which was never in it before. For that it is necessary to

---

[1] *Symb. rom.*: τὸν γεννηθέντα ἐκ πνεύματος ἁγίου καὶ Μαρίας τῆς παρθένου·
qui natus est de spiritu sancto ex Maria virgine.—*Symb. Nic. Const.*: σαρκωθέντα
ἐκ πνεύματος ἁγίου καὶ Μαρίας τῆς παρθένου καὶ ἐνανθρωπήσαντα.

[2] *Conf. Aug.* 8 : natus ex virgine Maria.—*Exp. simpl.* xi. p. 26 : non ex viri
coitu sed conceptum purissime ex spiritu sancto et natum ex Maria *semper
virgine.*—*Conf. Helv.* xi. p. 96 : carnem . . . ex intacta virgine Maria, spiritu
cooperante, sumens.—*Conf. Gallic.* xiv. p. 116 : cuius caro sit vere *semen
Abrahae et Davidis*, quamvis arcana et incomprehensibili spiritus sancti virtute
fuerit suo tempore in utero beatae illius virginis concepta.—*Conf. Anglic.* ii.
p. 127 : in utero beatae virginis ex illius substantia *naturam humanam* assumsit.
—*Conf. Belg.* xviii. p. 180 : conceptus in utero beatae virginis Mariae idque
virtute spiritus sancti absque viri opere.

[3] Even where the subject is not mentioned at all, as in the *Symb. Quic.* and
the *Conf. Hungar.*, no definite intention need be suspected.

[4] See § 69.

postulate, in addition to this reproductive power, a creative activity combined with the human activity ; only thus can the influence of the sexual activity in procreation be neutralized—an influence which would involve participation in the universal sinfulness. In this sense everyone who assumes in the Redeemer a natural sinlessness and a new creation through the union of the divine with the human, postulates a supernatural conception as well. But where natural procreation is inadequate, there its partial neutralization must also be inadequate. For the being of God in a life cannot be explained by its origin from a virgin without sexual intercourse ; and equally the absence of any paternal share in the new life cannot free that life from participation in the corporate life of sinfulness so long as the maternal share remains altogether what it is by nature. And so before long the complementary idea was formed, that in the same way Mary too must have been free from inherited sinfulness. But for one thing, the same affirmation must be made, and for the same reason, about the mother of Mary, and so right back through the generations. And for another, in so far as every psychical factor has also its physical counterpart, every actual sin of Mary must have exercised an influence upon the child so long as its life was enclosed within hers. Since, therefore, there is no doctrine or tradition of a continuous series of mothers who were conceived, and who remained, without sin, the absence of the male share in the begetting of the Redeemer is in both connexions inadequate ; and consequently the assumption of a Virgin Birth is superfluous. Consequently everything rests upon the higher influence which, as a creative divine activity, could alter both the paternal and the maternal influence in such a way that all ground for sinfulness was removed, and this although procreation was perfectly natural—as indeed only this creative divine activity could avail to give completeness to the natural imperfection of the child who was begotten. The general idea of a supernatural conception remains, therefore, essential and necessary, if the specific pre-eminence of the Redeemer is to remain undiminished. But the more precise definition of this supernatural conception as one in which there was no male activity has no connexion of any kind with the essential elements in the peculiar dignity of the Redeemer ; and hence, in and by itself, is no constituent part of Christian doctrine. Whoever accepts this definition, therefore, accepts it only on the ground of the narratives involving it contained in the New Testament writings ; hence belief in it, like belief in many matters of fact which have just as little necessary connexion with the dignity and the work of the Redeemer, belongs solely to the doctrine of Scripture ; and everyone has to reach a decision about it by the proper application of those principles of criticism and interpretation which approve themselves to Him.   But anyone who accepts a supernatural conception in our sense of the term can hardly, at least, find any reason in the supernatural element which they contain for denying the historical character of these narratives, or for departing from the literal interpretation of them.   Similarly anyone who cannot accept them as literally and historically true is still quite free to hold to the doctrine proper of the supernatural conception.   But if it is superfluous to set up a doctrine of the Virgin Birth proper, it is also inadvisable to do so, for this involves one all too easily in investigations of a purely scientific character which lie quite outside our sphere.[1]

And now in order to avoid misunderstanding, it is necessary to say only this further about a conception which has come to prevail everywhere in Christendom.   First, this physiologically supernatural element does not, in itself, imply what we demand of the divine influence in the conception of the Redeemer ; nor has it any influence upon the racial character of Jesus' personality—it neither abolishes, in itself, that which carries with it a participation in sinfulness, nor does it rob Him of what belongs to His historicity.   Secondly, for the same reasons, we must avoid spinning out the notion, which, as we have seen, has no other basis than the Gospel narratives, further than these narratives require ; hence the assertion that Mary remained a virgin is to be rejected as completely baseless.   Thirdly, the notion must not be based upon—and just as little made the basis of—a condemnation of the sexual impulse, as if its satisfaction were something sinful and productive of sin.   Lastly, even if we take the narratives literally and in a historical sense, we must not assume that their terminology is pedantically exact ; in particular, we must keep in mind that the angel could not then speak to Mary of the Holy Spirit in the more precise New Testament sense.[2] Therefore all ingenious explanations as to why this activity is attributed specially to the Holy Spirit are out of place.[3]   But only completely uninitiated persons could, in spite of the clear distinc-

[1] Consider, e.g., the expressions italicized in the quotations given above from the creeds.

[2] Joann. Damasc., rightly understood, agrees with this (i. 19, iii. 11) τῇ μὲν ἐνσαρκώσει τοῦ λόγου οὔτε ὁ πατὴρ οὔτε τὸ πνεῦμα κατ' οὐδένα λόγον κεκοινώνηκεν εἰ μὴ κατ' εὐδοκίαν, although elsewhere he speaks differently and less precisely.

[3] Cf. Gerh., loc. iii. p. 416, whose explanations depend principally upon Hilarius, de fid. trin. ii.

tion always made by the teachers of the Church,[1] so confuse the relation as to call Jesus the son of the Holy Spirit.

3. The second formula of our proposition, which describes the state of union of the two natures, can also be rightly understood only by the help of the canon we have laid down. Otherwise it would be easy to regard the association of the two natures as one on equal terms ; and, since an absolute equilibrium between them cannot be assumed, also to suppose an occasional preponderance on the side of the human nature. The nature of the association, however, must at every moment be such that the activity proceeds from the being of God in Christ, and the human nature is only taken up into association with it. If we think here of the antithesis—and it must certainly not be overlooked—between predominantly active and predominantly passive moments in human life, we might well be apprehensive that we are still losing, in this way, the completeness of the human nature in Christ, since of course passive states cannot proceed from the divine in Him, from which yet everything must proceed—and so passive states would necessarily be lacking in Him. To take this point now in its widest reference, we find one passive condition posited as necessary, almost as constant, in Christ, so that in a sense all His actions depend upon it—namely, sympathy with the condition of men ; yet at the same time in everything which proceeded from this we shall most distinctly recognize the impulse of the reconciling being of God in Christ ; which accordingly seems to be conditioned by a passive state which could only take its rise in the human nature. Now if that were really the case, and Christ could have come to all those actions, and therefore strictly speaking to the whole work of redemption, only through an almost accidental feeling [i.e. sympathy], then inevitably our whole idea of the Redeemer would thereby become something different from that which up till now we have represented to ourselves. But our canon also compels us to think of the human nature of Christ in such feelings, not as moved for and through itself, but only as taken up into association with an activity of the divine in Christ. Now this ' divine ' is the divine love in Christ which, once and for all or in every moment—whichever expression be chosen—gave direction to His feelings for the spiritual conditions of men. In virtue of these feelings, and in consequence of them, there then arose the impulse to particular helpful acts. So that in this interrelation every original activity belongs solely to the divine, and

---

[1] Many passages in Gerh., *loc. cit.*

everything passive solely to the human. For even the human activities conditioned by those impulses carry in themselves the quality of passivity. There must certainly, however, have been, even in the life of Christ, other passive states which did not proceed from any spiritual impulse, but only from the natural connexion of the human organism with external nature. Now to these states we must, also in accordance with our canon, apply the formula originally intended only for the act of union, that the human nature is not the personal nature of Christ before it has been taken up into union with the divine. For all such states were still impersonal so long as they were simply passive ; but their assumption into the innermost personal consciousness and their permeation by a divine impulse were so entirely one and the same thing that before such permeation they would have been assumed only as an external and alien element. So that, to sum up, we may say that there can have been no active state in Christ which, regarded as existing for itself, did not arise from the being of God in Him, and was not perfected by the human nature ; and similarly no passive state whose transformation into activity—which first made it a personal state—did not follow the same course.

Against this, of course, the objection might be urged, that if we distinguish individual moments, and ascribe to the divine in Christ the rise of all the activities which follow each other thus in time, then this divine in Christ, in contradiction to what can properly be asserted of a being of God, is being described as a temporal thing, with an activity which arises and passes away. But this difficulty too is resolved if, carrying further (under the guidance of our canon) the answer already [1] given to the same objection with regard to the act of union, we say that even during the union the Divine Essence in Christ retained its identity, only becoming active in temporal fashion, and that only that side of this activity is temporal which had already become human and passed over into the sphere of outward appearance. So that in Christ Himself the original assumptive divine activity and the divine activity during the union are not to be distinguished ; but all activities, in so far as distinguishable in time, are simply developments of the human activities. Every outward activity of Christ, whether it is to be regarded rather as an activity of the intellect or as one of the will, was in its aspect of human growth a result of the temporal development ; and only in so far as all emergent activity of Christ is to be regarded thus can we

[1] In 2 of this section.

rightly ascribe to Him a perfect human soul, but a soul inwardly impelled by this special being of God in Him, which, retaining its unchangeable identity, permeates that soul in the variety of its functions and moments, as that variety continually develops.[1] This, too, is the meaning of the phrase of the Schools, that *the union is a personal one.* It is not a special nature which comes into being in this way, one which could and must be distinguished from other human existence ; what comes into existence through the being of God in Christ is all perfectly human, and in its totality constitutes a unity, the unity of a natural life-story, in which everything that emerges is purely human, and one thing can be deduced from another, since every moment presupposes those which have gone before, yet in which everything can be completely understood only upon the presupposition of that union through which alone this Person could come into being, so that every moment also reveals the divine in Christ as that which conditions it.   And if, after all that has been said, we define the spheres of our two propositions in relation to each other, then we shall have to say that the first applies exclusively to the very earliest beginning of the existence of Christ when the life was coming into being as a simple entity, and consequently that it holds only of the time before the historical appearance of Christ. And similarly the latter applies exclusively after this appearance ; for only when the human element is absolutely complete, and there is no more growth in its coexistence with the being of God in Him, can it be purely co-operative in its action.   And so it is comprehensible that for the time filled by this historical appearance there should be two different modes of interpretation, which, although quite consistent with each other, yet when their true relation is not recognized, seem to be incompatible.   One of these pays such exclusive attention throughout to the initiatory divine factor that it is in danger of losing sight altogether of the human context ; the other attempts everywhere to grasp the human context so completely that it comes near losing sight of the underlying divine factor.

4. In agreement with both formulæ of our proposition are, further, the old canons—they have only a negative but no real

---

[1] The same view is expressed, among others, by Joann. Dam., if only he be rightly understood (iii. 7 ; p. 215 seq.) : Ἰστέον δὲ, ὡς εἰ καὶ περιχωρεῖν ἐν ἀλλήλαις τὰς τοῦ κυρίου φύσεις φαμὲν, ἀλλ᾽ οἴδαμεν ὅπως ἐκ τῆς θείας φύσεως ἡ περιχώρησις γέγονεν· αὔτη μὲν γὰρ διὰ πάντων διήκει καθὼς βούλεται καὶ περιχωρεῖ, δι᾽ αὐτῆς δὲ οὐδέν. καὶ αὔτη μὲν τῶν οἰκείων αὐχημάτων τῇ σαρκὶ μεταδίδωσι (of which more below) μένουσα αὐτὴ ἀπαθής, καὶ τῶν τῆς σαρκὸς παθῶν (to which everything temporal belongs) ἀμέτοχος.

positive value—which as a result of the discussions in the Councils are expounded even in the oldest systematic treatises.[1] It is obvious that underlying the earliest threefold statement of the points in question [2] is the idea that the divine nature in Christ cannot in any way be separated from the human nature in Him, so as to permit of the sundering of the two.   Every such separation, even if in accordance with these formulæ it were understood only in a temporal or spatial sense, could still be only a separation of the activities ; and if such a separation were possible, then there would have to be in Christ, on the one hand, human activities in no way dependent upon the impulse of the divine, and on the other, divine activities which would have nowhere betrayed themselves in His human nature.   But these could have given no proof of their derivation from the act of union, since they would bear in themselves no similarity to this ; accordingly these formulæ exclude just what our canon also excludes.   The other threefold statement [3] quite clearly has the purpose of rejecting any idea of an alteration of one nature by the other.   Through any such alteration—which of course could only have proceeded from the human nature—the divine would have become something conditioned in space and time ; and similarly, if the human had been altered by the divine, the Person would have lost its identity with the rest of the human race.   In neither case would there have been a union of the divine with the human.   Here too the aim, therefore, is the same as that which guides us in seeking to understand the divine factor in the union in the only way which is compatible with the integrity of the human, and *vice versa*.   None the less, these two formulæ are not for us to-day ; they are altogether based upon the conception of divinity as a nature, which can only serve to introduce confusion everywhere.

It is time that, along with these negative formulæ, we consigned to the history of dogma also the extremely empty and formal theory, that propositions about Christ, to be correct, must be differently constructed according as we are speaking of the whole Person of Christ, or only of one of the two natures.   Such rules, if they are to be normative for the language of edification, imposing the limits within which it must move, could only be of value in times of heresy-hunting ; but heresy-hunting in this form is hardly likely to recur.   In general, we must recognize that we are no longer

---

[1] *E.g.* Joann. Dam. iii. 3 ff.   [2] ἀχωρίστως, ἀδιαιρέτως, and ἀδιαστάτως.
[3] ἀναλλοιώτως, ἀτρέπτως, and ἀσυγχύτως.

at the same stage as the men of these far-off days, when the more exact technical terminology was only being gradually developed out of the popular presentations of eminent men.   Now that the system of doctrine has been completed, and development within the Schools goes its own way, Christian preachers must have the freedom granted to the poets, to make use of terms which cannot find a place in the terminology of technical theology, provided that in their immediate context, from which they must not be torn, they are unobjectionable, and that they involve nothing which would lessen the dignity of the Redeemer or offend people's feeling for that dignity.   If, on the other hand, these rules are meant to be used only in technical theology itself, in order that at every point it may more easily determine whether individual formulæ are or are not consistent with the general propositions, then they depend too much upon the use of the expression ' nature,' for the divine as well as for the human, to be useful when once that mode of expression has been abandoned.   And we possess a far better canon in the formula that in Christ the creation of man first reaches completion.   For what distinguishes Christ from all others is that which is innermost in Him ; hence the indwelling being of God in Him must be related to the whole human nature in the same way as that which previously was innermost was related to the whole human organism—an analogy which, even if not clearly expressed, runs through the whole foregoing presentation of the subject.

5. It follows at once from the character of the being of God in Christ as now set forth, and from the necessity of ceasing to treat the Supreme Being as a nature, as well as from our previous teaching on the divine attributes, that the theory of a mutual communication of the attributes of the two natures to one another also is to be banished from the system of doctrine, and handed over to the history of doctrine.   For in so far as we arrive at our ideas of divine attributes only by analogy, the attribution of these to human nature, if that nature is not to be destroyed by the infinity of these attributes, is merely an assertion of absolute human excellence. But on the other hand, in so far as each particular attribute is simply a negation of the essence of man, and it is only when viewed all together as one that they can represent the Divine Essence, it is impossible to predicate of human nature even the individual features of this collective view.   For example, if we were to attribute to human nature the identity of omniscience and omnipotence, so that one and the same omniscient omnipotence and

omnipotent omniscience of the divine nature should have permeated
the assumed human nature,[1] as heat permeates iron, then during
this communication nothing human could have been left in Christ,
since everything human is essentially a negation of omniscient
omnipotence.   If in consequence we fall back upon regarding the
divine attributes as altogether or for the most part quiescent—
though the former alternative alone is consistent, not even the
miracles being traced to an exceptional activity of the divine
attributes [2]—the emptiness of this whole theory comes out most
clearly.   For since divine attributes are simply activities, in what
consists the communication of these when they are inactive ?
Moreover, in that case the union of the natures would altogether
cease to be a dogmatic idea in the stricter sense, for it cannot possibly
be a statement regarding an impression received from Christ, since
the quiescent attributes cannot make themselves perceptible even
indirectly.   It is the same with the communication of human
attributes to the divine nature.   On the one hand, all statements
regarding our God-consciousness are just such an attribution,
inasmuch as all divine attributes are drawn, by analogy, from
human.   But apart from this, it would necessarily mean the
negation of the Divine Essence, if to the divine nature there were to
be ascribed any human quality (and in any way) which had to be
excluded in the original formation of our conceptions of divine
attributes.   If, for example, to the divine nature there were to be
communicated anything human in the way of capacity for suffering, in such a communication no room is left for anything divine ;
nay, every notable human excellence, even, is a diminution of the
capacity for suffering, and even what most inwardly resembles the
divine in man does not so much suffer as give its activity a re-
active form.   It has been believed that the capacity for suffering
must be attributed even to the divine nature in Christ, partly on
the ground that otherwise redemptive power would be lacking to
His suffering ; [3] not only, however, has this older assertions against
it,[4] but equally it depends, as we shall show later, upon wrong ideas

[1] See *Sol. decl.*, p. 778 : cum tota divinitatis plenitudo in Christo habitet
ut in proprio suo corpore etiam . . . in assumpta humana natura divinam
suam virtutem exerceat . . . idque ea quodammodo ratione qua . . . ignis in
ferro candente agit.

[2] See Reinh., *Dogm.*, § 97, 2 and 6.

[3] *Sol. decl.*, p. 771 : Si enim persuaderi mihi patiar ut credam solam
humanam naturam pro me passam esse, profecto Christus mihi non magni
pretii salvator erit, sed ipse tandem salvatore eget.

[4] Joann. Dam. iii. 7 : αὕτη μὲν (ἡ θεία φύσις) τῶν οἰκείων αὐχημάτων τῇ σαρκὶ
μεταδίδωσι μένουσα αὐτὴ ἀπαθής, καὶ τῶν τῆς σαρκὸς παθῶν ἀμέτοχος.

of the work of redemption.   And so it might well be said that this doctrine of the mutual communication of attributes, truly and completely worked out, must cancel again the union of the two natures, since in virtue of that communication each nature would cease to be what it is.   The rejection of this theory, however, by no means involves a preferring the Reformed school to the Lutheran. For if the former speaks, instead,[1] of contrasted attributes of two natures in one person, it is rightly met with the objection that it is dividing Christ, since contrasted things cannot be one, nor can the natures be one either, if their attributes are held apart.   But the other school is chargeable with a similar division.   For if the communication is to be a real one, then through it there arise in each nature two kinds of activities, which cannot really form a series—*e.g.* in the human nature of Christ there would have to be ideational activities both in the manner of a limited consciousness and in that of the communicated omniscience.   Both doctrines, therefore, are equally to be rejected, since they both depend upon the false idea of a divine nature to which it is possible to ascribe a group of attributes.

§ 98. *Third Theorem.—Christ was distinguished from all other men by His essential sinlessness and His absolute perfection.*

1. By essential sinlessness we are to understand a sinlessness which has its adequate ground within His personality itself, so that it would have been altogether the same whatever the outward relations might have been (and among outward relations we may include also whatever belongs to the body).   This expression at least sets forth with sufficient definiteness the point at issue, since it follows from what has been said that this inner ground can be none other than the union of the divine and the human in His Person.   That which in individual cases we experience immediately we must conceive to be possible also in general.   We have immediate experience of the fact that by a favourable combination of circumstances sin, even inward sin, may be prevented from becoming actual.   But this happens in such a way that therein we not only remain conscious of ourselves as sinful men, but are even confirmed in this consciousness through this very perception, for it implies a recognition that in our case the *inner* ground for the prevention of sin is lacking.   Such sinlessness, which in comparison with essential

---

[1] *Conf. Gall.* xv. p. 116 : manente tamen unaquaque illarum naturarum in sua distincta proprietate, etc.   Similarly, *Conf. Belg.* xix.

sinlessness is no more than accidental, would therefore not express
the peculiar excellence of the Redeemer ; and not only so, but
where the inward possibility of sinning is posited, there too is
posited in addition at least an infinitely small amount of the reality
of sin, in the form of tendency. So that one who can be content
with such accidental sinlessness in the Redeemer may also let pass
actual sin in Him, provided it does not make itself so perceptible [1]
that someone for a moment might claim superiority to Christ.
At the same time, the usual formulæ of technical theology do not
mark the distinction with the required sharpness, and the quarrel
which has been waged between them seems a perfectly empty one.
It is true that the formula, *potuit non peccare*, asserts the essential
pre-eminence of Christ, if taken as affirming a contrast to the state
of all other men. For these, one and all, can never not-sin ; sin
creeps into everything—which, strictly speaking, must then have
been the case with Christ also (to the extent of the infinitely small
amount referred to above), if a real possibility of sinning is ascribed
to Him. But the formula does not express that pre-eminence,
as soon as it is taken to mean something different from the other
formula, *non potuit peccare* ; for when made a contrast to this it
involves the possibility of sinning. But exactly the same holds
true of the latter formula ; it too may be used by one who is only
assuming a general divine protection exerted over the Redeemer.
Thus it too corresponds to the content of our formula only if it be
taken as the equivalent of the first in the sense indicated.

But, even on the basis of our formula, it remains difficult to determine what it excludes from Christ, and that in such wise as to preserve intact all that must belong to Him in virtue of His likeness to
us. And this point is indisputably one from which it must be
possible to develop much that is essential for Christian ethics ;
for everything depends on determining the point where sin begins.
A special difficulty arises here from the fact that even in the earliest
documents of the faith it is asserted that Christ was tempted in all
points, a statement which in the light of the conclusion reached
above [2] involves sin in Him, if we take it as meaning that there
was even an infinitely small element of struggle involved. On the
other hand, susceptibility to the contrast of the pleasurable and
the painful belongs to the reality of human nature, so that it must
be possible for pleasure and pain to exist in a sinless way, and the
beginning of sin must lie between the moment at which pleasure

---

[1] John 8⁴⁶.   [2] Cf. § 93, 4.

and pain exist in this sinless way and that at which struggle begins. If, at the same time, we remember that in Christ every impulse must have been determined by the God-consciousness, it follows that in Him, too, pleasure and pain must have been possible, but not so that they determined the impulse ; that is, they must have been present only as the result of an impulse which was determined in the manner appropriate to Him. They *are* such results when as sensation or feeling they remain wholly within the limits of the quiescent consciousness, but not when they pass over into desire or repulsion. Now temptation consists just in the approximation of these two, and Christ can have been tempted without prejudice to His essential sinlessness only if pleasure and pain came to Him as intensified sensation, while His essential sinlessness explains why they never could become anything more than symptoms of a state, but without any determinative or co-determinative power ; but not if they came so that the transition from the one sort to the other ever really took place.[1]   Only, as this rule must hold good for every moment of Christ's life without exception, it must be observed that this way of expressing it is applicable only to a developed consciousness, and that the childhood of Christ as well can only have had the character of perfect innocence if this rule held good then also in proportion to the stage of development reached at the moment.   So that in respect of sin Christ was at all times equally different from all other men, and at all times equally essentially free from sin.

It belongs further to this sinlessness, that Christ can neither have originated real error Himself, or even have accepted the error of others with real conviction, and as well-established truth.   Nor is it necessary to restrict this principle to the sphere of His proper vocation ; only we must hold fast to the distinction between the acceptance and the propagation of ideas which were definitely maintained by others (in regard to these one neither makes any investigation nor accepts any responsibility), and the forming of a judgment which in some connexion thereafter determines one's mode of action.   In the latter case, error always presupposes either a precipitancy which nothing but irrelevant motives could have

---

[1] In the treatment of this question I could take no special account of the story of the Temptation, for to me it is impossible to regard it as historical. Obviously its content, taken literally, is such that in comparison Christ must often have been much more strongly tempted in the course of His active life. And hence the narrator is by no means to be blamed who indicates (Luke 4[13]) that this is not to be regarded as for Him the end of all temptation.

occasioned, or an obscured sense of truth which partly has its basis in the universal sinfulness, but partly too is in each single case bound up with the special sinfulness of the individual.

Closely connected with this doctrine of the essential sinlessness of Christ is the idea of the *natural immortality* of Christ—namely, that Christ would not have been subject to death in virtue of His human nature ; an idea which has not, it is true, been fixed by being included in any of the creeds, nor is really based on passages in the Bible,[1] but yet has found very general acceptance. But the only basis for the conception is that when death is regarded as the wages of sin, he who is free from all connexion with sin must also have been free from the dominion of death. When we take into account what has already been said above [2] about the natural immortality of Adam and the connexion of all natural evils with sin, nothing more can be inferred from the sinlessness of Christ than that death can have been no evil for Christ. We must hold to this position, and instead of the idea in question take our side with those who acknowledge that immortality was conferred upon Christ's human nature only with the Resurrection.[3] All the more that mortality and the capacity for physical suffering are so closely connected that such a natural immortality in Christ would make the capacity of human nature in His Person for suffering a mere empty phrase, and no great worth could be attached to His physical sufferings without self-contradiction.

Yet this idea is not represented as simply an inference from the sinlessness of Christ ; it is held that it alone reveals to us the true significance of all the statements which set forth His death as a voluntary one, and thus brings out fully the higher significance of His suffering and death. But precisely from this point of view the idea is a highly dubious one. For one who cannot naturally die cannot be put to death by force either ; it would therefore have been necessary that Christ by a miracle should first have made Himself mortal, in order that it should be possible to put Him to death ; so that His death would have been, almost directly, His own act.

2. Now so far as the *absolute perfection* of His human nature during the period of His manhood is concerned, special emphasis is very often laid upon intellectual and physical excellence, especially

---

[1] What Christ Himself says in John 10[17-18] expresses, not a physical, but a social and ethical relation.

[2] Cf. § 59, *Postscript*.

[3] *Conf. Belg.* xix. p. 181 : et quamvis eidem naturae immortalitatem resurrectione sua dederit, etc.

in the older treatments of the subject.   But—since here no records
come to our aid which would transform every such proposition into
a historical one, and so remove it from the sphere of doctrine
altogether—it may well be doubted whether the impression which
we receive from Christ is sufficient to justify us in postulating for
Him qualities which we cannot deduce from the union of the divine
with the human nature.   Only one thing can be said if we deduce
the temporal appearance of this creative activity, as an individual
fact, from the general divine ordination.   And this is that, just
as the Redeemer could appear only at a particular time and only
out of the midst of this people, so, too, the divine activity would
not have assumed the human nature and created the Person of the
Redeemer in such a way that any deformity could have resulted.
It is natural enough, therefore, to ascribe to the Redeemer a
physical ideality also ; but since the physical aspect of His appearance was to be of no significance in itself, but only as the organ
of that union, the ideality must be restricted solely to this.   From
this assumption, and from the undisturbed and continuous influence of a pure will, there is to be inferred only a healthiness
which is equally remote from a disproportionate strength or
dominance of individual physical functions and from morbid
weakness, inasmuch as by both of these the balanced aptitude
of the organism for all demands of the will is impaired.   To this
accordingly we must restrict ourselves, and all the more reject all
prying questions,[1] because our ideas of the relation between body
and soul are still open to important corrections.   And thus, if the
ancients have not seldom something to say about the beauty of
the Redeemer,[2] this is an idea which lies very near the frontier
which we must not touch, and we may disregard it as an unconscious after-effect of heathen notions.

§ 99. *The facts of the Resurrection and the Ascension of Christ, and
the prediction of His Return to Judgment, cannot be laid down
as properly constituent parts of the doctrine of His Person.*

1. When we compare with the canon for dogmatic statements

---

[1] It is a divine provision, certainly of the highest significance, but not
sufficiently recognized, that neither a trustworthy tradition regarding the
external aspect of Christ's person, nor an authentic picture of it, has come
down to us. For the same reason, we may be sure, we lack an exact
description of His manner of life and a connected narrative of the events
of His career.

[2] *E.g.* Chrysost., *in ep. ad Col. Homil.* viii.: οὕτως ἦν καλὸς, ὡς οὐδὲ εἶναι
εἰπεῖν.

laid down above,[1] the propositions, on the one hand, concerning the Person of Christ which we have so far 'set forth, and on the other the statements contained in the oldest creeds [2] expressing these facts (*i.e.* Resurrection, Ascension, and Judgment), it will be seen that the former correspond to both the requirements insisted on, and the latter to neither. For if the redeeming efficacy of Christ depends upon the being of God in Him, and faith in Him is grounded upon the impression that such a being of God indwells Him, then it is impossible to prove any immediate connexion between these facts and that doctrine. The disciples recognized in Him the Son of God without having the faintest premonition of His resurrection and ascension, and we too may say the same of ourselves ; moreover neither the spiritual presence which He promised nor all that He said about His enduring influence upon those who remained behind is mediated through either of these two facts. This may well depend upon His sitting at the right hand of God—by which, however, since the expression may be strictly an impossible one, we must understand simply the peculiar and incomparable dignity of Christ, raised above all conflict —but not upon a visible resurrection or ascension, since of course Christ could have been raised to glory even without these intermediate steps ; and if so, it is impossible to see in what relation both these can stand to the redeeming efficacy of Christ. It is true, on the one hand, Paul seems to attribute to the resurrection, just as much as to the death, a share of its own in redemption ; [3] yet on the other, the way in which he brings it forward as a guarantee of our own resurrection [4] shows that he in no sense thinks of it as having an exclusive connexion with the peculiar being of God in Christ. Also, it is never adduced as an evidence of the divine indwelling in Christ ; for it is everywhere ascribed, not to Himself, but to God.[5] No more does John adduce the visible ascension as a proof of the higher dignity of Christ. Hence we may safely credit everyone who is familiar with dogmatic statements with a recognition of the fact that the right impression of Christ can be, and has been, present in its fulness without a knowledge of these facts.

So far as the Return to Judgment is concerned, we can treat of

---

[1] Cf. § 29, 3.

[2] *Symb. Nic.* : καὶ ἀναστάντα ἐν τῇ τρίτῃ ἡμέρᾳ κατὰ τὰς γραφάς· καὶ ἀνελθόντα εἰς τοὺς οὐρανοὺς καὶ καθεζόμενον ἐκ δεξιῶν τοῦ πατρὸς· καὶ πάλιν ἐρχόμενον μετὰ δόξης κρῖναι ζῶντας καὶ νεκρούς.

[3] Rom. 4[25].   [4] 1 Cor. 15[13, 16].

[5] Acts 2[24] 3[5] 4[10] 10[40], Rom. 4[24], 1 Cor. 6[14] 15[15], 2 Cor. 4[14].

the doctrinal significance of this idea only at a later point. Here it need only be remarked that although the Judgment, in so far as we regard it as a transferable divine act, is so closely bound up with the work of redemption that it is not easy to think that God could hand it over to any but the Redeemer, yet this implies nothing greater in the Person of Christ than already we ascribe to Him apart from this ; and in any case it does not really belong to the work of redemption itself, since of course those who believe do not come into judgment. But considered as the Return of Christ it is connected with the ascension as its counterpart. Just as the latter is only an accidental form for effecting the sitting at the right hand of God, so also the promise of return is only an accidental form for the satisfaction of the longing to be united with Christ. And just as the incomprehensible and miraculous in the ascension cannot be made dependent on the divine in Christ, which reveals itself as the impulse to all His free actions, and since the ascension is nowhere presented as His act, no more can the miraculous in the Return depend upon it. So that the dissimilarity between our propositions above (those, that is to say, which we have recognized as such) and these assertions must be clear to everyone.

It is somewhat different with Christ's so-called Descent into Hell.[1] This—according to its dominant idea—would certainly belong to His redemptive activities if only we could regard it as a fact. It would then have to be regarded as an exercise of His prophetic and high-priestly office towards those who had died before His appearance. But for one thing the only passage which seems to treat of this descent [2] is far from including anything of the kind, and for another the transaction, even with this extended interpretation of the passage, would not correspond to the task to be accomplished, as we are bound to understand it. For all those also who have died since His appearance without having heard the preaching of the Gospel have the same claims as the others. Moreover, the expressions used in that passage in no way compel us to assume such an otherwise unattested fact, any more than they fix the time at which it is supposed to have happened. For these reasons the Descent has been completely omitted from our proposition.

2. Belief in these facts, accordingly, is no independent element in the original faith in Christ, of such a kind that we could not

---

[1] *Symb. Rom.*: κατελθόντα εἰς τὰ κάτωτα only in one Greek, but in several old Latin copies ; *Symb. Quic.* 36: descendit ad inferos.
[2] 1 Pet. 3[19]. Eph. 4[9] should certainly not be adduced here.

accept Him as Redeemer or recognize the being of God in Him, if we did not know that He had risen from the dead and ascended to heaven, or if He had not promised that He would return for judgment. Further, this belief is not to be derived from those original elements ; we cannot conclude that because God was in Christ He must have risen from the dead and ascended into heaven, or that because He was essentially sinless He must come again to act as Judge. Rather they are accepted only because they are found in the Scriptures ; and all that can be required of any Protestant Christian is that he shall believe them in so far as they seem to him to be adequately attested. Here the sacred writers are to be regarded only as reporters ; accordingly belief in these statements belongs, immediately and originally, rather to the doctrine of Scripture than to the doctrine of the Person of Christ. Yet an indirect connexion with that doctrine is not to be denied to such belief, in so far, that is, as our judgment about the disciples as original reporters reacts upon our judgment about the Redeemer. Anyone, for example, who, in view of the miraculous element involved, and to avoid accepting the resurrection of Christ as literal fact, prefers to suppose that the disciples were deceived and took an inward experience for an outward, ascribes to them such weakness of intellect that not only is their whole testimony to Christ thereby rendered unreliable, but also Christ, in choosing for Himself such witnesses, cannot have known what is in men.[1] Or, if we suppose that He Himself wished or arranged that they should be constrained to regard an inner experience as outward perception, then He Himself would be an originator of error, and all moral conceptions would be thrown into confusion if such a higher dignity as His were compatible with this. With the ascension it is different, so far at least as we have no adequate reason for maintaining that we have before us a direct report from an eyewitness of what actually happened, and least of all from an apostolic eyewitness. If, nevertheless, it is affirmed that Christ did rise from the dead, but was not taken up into heaven, but lived in concealment for an indeterminate time, so that He must have arranged something which could be regarded as an ascension to heaven, then the case is just the same as with the resurrection. Least closely connected with the doctrine of the Person of Christ proper is the promise of His Return, especially as it is promised for the sake of an office to be fulfilled, and so far would belong to the next section, if only that office were one directly

[1] John 2²⁵.

belonging to His vocation as Redeemer. Only if exegesis brought out clearly that a time had been fixed for this Return which has now long since elapsed, or if it were described in a way whose impossibility we could prove, would this necessarily react, if not on the doctrine of the Scriptures, yet certainly on that of the Person of Christ.

Postscript to this Doctrine.—The presentation of the Person of Christ given above, first in our own quite independent form of expression, then in closer connexion with the accepted forms of the Church, is, in essentials, so widespread and so long current in the Christian Church, that it must be regarded as the general faith of Christians. All the more that even many of those who content themselves with a lesser idea of the Redeemer reject this dominant view only because they are suspicious of the miraculous in general —whether they overlook the distinction which we have laid down,[1] or reject it—or because they believe that along with it they must accept a doctrine of the Trinity which is offensive to them on account of its polytheistic complexion. It is therefore to be hoped that many will find it easier to accept, in a freer presentation, a view by which they are repelled when they find it invested in hard scholastic forms.

It cannot, however, be definitely proved that the same form of doctrine prevailed universally in Christendom where the same faith about the relation to the Redeemer underlay it, the reason being that neither understanding nor terminology had sufficiently developed for that. Also it is undeniable that alongside this view of the Redeemer other different and lesser ones were current in Christendom very early. For both these reasons the question cannot be avoided whether the view of the Church can really be vindicated as the original one by statements of Christ Himself and of the Apostles, or whether they are right who assert that it is a view which arose later. Here it must be premised, that even supposing the originality of our doctrine were not proved, it still would not follow that it is false or arbitrarily invented, provided only that those original testimonies are not demonstrably at variance with it. But the question itself, it must be admitted, is so complicated that it cannot be decided in a manner which could win general acceptance, so long as, on the one hand, the most various opinions exist alongside each other as to the way in which the New Testament writings came into existence and as to who their authors were, and,

[1] Cf. § 13.

on the other hand, exegetical methods are so various and so arbitrary. So long as it is possible to dispute interminably over the meaning of particular passages, it is useless to have recourse to particular sayings of Christ's own to prove His essential sinlessness [1] or the being of God in Him.[2] But anyone who in the interpretation of particular passages is not content merely with a sense in harmony with his own theory, but keeps an open mind for a true impression of the whole, will scarcely be able to ascribe to the sayings of Christ about His relation to men and to His Father [3] (having regard to the way in which they complete and pervade each other) a lesser content than that set forth in our propositions, although perhaps not precisely in the sense of the ecclesiastical formulæ relating to the doctrine of the Trinity.   And at the same time these sayings are not of such a kind that they destroy the reality of Christ's human existence, as if in His temporal consciousness He had, say, a recollection of a separate existence of the divine in Him, before His incarnation.[4]

In entire agreement with this is the double appellation, Son of Man and Son of God, which Christ gives to Himself. For He could not have given Himself the first name, if He had not been conscious of sharing completely in the same human nature as others ; but it would have been meaningless to claim it specially for Himself, if He had not had a reason for doing so which others could not adduce— if, that is, the name had not had a pregnant meaning, which was meant to indicate a difference between Him and all others.[5] Similarly the connexion between the appellation Son of God and what Christ says about His relation to His Father shows that He did not use it of Himself in the same sense in which it had already been used of others [6]—as indeed is clearly involved in the expression ' only-begotten ' which comes from Christ Himself.[7] Only if we destroy this natural connexion between two designations which manifestly refer to each other, will it become easier to admit lesser

---

[1] John 8[46].   [2] John 10[30-38].

[3] John 5[17. 21. 26] 8[24. 36] 14[11. 20] 17[10. 21-23].

[4] An indication of this sort might be found in John 17[5], but John 5[19. 20] makes this interpretation almost impossible. But even apart from that it would be open to suspicion, because the petition has remained unfulfilled, since in spite of all the labour expended no one has yet reached a clear consciousness on the matter, and no one ever will.

[5] It is a strange idea that this designation was intended to refute the popular opinion that no one would know whence the Messiah came ; not less strange is the other, that it was intended to refer to a vision in Daniel (7[13]) where one *like* a Son of man—manifestly by contrast with the beasts mentioned earlier—comes in the clouds of heaven before the Ancient of days.

[6] Compare especially John 10[35 ff.].

[7] John 3[16].

interpretations and to associate them with Ebionite theories.   While, on the other hand, those passages in which a high degree of grief is ascribed to Christ,[1] or in which something is told of Him which seems to imply passionate excitement,[2] are really only details which —so far from being evidence against His sinlessness, or incompatible with the being of God in Him—manifestly caused no one to doubt Him, because everyone habitually interprets such individual moments in harmony with the total impression he has already received.   So they serve only to remind us that faith in Jesus as Redeemer was not based on details, but develops out of a total impression—from which it follows only that there are no details in existence which could have prevented that impression.   But that the faith even in the first generation of His disciples had the same content as we have set forth here, is proved, not only by the most various testimonies which ascribe to Christ perfect purity [3] and fulness of power,[4] but also by the way in which Paul describes Him, in contrast with Adam, as the originator of a new human worth, and by the Johannine presentation of the λόγος, as well as by the theory set forth in the Epistle to the Hebrews.

Now of course even these testimonies could be weakened by artificial interpretations, by tearing them out of their context and combining them with what is irrelevant.   But it is not sufficient to show merely that this expression and that other may have less significance ; it must also be made clear how it can have come about that an ordinary relation was described in extraordinary and inappropriate terms, and how the original sense of these was so early lost in the tradition.   So long as this cannot be done better than it is by entirely arbitrary hypotheses, the belief will probably hold the field that the faith of the Church is also the original faith and is founded upon the sayings of Christ about Himself.

Now if this is in general the sufficiently clear result of an examination of Scripture, our Dogmatic can not only easily dispense with the whole arsenal of particular statements which have been set forth under various rubrics [5] as proving the being of God in Christ, but put them aside all the more readily that they give no help in presenting the subject in the best way, but rather hide what is important and certain under what is untrustworthy.   For what is the use of ascribing divine titles to Christ, if He Himself calls attention to an

---

[1] Matt. 26[37], Luke 19[41].   [2] John 11[33, 38].
[5]2 Cor. 5[21], 1 Pet. 2[22], Heb. 1[3] 7[26-27] 9[14].   [4] Phil. 4[13].
[5] ὀνομαστικῶς, ἰδιωματικῶς, ἐνεργητικῶς, and λατρευτικῶς.

improper use of the word ' God ' [John 10³⁴⁻³⁶] ? But appellations which express the unity of the divine and the human in so definite and unambiguous a way as the later ' God-man ' do not occur in Scripture ; all the predicates which can be cited in this connexion are more or less uncertain in meaning.[1] So, too, as far as the divine attributes are concerned, it is natural that, since Christ is always spoken of as a man, only such attributes are ascribed to Him as express exalted humanity, so that it is easy to explain them as nothing but very permissible hyperbolical expressions. Since, further, it is difficult to distinguish between worship in the strict sense and the utterances of a deep, but not properly divine, adoration, if we were to proceed on that line everything would depend upon the divine activities asserted of Christ. But creation and preservation are only ascribed to Christ [2] in such a way that it must remain doubtful whether they do not mean that He is active cause only in so far as He is final cause. Finally, in the Resurrection and the Last Judgment, Christ is everywhere distinguished from God, for He appears only as a deputy with full powers, and hence His power is represented as resting in the Father, just as the appointment proceeds from the Father originally. Exactly the same is true of the sending of the Spirit, which Christ ascribes, now to Himself, now to the Father, who sends it at His request.[3] So that without those great supreme testimonies all these details would have little effect.

[1] It is obvious that no reference can be made here to the miraculous signs of the Old Testament, heavenly voices and appearances, by which the Son of God is to be recognized. For in any case they could have nothing to say about the Person of Christ ; at most they might have to be considered *apropos* of the doctrine of the Trinity.

[2] 1 Cor. 8⁶, Col. 1¹⁵⁻¹⁷, Heb. 1⁴.

[3] Luke 24⁴⁹ and John 15². ⁶ ; cf. John 14¹⁶. ³⁶.

SECOND DOCTRINE: THE WORK OF CHRIST

§ 100. *The Redeemer assumes believers into the power of His God-consciousness,*[1] *and this is His redemptive activity.*

1. In virtue of the teleological character of Christian piety, both the imperfect stage of the higher life, as also the challenge of it, appear in our self-consciousness as facts due to our own individual action—though we do not feel responsible for the latter in the same way as for the former. In virtue, however, of the peculiar character of Christianity this challenge is also apprehended in our self-consciousness as the act of the Redeemer.[2] These two points of view can be reconciled only by supposing that this challenge is the act of the Redeemer become our own act. And this, accordingly, is the best way of expressing the common element in the Christian consciousness of the divine grace. Hence, from this point of view, the peculiar work of the Redeemer would first be to evoke this act in us. But if we regard the matter more closely, it is clear that what we have thus described is in every case an act both of the Redeemer and of the redeemed. The original activity of the Redeemer, therefore, which belongs to Him alone, and which precedes all activity of our own in this challenge, would be that by means of which He assumes us into this fellowship of His activity and His life. The continuance of that fellowship, accordingly, constitutes the essence of the state of grace; the new corporate life is the sphere within which Christ produces this act; in it is revealed the continuous activity of His sinless perfection.

But His act in us can never be anything but the act of His sinlessness and perfection as conditioned by the being of God in Him. And so these too in addition must become ours, because otherwise it would not be His act that became ours. Now the individual life of each one of us is passed in the consciousness of sin and imperfection. Hence we can know the fellowship of the Redeemer only in so far as we are not conscious of our own individual life; as impulses flow to us from Him, we find that in Him from which everything proceeds to be the source of our activity also—a common possession,

[1] Cf. § 88.   [2] Cf. § 63, 1 and 2.

as it were. This too is the meaning of all those passages in Scripture which speak of Christ being and living in us,[1] of being dead to sin,[2] of putting off the old and putting on the new man.[3] But Christ can only direct His God-consciousness against sin in so far as He enters into the corporate life of man and sympathetically shares the consciousness of sin, but shares it as something He is to overcome.[4] This very consciousness of sin as something to be overcome becomes the principle of our activity in the action which He evokes in us. But our own immediate experience in being thus assumed into the fellowship of Christ will be explained in the first Doctrine of the second main Division, which deals with forgiveness. And the further development of this fellowship in time, through a series of common actions, is the subject of the second Doctrine, dealing with sanctification. Here we have only to explain more exactly what the Redeemer does and how He accomplishes it.

2. All Christ's activity, then, proceeds from the being of God in Him. And we know no divine activity except that of creation, which includes that of preservation, or, conversely, that of preservation, which includes that of creation. So we shall have to regard Christ's activity too in the same way. We do not, however, exclude the soul of man from creation, in spite of the fact that the creation of such a free agent and the continued freedom of a being created in the context of a greater whole is something which we cannot expect to understand ; all that we can do is to recognize the fact. The same is true of the creative activity of Christ, which is entirely concerned with the sphere of freedom. For His assumptive activity is a creative one, yet what it produces is altogether free. Now the being of God in Him as an active principle is timeless and eternal, yet its expressions are all conditioned by the form of human life. It follows that He can influence what is free only in accordance with the manner in which it enters into His sphere of living influence, and only in accordance with the nature of the free. The activity by which He assumes us into fellowship with Him is, therefore, a creative production in us of the will to assume Him into ourselves, or rather—since it is only receptiveness for His activity as involved in the impartation [5]—only our assent to the influence of His activity. But it is a condition of that activity of the Redeemer that the individuals should enter the sphere of

---

[1] Gal. 2[20], Rom. 8[10], John 17[23], 2 Cor. 13[5].
[2] Rom. 6[2. 6. 11], 1 Pet. 2[24].
[3] Col. 3[10], Eph. 4[22. 24].   [4] John 16[33].   [5] John 16[19].

His historical influence, where they become aware of Him in His self-revelation. Now this assent can only be conceived as conditioned by the consciousness of sin ; yet it is not necessary that this should precede entrance into the sphere of the Redeemer. Rather it may just as well arise within that sphere as the effect of the Redeemer's self-revelation, as indeed it certainly does come to full clarity only as we contemplate His sinless perfection. Accordingly, the original activity of the Redeemer is best conceived as a pervasive influence which is received by its object in virtue of the free movement with which he turns himself to its attraction, just as we ascribe an attractive power to everyone to whose educative intellectual influence we gladly submit ourselves. Now, if every activity of the Redeemer proceeds from the being of God in Him, and if in the formation of the Redeemer's Person the only active power was the creative divine activity which established itself as the being of God in Him, then also His every activity may be regarded as a continuation of that person-forming divine influence upon human nature. For the pervasive activity of Christ cannot establish itself in an individual without becoming person-forming in him too, for now all his activities are differently determined through the working of Christ in him, and even all impressions are differently received—which means that the personal self-consciousness too becomes altogether different. And just as creation is not concerned simply with individuals (as if each creation of an individual had been a special act), but it is the world that was created, and every individual as such was created only in and with the whole, for the rest not less than for itself, in the same way the activity of the Redeemer too is world-forming, and its object is human nature, in the totality of which the powerful God-consciousness is to be implanted as a new vital principle. He takes possession of the individuals relatively to the whole, wherever He finds those in whom His activity does not merely remain, but from whom, moving on, it can work upon others through the revelation of His life. And thus the total effective influence of Christ is only the continuation of the creative divine activity out of which the Person of Christ arose. For this, too, was directed towards human nature as a whole, in which that being of God was to exist, but in such a way that its effects are mediated through the life of Christ, as its most original organ, for all human nature that has already become personal in the natural sense, in proportion as it allows itself to be brought into spiritual touch with that life and its self-perpetuating organism. And this in order that the former personality may be slain and human nature, in vital fellowship with Christ, be formed into persons in the totality of that higher life.

Let us now look at the corporate life, or at the fellowship of the individual with the Redeemer. We may best describe its beginning, since it is conditioned by a free acceptance, by the term *calling*—the whole official activity of Christ began with just such a call. But the share of the Redeemer in the common life, viewed as continuing, we are fully justified in calling *soul-bestowal* (*Beseelung*), primarily with reference to the corporate life—as indeed the Church is called His Body. In just the same way Christ is to be the soul also in the individual fellowship, and each individual the organism through which the soul works. The two things are related as in Christ the divine activity present in the act of union is related to that activity in the state of union, and as in God the activity of creation is related to that of preservation. Only that here it is still clearer how each moment of a common activity can be regarded also as a calling, and likewise how the calling proper can be regarded as soul-bestowal. But this formula, too, we shall employ in another place.

3. This exposition is based entirely on the inner experience of the believer ; its only purpose is to describe and elucidate that experience. Naturally, therefore, it can make no claim to be a proof that things must have been so ; in the sphere of experience such proof is only possible where mathematics can be used, which is certainly not the case here. Our purpose is simply to show that the perfect satisfaction to which we aspire can only be truly contained in the Christian's consciousness of his relation to Christ in so far as that consciousness expresses the kind of relation which has been described here. If this content be lacking in the Christian consciousness, then either the perfect satisfaction must come from some other quarter, or it does not exist at all, and we must be content with an indefinite appeasement of conscience, such as may be found without any Redeemer ; and in that case there would be no special possession of divine grace in Christianity at all. Now these negations cannot be logically refuted ; they can only be removed by actual facts : we must seek to bring doubters to the same experience as we have had.

Now such a presentation of the redeeming activity of Christ as has been given here, which exhibits it as the establishment of a new life common to Him and us (original in Him, in us new and derived), is usually called by those who have not had the experience, 'mystical.' This expression is so extremely vague that it seems better to avoid it. But if we are willing to keep so close to its original use as to understand by it what belongs to the circle of doctrines which only a few share, but for others are a mystery, then we may accept it. Provided that we recognize that no one can be received into this circle arbitrarily, because doctrines are only expressions of inward experiences—whoever has these experiences *ipso facto* belongs to the circle ; whoever has not, cannot come in at all. But an analogy to this relation may be pointed out in a sphere which is universally familiar. As contrasted with the condition of things existing before there was any law, the civil community within a defined area is a higher vital potency. Let us now suppose that some person for the first time combines a naturally cohesive group into a civil community (legend tells of such cases in plenty) ; what happens is that the idea of the state first comes to consciousness in him, and takes possession of his personality as its immediate dwelling-place. Then he assumes the rest into the living fellowship of the idea. He does so by making them clearly conscious of the unsatisfactoriness of their present condition by effective speech. The power remains with the founder of forming in them the idea which is the innermost principle of his own life, and of assuming them into the fellowship of that life. The result is, not only that there arises among them a new corporate life, in complete contrast to the old, but also that each of them becomes in himself a new person—that is to say, a citizen. And everything resulting from this is the corporate life—developing variously with the process of time, yet remaining essentially the same—of this idea which emerged at that particular point of time, but was always predestined in the nature of that particular racial stock. The analogy might be pushed even further, to points of which we shall speak later. But even this presentation of it will seem mystical to those who admit only a meagre and inferior conception of the civic state.

Let us be content, then, that our view of the matter should be called mystical in this sense ; naturally everything to be derived from this main point will be called mystical too. But just as this mystical view can substantiate its claim to be the original one, so too it claims to be the true mean between two others, of which I shall call the one the magical way, and the other the empirical. The former admits, of course, that the activity of Christ is redemptive, but denies that the communication of His perfection is dependent on the founding of a community ; it results, they maintain, from His immediate influence upon the individual : and for this some take the written word to be a necessary means, others do not. The latter show themselves the more consistent, but the more completely they cut themselves loose from everything originating in the community the more obvious becomes the magical character of their view. This magical character lies in an influence not mediated by anything natural, yet attributed to a person. This is completely at variance with the maxim everywhere underlying our presentation, that the beginning of the Kingdom of God is a supernatural thing, which, however, becomes natural as soon as it emerges into manifestation ; for this other view makes every significant moment a supernatural one. Further, this view is completely separatist in type, for it makes the corporate life a purely accidental thing ; and it comes very near being docetic as well. For if Christ exerted influence in any such way as this—as a person, it is true, but only as a heavenly person without earthly presence, though in a truly personal way—then it would have been possible for Him to work in just the same way at any time, and His real personal appearance in history was only a superfluous adjunct. But those who likewise assume an immediate personal influence, but mediate it through the word and the fellowship, are less magical only if they attribute to these the power of evoking a mood in which the individual becomes susceptible to that personal influence. They are more magical still, if these natural elements have the power of disposing Christ to exert His influence ; for then their efficacy is exactly like that attributed to magic spells. The contrary empirical view also, it is true, admits a redemptive activity on the part of Christ, but one which is held to consist only in bringing about an increasing perfection in us ; and this cannot properly occur other wise than in the forms of teaching and example. These forms are general ; there is nothing distinctive in them. Even suppose it admitted that Christ is distinguished from others who contribute in the same way to our improvement, by the pure perfection of His teaching and His example, yet if all that is achieved in us is something imperfect, there remains nothing but to forgo the idea of redemption in the proper sense—that is, as the removal of sin— and, in view of the consciousness of sin still remaining even in our growing perfection, to pacify ourselves with a general appeal to the divine compassion. Now, teaching and example effect no more than such a growing perfection, and this appeal to the divine compassion occurs even apart from Christ. It must therefore be admitted that His appearance, in so far as intended to be something special, would in that case be in vain. At most it might be said that by His teaching He brought men to the point of giving up the effort, previously universal, to offer God substitutes for the perfection they lacked. But since the uselessness of this effort can be demonstrated, already in our natural intelligence we have the divine certainty of this, and had no need to obtain it elsewhere. And probably this view is chiefly to blame for the claim of philosophy to set itself above faith and to treat faith as merely a transitional stage. But we cannot rest satisfied with the consciousness of growing perfection, for that belongs just as much to the consciousness of sin as to that of grace, and hence cannot contain what is peculiarly Christian. But, for the Christian, nothing belongs to the consciousness of grace unless it is traced to the Redeemer as its cause, and therefore it must always be a different thing in His case from what it is in the case of others—naturally, since it is bound up with something else, namely, the peculiar redemptive activity of Christ.

§ 101. *The Redeemer assumes the believers into the fellowship of His unclouded blessedness, and this is His reconciling activity.*

1. If this assumption into the fellowship of Christ's blessedness were independent of the assumption into the power of His God-consciousness, or even if the former were to follow from the latter, the teleological nature of Christianity would be changed. But just as in God blessedness and omnipotence are balanced, mutually conditioned, and yet also independent of each other, so also in the Person of Christ blessedness and the power of the God-consciousness must be balanced in the same way, one conditioning the other and each independent of the other. Accordingly we can say that it must be the same with the effective influence of Christ. Either this must be simply admitted, or else there must be two contrasted ways of regarding Christianity, complementary to each other, one of them presenting it as an effort after blessedness for the sake of the power of the God-consciousness, the other *vice versa*. But since the effective influence of Christ arises only in so far as a receptivity or a longing for it pre-exists in its object, so the reconciling activity can only manifest itself as a consequence of the redemptive activity because the consciousness of sin, in itself

and not as a source of evil, forms the necessary basis of that longing, inasmuch as in the case of the individual evil is not connected with sin. So if we think of the Redeemer's activity as an influence upon the individual, we are bound to make the reconciling factor follow upon the redemptive and issue from it. But we equate the two thus far, that the communication of blessedness no less than the communication of perfection is given immediately in the assumption into vital fellowship with Christ.

2. Now in view of the exact parallel between this proposition and the preceding one, so that regarded in and by themselves they might fittingly have been run together into one, this seems hardly to need explanation. On the one hand, every activity in Christ proceeded from the being of God in Him, and this activity was never hindered by any resistance of His human nature. Similarly, the hindrances to His activity never determined any moment of His life until the perception of them had been taken up into His inmost self-consciousness, which was so completely one with His powerful God-consciousness that they could appear in it only as belonging to the temporal form of the perfect effectiveness of His being. On the other hand, it was still less possible that hindrances arising out of His own natural or social life could be taken up in this innermost consciousness as hindrances ; they could be no more than indications of the direction set for His activity. Similarly, the redeemed man too, since he has been assumed into the vital fellowship of Christ, is never filled with the consciousness of any evil, for it cannot touch or hinder the life which he shares with Christ. All hindrances to life, natural and social, come to him even in this region only as indications. They are not taken away, as if he were to be, or could be, without pain and free from suffering, for Christ also knew pain and suffered in the same way. Only the pains and sufferings do not mean simple misery, for they do not as such penetrate into the inmost life. And this holds good also of his consciousness of the sin still occurring in his life. It cannot have its source in his new life ; he refers it therefore only to the corporate life of general sinfulness, which still has a place in him. Not that it is not pain and suffering, so far as he clings to his own personality ; but it reaches the life of Christ in him only as an indication of what he has to do ; consequently there is in it no misery. The assumption into vital fellowship with Christ, therefore, dissolves the connexion between sin and evil, since morally

the two are no longer related to each other, even if from the merely
natural point of view the one is the consequence of the other.
Morally, however, each of them by itself is' regarded solely in
relation to the task of the new life.   Hence, just as the redemptive
activity of Christ brings about for all believers a corporate activity
corresponding to the being of God in Christ, so the reconciling
element, that is, the blessedness of the being of God.in Him, brings
about for all believers, as for each separately, a corporate feeling
of blessedness.   Therein, too, their former personality dies, so far as
it meant a self-enclosed life of feeling within a sensuous vital unity,
to which all sympathetic feeling for others and for the whole was
subordinated.   But what remains as the self-identity of the person
is the peculiar way of apprehending and perceiving, which as individualized intelligence so works itself into the new common life
that relatively to this factor also the activity of Christ is person-
forming, in that an old man is put off and a new man is put on.
Here too, if we wish to note similarities between the activity of
Christ in forming the new corporate life and the divine activity in
forming the personality of Christ, we shall be able to distinguish
a first moment, which corresponds to the act of union as first
beginning, and as such can only look back to what preceded, and
a second, which represents the state of union, and, as expressing
continuance, also looks forward to the future.   Now here the beginning is the disappearance of the old man, and so also of the
old reference of all evil to sin, that is, the disappearance of the
consciousness of deserving punishment.   Consequently the first
thing in the reconciling aspect is the forgiveness of sins.[1]   For in
the unity of life with Christ all relation to the law ceases, since the
general movement contrary to sin, proceeding from Him, begins.[2]
But the state of union is the real possession of blessedness in the
consciousness that Christ in us is the centre of our·life, and this in
such a way that this possession exists solely as His gift, which,
since we receive it simply by His will that we should have it, is
His blessing and His peace.   But the same thing is true here again,
that each moment or aspect may at the same time be regarded in
accordance with the formula of the other.   For in the first moment
the whole development is already implicitly contained, but at the
same time in every later moment the first persists ; for the fact
that this possession of blessedness is pervaded throughout by sin
(a fact which our recurrence to Christ makes it all the more

[1] Rom. 8[1], 1 John 1[8]. [9] 2[1]. [2].   [2] Gal. 2[19-21] 5[22-24].

impossible for us to overlook) always points on in turn to the forgiveness of sins.

3. Obviously our proposition is mystical in the same sense as the previous one, and its truth also can only be proved in experience. But in the same sense it too stands intermediate between a magical view, which destroys all naturalness in the continuous activity of Christ, and an empirical, which reduces it altogether to the level of ordinary daily experience, and thus does not make its supernatural beginning and its distinctive peculiarity the fundamental things in it.

The latter view likewise starts from the connexion between sin and evil, and rightly infers that when sin is taken away so also is evil. But since this connexion principally holds good for social evil alone, and is exact even for this only if we consider a large corporate life as a rounded whole, whereas in every individual part of that life inward improvement may well be accompanied by increasing evil, because of its connexion with the rest, the growing improvement of the individual can furnish no guarantee at all that he is being set free from evil and cannot form a basis of blessedness. Even along with increasing perfection the fact remains not only that he encounters hindrances to life, but that they are such as in the light of the sin still present in him have the aspect of punishment. It follows that this reconciliation only very accident- ally takes the form of enjoyment and possession ; in essence it can never be set forth as more than hope. But in either form it is not, so far as content is concerned, anything peculiarly Christian, nor can it as enjoyment have a greater strength, or as hope possess a higher degree of certainty, within Christianity than without. And how slight this is everywhere, history clearly shows. For, alto- gether apart from Christianity, the dispute is constantly recurring as to whether evil in the world is really growing less, or only changing its form while in sum remaining what it has ever been. Not only so, but within the Christian Church itself the same doubt constantly reappears, and this the more strongly the less experience there is of the enjoyment of the unclouded blessedness of Christ, and the more recourse is had to that general hope. And, quite contrary to Christ's own assurance,[1] that blessedness is relegated to the life beyond time, and thus clearly declared to be independent of the gradual improvement. But in that case Christ has part in our blessedness or salvation only through His influence upon this pro-

[1] John 5²⁴.

gressive improvement, which means that a specific difference between Him and other men is of little importance.

Only those views of Christ's reconciling activity appear to be magical which make the impartation of His blessedness independent of assumption into vital fellowship with Him. This means that the forgiveness of sins is made to depend upon the punishment which Christ suffered, and the blessedness of men itself is presented as a reward which God offers to Christ for the suffering of that punishment. Not, of course, that the thought of our blessedness as a rewarding of Christ is altogether to be rejected—on the contrary, we shall have to speak of that later. Nor that all connexion between the suffering of Christ and the forgiveness of sins is to be denied. But both ideas become magical when blessedness and forgiveness are not mediated through vital fellowship with Christ. For within this fellowship the impartation of blessedness, as explained above, is a natural one ; whereas without this the rewarding of Christ is nothing but divine arbitrariness. And this in itself is always something magical, but it is especially so when something so absolutely inward as blessedness is supposed to have been brought about externally, without any inner basis. For if it is independent of life in Christ, then, since man does not have the source of blessedness in himself, it can only have been infused into each separate individual somehow or other from without. In no less magical a way is the forgiveness of sins achieved, if the consciousness of deserving punishment is supposed to cease because the punishment has been borne by another. That in this way the expectation of punishment might be taken away is conceivable ; but this is merely the sensuous element in the forgiveness of sins. The properly ethical element, the consciousness of deserving punishment, would still remain. And this therefore would have to disappear as if conjured away, without any reason. And to what extent something even of this view has passed over into Church doctrine is a question we shall have to discuss below.

4. Now if we compare the connected view here set forth with the two alternative views which have just been cited, they certainly suggest the reflection that in our view, the suffering of Christ has nothing to say, so that there has not even been an opportunity to raise the question whether, and to what extent, it belongs to redemption or to reconciliation. But the only conclusion to be drawn from this postponement of the question is that no reason existed for adducing it as a primitive element either in the one

place or in the other. And this is so far correct, that otherwise no complete assumption into vital fellowship with Christ, such as makes redemption and reconciliation completely intelligible, would have been possible before the suffering and death of Christ. As an element of secondary importance, however, it belongs to both ; immediately to reconciliation, and to redemption only mediately. The activity of Christ in founding the new corporate life could really emerge in its perfect fulness—although belief in this perfection could exist even apart from this—only if it yielded to no opposition, not even to that which succeeded in destroying His person. Here, accordingly, the perfection does not lie properly and immediately in the suffering itself, but only in His giving up of Himself to it. And of this it is only, as it were, a magical caricature, if we isolate this climax, leave out of account the foundation of the corporate life, and regard this giving up of Himself to suffering for suffering's sake as the real sum-total of Christ's redemptive activity. But so far as reconciliation is concerned, our exposition makes it obvious that, in order to effect assumption into the fellowship of His blessedness, the longing of those who were conscious of their misery must first be drawn to Christ through the impression they had received of His blessedness. And here too the situation is that belief in this blessedness might be present even apart from this, but that none the less His blessedness emerged in its perfect fulness only in that it was not overcome even by the full tide of suffering. The more so that this suffering arose out of the opposition of sin, and that therefore the Redeemer's sympathy with misery, ever present, though without disturbing His blessedness, from the time of His entrance into the corporate life of sin, had here to enter on its greatest phase. And here it is not the giving up of Himself to suffering, as something that forms part of the redemptive activity, but the suffering itself which is the full confirmation of belief in the Redeemer's blessedness. But here again it is only a magical caricature of this which, completely overlooking the necessity of an imperturbable blessedness in Christ, finds the reconciling power of His suffering precisely in the fact that He willingly gave up even His blessedness, and experienced, even if only for moments, real misery. So far as Church doctrine is not wholly free from this idea either, we shall return to the matter below.

The ·climax of His suffering, we hold then, was sympathy with misery. This, however, at once involves the further conclusion that no suffering which is not bound up with the redemptive activity of Christ can be regarded as belonging to reconciliation, because suffering of that sort would also have no connexion with the Redeemer's opposition to misery, and so it could belong to the reconciliation only in a magical way. Now Christ's sufferings can be thought of in this connexion with His redemptive activity only when regarded as a whole and a unity ; to separate out any particular element and ascribe to it a peculiar reconciling value, is not merely trifling allegory if done in teaching, and worthless sentimentality in poetry ; probably it is also seldom free from a defiling admixture of superstition. Least of all is it proper to ascribe such a special reconciling value to His physical sufferings ; and that for two reasons. On the one hand, these sufferings in themselves have only the loosest connexion with His reaction against sin. On the other hand, our own experience teaches us that an ordinary ethical development and robust piety have as their reward the almost complete overcoming of physical sufferings in the presence of a glad spiritual self-consciousness, whether personal or corporate. Certainly they can never suppress that consciousness, nor make a moment of blessedness any less blessed. But in order that the exposition just given may serve as an all-round test in scrutinizing Church formulæ, it must be brought into relation to our general formula of the creation of human nature as completed through Christ, so as to convince ourselves that in this twofold activity of Christ such creation is really fully accomplished. For whatever in human nature is assumed into vital fellowship with Christ is assumed into the fellowship of an activity solely determined by the power of the God-consciousness, therefore adequate to every new experience and extracting from it all it has to yield. It is at the same time assumed into the fellowship of a satisfaction which rests in that activity and which cannot be disturbed by any outside influence. Now that each assumption of this sort is simply a continuation of the same creative act which first manifested itself in time by the formation of Christ's Person ; that each increase in the intensity of this new life relatively to the disappearing corporate life of sinfulness is also such a continuation, must now be clear ; and that in this new life man achieves the destiny originally appointed for him, and that nothing beyond this can be conceived or attempted for a nature such as ours—all this requires no further exposition.

However exactly this presentation of the subject may correspond to the immediate consciousness of the Christian, so that it recognizes itself in it, still it is inevitable that, as it stands half-way between the empirical and the magical interpretations, it should be mistaken by each of these for the opposite one.   For, on the one hand, since a spiritual thing like the foundation of a corporate life must be spiritually achieved, and there is no spiritual influence but the presentation of oneself in word and deed, the Redeemer could only enter into our corporate life by means of such self-presentation, thereby attracting men to Himself and making them one with Himself.   Now to warn those who lean to the side of magic, this touchstone must be kept before them, whether their conception really agrees with the possibility of conceiving the effective influence of Christ under this historical natural form.   And nothing is easier than for them to misunderstand this, and to imagine that Christ must work simply in the ordinary human way as teacher and example, the divine in Him being altogether left out of account.   But on the other hand, the distinction between such a Christ and Christ as we here understand Him, can only be made plain by reference to ' Christ in us,' whereas the relation of teacher and pupil, like that of pattern and imitation, must always remain an external one.   If, however, those who lean to the empirical view were asked whether they too had a real experience of vital fellowship with Christ, they would only too easily misunderstand the question, and suppose that they were being asked to assent to the objectionable magic view.   For that reason we shall leave wide room on both sides open, not only for the Christian Church as a whole, but also for the Protestant Church, in which all these differences are present, in order that, wherever there is a recognition of Christ—and the danger of letting this go is just as great on the side of the magical extreme as on that of the empirical—and so long as such an extreme has not yet been reached, we may always be able to maintain fellowship, and by means of it bring all ever nearer to the centre.

§ 102. *Church doctrine divides the whole activity of Christ into three offices, the prophetic, the priestly, and the kingly.*

1. At first sight this division has against it the appearance of being very arbitrary.   It looks as if from the great number of Biblical expressions used by Christ Himself one in particular had been chosen and the others set aside, and to this one two others added, which were used, not by Christ Himself, but only by His

disciples.[1] If then pictorial expressions are to be used at all, unquestionably the picture of the Shepherd, which was used by Christ Himself and repeated by Peter, has a better right (it will be said) than the expressions ' High Priest ' and ' Prophet.'   Now if this really were the case—that out of a number of equally justifiable expressions, all of them pictorial, these had been selected, more or less by accident—then it would be surprising (since pictorial expressions are always hard to define, and therefore in a dialectical discussion almost inevitably involve great inconveniences) that such a presentation had been able to maintain itself for so long without being supplanted by some other even if it were one no less arbitrary ; and not only so, but one would reasonably hesitate to make any further use of this form of expression in a strictly theological treatment.   But these expressions are not to be put on one level with other pictorial expressions ; manifestly their purpose is to be sought in the comparison they indicate between the achievements of Christ in the corporate life founded by Him and those by which in the Jewish people the theocracy was represented and held together, and this comparison is not even to-day to be neglected in the system of doctrine.   For even if it is equally true that this presentation is rather characteristic of the earliest formative period of the faith (when it certainly was necessary to bring the anti-Jewish element in Christianity into evidence under the Jewish form itself) than fitted to be a persistent type of doctrine, this would only mean that these forms alone cannot suffice for us.   When we have, however, developed the subject in our own way, as above, on the basis of our own Christian experience, it is still worth while to preserve a continuity with those original presentations, for the first theoretical interpretation of Christianity was based upon a comparison of the new Kingdom of God with the old.   And so we have to show that our conception is in agreement with that which the earlier Christians formed for themselves, when they represented the offices of Christ as new and intensified forms of those through which in the old covenant the divine government was revealed.

2. Of course we are here concerned rather with the idea of these authorities [prophet, priest, and king] in Judaism than with

[1] Apart from the Epistle to the Hebrews, the conception of the ' High Priest ' occurs (but only indirectly) in Paul (Rom. 5[11]), and in Peter (1 Pet. 2[21]), and in John (1 John 2[1]); Christ calls Himself a prophet in Luke 13[33],.and less directly in similar passages.

their historical development. The kings were properly the representatives of the God of Israel ; to them the government was entrusted, in order that the people might be held together and the common life, where necessary, renewed and purified. The priests were the guardians of the temple and the shrines, and presided over the immediate relation of the people to God, bringing requests and offerings before Him, and bringing back from God forgiveness and blessing. The prophets were men specially called and sent forth by God, belonging to both sides, God and man, and mediating between them, but not so constantly as the priests. For although there were schools of the prophets, yet there was no uninterrupted succession of prophets in the narrower sense. In the hour of need the prophet arose, now from the ranks of either kings or priests, now from the midst of the people, with a message of warning when one of the appointed authorities had erred from the right path, of revival when the original spirit threatened to be extinguished by the dead letter. Now in order to make clear the relation of the Kingdom of heaven to this earthly theocracy, Christ, on whom alone the Kingdom rests, is represented as uniting all these three offices in Himself. The meaning of this is that in this Kingdom of God (which, it is always understood, is not of this world) the establishment and maintenance of the fellowship of each individual with God, and the maintenance and direction of the fellowship of all members with one another, are not separate achievements but the same ; and further, that these activities and the free dominion of the Spirit in knowledge and doctrine do not spring from a different source but from the same.

3. Now in what way the whole redemptive and reconciling activity of Christ, as just described,[1] is completely reproduced in terms of these three offices, can be shown only in the exposition which follows. But so much at least we can point out here and now—that if we ascribe to the Redeemer only one of these three functions, and neglect the others, or, alternatively, completely exclude one of them, then that harmony between the old covenant and the new is destroyed, and the peculiar quality of Christianity is endangered. For to claim for Christ the prophetic office alone means limiting His effective influence to teaching and admonition relatively to a form of life already in existence either before Him or apart from Him, and to a relation to God already established apart from Him at some other point ; and on such an interpretation the

[1] §§ 100 and 101.

peculiar element in Christianity is seriously overshadowed. It is just the same if we ascribe to Him the two formative activities, but exclude Him from the prophetic activity, with its character of direct spiritual stimulation. For then one cannot see how, if the power of the living word is to have no share in the work, the Kingdom of God can arise except in some magical way. If, on the other hand, we exclude the kingly office, then the other two taken together, though certainly they unite each redeemed individual closely to the Redeemer, yet supply no relation to a corporate life, and so produce only an unpleasing and even, when more closely observed, an unchristian separatism. Lastly, if the high-priestly office is passed over, but the other two retained, then the prophetic activity could be related only to the kingly, and consequently, if we are to remain true to the original type, all religious content would be lacking. On the other hand, if Christ be represented solely as High Priest, it would be almost impossible to avoid the magical conception of His influence. Similarly, if we retain only the kingly dignity, and think of Christ solely as forming and directing the Church, the immediate relation of the individual to the Redeemer would be endangered, and we should have strayed in the direction of the Roman Church, which makes this relation dependent at once upon the Church and upon those who direct its government. Now where there is revealed an interdependence of this sort, there is also a presumption that what is so bound up together is also complete.

§ 103. *First Theorem.—The prophetic office of Christ consists in teaching, prophesying, and working miracles.*

1. These three activities also constituted the dignity of the Old Testament prophets. Certainly the essential thing was always stimulus by means of teaching and admonition ; but in all important instances, where the teaching had some definite occasion, it at once became prophecy (since the idea of the divine retribution was dominant), now threatening, now promising, in agreement with the original type created when the law was given. But since the prophets never appeared except in connexion with crimes or public misfortunes, which might be supposed always to involve the guilt of those to whom they had to speak, they required, in default of an outward vocation to which they might have appealed, some special proof of their authority. Hence miracles were expected or assumed as a token of their divine mission. It was only

the absence of this third mark of a prophet that made it possible for the Baptist to say that he was no prophet,[1] in spite of his very definite divine vocation. For he certainly had taught and prophesied,[2] but the gift of miracles had not been granted him,[3] and hence he would not be troubled with a useless question about it.

In Christ these three signs of a prophet did not follow one from the other ; all three were one from the very outset. For the preaching of the Kingdom of God was both teaching and prophecy, and the Kingdom of God itself is properly the miracle accomplished by Christ ; but since its fulfilment began simultaneously with the preaching, all three elements were present in one and the same germ, and we can differentiate them only as this germ develops further.

2. That the prophetic voice had fallen silent was a fact which had long been generally admitted when Jesus appeared. Instead, there was then a tradition of doctrine in the schools of the scribes. This made no claim to be anything more than tradition ; it was gradually extended by the subtle combinations of distinguished scholars, and in connexion with it there was also an official practice of teaching in the synagogues. But Christ could not belong to any of the sects into which the scribes were divided ; as little could He undertake any official activity which would have involved Him in other duties, and have limited Him in a way incompatible with His appointed work. But since, outside the activity of the scribes, there was complete freedom of teaching, He was able to come before the people in a regular way, as soon as He had reached the age required by custom. Thus no exception to His competence to teach could be taken by any public authority. The *teaching office* of Christ, therefore, means only His determination to make the fullest possible use of this freedom. Thus for Him no other occasion was needed for any particular act of teaching than the presence, individually or in groups, of those who were anxious to be taught ; His conversation was all of the nature of teaching, so far as the subject and the conditions permitted. And to this extent it must certainly be admitted that Christ taught, in this wider sense, even before His public ministry began ; still, that He taught publicly as a boy remains a mistaken view, and one entirely without foundation in the Gospel story,[4] but resembling the apocryphal stories. Similarly, there is really only one Gospel

[1] John 1[21].
[2] Matt. 3[10. 16. 17].
[3] John 10[41].
[4] Luke 2[46. 47].

testimony [1] which connects the beginning of His public appearance with His reception of the baptism of John ; and the explanation which Jesus Himself gives of this circumstance forbids the supposition that by this baptism He became something which He had not been before, or that He received an authority or a consecration which was not already His.   The former supposition is incompatible with belief in the originality of the divine in His person ; and for the latter there is no external authority of any kind in the rite instituted by John.   The only value, therefore, which we can attribute to this transaction is that it helps us to understand His public appearance historically : He marked His more open transition from seclusion to public life by an act of confession which inevitably evoked a more definite opinion about Him, to which He was able to attach His teaching.   For the people His work as a teacher came to an end with His arrest, but for the disciples only with His ascension.   It seems to have been His chief work in the days of the resurrection, partly to expound the Scripture to His disciples, without doubt establishing the way in which they were afterwards to make use of it among their people ; partly also to complete His injunctions as to the corporate life deriving from Him, and so to establish that life more securely.   It is obvious, therefore, how essentially this teaching activity on Christ's part belonged to the redemptive activity described above.   But so far as the *source* of the teaching is concerned, that of the prophets' teaching (although their participation in teaching came to them in the form of a special divine call) was always simply the law ; their calling was entirely concerned with the relation between God and the people, and the end to which they worked was a purely national one.   Now it was part of Christ's regard for the law not to destroy the law ; hence He recognized and affirmed the national obligation towards it.   Nevertheless, just as His inspiration was not a transient one, dependent on individual occasions supplied by the state of the people, and just as He is not to be regarded as merely a product of human nature in a specifically national form, so too the inner development of His thoughts could not be dependent on the law.   Moreover, to regard His teaching as a purification and a development of the ethics current among the people, springing out of universal human reason, is part of the empirical conception we have rejected.   Rather, the source of His teaching was the absolutely original revelation of God in Him.   In Him the contrast

[1] Luke 4[11] ; but compare also Acts 1[21. 22].

between learning and teaching was only the contrast between the influence of the divine principle in Him upon the receptivity of His spiritual organ (so as to yield a pure apprehension of the human conditions confronting Him in their bearing on man's relation to God) and the influence of the same principle upon the spontaneity of His spiritual organ. But since receptivity always involves spontaneity, His teaching was already forming itself imperceptibly in His learning ; and this first development of His own thought was already the source of His astonishing questions.[1] Naturally, however, after spontaneity had gained the upper hand, and teaching had come to be His constant preoccupation, the law no less than the Messianic hopes was the point of connexion at which He developed His preaching of the new corporate life to be founded by Him—the Kingdom of God.

Hence, if the *content* of Christ's teaching is to be specially stated here (although in point of fact our task throughout has been simply to expound that teaching), then here also we should first have to recur to the prophetic element. The prophet felt it incumbent on him to do full justice by his preaching to the impulse which he felt had come to him from God, and to pass on its full content to his hearers—always a limited and definite task. In the same way, Christ's self-determination to teach was the task of satisfying fully the powerful (which also means the creative) God-consciousness, as it took shape in His spiritual organ, and of so reproducing it in His teaching that thereby the assumption of men into His fellowship might be effected. No other measure is applicable here of the success of His teaching, and consequently of its perfection. Naturally His discourses were sometimes more general in character, sometimes more detailed ; sometimes they were more the pure outflowing of what was in Him, sometimes they had a closer bearing on some outward occasion ; and the attempt has for long been made to distinguish the more essential from the more subordinate and accidental, though in very different ways. We can only say that everything is essential so far as it is connected with His self-presentation, for it was only by the proclamation of His peculiar dignity that men could really be invited to enter into the fellowship offered them. And so these three parts are inseparable from one another as constituting the essence of His teaching—the doctrine of His Person, which is at the same time, in its outward aspect, the doctrine of His calling, or of the communication of eternal life in the Kingdom

[1] Luke 2⁴⁷.

of God, and in its inward aspect, the doctrine of His relation to Him Who had sent Him, or of God as His Father, revealing Himself to Him and through Him.   So that everything which belongs to His high-priestly and kingly office must likewise appear in His teaching, since He proclaimed His mission to raise men to fellowship with God and to rule spiritually.   And only that is accidental in His teaching which contains least of this, and keeps most to the historical situation, and bears on the given national factor.   To emphasize the latter above the former leads very easily to a dangerous distinction between a teaching *of* Christ and a teaching *about* Christ (as something merely additional), and undeniably imperils what is specifically Christian, as if all that is involved were some improvements upon natural ethics and natural theology —which, besides, are represented as if human reason must have found them out by itself.   But with this proviso, there is room enough for Christians of different temperaments to hold for their own use predominantly to one or another of these elements.

But further, this original revelation of God in Christ is so adequate and also so inexhaustible, that, so far as this first aspect is concerned, Christ is manifestly at once the climax and the end of all prophecy.   No presentation of our relationship to God can arise outside the sphere in which Christ is recognized, which would not fall short of that revelation ; nor can any possible advance within the Christian Church ever bring us to the point either of perceiving anything imperfect in the teaching of Christ Himself, for which we could substitute something better, or of conceiving anything which aids man's understanding of his relation to God more spiritually, more profoundly, or more perfectly than Christ has done.   Indeed, with the assumption that Christian doctrine is capable of being perfected in a way which implies our transcending Christ, the assumption of Christ's peculiar dignity would have to be given up. Even the most admirable later achievements in this sphere can never be more than a correct development of what lies undeveloped in His utterances, as we possess them, or, as the connexion of thought assures us, must even then have been before His mind. Now if Christ is the climax of all prophecy because of the perfection of His preaching, proceeding from a divine impulse, He is so also because even as teacher He is not one among many of His like. And He is the end of all prophecy, because no new teaching can arise which, after His, would not be false ; that is to say, from now on all true teaching in this sphere goes back, not to Moses and the law, but to the Son.   He is also the end of prophecy for this reason, that now there can be no such thing as an independent personal inspiration, but only a being inspired by Him.

This only remains to be said, that, like the teaching of the pro-phets, His too was always the direct utterance of His whole being, hence not to be separated from the total impression His being made. And from this it follows for His teaching, that (since His inspiration was not transient but constant) every utterance of His moved spirit in speech and accompanying expression contains elements of teaching, and serves as confirmation of His teaching proper, inas-much as it bears witness to the being of God in Him.

3. The prediction of the Old Testament prophets, so far as we can form conclusions about the whole from what remains to us, was of two kinds.   One kind was special prediction, directed to an individual event ; since it rested upon the two chief concepts of the Jewish religion, the divine election of the people and divine retribution, it was for the most part hypothetical, and formed an addition to teaching which conveyed warning, encouragement, and comfort, in accordance with the spirit of the law.   The other kind rose above the individual event to an exposition of the universal, and as such claimed absolute value—this was Messianic prediction. The first kind was a foretelling in the proper sense ; in its more or less definite assertions it attained now a higher, and now a lower degree of accuracy.   In Messianic prophecy, the individual assertions, more or less, are nothing but an external vesture, so that it often remains uncertain whether this point or that does or does not really belong to the prediction itself.   But its essence consists in this, that it spoke of the future of God's true messenger. The idea of that messenger could be grasped by individuals only in limited fashion, by each in his own way ; but rightly under-stood it always involved the end of those two Jewish conceptions of retribution and election.   Now Christ, as the Messiah appearing in person, could only predict messianically concerning what had not yet appeared but would be fulfilled by means of the same activity as that from which the prediction itself proceeded ; that is, He could predict only concerning the further development of His Kingdom or its completion.   Hence this prediction was pre-cisely the same thing as His teaching ; in this sense He prophesied without foretelling.[1]   But neither could He foretell the merely accidental, for everything so to be described is without value in

[1] Acts 1[7].

His Kingdom, and thus could not be the object either of investigation or of premonition. He could foretell, therefore, only the
end of such institutions as rested upon those limited concepts
of election and retribution ; and this He did, not hypothetic-
ally, but with the perfect accuracy belonging to His infallible
perfection. His certainty in this foretelling, indeed, must be
identical with the certainty of His own mission. In both connexions, therefore, Christ is the climax of prophecy. And just as
He is the climax, so too He is the end. For essential prophecy has
now been completely fulfilled, since the Spirit has been poured out ;
nothing essential can be thought of which is still lacking to the
kingdom of God ; to point forward to anything new which is still
to occur would necessarily be to preach another gospel. It is just
the same with the foretelling. Apostolic prediction—what there
is of it [1]—we can regard only as an interpretation or an echo of
Christ's prediction ; there was only one occasion for it which did
not yet exist in His time—namely, the application to hostile
heathendom of prophecies similar to those which He had uttered
against Judaism. For the rest, along with those limited concepts
there disappeared the basis and support for all prophecy such as is
attached exclusively to a heightened excitation of the devout soul.
All that remains is such prophecy as can arise from an intelligent
and comprehensive view of human relations and from a true and
deep sympathy. But to no prediction, whatever its content, and
however great its accuracy, and however wonderfully the pictures
of an excited faculty of premonition may occasionally come true,
can we ascribe a sacred character.

If this proposition has not hitherto received such definite
doctrinal expression in the Protestant Church as in consistency it
has been given here, perhaps such expression is also more necessary
now than before, and in all likelihood it will meet with little opposition in the Church itself. And this, not only because it essentially
belongs to the naturalization of the Kingdom of God in the world,
but because the whole previous practice of our Church shows that it
invariably regards any claim to the gift of prophecy as symptomatic
of fanaticism. For us at present, therefore, it remains only to
interpret the prophecies of Christ and the Apostles. But that is a
task which can only be done in accordance with the rules of the art
of interpretation, not with an arbitrariness which would be justified

---

[1] I do not include here the Revelation of John ; I cannot admit its apostolic
origin.

only in the measure in which it itself was prophecy. But all fore-tellings, both those derived from the historical sense and those derived from inexplicable capacities for premonition, must be left to the natural science of mind.

4. Although it was laid down that even wonders and signs were not to protect the prophet who spoke against Jehovah and His law,[1] yet this very fact makes it clear that when people thought of a prophet they always thought also of wonders and signs.[2] With reference to the Redeemer, we might of course [3] surmise it to be natural in a higher order of things that He should have even miraculous powers at His command ; but from this comparison with the Jewish prophets it is clear in what sense Christ Himself and His disciples could appeal to His miracles, and yet why Christ, when signs and wonders were demanded of Him, refused to do them. For even the wonders of the prophets were not intended to evoke faith in their Messianic prophecies, and could not do so ; their purpose was to evoke faith in their conditional predictions in order to induce people to do what had to be done. But Christ gave no such conditional predictions about Himself, and faith in His relation to the Messianic idea was meant to proceed solely from the direct impression made by His Person.[4] That is why Christ never availed Himself of His miraculous powers in any definite connexion with the demands He made or His statements about Himself,[5] but (in the same way as everyone avails himself of his natural powers) according as opportunity offered of doing good by them.

In those days the true recognition of Christ might in individual instances be evoked by miracles ; elsewhere it found a confirmation in them ; but it might never be properly based upon them. Hence for us, so far as our faith is concerned, they cannot but be altogether superfluous. For miracles can only direct the spiritual need to a definite object in virtue of their immediate impressiveness, or, if it has already been directed thither, justify this inner relation in an external way.[6] This impressiveness, however, is lost in proportion as the person who is to believe is at a distance from the miracle itself in space and time. What takes the place of miracles for our time is our historical knowledge of the character, as well as of the scope and the duration, of Christ's spiritual achievements.

---

[1] Deut. 13[1-5].   [2] See above (§ 103. 1).
[3] Cf. § 14, *Postscript*, pp. 70 ff.   [4] Matt. 16[16], John 1[14. 16] 4[42] 6[68. 69] 7[25. 26].
[5] Even John 11[42] is no exception to this, although I cannot argue the point here.
[6] This last must also be the sense of John 20[30. 31].

In this we have an advantage over the contemporaries of the Redeemer, and a witness whose power increases exactly in proportion
as the impressiveness of the miracles is lost. But what does this
mean except that our attention is directed away from the individual,
more physical, miracles to the general spiritual miracle, which
begins with the person of the Redeemer and is completed with the
completion of His Kingdom ? Our faith in the external miracles
wrought by Christ, as deeds which were not wrought by Him in
accordance with rules learned anywhere, and whose success cannot
be traced to natural laws recognized by us as valid for all time—
this faith belongs not so much to our faith in Christ directly as to
our faith in Scripture.

For we cannot include these phenomena in the field of nature
familiar to us without having recourse to presuppositions such that
the trustworthiness of the whole body of our records concerning
Christ is imperilled.[1] And this conviction will probably be the result
of the controversy now being waged on this question, and as a conviction will be the more living and the more universal the greater
the candour and the intelligence with which the controversy is
carried on.

If we confine ourselves to these individual miracles, then we
cannot make it so clear as we did in the case of teaching and prophecy
that Christ is also the climax of miraculous activity. For in Christ's
miracles we have nothing which definitely raises them, in and by
themselves, above other similar miracles of which we have stories
from many various times and places. But if we consider the total
spiritual miracle, then we must declare Him to be the climax, all
the more definitely that we recognize that—apart from Him—this
total spiritual miracle could not have been achieved by all the powers
of spiritual nature as we know it. But equally certainly Christ is
also the end of miracle. For the surer it is that by Christ redemption
has been completed, so that whatever is yet in store for the human
race, so far as fellowship with God is concerned, is to be regarded
only as a further development of Christ's work, not as a new revelation, the more reason we have for rejecting everything that claims
to offer miraculous evidence for a new achievement in the sphere
of spiritual life. Only new natural epochs—or even new historical
epochs, so long as they are not in the sphere of religion—could still
be announced by miracles ; and in that case to pass judgment
on such miracles is purely a matter for natural science.

[1] Cf. § 99.

On this point too we can scarcely say there is a fixed doctrine in the Protestant Church. Yet Luther's words [1] on the matter show clearly enough that he did not regard the great change in the Church which he helped to bring about (in spite of the fact that, at least in a subordinate sense, it was the beginning of a new corporate life) as a point of development such that it needed to be supported by the power of working miracles. Also this doctrine has the support of a maxim which we may regard as having become dominant in the Protestant Church by tacit agreement, namely, that we assume the presence of superstition wherever new miracles are represented and believed to have occurred for the confirmation of Christianity. Against this it might be objected that our proposition certainly cannot be admitted strictly and literally, since the miracles of the disciples of Christ were just as well attested as His own, and He manifestly bequeathed to them His power of working miracles. And since (it might be argued) it can in no sense be proved that these miraculous gifts were suddenly to die out with the death of the Apostles, so much anyhow is certain, that Christ Himself did not claim to be the end of miraculous powers, while it must be left undecided whether these gifts really have gradually died out, or whether perhaps they do not still persist in the Church, or at least revive periodically. To this the answer is that the same thing holds true of the miracles of the Apostles as of their prophecies, and that Christ transmitted to them the power of working miracles only as a sign to accompany the earliest preaching. Even if it cannot be strictly proved that the Church's power of working miracles has died out (and this the Roman Church denies), yet in general it is undeniable that, in view of the great advantage in power and civilization which the Christian peoples possess over the non-Christian, almost without exception, the preachers of to-day do not need such signs. And in every individual case it will always be possible to show that alleged miracles, whatever spiritual aim may be ascribed to them, would always be inadequate to it, and consequently that they are superfluous. Indeed, the Roman Church itself, by the manner in which in one case it limits miracles, and in another scrutinizes them, betrays no great confidence in the principle which it sets up.

----

[1] 'The same signs as the Apostles did might easily happen even to-day if there were any need' (*W.A.* xi. pp. 1294, 1339).

§ 104. *Second Theorem.—The priestly office of Christ includes His perfect fulfilment of the law* (i.e. *His active obedience*), *His atoning death* (i.e. *His passive obedience*), *and His intercession with the Father for believers.*

1. The difficulty of presenting the total activity of Christ under these forms of the old covenant occurs chiefly in this section. For one thing, the analogy between that part of the effective influence of Christ which must be assigned to this section, if a place is to be found for it at all, and the functions of the High Priest, is less conspicuous. For another, many aspects of the functions of the High Priest, which must be paralleled in Christ, reveal themselves in activities of the Redeemer which one would be more inclined to assign to one of the other two offices. Thus the extraordinary, but most significant, function of the High Priest, that of receiving instructions from Jehovah in the Holy of Holies, has no direct analogy in the work of Christ. In so far as Christ received from His Father all instructions which He imparted to His followers,[1] this must be reckoned chiefly to His prophetic activity. The benedictions which the High Priest pronounced over the people remind us of what we have already ascribed to the reconciling activity of Christ, but Church doctrine does not expressly include it in that activity. Yet since the benediction of Christ cannot be simply a wish, but must be a real gift, His benediction must be involved in His governing and directing activity ; indeed, the Epistle to the Hebrews undoubtedly conceives of a kingly activity in addition to the high-priestly. So there remain only symbolical actions. Among these the functions of the Day of Atonement are the most impressive. But we cannot think of relating any of these to the special functions of Christ which have just been mentioned. While if we regard the High Priest as being at the same time the head of the priesthood, so that its performances are traceable to him, then he would be the agent of the people with Jehovah, and this would be completely expressed by the idea of representation. On the other hand, nothing is said directly about a legal perfection of the High Priest, and the atoning death of Christ, regarded as a sacrifice, has nothing corresponding to it. So far as the first point is concerned, two things should be kept in mind. First, that personal physical perfection was essential in the High Priest. The nearest direct parallel to this in the doctrine of the person of Christ

[1] John 7[16] 8[26] 17[8].

is, of course, His sinless perfection.   And second, and chiefly, that
before the High Priest entered upon the official performances of the
Day of Atonement—and to these, as his most characteristic duties,
we must pay particular attention—he had to purify himself in
many different ways, and to bring a sin-offering for himself and his
house, in virtue of which he was then held to be legally perfect.
And so far as the other point is concerned, the fact that Christ
offered *Himself* is to be disregarded in this connexion.   For in so far
as He Himself was the offering, He is to be compared to the sacri-
ficial animal.   Not only is this mode of expression found in various
places in the Bible,[1] but this twofold reference has also passed over
into confessional documents,[2] so that it is the more necessary for us
to distinguish the two aspects from each other ; and yet here we
should have to think of Christ principally as the sacrificer, not as the
offering.   As the sacrificer, however, He is active, and His suffering
can be only an accompaniment, and can have its ground solely
in sympathy with sin, which of course we may also presuppose
in the High Priest, especially in his acts of atonement.   Yet here a
new difficulty arises, namely, that both the active and the passive
obedience of Christ belong entirely to His self-presentation, and
consequently to His prophetic office ; just as His intercession or
representation, since it cannot be thought of as lacking in effect,
seems to coincide wholly with His government.   Here too, then,
we shall have to make a distinction on both sides, and set forth the
representation of Christ here only in so far as it is something different
from His government, and His twofold obedience only in so far as
it is something different from His self-presentation or His proclamation of the divine will by word and deed.

2. If we begin by dividing the obedience of Christ into active
and passive, we are by no means to imagine that these two are
so divided that they occupied different parts of His life, as is
commonly supposed—that the passive obedience began only with
His arrest, while the active had expressed itself from the beginning
of His public life up to that point.   For not only can there be no
suffering at all without reaction, which is always activity ; we have
already established the special conclusion with regard to Christ,[3]

[1] Eph. 5[2], Heb. 9[26].
[2] Maneat ergo hoc in causa, quod sola mors Christi est vere propitiatorium
sacrificium (*Apol. Conf.* p. 255).   Oblatio Christi semel facta, perfecta est
redemtio propitiatio et satisfactio pro omnibus peccatis (*Conf. Angl.* xxxi.
p. 138).   Similarly *Conf. Tetrap.* xix. p. 354 ; *Declar. Thorun.* p. 425.
[3] See § 94, 2.

that we can separate off no moment in His life which does not contain His powerful God-consciousness, and that this can manifest itself only as activity—activity which, even where it appears as reaction (and this of course it does in His sufferings proper), could never be anything else than the most perfect fulfilment of the divine will ; as indeed His perfect submission, without complaisance on the one side, or bitterness or ill-humour on the other, is the crown of His active obedience.   Similarly, there is never any activity without some definite occasion — which always presupposes a passive state ; and just as little is there ever any activity without limits to what is effected by it—and these limitations also are felt as suffering.   Now both those occasions and those limitations came to Christ out of the corporate life of universal sinfulness ; and thus every instance of opposition which He experienced during His active life, every snare of His adversaries, and equally the in-difference with which many passed Him by, became for Him suffer-ing, because in it He had a sympathetic feeling of the world's sin, and thus carried that sin ; so that this suffering accompanied Him throughout His whole life.   Looked at more closely, then, active and passive obedience were bound up with each other at every moment.   The one term, therefore, describes simply the condition, pleasing and completely satisfying to God, in which Christ was receptive towards everything which came to Him from the corporate life of sin, in that He accepted everything solely as it was related to the task to be discharged by means of the potency of his God-consciousness, in the most perfect and the purest way.   The other describes the parallel condition of His self-activity relatively to everything which it was incumbent on Him to do for the corporate life which He had come to call into being—the meaning of all this being that He never conceived any other purpose than this.   But both receptivity and self-activity, and hence both active and passive obedience, were present in all the moments of Christ's life.   The action of Christ without the suffering could not have been re-demptive, nor the suffering without the action reconciling ; and on that account redemption cannot be ascribed to the active obedience alone, nor reconciliation to the passive obedience alone, but both to both.

3. In comparing Christ, as regards His active obedience as thus defined, with the High Priest, we must, of course, consider only the original institution of this office, not what it degenerated into in reality.   The High Priest, in virtue alike of his setting-apart and

of the seclusion of his life in the precincts of the temple, was very favourably situated. It was not easy for him to neglect anything pertinent to his calling, nor was anything likely to be demanded of him which was out of keeping with his dignity and thus apt to injure it. Also it was much easier for him than for anyone else to keep clear of ceremonial defilements. These privileges had to be granted to human weakness if, in relation to his people, he was to represent even symbolically that which Christ actually was in relation to men. For the people were in constant danger, indeed almost in constant consciousness, of defilement. But the High Priest through his setting-apart was relieved of all worldly affairs, and even of the most natural duties, if to fulfil them involved even a slight defilement. It was his function to represent the pure man, who as such was alone authorized to officiate at the yearly sacrifice of atonement, by way of supplement to all the sacrifices which the people were ceaselessly offering through the priesthood as a whole. Thus the people, living at a greater or less distance from the temple, seemed to itself to be living also at a greater distance from God—a distance which was only temporarily lessened by the alternation of the times of divine service and those of ordinary business. But the function of the High Priest was to counter-balance these fluctuating movements by remaining constantly in the immediate neighbourhood of the temple, even although he actually entered it only at prescribed times and for prescribed purposes. Now just this is the essential thing in the high-priestly significance of the active obedience of Christ. For that it is His action alone which completely corresponds to the divine will, and gives pure and full expression to the dominion of the God-consciousness in human nature—this is the basis of our relationship to Him ; and on the recognition of this everything specifically Christian is based. What this implies is that, apart from connexion with Christ, no individual man, nor yet any part of the corporate life of men is at any time, in and for itself, righteous before God or an object of His good pleasure. And just as of the whole Jewish people the High Priest alone appeared immediately before God, and God saw the whole people as it were only in him, so Christ too is our High Priest because God sees us, not each of us for himself, but only in Christ. In living fellowship with Christ no one wishes to be anything for himself, nor yet to be regarded by God as any-thing. Each one wishes to appear only as animated by Christ, and as a part of His work which is still in process of development ;

so that even that which has not yet been altogether united with Him is still related to the same animating principle, because it is yet to be animated by Him some day. Thus, just as the High Priest was then, so Christ is now, the One who presents us pure before God in virtue of His own perfect fulfilment of the divine will. Because of His life in us, the impulse to the fulfilling of that will is also active in us, so that in this connexion with Him we too are objects of the divine good pleasure. This is the meaning (characteristic of our view, and from a Christian standpoint unobjectionable) of the often misunderstood expression, that Christ's obedience is our righteousness, or that His righteousness is imputed to us.[1] Such an expression is very easy to misunderstand, and it certainly cannot be thoroughly defended except on the assumption of a common life—which for that matter is also most definitely assumed in the conception of the High Priest. Thus we are also enabled to distinguish the prophetic value of Christ's obedience from the high-priestly. To the prophetic office of Christ belongs everything which is proclamation, and so self-presentation as well, not in words only, but also in deed. This, however, is addressed to men in view of their opposition to Christ, in order to make them susceptible of union with Him. Hence the obedience of Christ in this aspect of it is held up[2] even for all who are in the Church, and bears on the distinction between Christ and them which still persists. But the high-priestly value of His obedience relates to His union with us, in so far, that is, as in virtue of the vital fellowship existing between Him and us His pure will to fulfil the divine will is active in us also, and we therefore share His perfection, if not in execution, at least in impulse.[3] Our union with Him, accordingly, although it never attains more than relative manifestation, is yet recognized by God as absolute and eternal, and is affirmed as such in our faith.

There are only two things in the ordinary presentation against which we must still be on our guard. First, the active obedience of Christ must not be presented as the perfect fulfilment of the divine *law*. For law always denotes a distinction and a severance between a higher will which commands, and an imperfect will

---

[1] Eam ob causam ipsius obedientia . . . qua nostra causa sponte se legi subjecit, eamque implevit, nobis ad iustitiam imputatur (*Sol. decl.*, p. 585). Jesus Christus nobis imputans omnia sua merita, et tam multa sancta opera, quae praestitit pro nobis ac nostro loco est nostra iustitia (*Conf. Belg.* xxii. p. 183).

[2] Phil. 2^{5-8}, 1 Pet. 2^{21}.

[3] Cf. § 88, 3.

which is subordinate to it. In this sense the claim must certainly be made for Christ that He was not subject to the law, since, even if in view of the two natures a twofold will be ascribed to Him, yet the two even so must be in complete agreement.[1] But just as little can it be said that He willingly subjected Himself to the law ; for not even willingly could He bring Himself so to differ from the divine will that it could become a law for Him. The active obedience of Christ was rather His perfect fulfilment of the *divine will*.[2] But if what is in question is the Mosaic law, in so far as it chiefly prescribed performances and abstentions, then to this He certainly was subject so far as His personality was concerned,[3] so that it cannot be said that He undertook its fulfilment willingly. But the high-priestly worth of His obedience could not have consisted in this alone, except in so far as it was part of His fulfilment of the divine will. The second point is this, that if we are to express ourselves with any accuracy we cannot say, either, that Christ fulfilled the divine will *in our place* or *for our advantage*. That is to say, He cannot have done so *in our place* in the sense that we are thereby relieved from the necessity of fulfilling it. No Christian mind could possibly desire this, nor has sound doctrine ever asserted it. Indeed, Christ's highest achievement consists in this, that He so animates us that we ourselves are led to an ever more perfect fulfilment of the divine will.[4] Not only so ; but He cannot have done it in the sense that the failure to please God which is present in us in and for ourselves, should or could, as it were, be covered by Christ's doing more than was necessary to please Him. For only that which is perfect can stand before God ; hence even Christ Himself had (to put it so) nothing to spare, which could be distributed among us, whether we regard the completeness of His fulfilment in outward acts (which, moreover, for reasons which will emerge more clearly later, would be quite un-Protestant) or whether we regard only the purity of the inward sentiment.

Neither can He have fulfilled the divine will in any way *for our advantage*, as if by the obedience of Christ, considered in and for itself, anything were achieved for us or changed in relation to us. The true view is that the total obedience—δικαίωμα—of Christ avails for our advantage only in so far as through it our assumption into vital fellowship with Him is brought about, and in that fellow-

---

[1] But this, of course, is not what is meant in *Sol. decl.*, p. 605 : tam non fuit legi subjectus, quam non fuit passioni et morti obnoxius, quia dominus legis erat.

[2] John 4[34] 5[19. 30] 6[38].   [3] Gal. 4[4].   [4] John 15[2. 5. 8. 11].

ship we are moved by Him, that is, His motive principle becomes ours also—just as we also share in condemnation for Adam's sin only in so far as we, being in natural life-fellowship with him and moved in the same way, all sin ourselves.[1]

4. We come now to the *passive obedience* of Christ. It has already been stated above that the resemblance to the High Priest is here only a very general one. So we cannot use it to explain the connexion between the passive obedience of Christ and His redeeming and reconciling activity, especially since nothing is said about the High Priest enduring evil, while this is assumed to be the important element in the passive obedience of Christ, with the result that His feeling as sacrificer and His suffering as sacrificed or as sacrifice are confused. If for the present we allow this confusion, we are thrown back upon the fact that in every human society, so far as it can be regarded as a self-enclosed whole, there is as much evil as sin ; and that while the evil is certainly the punishment of the sin, yet each individual does not wholly and exclusively suffer precisely the evil which is connected with his personal sin.[2] Therefore it can be said, in every case in which anyone suffers evil not connected with his own sin, that he suffers punishment for others ; and as the causality of this sin has now exhausted itself, these others, in virtue of his punishment, can no longer be affected by the evil. Now in order that Christ should assume us into the fellowship of His life, it was necessary that He should first have entered into our fellowship. He without sin, so that no evil could arise from the presence of sin in Him, must enter into the fellowship of the sinful life where, along with and as a fruit of sin, evil is constantly arising. Hence it must be said of Him, that His suffering in this fellowship, if occasioned by sin—and from merely natural evils He never suffered—was suffered for those with whom He stood in fellowship, that is, for the whole human race, to which He belongs, not only because no particular fellowship within the human race can be completely isolated, but also by His own deliberate choice. Not only was the distinction between Jews and Gentiles abolished, in real fact, alike by His manifestation as ideal man and more particularly in His consciousness ; but for one thing His activity had already, at least indirectly, a bearing on the Gentiles, and for another thing, and especially in the last days of His life, He was surrounded by Judaism and heathendom, as political and religious authorities, causing His suffering, and representing

---

[1] Rom. 5[12. 18].　　　　　　　　　　　　　[2] Cf. § 77.

the sin of the whole world. If we abstract from those evils which
did not properly have any high-priestly character, and regard
only the suffering which He experienced as High Priest, it is obvious
that the sympathy with sin, conditioned as it is in Him as human
experience by this situation, must have been brought to its climax
in this alliance of the two chief classes of sinners against His sinless
personality. Now just as this sympathy with human guilt and
liability to punishment was the initiatory motive in redemption
(as every definite human activity is preceded by a determining
impression), so too the highest degree of just this sympathy was the
direct inspiration of the greatest moment in the work of redemption.
And as victory over sin rose out of this,[1] and along with sin its
connexion with evil has also been overcome, by the substitution of
equivalents we may say that through the suffering of Christ punishment is abolished, because in the fellowship of His blessed life even
the evil which is in process of disappearing is no longer at least
regarded as punishment.[2]

What has now been set forth is the real meaning of the statements that Christ by His willing surrender of Himself to suffering
and death satisfied the divine justice, as that which had ordained
the connexion between sin and evil, and thus set us free from the
punishment of sin.[3] Everywhere within the specific sphere of
Christianity this is easily intelligible and easily defensible, though
the statements are often criticized from without. And from this
presentation it must be possible to deduce whatever in the way of
appropriation of Christ's suffering (as distinct from its exemplary
value, which belongs to His prophetic office) has proved fruitful in
Christian piety. Even that form of the doctrine which sometimes
appears one-sided, and which concentrates the whole power of
redemption almost exclusively in the suffering of Christ, and so
finds satisfaction in this alone, may readily be understood in this
light. For in His suffering unto death, occasioned by His steadfastness, there is manifested to us an absolutely self-denying love ; and
in this there is represented to us with perfect vividness the way in
which God was in Him to reconcile the world to Himself, just as it

---

[1] John 12[24].   [2] Rom. 8[28].

[3] Deus ergo propter solum Christum *passum* et resuscitatum propitius
est peccatis nostris, etc. (*Expos. simpl.* xv. p. 41). Hunc . . . credimus . . .
unica sui ipsius oblatione Deo . . . pro nostris . . . peccatis satisfecisse . . .
sicque morte sua triumphum egisse, etc. (*Conf. Mylhus.* iv. p. 104). Profitemur quod . . . anima et corpore passus est, ut pro populi peccatis plane
satisfaceret, etc. (*Conf. Scot.* ix. p. 149). Ad haec passus mortuus et sepultus,
ut pro me satisfaceret meamque culpam persolveret (*Catech. maj.*, p. 495).

is in His suffering that we feel most perfectly how imperturbable was His blessedness. Hence it may be said that the conviction both of His holiness and of His blessedness always comes to us primarily as we lose ourselves in the thought of His suffering. And just as the active obedience of Christ has its properly high-priestly value chiefly in the fact that God regards us in Christ as partners in His obedience, so the high-priestly value of His passive obedience consists chiefly in this, that we see God in Christ, and envisage Christ as the most immediate partaker in the eternal love which sent Him forth and fitted Him for His task.

Although it seems now hardly necessary to stay to compare this simple presentation with those artificial constructions [1] which never tire of bringing together all sorts of reasons to prove the necessity or the appropriateness of Jesus' suffering and death, yet there still remain serious misunderstandings which we must dispose of. The first is this, that although it is in a specially impressive way from His suffering that we gain a true understanding of Christ, yet this is no justification for the triviality of the so-called ' wounds-theology,' once very widespread but now almost obsolete, which thought to find the deep import of the suffering of Christ in its sensuous details, and hence, for the sake of allegorical trivialities, broke up into details the totality of Christ's suffering. Underlying this was a confusion of thought ; what can only be attributed to Christ as a sacrifice or victim was transferred to His high-priestly dignity. The victim has no independent activity ; it is completely passive in everything which happens to it. So Christ too was perfectly passive in respect of those details of His suffering as to which He had no choice, and which consequently are not to be regarded as being for Him significant elements in experience. The second misunderstanding is to take the formula, that through the suffering of Christ the punishment of sin is taken away—a formula perfectly correct when interpreted as explained above—to mean that He bore the punishment, that is, that His suffering was equal to the sum of the evils constituting the amount of the punishment for the sins of the human race, since otherwise the divine righteousness would not have been satisfied. From which it naturally follows, since the total sin of the human race cannot be reckoned anything less than infinite, that the suffering also was infinite. If now the suffering of Christ and His death, although limited to a definite space of time and relative to a capacity for suffering infinitely diminished

[1] Among others, Reinhard, *Dogm.*, §§ 107 and 108, pp. 401 ff.

by His higher spiritual power, is thus to be equated to the total of human suffering for sin, postulated as infinite, then it is scarcely possible to avoid the supplementary assumption that the divine nature in Him also shared in the suffering.[1] This presentation of the matter, contradicting as it does the incapacity of the divine nature for suffering (a truth long recognized even in this doctrine), certainly can offer no defence to any serious attack by its opponents. But this misunderstanding only reaches its height in the view that the suffering of Christ is a transference of punishment in the still more exact sense that God (who nevertheless, according to the doctrine of the Church itself, is not in general the Author of punishment) appointed His suffering for the Redeemer as punishment, so that Christ is supposed to have felt the primary and most direct punishment of sin, namely, the divine wrath, as striking Him and resting upon Him. This theory, on the one hand, deprives the human consciousness of Christ of all human truth, by regarding as His personal self-consciousness what from the nature of the case could in Him be only sympathy.[2] And, on the other hand, it is obviously based on the assumption that there is an absolute necessity in the divine punishment, without any regard to the natural connexion of punishment with moral evil. This again can hardly be divorced from a conception of the divine righteousness which has been transferred to God from the crudest human conditions. Now if we take these two elements together, as they are united in the phrase *vicarious satisfaction*, we must surely admit that it is not fitting to stamp it as *the* phrase in which these aspects of the high-priestly work of Christ should be comprised. But perhaps the protest against this expression (which, of course, has already been attacked on many sides, yet continues to be the expression current in the Church) cannot be set forth more effectively than by demon-

[1] This is expressed, not obscurely, in the whole context of the passage quoted above from the *Sol. decl.*, p. 696, although throughout, so far as words are concerned, the proposition that the divine nature does not suffer is not abrogated. For it is at the same time maintained that the human nature became capable of suffering this only through its union with the divine, which is the same as saying, through the divine. With this, further, agrees the fact that this credal document—which of course is open to serious criticism—also teaches practically the opposite of the view here set forth : Reiicimus . . . quod fides non respiciat tantum obedientiam Christi, sed divinam ipsius naturam, quatenus videlicet ea in nobis habitet et operetur, et quod per hanc inhabitationem nostra coram Deo peccata tegantur (p. 697).

[2] It has given me much pleasure to read that the late J. J. Hess, too, could not bring himself to regard the passage Matt. 27[46] as a description by Christ of His own state of misery, but only as the first words of the Psalm, quoted with reference to what follows.

strating how it would have to be reinterpreted if it is to be accepted at all. Instead of taking it as a single expression which refers equally both to the active and to the passive obedience—as it claims to do—we must divide it up, and apply ' vicarious ' only to the passive, and ' satisfaction ' only to the active obedience. For Christ certainly made *satisfaction* for us by becoming, through His total action, not only the beginning of redemption in time, but also the eternally inexhaustible source, adequate for every further development, of a spiritual and blessed life. But this satisfaction is in no sense ' vicarious ' ; it could not have been expected of us that we should be able to begin this life for ourselves, nor does the act of Christ set us free from the necessity of pursuing this spiritual life by our own endeavour in fellowship with Him. On the other hand, the suffering of Christ is certainly *vicarious*, and that with respect to both its elements. For He had sympathy with sin in perfect measure even in regard to those who had not yet themselves become miserable through consciousness of it. While the evils which He suffered were vicarious in this general sense, that one in whom there is no moral evil ought not to suffer ; hence when he does experience evil, *he* is struck instead of those in whom the moral evil is. But this ' vicarious ' quality in no way makes ' satisfaction ' ; so far as the first element is concerned, because those who are not yet miserable must first become so in order to be able to be received by Christ ; so far as the other element is concerned, because it does not exclude other suffering of the same sort. Rather, all those who are assumed into the fellowship of Christ's life are called to share the fellowship of His suffering,[1] until the time when sin has been completely overcome and through suffering satisfaction has been made in the corporate life of humanity. Until then all suffering, even on the part of one who is only relatively innocent, always has a vicarious character. If, however, we wish to regard these two aspects of the high-priestly office of Christ in their indivisibility (that is, so far as it is possible to include the suffering under the activity), then we may turn the expression about, and call Christ our *satisfying representative* : in the sense, first, that in virtue of His ideal dignity He so represents, in His redemptive activity, the perfecting of human nature, that in virtue of our having become one with Him God sees and regards the totality of believers only in Him ; and, second, that His sympathy with sin, which was strong enough to stimulate a redemptive activity sufficient for the assumption of all men into His vital

[1] Matt. 10^{24-28}, John 15^{18-21}.

fellowship, and the absolute power of which is most perfectly
exhibited in His free surrender of Himself to death, perpetually
serves to make complete and perfect our imperfect consciousness
of sin. It was just like the complementary sacrifice of the High
Priest : that had special reference to those trespasses which had
not been consciously recognized, so that his sympathy, regarded
as the source of his action, took the place of that consciousness,
and the people then felt themselves as free from all anxiety about
divine punishment for the sins they had committed as if each one
himself had fulfilled everything that the law required where there
was consciousness of sin.

Only one misunderstanding still remains to be guarded against
at this point ; we must not set forth Christ's surrender of Himself
to death as a free decision on His part in any other sense than
that which is here taken as fundamental, namely, that His self-
surrender was identical with His persistence in redemptive activity.
For otherwise the suffering of Christ, so far as it must be regarded
as His own act, appears arbitrary, because in that case He must
simply have appointed Himself to the suffering as such ; and that
which, if regarded as a divine ordinance, would be that irrational
necessity of retribution which we have already disposed of, would,
as the free act of Christ, be an arbitrary self-torture—a pattern
for the arbitrary mortifications of the Roman Church, by the
transference of which it is possible for one person to set another
free from punishment. But in addition to this, we should still
need to take precautions—and it is impossible to see how our
precautions could be successful—lest the example of Christ might
be taken to afford a justification of voluntary death, even of the
sort which is absolutely unchristian. For if we wish to assert the
reality of human moral nature in Christ, we must not ascribe to
Him, even in this connexion, any other rules of conduct than
such as we have to recognize as valid for us all ; otherwise
there would be a danger that His life would cease to be an example, and consequently that it would cease to be an ideal. Thus,
so far as self-preservation is a duty at all, it must be true of Christ
also that if He foresaw His death, and if there was any means
of avoiding it without dereliction of duty, He was bound to make
use of it, as He had done previously.[1] The only thing He was *not*
bound to do was to ask for the help of angels,[2] or in this struggle to
call to His aid any miraculous power. He must therefore have

---

[1] Luke 4[30], John 8[59].   [2] Matt. 26[53].

accepted it as a duty involved in His vocation to appear in the holy city for this feast, in spite of the foreknowledge He possessed ; [1] and beyond question it was an element in the development of this great crisis that Christ met His death in His zeal for His vocation relatively to His Father's law, just as truly as His opponents —at least the best among them—condemned Him to death in their professional zeal for the law. If, nevertheless, we wish to regard even this from the standpoint of the divine decree, then we must concede that it behoved the Perfecter of faith to die a death which should be not simply an occurrence, but at the same time a deed in the highest sense of the word, in order that in this too He might proclaim the full dominion of the spirit over the flesh. By a natural death, whether due to accidental illness or the result of the weakness of old age, this could have become evident only accidentally and in a lesser degree. But this danger, too, of presenting the voluntary character of Jesus' death in a doubtful light, will best be avoided by keeping to the method we have hitherto followed, and making real use of it. For the atoning sacrifice of the High Priest was also a free action, though a professional one, on the one side conditioned by the sin of the people, and on the other following an established divine ordinance without arbitrariness of any kind.

5. Finally, Christ's *representation* of us before God, if we take the word in its usual meaning (that is, as either, more generally, the direction of another's business, or, more specifically, and more in the dominant Biblical sense, the bringing of the wishes of another before a third party and urging him to grant them), seems hardly to be at all separable from His kingly office. For how can that which Christ is thought of as obtaining from His Father be separated from that which He Himself as king brings about, and determines by laws and ordinances of government ? If then the phrase is to have any reality, if it is not as an undefined middle term to introduce confusion into our treatment, it must be confined to things which either do not belong at all, or at least do not wholly belong, to the Kingdom of Christ ; either this, or as a part of His activity it too must have been carried on during His earthly life, just like other parts—otherwise He would not have been a perfect High Priest. The New Testament passages upon which the use of the term is chiefly based [2] give little definite guidance, since it is not

---

[1] Matt. 16[21] and elsewhere ; cf. John 11[7-9] ; cf. ver. 56.

[2] Rom. 8[34], Heb. 7[25], 1 John 2[1] ; but it is to be noticed that both the expressions found here, $\dot{\upsilon}\pi\epsilon\rho\epsilon\nu\tau\upsilon\gamma\chi\acute{\alpha}\nu\epsilon\iota\nu$ and $\pi\alpha\rho\acute{\alpha}\kappa\lambda\eta\tau\sigma\varsigma$, are also used elsewhere of the Holy Spirit.

clear that in all of them the reference is to the High Priest ; they seem rather to proceed from different points of view. Hence we had better keep to the conception of the high-priestly function, and bring in chiefly His appearing before God on our behalf.[1] And, if in doing so the distinction mentioned above is observed, then the representation will consist chiefly of two things : Christ appears before the Father, first, to establish our fellowship with Him, and then, further, to support our prayer before the Father. For the Kingdom of Christ extends only over those who have already been assumed into vital fellowship with Him ; while the gradual addition of individuals to this realm depends upon the divine Providence with regard to them. But just as in general this fellowship is sought for us by Christ, and is granted by God for His sake, so it is not only in His high-priestly prayer that we have the memorable fact of this representation ; that is indicated also in everything which He says about His prayer,[2] not even excluding statements which seem to be contradictory, and also in what is said about His prayer by others.[3] As regards the rest, if we proceed wholly on the principle that whatever does not belong to the Kingdom of God must also be excluded from the subjects of our prayer,[4] then in the spiritual sphere there are some things which are not so exclusively spiritual in character that they are not also interwoven with the general world order, and some which are not entirely determined by the general rules and ordinances properly to be deduced from the kingly dignity of Christ. And when He bids us pray to the Father ourselves, the fact that it is to be prayer in His name involves the certainty of a co-operation on the part of Christ which hallows our prayer by purifying and perfecting our consciousness of God. Now this co-operation is His representation of us, in the sense that it is only through Him that our prayer comes acceptably and effectively before God. In virtue, therefore, of that relation to us which is based upon His peculiar dignity, He remains the representative of the whole human race, for, like the High Priest, He brings our prayer before God and conveys to us the divine blessings. Faith in that part of this work which lies beyond Christ's earthly career is in no sense dependent on knowledge—which is denied us—of the character of His exalted life, but only on the

---

[1] Heb. 9[24].
[2] John 14[16] 16[26] 17[9], Luke 22[32],
[3] Luke 6[12] and elsewhere ; Heb. 5[7].
[4] Matt. 6[33].

content and dignity of His personality in relation to God and to us, as these have been set forth above.-

6. Now just as, in accordance with all that has been said, Christ is the climax of the priesthood, and far beyond all comparison even with the High Priest, so He is also the end of all priesthood. For that which is the essential thing in the conception of priesthood, that of which every earlier priesthood was only an imperfect indication, has been given absolutely and once for all in Christ ; for He is the most perfect mediator for all time between God and every individual part of the human race, of which no one, in and for himself, could be in any sense an object for God, nor could enter into any connexion with Him. Hence, now that the true and eternal priesthood is known, there is no place for any arbitrarily devised priesthood—a mere copy of the real—nor for any further sacrifice : all human institutions of this sort are abolished. But at the same time, the high-priesthood of Christ has passed over to the fellowship of the faithful, so that Christians as a whole are called a priestly nation.[1] Two things are clearly involved in this. First, that among themselves all distinction between priests and laity is abolished. Even the Apostles never claim for themselves anything that can properly be called priestly, so that the revival of the priesthood in the Church must be viewed as one of the greatest misapprehensions. But second, Christendom as a whole, as the human race already united to the Redeemer, stands to the rest of humanity in the relation in which the priests stood to the laity. For it is only in so far as there exists a real vital fellowship with Christ at least in one part of the race that there is also a relationship between Him and the rest. Hence in this sense the Christian community, as inseparable from Christ, appears before God for the whole race and represents it. On the other hand, there can be no talk at all of any special intercession and representation on the part of individuals in the community of the perfected.[2] Similarly, all the activity of Christendom as a whole on behalf of the Gospel belongs to the active obedience of Christ, but nothing follows from this as to a meritoriousness of individual good works done by the faithful. The same is true also of all sufferings for the sake of the Gospel in the widest sense : they belong to the atoning suffering of

---

[1] 1 Pet. 2[9].

[2] Credimus quoniam Jesus Christus datus est nobis unicus advocatus . . . quicquid homines de mortuorum sanctorum intercessione commenti sunt nihil aliud esse quam fraudem et fallacias satanae, ut homines a recta precandi forma abduceret (*Conf. Gallic.* xxiv. p. 119).

Christ,[1] but nothing follows from this as to arbitrary mortifications —any more than there was anything arbitrary in Christ's suffering. Hence Christ remains the end of the priesthood, for all this is high-priestly only in so far as it is really at the same time Christ's doing and suffering. These last-mentioned inferences—and they are perfectly natural—ought surely of themselves to suffice to secure its place in our system for a mode of presentation which has been attacked by almost all modern dogmatic theologians since Ernesti.[2]

§ 105. *Third Theorem.—The kingly office of Christ consists in the fact that everything which the community of believers requires for its well-being continually proceeds from Him.*

1. The term ' king ' has, and had in the time of Christ, many meanings ; and there is a great difference between its strict official use and its vague polite use. It is, therefore, impossible to base our presentation upon an exegetical decision on the questions in what sense Christ was asked whether He was a king,[3] and whether He answered in the same sense or another. Rather we must keep to the recollection, not yet extinct, that the conception of king was opposed on the one hand to that of a tyrant, whose power was just as unlimited, but not natural ; and on the other hand, to that of the authorities of a society, who possessed only a limited and delegated power, conferred on them by the governed themselves. A tyranny, on the other hand, always involved the possibility, not to say the assumption, that the power which had been arbitrarily seized was also selfish, and might have other aims than the free development and the natural prosperity of those over whom it was exercised. In contrast with both, the lordship of Christ is as unlimited as that of the animating principle always is when it is neither outwardly hindered nor inwardly weakened. Moreover, it is in the interest of those over whom it is exercised, as obviously follows from the facts that it is nothing but the lordship of that element whose weakness in themselves men deplore, and that submission to His lordship must always be voluntary. But the kingly power has this in common with the other two, that its object cannot be an individual as such, but only a society, and the individual only in so far as he belongs to the society. Individuals, then, submit voluntarily to the lordship of Christ ; but in so doing they at the same time enter a society to which they did not previously

[1] 2 Cor. 1[5] 4[10]. [2] See his *Diss. de triplici munere Christi.*
[3] John 18[33], Matt. 27[11].

belong. So that, in attributing a kingly dignity to Christ, we are
eo ipso declaring ourselves definitely opposed to the contention that
Christ did not intend to found an organic community, but that the
society of believers came into being, or was formed, later, without
His injunction. But since, at the same time, no one enters this
community except by submitting himself to Christ's lordship, it
follows that Christ Himself initiated this Kingdom, and is thus
without any predecessor in His kingly dignity.

Christ Himself, however, indicates still another contrast, when
He describes His Kingdom as not of this world, and so distinguishes
it in yet another way from both those others. This negative
description involves in the first place that His kingly power is not
immediately concerned with the disposal and arrangement of the
things of this world—which means that nothing remains as the
immediate sphere of His kingship but the inner life of men individually and in their relation to each other. It involves further,
that for the exercise of His lordship He makes use of no means
which are dependent upon the things of this world, *i.e.* of no constraint which requires superiority in material forces, nor yet of
enticements or threatenings of any kind which require support of
that kind and make a merely sensuous appeal—for that, too,
belongs to this world. But this is by no means to say that the
kingly power of Christ began only after He had been raised above
the earth, still less—as might be held—that it covers only His
exalted life ; He Himself says, not that He will be a king, but that
He is one ; and not only did He prove Himself a king during His
earthly life—by giving laws for His community, by sending out
His servants for its extension, by imposing rules of conduct and
giving directions as to the way in which His commanding will
should be carried out [1]—but His kingly power is and remains
everywhere and always the same. For those laws and directions
do not grow old, but remain valid, with undiminished force, in the
Church of Christ ; and if for the future He refers His disciples to
His spiritual presence, yet even that does not make a distinction
between different times. For even His original influence was
purely spiritual, and was mediated through His bodily appearance
not otherwise than even now His spiritual presence is mediated
through the written Word and the picture it contains of His being
and influence—so that even now His directive control is not simply a
mediate and derived one. So that, keeping in mind what was said

[1] Matt. 10[5-14] 18[15-20] 28[19-20].

above, we may say that His government of us bears the same relation to our activity in His name as His representation of us does to our prayer in His name.   Indeed, it is also obvious that since He stands to the totality of believers in exactly the same relation as the divine nature in Him does to the human, animating and taking it up into the fellowship of the original life, His lordship too is in the strictest sense a sole lordship, for no one else is in a position to share it. Thus, just as Christ has no predecessor in the society governed by Him, but is its original founder, so too He has in it no successor and no representative.   For He exercises His lordship through ordinances which He Himself established,[1] and has Himself declared these to be sufficient,[2] so that nothing is now necessary but the right application of these ; and to apply them is the common task of those who are ruled by Christ, just because they are His subjects. Even if at any time they could transfer this task, either to one individual or to several—though of course they could not do so without giving up their vital relation to Christ—yet any such individual would be only their representative, and not a representative of Christ.[3]   So that among believers there is nowhere any lordship other than His alone.

2. The difficulty in regard to this part of the work of Christ consists especially in defining aright the kingly power of Christ in relation to the general divine government (a difficulty which cannot be overlooked once the subject is somewhat more closely scrutinized from a *theoretical* point of view), and further in defining it aright relatively to secular government (a difficulty which at once emerges in the *practical* treatment of the question).

The customary division of the Kingdom of Christ into the kingdom of power, the kingdom of grace, and the kingdom of glory helps us little.   We have first to break it up so as to comprehend under the two latter the proper object of Christ's kingly activity, namely, the world which has become participant in redemption, while under the kingdom of power we understand the world as such, and in itself.   But in taking this position, we seem to lend ourselves to the extravagant notion that there belonged to Christ a kingdom of power, as it were, before the kingdom of grace, and independent of it. Now, to say the least, such a kingdom could not possibly belong to His redemptive activity ; and if the Apostles knew of such a

---

[1] Eph. 4[11-16].   [2] Matt. 21[20], John 15[9. 10] 17[4].
[3] *Expos. simpl.* xvii. p. 50 : Ecclesia non potest ullum aliud habere caput quam Christum . . . Nam ut ecclesia corpus est spirituale, ita caput habeat sibi congruens spirituale utique oportet.

kingdom belonging to the Word,[1] it must have been a knowledge which, because unconnected with redemption, could not belong to Christian piety either.   Anyone who thinks it necessary to inter- pret the expressions which they use with reference to Christ as the Word made flesh, the God-man and the Redeemer,[2] or which Christ uses of Himself,[3] as if they attributed to Him the governance of the whole world, involves himself in a contradiction, not only with all the passages in which Christ Himself offers petitions to the Father and refers to what the Father has retained in His own power, but also with all passages which express His intention to establish an immediate relationship, both of petition and response, between believers and the Father.   It is true that occasionally there is to be found even within the Protestant Church a form of doctrine, and here and there, in conjunction with it, even a type of Church service which leaves room (all the prayers being addressed solely to Christ) only for a relationship of believers to Christ, to the exclusion of the Father.   But we must, with Scripture and very much more with the Church, pronounce this a dubious innovation. If, however, this rock is to be avoided, by the power of Christ we can understand only that power which begins with the kingdom of grace and is essentially included in it.   And this itself is a power over the world only in so far as believers are taken out of the midst of the world, and the fellowship of believers or the kingdom of Christ can increase only as the world (as the antithesis of the Church) decreases, and its members are gradually transformed into members of the Church, so that evil is overcome and the sphere of redemption enlarged.   But even this is a power of Christ over the world which proceeds only from the kingdom of grace, *i.e.* it exists in virtue of the influence of the command to preach given by Christ and perpetually valid in the Church.   On the other hand, what part of the world, or what individual, becomes ripe for the fruitful- ness of this preaching before other parts, or before other individuals, is a matter belonging to the kingdom of power, which the Father has retained for Himself.[4]   Accordingly, the only things which remain subject to Christ's direct control are the forces of redemption implanted in the Church ; and it would be a rather unfruitful distinction, and not even correctly described, if we called His King- dom a kingdom of grace in so far as these forces show themselves effective in a purely inward way, for sanctification and edification,

---

[1] John 1[2. 3].
[2] Heb. 1[2. 3].
[3] Matt. 11[27] 28[18] ; cf. John 17[5. 22. 24].
[4] Acts 1[7], John 6[44].

and a kingdom of power in so far as they are employed in the overcoming of the world ; for these two things it is quite impossible to separate from each other. The distinction, however, between the kingdom of grace and the kingdom of glory is usually taken to be that the latter follows upon the former, so soon as all Christ's subjects have been placed in full possession of all the benefits won for them, and no longer have any contact with the world—an assumption which we shall consider more closely later. Here it need only be remarked, with reference to the kingly dignity of Christ, that if the assumption is taken strictly then there can be no other activity in this Kingdom than one of expressive representation, in which case the exercise of a general directive power is reduced to a minimum. Hence we can certainly regard it as a glory of Christ that He has no more to suffer, even in sympathy, with the whole body of believers, because it has been finished and perfected ; but in no sense is this a condition which should be described as a Kingdom. Thus there remains only the one kingdom of grace as Christ's true kingdom, as indeed it is the only one a consciousness of which really emerges in our moods of devotion, the only one of which we require knowledge for our guidance, because our active faith must be directed towards it. The two other terms in the customary division we can use only to determine the scope of this very kingdom of grace. In calling it a kingdom of power we are asserting, not only that the extension of the influence of Christ over the human race knows no limits, and that no people is able to offer it a permanently effective opposition, but also that there is no stage of purity and perfection which does not belong to Christ's Kingdom. And in calling it a kingdom of glory we are confessing our belief —of course in connexion with that highest purity and perfection, only approximately given in experience—in an unlimited approximation to the absolute blessedness to be found in Christ alone.

So far as the distinction between the kingly power of Christ and civil government is concerned, it would seem, after what has been said, that nothing is easier than to distinguish exactly between the two in conception. For civil government is unquestionably an institution which belongs to the general divine government of the world,[1] and even by His own declaration is accordingly as such alien to Christ's Kingdom. On the other hand, civil government is a legal thing, and exists everywhere, even where there is no

[1] Rom. 13[1, 2].

Christian religion. Hence, since it springs out of the corporate life of sinfulness, and everywhere presupposes this (for of course for the sanction of its laws it reckons upon the force of sensuous motives), it cannot as such have the slightest authority in the Kingdom of Christ. On this view the two powers seem to be held entirely apart from each other, so that the sole lordship of Christ in His Kingdom remains secure although His followers conduct themselves in worldly affairs in accordance with the regulations of the secular government, and regard everything that comes to them from it as coming from the divine government of the world.[1] But how greatly the situation is altered as soon as we think of the secular government as exercised by Christians over Christians, is clearly to be seen in the fact that, on the one side, the Church has attempted to control the secular government in the name of Christ, while on the other, the Christian magistracy as such has claimed for itself the right to regulate the affairs of the society of believers.   In order not to introduce at this point anything which belongs to Christian Ethics—from which even the theological principles of Church Law must be derived—the only question we shall here have to propound is whether the Kingdom of Christ is changed in extent through the entrance of this new material relationship.   Now it is certainly true that Christ must completely control the society of believers, and consequently that every member of the society must show himself, wholly and in every part of his life, to be governed by Christ.   But since this depends entirely upon the inner vital relationship in which each individual stands to Christ, and since there can be no representative who exercises the kingly office of Christ in His name, this simply means that everyone, whether magistrate or private citizen, has to seek in the directions given by Christ, not indeed right directions for his conduct under civil government (for this is always a matter of the art of politics), but certainly the right temper of mind even in this relationship. On the other hand, it also remains true that no one can exert influence upon the society of believers except in the measure in which he is a pre-eminent instrument of Christ's kingly power,[2] since otherwise the sole lordship of Christ would be imperilled.   And this

---

[1] *Aug. Conf.* xvi. : Quia Evangelium tradit iustitiam aeternam cordis, interim non dissipat politiam aut oeconomiam, sed maxime postulat conservare tanquam ordinationes Dei et in talibus ordinationibus exercere caritatem.

[2] This is also the basis of the rule of Peter, Acts 1[21], and of the procedure of the Church as related in Gal. 2[7 9].

does not at all depend on his outward vocation ; [1] one who is called
as a bond-servant is not therefore a bond-servant in the society, but
a freedman of the Lord, and similarly he who is called as a lord does
not therefore become a lord in the society, but only a bond-servant
of Christ like everyone else.[2] So that the civil contrast between
magistrate and private citizen loses all significance in the Church ;
it makes no difference to a man's relationship to the kingly power
of Christ.

3. In this way, then, we have separated the kingly power of
Christ, on the one hand, from the power which the Father has retained for Himself, while on the other we have set it beyond all the
resources of the civil power.   The latter is undoubtedly the way in
which what Luther called ' the two swords ' should be kept separate
from each other. We may therefore say of this part also of the
work of Christ, as of the former ones, that He is the climax and the
end of all spiritual kingship ; and this will hold true in and for itself
as well as relatively to this separation.   In and for itself we must
compare His lordship with every other purely spiritual power, and
all the relationships of master and scholars, pattern and imitators,
law-giver and law-receivers, we must put far below it—they stand
on a vastly lower level, and are only concerned with individual
parts of the life of the human spirit.   The same is true of the
founders of other religions, who neither evoked a temper of mind
opposed to former habits and customs, as Christ did (rather they
accommodated themselves to these in various ways), nor, as Christ
did, called the whole human race under their lordship.   In the
same way He is the end of all such kingship, for there is just as
little possibility of a similar kingdom after His,[3] as there is that a
similar one should now exist or should ever have existed alongside
of it.   But He is both climax and end, only in so far as the above-
mentioned separation is maintained.   For it is part alike of the
purity and of the perfection of His spiritual power that sensuous
motives can have no share whatever in it.   That is why Christianity
is neither a political religion nor a religious state or a theocracy.
The former are those religious fellowships which are regarded as
the institutions of a particular civil society, and which rest upon
the assumption that the religion is derived from civil legislation, or

---

[1] *Expos. simpl.* xxx. p. 91 : Si magistratus sit amicus adeoque membrum
ecclesiae, utilissimum excellentissimumque membrum est, quod ei permultum
prodesse eamque peroptime iuvare potest.
[2] 1 Cor. 7^{22}.
[3] Heb. 12^{27} : even 1 Cor. 15^{28} does not contradict this.

is related as a subordinate movement to the same higher impulse which first called the civil organization into being, so that for the sake of the civil society its members also unite in a religious fellowship, which therefore is animated by the common spirit of the society and by patriotism—these being ' fleshly motives ' in the Scriptural sense. Theocracies, on the other hand, are religious fellowships which as such have subordinated the civil society to themselves ; in which consequently political ambition aims at preeminence within the religious fellowship, and there is the underlying assumption that the religious society, or the divine revelation upon which it rests, was able to call into being the civil society—which in this sense is possible only for religious fellowships which are nationally limited. To both, then, political religions as well as theocracies, Christ puts an end through the purely spiritual lordship of His God-consciousness ; and the stronger and the more extensive His Kingdom becomes, the more definite becomes the severance between Church and State, so that in the proper outward separation —which, of course, may take very different forms—their agreement is ever more perfectly worked out.

Postscript to this Division.—Only after we have concluded our treatment of the whole of the doctrine of Christ are we in a position to see what kind of meaning is to be given to the two contrasted *states of humiliation and exaltation* ascribed to Him. For these expressions, when taken as precisely as a place in the system must involve, cannot be applied either to the relationships of the Person by itself, or of the Work by itself, nor to the relationship of the Work to the Person. In the first place, the term ' humiliation,' taken strictly, presupposes a higher being which existed previously. But what this is, we cannot discover, so long as we abide by the unity of the Person. It may rightly be called an exaltation, that Christ became the first-fruits of the resurrection, and sits at the right hand of God ; and in comparison His earthly condition may be called a lower one—but not a humiliation, for the Person of Christ began only when He became man. On such terms the Person of Christ is divided, and since the divine in Him is regarded as something special existing from eternity, its descent to earth takes on the appearance of a humiliation. But to the absolutely highest and eternal — which necessarily remains always self-identical — no humiliation can possibly be attributed. It would follow from this that, from the same point of view, the indwelling of the Holy Spirit in the fellowship of believers must also be a humiliation—all the

more that human nature in us is not pure and sinless as it was in
the Person of Christ. Nay more, in view of the omnipresence of
God in all finite creatures, creation itself would be a humiliation ;
and this, although the glorification of God is actually given as the
purpose of creation. But if we accept the term ' humiliation ' instead
of the more exact ' state of lowliness,' but hold fast to the unity of
the Person, even so the antithesis reveals itself as a mere deception,
or at least as merely an appearance for others but not a reality for
Christ Himself. For how can one have been conscious of the lowliness of His state who speaks of His relationship to God the Father
in such a way [1] that even to be set at His right hand could not be
regarded as an exaltation ? If, further, we think of the customary
conception of the two natures and of a mutual impartation of the
attributes of each, we cannot refer the humiliation to the union of
the two natures (for that remains even if the humanity of Christ
be exalted to the right hand of God), but only to the divine nature,
either in so far as it refrains from the use of its attributes, or in so
far as along with them it must accept those of the human nature.
Now the latter circumstance remains unaltered in the state of exaltation as well. For since the distance between God and every finite
being is infinite, it remains unchanged whether we think of humanity
in its present state or in advanced development. The former has
only slightly more plausibility. For if (and this is involved in this
mode of presentation) even in the state of lowliness exceptions to the
non-use of divine attributes occurred in virtue of the free will of
Christ,[2] then of course the renouncement of them itself must have been
voluntary. Indeed, we must assert this, even without any regard
to exceptions ; for no compulsion can be laid upon the divine nature.
In fact, we must rather say that a compulsion to make use of those
attributes against His free will would have been a humiliation. But
we cannot imagine that even in the state of exaltation Christ makes
a more complete use of them. For if all the attributes of the divine
nature are active without intermission in the human nature, then
all activities of the human nature must be at rest without intermission ; which is the same as saying that so far as its activity was
concerned the human nature was absorbed by the divine, and there
remained only its passive aspect—and this is quite contrary to the
original assumption. But how, again, could we conceive an un-

---

[1] John 1^{51} 4^{34} $5^{17. 20ff.}$ 6^{57} 8^{29} $10^{30. 36}$, etc. etc.
[2] Sol. decl., p. 767 : divinam suam majestatem pro liberrima voluntate
quando et quomodo ipsi visum fuit etiam in statu exinanitionis manifestavit.

interrupted use of the divine qualities, if we are really to think of Christ as representing us before the Father, and making requests for us in view of sin—that is, as sympathetically sharing in the conflicts of the warring Church ?   So that even here there remains only a less or more, which cannot justify the use of such expressions. And it hardly need be said that this antithesis cannot be related to the functions of Christ either.   For even if we were to say that the kingly function is by far the highest, even so the prophetic and the priestly were next to it, and were not opposed to it as lowly functions—for it was in no lowly attitude that Christ exercised the prophetic activity.

If now, in view of the complete untenability of this formula, we inquire what its origin was, the answer is that its only basis is a passage of Scripture,[1] whose devotional and—when we regard the whole context—rhetorical character indicates no intention that the expressions used should be set up as a fixed didactic formula. Besides, it would follow from this passage that the exaltation of Christ is simply a reward appointed Him by God for the humiliation, without direct connexion either with His peculiar dignity or with the completion of His work.   But the way in which Paul here sets up Christ as an example is quite compatible with the view that his starting-point was simply the appearance of lowliness in Christ's life as well as in His death.   In the transmission of doctrine, accordingly, we are perfectly entitled to set this formula aside ; it may justly be entrusted to history for safe keeping.

---

[1] Phil. 2^{6-9}.   None of the other passages cited in this connexion contributes anything to the question.

SECOND DIVISION : THE MANNER IN WHICH FELLOWSHIP WITH
THE PERFECTION AND BLESSEDNESS OF THE REDEEMER
EXPRESSES ITSELF IN THE INDIVIDUAL SOUL

§ 106. *The self-consciousness characterizing those assumed into living
fellowship with Christ may be set forth under both conceptions,
Regeneration and Sanctification.*

1. If it be the essence of redemption that the God-consciousness
already present in human nature, though feeble and repressed,
becomes stimulated and made dominant by the entrance of the
living influence of Christ, the individual on whom this influence is
exercised attains a religious personality not his before.   Before this
the God-consciousness was evinced only casually in isolated flashes,
never kindling to a steady flame.   The God-consciousness was not
in a position to take constant control of the various elements of
life.   Even those elements actually controlled by it were in fact
always quickly submerged by elements of a contrary nature ; whereas
a devout personality must be taken to mean one in which every
mainly passive element is part of the relation to the God-consciousness produced by the influence of the Redeemer ; and every active
element is due to an impulse of the same God-consciousness.   Life
thus comes under a different formula, making it a life that is new ;
hence the phrases ' a new man,' ' a new creature,' [1] which bear the
same sense as our phrase ' a new personality.'   This new life of
course presents itself as something in process of becoming, for the
individual identity persists and the new life can only, as it were,
be grafted on to the old.   And yet the situation in which the new
life is present as something in process of becoming, when related in
memory to the situation in which it was not present at all, can be
attached and bound together with the old into one continuous
personal life only by assuming a turning-point at which the continuity
of the old ceased, and that of the new began to be in process of
becoming.   This is the essence of the conception ' regeneration.'
Similarly from another point of view the growing continuity of the
new life in which the elements answering to its formula are more

[1] 2 Cor. 5[17], Eph. 4[24].

and more integrated and the elements representing the old life recur ever more feebly and rarely is denoted by the expression ' sanctification.'

If now in this connexion we recall what was said before, namely, that the relation of Christ to the rest of humanity is exactly the same as the relation within His personality of its divine to its human element, we may add that these two conceptions, regeneration and sanctification, set forth just the same distinction as between the act of uniting and the state of union ; except that in that instance first of all one Person originated intact, and so the state of union too was an unbroken continuity, and an uninterrupted diffusion through the human nature ; which would, accordingly, happen in this instance too were it not that, through the identity of the subject with the earlier personality, elements from the life of sinfulness are still present as a hindrance.   And as in that former instance one could not exist without the other, so here we cannot isolate regeneration or sanctification.

2. The formulation of this division being thus generally justified, we need only add to what has already been said [1] one remark about the order adopted.   The part which has just been concluded, dealing with the kingly office of Christ, might of itself have led in the most natural way to a description of the new corporate life over which He holds sway ; and as the incitements that bring about this assumption into living fellowship with Christ come to each man only from this corporate life, and as the sanctification of each depends on the effective influence upon him of the whole, this doctrine might very well have been treated in the next section.   But the other arrangement is equally correct.   For, the entrance of Christ into humanity being its second creation, humanity thus becomes a new creature, and one may regard this entrance as also the regeneration of the human race, which to be sure only actually comes to pass in the form of the regeneration of individuals.   And as the community of believers in its true essence consists only of the totality of the sanctified elements of all who are assumed into living fellowship with Christ, so again the sanctification of the individual includes everything by which the fellowship is constituted and maintained and extended.   In view of this symmetrical interlocking, the order taken justifies itself for one reason, because while individuals are indeed originally laid hold of by Christ, yet at the same time it is always by an influence of Christ Himself,

[1] Above, § 90, 1 and § 91, 2.

mediated by His spiritual presence in the Word, that individuals
are assumed into the fellowship of the new life ; but, above all,
because the earlier place is more suitable for what in one aspect
relates back to the old corporate life of general sinfulness but in
another aspect lies at the base of the new common life under grace.
This double reference holds for both of the conceptions to be discussed in this Division.   While regeneration is for the individual
the turning-point at which the earlier life as it were breaks off and
the new begins, it can also be regarded as the vanishing of the old
life in a fashion explicable only by the redeeming activity of Christ,
which, be it noted, takes effect in such wise that simultaneously
therewith the power of the new life is implanted in the soul.   The
treatment of the theme has therefore both a backward reference to
the previous division of the subject and an anticipation of the
main lines of the next Section, where the power of the new life is
considered as the common spirit which animates the whole.   Sanctification also has two aspects : from one point of view it is measured
by the degree in which the common sinfulness is more or less rapidly
overcome in the individual soul ; from the other it is measured
by the relation of the individual soul to the new corporate life in
the service of which it makes more or less rapid progress.

FIRST DOCTRINE : REGENERATION

§ 107. *Assumption into living fellowship with Christ, regarded as a
         man's changed relation to God, is his Justification ; re-
         garded as a changed form of life, it is his Conversion.*

1. Seeing that we are here concerned simply with the situation
of the individual in his transition from the corporate life of sinfulness to a living fellowship with Christ, we must use this situation
to explain the necessary connexion of the two elements just specified.
' Form of life ' is to be understood simply as the fashion in which
the time-elements of life happen and arrange themselves ; and self-
consciousness is viewed as passing into action, that is to say, as
basis of the will.   In the condition left behind, the stirrings of a
self-consciousness suffused with a consciousness of God were never
determinative of the will, being but casual and fleeting ; the
sensuous consciousness alone was determinative.   When life is
linked to Christ it is the other way about, and this change is expressed by the term ' conversion.'   As a matter of fact, our relation
to God is really an affair of the quiescent self-consciousness, looking

at itself reflected in thought and finding a consciousness of God included there. Now we know that only one relationship to the divine holiness and righteousness is proper to the corporate life of sinfulness, namely, the self-consciousness of guilt and merited punishment.[1] Obviously this relation must vanish at the very beginning of living fellowship with Christ, and not at some later stage of its development towards perfection, for the two are contradictory ; there can be no true consciousness of fellowship with Christ as long as that other consciousness persists.

It is clear also that the two elements cannot be held separate in such a manner that a conversion could even be imagined without justification, or a justification without conversion. Justification would then be a resolve to forgive oneself on the ground that sin is unavoidable, a vanishing of the old relation to God without any new relation taking its place, and therefore not really justification at all but a complete cessation of the God-consciousness within the self-consciousness—that is, hardening. A new relation can arise only through the union with Christ which effects conversion too. Equally inconceivable is a new direction of the will, based on becoming one with Christ, in which the consciousness of guilt and punishability persists. The new man would then have to remain altogether unconscious, or, to put it otherwise, there would have to be an assumption into fellowship with the perfection of Christ that did not include fellowship with His blessedness. If this ever seems to happen, the explanation is either that the consciousness of guilt is merely a delusive carrying-forward of past feelings into the present, or that ' conversion ' has been a mere desire to become better by one's own resources, without any genuine living fellowship with Christ. Conversion and justification, being thus utterly inseparable, must also be regarded as happening simultaneously, and each is the infallible criterion of the other.

2. In the fuller treatment of these matters much diversity is found in the text-books, identical expressions being taken by different writers in different senses ; and the present writer may be open to the charge that he, too, chooses his terms arbitrarily. For, to compare the expressions ' regeneration ' and ' conversion,' there is no real indication that the second conception is just a part of the first ; it is quite as legitimate to put it the other way about. Still less is there anything in the expression ' justification ' pointing to the beginning of a new form of life ; if we consider that the

---

[1] Cf. §§ 83 and 84.

condition being superseded is one governed by law, the expression rather suggests that this condition is to continue than that it is to lapse.   Moreover, other expressions as significant and as scriptural as conversion might also put in a claim to be preferred ; and in view of the great wealth of expression, mainly pictorial, of which Biblical writers [1] avail themselves in this connexion, variation is unavoidable.   The important matter is the exact exposition of the actual meaning of the expressions rather than any particular choice of words.   The choice made here is justifiable on the one hand because regeneration expresses in the most definite way the beginning of a consistent life ; and on the other hand because the relation to the past, which in the general expression ' regeneration ' falls very much into the background, comes to be the ruling consideration in the more particularized expressions ' conversion ' and ' justification.' The use of the word ' conversion ' for the transformation, the right-about-turn to better things, makes evident that it is the beginning of a new page, a new order in contrast to the old.   Justification, too, presupposes something in respect of which a person is justified ; and since no error is possible to the Supreme Being it must be assumed that something has happened to a man between his former and his present state by which the divine displeasure has been removed and without which he could not have become the object of divine favour.   However, it seems inadvisable to introduce still other figurative expressions from the Bible ; for without a fine-spun and unprofitably lengthy discussion one could not distinguish all the various aspects of what is, after all, only a momentary point of departure ; not to speak of the fact that enlightenment and renewal can be used just as well of what is continuous and permanent, and referred to the sphere of sanctification.

The order seems, in view of the symmetry of the definition, a matter of entire indifference ; many considerations, however, make it more convenient to begin with conversion.

FIRST THEOREM : CONVERSION

§ 108. *Conversion, the beginning of the new life in fellowship with Christ, makes itself known in each individual by Repentance, which consists in the combination of regret and change of*

---

[1] *E.g.* ' enlightenment,' Eph. 3[9] 5[14], Heb. 6[4-6] ; ' renewal,' Eph. 4[23], Tit. 3[5] Heb. 6[6].

*heart ; and by Faith, which consists in the appropriation
of the perfection and blessedness of Christ.*

Conf. Aug. xii. : Constat autem poenitentia proprie his duabus partibus,
altera est contritio seu terrores incussi conscientiae agnito peccato, altera est
fides.—*Apol. Conf.* v. : Nos igitur constituimus duas partes poenitentiae
videlicet contritionem et fidem. Si quis volet addere tertiam videlicet . . .
mutationem totius vitae ac morum in melius non refragabimur.—*Expos. simpl.*
xiv. p. 36 : Per poenitentiam autem intelligimus mentis in homine peccatore
resipiscentiam verbo evangelii et spiritu s. excitatam fideque vera acceptam,
qua protinus homo agnatam sibi corruptionem peccataque omnia sua . . .
agnoscit ac de his ex corde dolet, eademque coram Deo deplorat et . . .
execratur cogitans iam sedulo de emendatione. Et haec quidem est vera
poenitentia, sincera nimirum ad Deum et omne bonum conversio, sedula vero
a diabolo et omni malo aversio. Diserte vero dicimus hanc poenitentiam
merum esse Dei donum et non virium nostrarum opus.—*Ibid.* xv. p. 48 : Qua
propter loquimur in hac causa . . . de fide viva vivificanteque, quae propter
Christum quem comprehendit viva est.—*Repetit. Conf.* p. 147 (Twesten):
Ostendimus supra, fide significari fiduciam acquiescentem in filio Dei, propter
quem recipimur et placemus.—Melanchth., *loc. s. t. de voc. fides* : Fides est
fiducia applicans nobis beneficium Christi . . . fiducia est motus in voluntate,
quo voluntas in Christo acquiescit.—*Ibid.* : Quibuscunque verbis alii uti volent,
rem retinere cupimus.

1. The definition found in these citations from confessional
literature certainly does not appear to tally with that given formally
here ; for the word *pœnitentia* rather corresponds merely to repentance—that is, to only one part of conversion ; and in the Swiss
Confession the word *conversio*, which corresponds to our word
conversion, expresses only one part of it, namely, *pœnitentia*.
And even if we enter the caveat that although turning away from
evil is not explicitly mentioned, it is understood to be implied,
still these two together—turning away from evil and turning to God
and the good—include only that part of conversion which we define
as change of heart. It must be noted, too, that while *aversio* and
conversio taken together are here regarded as equivalent to the
whole experience, yet, in fact, this experience is already reckoned
to include both the painful recognition of sin which precedes the
turning away, and the faith which precedes the turning towards,
so that turning away and turning towards do not really give a complete account of the matter. In the *Augsburg Confession*, besides
faith we meet only contrition, equivalent to our regret. But in the
Apology ' change for the better ' is added, which of course in its
permanent aspect means sanctification, but, regarded as a new
beginning, has its place here and corresponds to our expression
' change of heart.' If we gather all the elements of the Con-

fessions together, the general result is identical with our own statement. Our general definition is sufficiently justified by prevalent
devotional usage, and certainly is greatly to be preferred to the
expression *pœnitentia* or repentance, because that word has no
definite reference to the actual beginning of a new form of life, and
also because it sounds very awkward to hear faith (a word that we
obviously use in exactly the same sense as the Confessions) reckoned
as a part of repentance. And indeed we find the expressions
'repentance' and 'conversion' made interchangeable in other places
in the *Apology*.[1] Another point of difference is best seen in certain
passages in the confessional documents where contrition and faith
as the two constituents of conversion are alluded to as 'mortification'
and 'revival.'[2] Clearly 'mortification' here is regret or contrition
and 'revival' is faith ; but if so, no notice is taken of what we have
called change of heart. Nevertheless, no genuine laying hold of
Christ in faith is even conceivable without such an alteration in the
innermost aspirations and endeavours, nor any contrition other than
a passing wave of emotion ; and so in both connexions change
of heart too is silently taken for granted. Lastly, it must be
emphasized that our general expression 'conversion,' as well as the
narrower terms 'repentance,' 'regret,' and 'change of heart,' are all
employed in Church usage, not only as denoting what happens at the
beginning of the new life, but also for what occurs in the course of
the new life in connexion with the sin that still remains. All the
same, it follows from the explanations previously given [3] that there
must be a very great difference between what constitutes turning
away from sin in the two differing cases of one who is not yet, and
one who already is, in fellowship with the Redeemer. In the latter
case, the connexion with the Redeemer and the correspondingly
changed disposition may become clouded over and less effective, but
neither is utterly lost. In their case no sin can come to consciousness unaccompanied by regret, yet they do not require to begin the
new life all over again, nor is change of heart in the strictest sense
necessary. On the other hand, in regard to faith, it is clear that
faith is a permanently enduring state of mind, and that at this
point in the treatment of the doctrine of conversion, strictly under-

---

[1] See p. 168 : Ostendendum est quod scriptura in *poenitentia* seu *conversione* has duas partes ponit.

[2] *Apol. Conf., ibid.* : Paulus fere ubique cum describit conversionem, facit
has duas partes mortificationem et vivificationem . . . sunt ergo hae duae
partes contritio et fides.

[3] § 74.

stood, only the origin of faith is in question. For appropriation,
taking possession,[1] is a single act ; whereas faith in its duration is
the resulting, abiding consciousness of being in possession. Thus
the beginning of divinely created faith essentially belongs to conversion ; its duration is the constant basis of the new life. Thus,
even though treating regeneration and sanctification more or less
separately, we begin by bringing out their necessary interconnexion,
and the continuity of the divine action throughout the whole course
of the new creation.

The Roman Church does not count faith as an element in conversion, but puts in its stead confession and satisfaction, in spite of
the fact that confession, rightly understood, is included in regret,
and that satisfaction is a sheer impossibility. The reason lies
partly in her doctrine of the Church and partly in the different
sense in which the Church uses the word ' faith,' understanding by
it only the divinely imparted and humanly accepted knowledge of
man's destiny ; its assertion being accordingly that faith precedes
repentance and conversion.[2] This difference of language is unfortunate, increasing, of course, the difficulty of comparing clearly
the points of divergence ; and it is unfortunate too that in ordinary
life this same word ' faith ' is so often used for a conviction that is
without either influence on the will or adequate foundation.
Nevertheless, we cannot let the word drop, but must rather maintain
all the more strenuously its well-won title. The justice of our own
usage is easily demonstrable. The expression has become established among us as the translation of the word by which the original
language of Scripture defines the inward condition of one who
feels content and strong in fellowship with Christ. Moreover, the
controversy with the Roman Church about good works has given
the word an additional historical value for us.

2. Repentance and faith, then, are to be taken as covering the
whole experience of conversion. Now, since every turning-point
is at once the end of one movement and the beginning of the reverse,
in these two things, taken together, existence in the common life
of sin ceases, and existence in fellowship with Christ begins. Since
some activity of the self is an essential element in both, and opposed

[1] *Expos. simpl.* xv. p. 42 : fides Christum recipit.
[2] *Catech. Rom. praef.* 27 : Cum enim finis qui ad beatitudinem homini
propositus est altior sit, quam ut humana mentis acie perspici possit, necesse
ei erat ipsius a Deo cognitionem accipere. Haec vero cognitio nihil aliud est
nisi fides.—*Ibid.* p. II. de poenit. 8 : Verum in eo quem poenitet, fides poenitentiam antecedat necesse est . . . ex quo fit, ut nullo modo poenitentiae pars
recte dici possit.

activities cannot accompany, but must succeed one another, the turning-point must be a twofold inactivity, a state of being no longer active in one direction and not yet active in another. In the spiritually living existence of the subject nothing is left in place of the vanishing activity except its inert echo in feeling, and nothing is present in respect of the activity not yet begun except inert antici-pation of it in desire. The first is regret—which certainly expresses an existence in fellowship with sin, an existence, however, in which there is no activity of the self—for where regret is, the regretted condition has been abjured—but simply the retention in consciousness of something that is past. At every moment in which it is no more than an approach to complete transition, this consciousness witnesses to a disturbance and obstruction of life proper, and is felt as pain. The regret that goes with conversion, relating not to particulars but to a general condition, and abjuring that condition finally is, considered apart from everything else, the purest and most perfect pain, which, if allowed to reach its limit, might bring life itself to an end.[1] This is to be noted, how-ever, that regret arising out of the knowledge of sin given by the law is not the same as that directly appertaining to conversion. The law, after its wont, goes into particulars, and the regret evoked by it is only regret for particular motions and affections and not for the general condition and its deepest cause. Nor is there anything in this connexion out of which a new and opposite movement of life might develop. The outcome of such regret is therefore death or despair. However large the previous experience of this regret may have been the true conversion-regret must always eventually arise out of the vision of the perfection of Christ, and this beginning of regeneration must be due to Christ's redeeming activity. It is only on this view of repentance and faith that their interconnexion is clear, their origin thus being the same. Christ awakens a wholly perfect regret just in so far as His self-imparting perfection meets us in all its truth, which is what happens at the dawn of faith. And Christ can, in fact, lay hold of us in His receiving activity only if and when His soul-stirring exhibition of Himself to us leads us to abjure utterly our previous condition. In the same way, regret and faith being directly interdependent, the beginning is present of existence in living fellowship with Christ. For our attitude here

---

[1] *Apol. Conf.* v. p. 169 : Mortificatio significat veros terrores quos sus-tinere natura non posset, nisi erigeretur fide. Ita hic (Col. 2[11]) exspolia-tionem corporis peccatorum vocat, quam nos usitate dicimus contritionem, quia in illis doloribus concupiscentia naturalis expurgatur.

cannot be different from that of the human nature of Christ in its act of uniting with the quiescent consciousness of being accepted. This attitude is not only originally joyful and—unlike regret— uplifting,[1] but it includes also in its steady progress a stimulation of the will, and develops into an activity of the will ; and so with the dawn of faith conversion is complete. Still, in between that quiescent consciousness and real activity there comes desire, in two interconnected forms. There remains over from regret the continual abjuration of the fellowship of the sinful life, and there is also the desire to receive the impulses that come from Christ. This desire, acting in two directions, is the change of heart effected by Christ which binds regret and faith together and represents the true unity of conversion. One may include the negative ray of desire along with regret in the concept repentance, and count the positive ray as a part of revival, or one may with equal justice give desire a middle place of its own.

Regret that lies outside Christianity and has no reference to the consciousness of God is beyond the scope of our discussion. But within the sphere of Christian piety, if we carry our examination further back into the common life of sinfulness, we find many sorts of regret. Such regrets, too, can be traced back more or less directly to the vision of Christ, and are not always limited to some particular, but may show genuine pain at the general human state of sinfulness as illustrated in one's own person ; but they do not develop into a continuous inward movement amounting to the dawn of living faith. All the same such stimulations, arising as they do from the influence of the common Christian life, even though they are only an unconnected and casually-appearing mixture of elements, are to be regarded as divinely caused, and indeed involved in the divine ordinance which places all men in relation to the Redeemer ; and in this sense such a condition is ascribed to *the prevenient grace of God*.[2] In the same way a change of heart may appear before it is permanently bound up with conversion ; and, all the more because the insight which rejects former desires is looking back to the figure and teaching of Christ, this too is to be regarded as a work of preparatory grace. Nor do we find such regret and change of heart always separately ; they may be

---

[1] *Ibid.* : Et vivificatio intelligi debet . . . consolatio quae vere sustentat fugientem vitam in contritione.

[2] This is never more than an inexact phrase, for according to our general formula all divine grace is always prevenient ; and it would be more correct to say ' preparatory.'

related to one another without losing their preparatory character. The higher character which both possess is only recognized from the simultaneous dawning of faith ; and perfect and *effective* divine grace is seen only in the union of all three—regret, change of heart, and faith.   There are similar preliminary approximations to faith.   For, even when the perfection of the Redeemer is not recognized as more than human, it would be wrong to regard as an adverse judgment of human reason such a sense of its compelling power as sets Him on a different plane from other sages or God-gifted men, and such a satisfaction in the idea of His Kingdom as sets it high above other earthly aims.   A presentiment of His higher dignity may be already implied in this, and an inward surrender may arise out of it.   This, too, is a gracious work of preparation, and of faith also it is true that its higher character, as it dawns, is recognizable only in its unity with the other elements of conversion.

From all this it follows naturally that since imperfect regret and change of heart may quite easily occur even when the soul has conceived a higher idea of the Redeemer, conversion cannot be distinguished either in and for itself, or by any particular mark, from the effects of preparatory grace.   Only gradually can each consciousness reach certainty for itself, and its peace of heart become fixed.   Even approximations to faith are bound to have an influence on conduct indistinguishable with any certainty from the beginnings of sanctification, because in accordance with the laws of organic nature the true life of Christ in us announces itself at first only in weak and intermittent impulses, and then gradually a unified activity emerges.   The only marks we can point to are steady progress in sanctification taken in its full meaning, and active participation in the extension of Christ's Kingdom.   What is incomplete is usually in its very nature fluctuating.   And it is scarcely thinkable that a man should be received into unity of life with Christ without very soon actively proving himself an instrument of His redeeming activity.   When therefore the Redeemer calls the decisive working of divine grace a new birth, we must take part of the meaning to be that just as in the natural life birth is not the absolute beginning, so here a period of hidden life precedes it, and at first even the newly-born life remains unconscious, only gradually learning to know itself as a real personality in a new world. Keeping to the illustration given us by the Redeemer Himself, we must rest assured that even though neither we nor others can point out the very beginning of our new life, and its moment in time is as little to be determined as the point in space from which the wind begins to blow, still the fact of the distinction between the new life and the old remains, and of our share in the new we become ever more certain.

3. The idea that every Christian must be able to point to the very time and place of his conversion is accordingly an arbitrary and presumptuous restriction of divine grace, and can only cause confusion. In its most definite form it is found in the assertion of an otherwise worthy party in the Church that every true Christian must be able to allege, as the beginning of his state of grace, a penitential crisis of soul, that is to say, a surging up of regret to the limit of despairing self-abhorrence, followed by a feeling of divine grace reaching to the limit of inexpressible felicity ; all steadfastness of heart being mere illusion, and all evidences of sanctification deceitful works of men. This view never became part of the general teaching of the Church ; it is no more than a dubious aberration. In this connexion two points can be made here. In the first place, the true change of heart, complete because covering all the ground from regret to faith, need by no means invariably spring from a flood of regret that almost wrecks the whole being by its painful emotion. On the one hand, the capacity of people for emotion is very various. What to an insusceptible nature is a very intense degree of excitement seems but a trifle to one more emotionally constituted, and in this respect the same person differs from time to time. In such a matter no definition or summary statement is possible. On the other hand, the experiences recorded in the autobiographies of many religious men show that even if a shattering storm of feeling occur which is reckoned by themselves to be the moment of their conversion, often enough they sink back again into a state of futility and uncertainty ; and so the supposed value of that moment seems entirely doubtful. Even in these cases steadfastness of soul comes only gradually. Further, self-abasement being not a pure judgment but also feeling must as the spiritual side of regret be distinguished from pain, its sensuous side, and these may stand in very various relations to each other. One practised in the estimation of sensuous susceptibilities may have the strictest and profoundest judgment of self-abasement without any corresponding intensity of feeling. So, on the one hand, care must be taken, if intensity of feeling gives a predominantly sensuous colouring to the whole condition, lest regret,

being not yet pure and in its inmost fibre free from sensuous admixture, may thereby be unfitted to have life-giving faith as its immediate result. And, on the other hand, the oftener and more strongly such imperfect regret occurs before conversion, the easier it is for the relation between self-abasement and pain to take a quite different form within genuine repentance. The very thing that evokes the utter self-abasement to which faith and the positive pole of change of heart attach themselves, may be allowed a place only as a kind of memory of former suffering and a shadowy image of already felt pain. This is new evidence of the inadmissibility of the demand that everyone must be able to distinguish, in the phenomena of consciousness, between the working of grace as initiating the new life and the preparatory work of grace. Hence we can concede the reality of this conception of an agonizing crisis of repentance only as denoting the whole change of conditions, from the first challenging and preparatory effects of grace on to the unchangeable fixing of the heart in faith. Whether these are spread over a longer or compressed into a shorter interval, and how far during this period particular oscillations may differ in amplitude, and whether the final oscillation must be the largest—all these questions are left quite undetermined.

The second point we can determine is this. A constituent part of living fellowship with Christ is a share in His blessedness. This too, then, must be included from the very beginning in the dawn of faith ; all the more because the unblessedness that clings to regret can be relieved only by its opposite, namely, blessedness. The two chief elements in conversion can still be very closely linked together, and even in perfect regret no great pain need be felt. Thus many and various relations are possible between the pain of repentance and the joy of conscious fellowship with Christ ; among them this one, that if a glorious outpouring of joy be found along with a faint measure of sorrow, the suffering may become almost imperceptible. Undeniably there are types of conversion which seem to be mainly a happy rescue from despair. But there are others in which no such agonizing crisis occurs, and which are experienced as an almost unalloyed blessing from above, the painful element in regret being suppressed to a point just short of actual disappearance.

4. Although some teachers in English and German Churches have recently declared that no conversion whatever is needed in the case of those born in the bosom of the Christian Church and

already as children received into its fellowship, since they are already members of the body of Christ and recipients of regeneration in baptism, we must in accordance with almost the whole trend of our discussion withhold our agreement. For everything we said regarding the original cause of the beginning of sin in man holds good just as much about those born within the Christian Church as about others. The former, too, reveal a tendency to drag down the divine, which of course influences them like others through the Christian community, to the sphere of the sensuous. It may, indeed, be fitly said that in Christian children sensuous representations of the divine spontaneously develop, sometimes of the pagan, idly frivolous kind, sometimes Judaic and gloomily fearful. If, therefore, in spite of infant baptism, sin thus shows its power in them, they need conversion as much as anyone born outside the Church. The only difference really present is that in the case of others it is a matter of chance how and when the gospel call reaches their ears, whereas Christian children are already called in virtue of their standing in a natural and orderly relation to the working of divine grace. This in no way invalidates the natural order we described, namely, the sequence of preparatory and quickening grace ; and where this order obtains conversion takes place. Furthermore, the opinion referred to finds at most an apparent support in our confessional statements ; fundamentally they are in entire agreement with our position. This may be seen partly in the fact that they never raise any distinction in connexion with the doctrine of conversion, between those born inside and outside the Church,[1] and partly because they expressly ascribe to our baptism only the beginning of the divine work of grace.[2] That the same effect occurs within the Church even without previous baptism is evident from the facts about persons baptized in heart alone. It is true that some passages seem to approach more nearly to the opinion in dispute.[3] But if we recall how differently they speak of regeneration, saying that in it the Holy Spirit opens our eyes to the

[1] Compare, in the *Apology for the Augsburg Confession*, the whole treatment of the conceptions repentance, confession, and satisfaction.
[2] *Apol. Conf.* i. : Addidit etiam (Lutherus) de materiali quod spiritus sanctus datus per baptismum *incipit* mortificare concupiscentiam et novos motus creat (and obviously only *incipit creare*) in homine.—*Ibid*. iv. : Igitur necesse est baptizare parvulos, ut applicetur iis promissio salutis.
[3] *Expos. simpl.* xx. : Assignantur haec omnia baptismo. Nam intus regeneramur purificamur et renovamur a Deo per spiritum sanctum, foris autem accipimus obsignationem, etc. — *Conf. Gallic.* xxxv. p. 123 : Quamvis baptismus sit fidei et resipiscentiae sacramentum, tamen . . . affirmamus . . . infantes . . . esse baptizandos.

understanding of divine mysteries,[1] and that sanctification begins with regeneration, it is clear that they are really seeking to connect with regeneration the original baptism of adults who asked for it, and only loosely by indulgence let their statement serve for infant baptism too.   Nowhere in the testimony of such Churches is anything more intended than what Calvin [2] himself has said.   With him indeed we have been in pretty close agreement ; his phrase ' seed of repentance and faith ' might have been our text.

It is evident enough that one can all too easily lapse unawares into the region of magic, if regeneration be brought into connexion with our particular method of administering the sacrament of baptism.   We need only look at the answer we should have to give to the question how, in our commonly adopted practice of the rite, the receiving activity of Christ and the passive condition of him who is received are related to one another.

5. As regards the first of these, we again become conscious of an inconvenience in our arrangement, for in the public teaching of the Church regeneration is usually ascribed to the Divine Spirit, of whom we have not yet treated, and, to mention what we have already said would be our next topic, the divine activity in justification is usually ascribed to God the Father.   But here again we must recall our fundamental proposition, that the whole procedure in redemption, the same for all races, Jew and Gentile, is also the same for all ages, and that the essential identity of redemption and of the Christian fellowship would be imperilled if our faith had either another content or another origin—the one implies the other—than it had in the case of the first disciples.   If faith arises in the same way, conversion must happen in the same way.   Now in the first disciples both were effected by the Word in its widest sense, that is, by the whole prophetic activity of Christ.   And we must be able to understand this that we have in common with them, if need be without a doctrine of the Holy Spirit, just as the disciples understood their own condition without any such doctrine.   The constant factor is above all the divine power of the Word—taking the expression in its widest sense—by which conversion is still effected and faith still arises.   The difference is simply that the self-revelation of Christ is now mediated by those who preach Him ; but they

---

[1] *Expos. simpl.* ix. : In regeneratione intellectus illuminatur per Spiritum sanctum ut et mysteria et voluntatem Dei intelligat.

[2] *Institutt.* ix. 16. 20 :   Baptizantur in futuram poenitentiam et fidem, quae etsi nondum in illis formatae sunt, arcana tamen spiritus operatione utriusque semen in illis latet.

being appropriated by Him as His instruments, the activity really proceeds from Him and is essentially His own. This is definitely and uncompromisingly asserted in most of our Confessions, though with references to the Holy Spirit which will become clear to us only later in our discussion.[1] If other passages [2] seem to be less convincing, still they draw attention to exceptions which when looked at more closely are only apparent. For if one ventures to make a merely relative separation between the Word itself and the public ministry of the Word, and to recall that all Christians are summoned to a common ministry of the Word, it is with a view to affirming boldly that no example can be given of conversion apart from the mediation of the Word : and we need cherish no misgiving that to assert this strenuously is to limit the divine omnipotence. For the second creative act is recognized as a work of the divine omnipotence just because only through the power revealed in it the business of conversion is carried through in all believers. The miracle of the appearance of Christ, who could Himself work only in the form of the Word, would be insufficient if some had to be converted otherwise than through influences proceeding from Him ; indeed, in that case they would not be included in the priestly intercession of Christ.[3] Again, if it were possible that Christ should reveal Himself to some immediately and inwardly without the Word, this could happen to all ; which would amount to redemption through the mere idea of the Redeemer,

---

[1] *Augsb. Conf.* v : To win such faith God has appointed preaching, by means of which the Holy Spirit awakens and comforts the heart and imparts faith.—*Art. Smalc.* vii. : Constanter tenendum est Deum nemini spiritum vel gratiam suam largiri nisi per verbum et cum verbo externo et praecedente : and it is here to be remarked that the communication of the Spirit is described as a consequence or result—ut ita praemuniamus nos contra Enthusiastas, qui iactitant se ante verbum et sine verbo spiritum habere.—*Expos. simpl.* xiv. : Per poenitentiam autem intelligimus mentis in homine peccatore resipiscentiam, verbo evangelii et spiritu sancto excitatam. *Ibid.* xvi. : Haec autem fides merum est Dei donum, quod solus Deus ex gratia sua . . . donat, et quidem per Spiritum sanctum mediante praedicatione Evangelii.—*Conf. Gall.* xxv. : Credimus quoniam non nisi per Evangelium fimus Christi compotes.—*Conf. Belg.* xxiv. : Credimus veram hanc fidem per auditum verbi Dei et Spiritus sancti operationem homini insitam eum regenerare.

[2] *Expos. simpl.* i. : Quamquam enim nemo veniat ad Christum, nisi qui trahatur a patre ac intus illuminetur per spiritum sanctum, scimus tamen Deum omnino velle praedicari verbum Dei. Equidem potuisset per spiritum sanctum suum aut per ministerium angeli instituisse Cornelium, etc.—Agnoscimus interim Deum illuminare posse homines etiam sine externo ministerio, etc.—*Conf. Helv.* xiv. : Quae (ecclesia) externis . . . ritibus ab ipso Christo institutis et verbi Dei . . . publicâ disciplinâ . . . ita construitur, ut in hanc sine his nemo *nisi singulari Dei privilegio* censeatur.

[3] John 17[20].

making the actual appearance of Christ superfluous. For the present day this is the specially relevant reason for the position we take, which has behind it the whole apostolic usage and the express witness of Scripture,[1] and is no mere design of strengthening our case in opposition to certain visionaries. All the same, this statement was needed in order to expose fully the danger of fanaticism on this point. For if it be allowed that there are divine workings of converting grace in no actual historical relation to the personal efficacy of Christ (even though it is as workings of Christ that they come to consciousness), there would be no security that this inward mystic Christ was identical with the historical Christ. Every exposition of the matter, therefore, which deprives the Word of its sole place in conversion not only wipes out all lines of demarcation (for then everyone with unrestrained caprice can profess that anything and everything is Christian and due to Christ), but also dissolves all fellowship ; for every individual, who is inwardly and independently enlightened, must also be perfectly complete in himself, with no inducement to, or need of, fellowship. All essentially separatist tendencies spring from ideas of this kind. The influence of Christ, therefore, consists solely in the human communication of the Word, in so far as that communication embodies Christ's word and continues the indwelling divine power of Christ Himself. This is in perfect accord with the truth that, in the consciousness of a person in the grip of conversion, every sense of human intermediation vanishes, and Christ is realized as immediately present in all His redeeming and atoning activity, prophetic, priestly, and kingly. In this sense everything that in any way contributes to conversion, from the first impression made on the soul by the preaching of Christ on to its final establishment in faith, is the work of Christ. These divine workings of grace are supernatural in so far as they depend upon and actually proceed from the being of God in the Person of Christ. At the same time, being historical and formative of history, they are natural in so far as they have a general natural connexion with the historical life of Christ ; and in detail each working that establishes a new personality is bound up in its efficacy with the historical totality of Christ's effects.

6. As regards the state of the subject himself during conversion, we may take conversion to be the moment at which the entry into living fellowship with Christ is complete. This moment is the

[1] Rom. 10[17], Tit. 1[3].

beginning of a higher form of life which only Christ can communicate, because only in Him is it originally present.   It seems obvious, then, that here no causal agency can be attributed to the person who is being taken up into fellowship, for the higher form cannot be in any way derived from lower stages of life as present either in the individual or in a group of people yet to be converted.   On the other hand, if we remember that the converted person, both after-wards within the living fellowship of Christ and even beforehand in the common life of sin, is, as an individual of reasonable perceptions, spontaneously active, and that in general there is never in any living being a complete moment wholly devoid of spontaneous activity, two questions are inevitable.   The first is : How is the ordinary natural action of the subject going on at the moment of conversion related to the work of Christ which produces change of heart and faith ?   The second is : How is the presupposed passive condition during conversion related to the spontaneous activity which ensues in fellowship with Christ ?

In regard to the first question, we may, without abandoning our fundamental assumption, regard the natural spontaneous action of the subject in that moment as non-co-operative.   All that prepara-tory grace has already brought to pass within him of course co-operates, but this is itself part of the divine work of grace and not of his own action.[1]   Anything proceeding purely from his own inner life could co-operate only so far as the efficacy of divine grace was actually conditioned by these activities of his own.   It cannot indeed be denied that this may happen.   For the Word through which the influence of Christ is mediated can mediate only by making an impression on men, and for this the activity of his sense-faculties as well as of the inner functions of his consciousness is required.   In so far as the activity of all these functions depends on the free will of man, the capacity of apprehension must therefore be allowed to exist in his natural condition.[2]   But as regards what

---

[1] *Sol. decl.*, p. 674: Ex his consequitur, quam primum Spir. s. per verbum et sacramenta opus suum regenerationis et renovationis in nobis *inchoavit*, quod revera tunc per virtutem Spir. s. cooperari possimus ac debeamus.—Hoc vero ipsum non est ex nostris carnalibus et naturalibus viribus, sed ex novis illis viribus, quae Spir. s. in nobis in conversione inchoavit.   What is said expressly of the period after conversion holds good all the more for the period preceding it.—*Ibid.*, p. 681 : . . . hominem ex se ipso aut naturalibus suis viribus non posse aliquid conferre vel adjumentum adferre ad suam con-versionem.

[2] *Ibid.*, p. 671 : In eiusmodi enim externis rebus homo adhuc etiam post lapsum aliquo modo liberum arbitrium habet, ut . . . verbum Dei audire vel non audire possit.

happens after the Word has made its impression on the soul, in the attainment of its aim for men, here we cannot concede man's natural co-operation. Even the consent accompanying the reception of the Divine Word, as far as it is directed to what is essential and characteristic in it, can be ascribed only to the antecedent work of grace. On the other hand, if it should be held that the natural activity which goes on during Christ's working of conversion is of the nature of resistance, it must be, if not disapproval, at least indifference ; that is to say, the activity remains directed to other matters, and as far as the operation of Christ is concerned, negligible. If conversion is effected during such a condition it is certainly not in virtue of the Word so received. To assume an entire lack of relation between man's personal activity and the higher operation of Christ therefore yields no satisfactory result, and the problem remains to find room for an activity in real relation to the work of Christ, and yet neither co-operation nor resistance. If now we take as starting-point that organic co-operation which we admitted to go on before apprehension of the Word, and that minimum of opposition consisting in the direction of the will to other things, which we rejected, it is clear that the two cannot coexist. That co-operation of the mental organism in the reception of the Word implies a consent of the will ; and this is just a surrender to the operation of Christ or giving rein to a lively susceptibility thereto. This middle stage, to which we have recourse in all similar cases— a passive condition, yet including that minimum of spontaneous activity which belong to every complete moment—meets the conditions of the problem perfectly. The solution, however, is invalidated if this susceptibility be again divided into active and passive, and only the latter allowed as applicable to our case ; for then one would simultaneously have to find room for another spontaneous activity, and the whole difficulty would return.[1]

Let us now go back to the other question. Since the whole life of the Redeemer, because solely determined by the being of God in Him, is activity, and not passivity, it is clear that in fellowship with His life no moment can be purely passive, because everything in it that proceeds from Him and becomes an impulse is necessarily activity. Spontaneous activity in living fellowship with Christ begins in the moment of being received into His fellowship. There

[1] Cf., *inter alia*, Gerhard, t. v. p. 113, and *Sol. decl.*, p. 662 : Et hoc ipsum vocat (Lutherus) capacitatem non activam sed passivam, which are not really Luther's words.

is no interval. Conversion may be said to be just the evocation of this spontaneous activity in union with Christ. The lively susceptibility passes into quickened spontaneous activity. Every heightening of that lively susceptibility is a work of preparatory grace. The grace that effects conversion changes it into quickened spontaneous activity. If we trace this element backwards from the point at which it first appears already heightened by the preparatory work of grace, and ask in what the first beginning of life has consisted by which it can be differentiated from pure passivity, we can only point to that desire for fellowship with God, never entirely extinguished, though pushed back to the very frontiers of consciousness, which is part of the original perfection of human nature. As this is what we regard as the first point of attachment for every operation of divine grace, the only thing we are ruling out is a passivity that would be entirely foreign to human nature, in virtue of which a person would resemble a lifeless object in the matter of conversion,[1] and we are saying nothing about that in our Christian self-consciousness which we ascribe to the grace of God in Christ. For mere desire is not an act ; it is but the anticipatory feeling of an act that may possibly happen if a certain impulse occurs later. It is exactly what shows itself as the feeling of need for redemption, a feeling without which there could be no dissatisfaction with the common state of sinfulness, but only a universal complacent recognition of the inevitability of sin. Hence this desire is simply the ineradicable residuum in human nature of the original impartation of the divine which makes human nature what it is, and not in itself but only in so far as it is stirred up to some definite degree of strength does it give rise to the contrast between nature and grace. Indeed, the parallel between the beginning of the divine life in us and the incarnation of the Redeemer comes out here too. In Him the passivity of His human nature in that moment was just such a lively susceptibility to an absolutely powerful consciousness of God, accompanied by a desire to be thus seized and determined, which became changed through the creative act into a spontaneous activity constituting a personality. In the same way our desire is heightened in conversion by the self-communication of Christ till it becomes a spontaneous activity of the self that constitutes a coherent new life.

---

[1] *Sol. decl.*, p. 662 : Antequam autem homo per Spir. s. . . . . regeneratur . . . ex sese ad conversionem nihil . . . cooperari potest, nec plus quam lapis truncus aut limus.

SECOND THEOREM : JUSTIFICATION

§ 109. *God's justifying of one who is converted to Him includes the forgiving of his sins, and the recognizing of him as a child of God. This transformation of his relation to God, however, follows only in so far as he has true faith in the Redeemer.*

Augsb. Conf. iv. : ' And it is taught that we attain the forgiveness of sins and are counted just before God out of grace for Christ's sake through faith.'— *Conf. Tetrap.* iii. : . . . nostri hanc totam (iustificationem) divinae benevolentiae Christique merito acceptam referendam solaque fide percipi docuerunt.—*Expos. simpl.* xv. : Iustificare significat peccata remittere, a culpa et poena absolvere in gratiam recipere et iustum pronunciare. . . . Certissimum est autem omnes nos . . . iustificari solius Christi gratiâ, et nullo nostro merito aut respectu . . . Quoniam vero iustificationem hanc recipimus non per ulla opera sed per fidem . . . ideo docemus . . . hominem iustificari sola fide in Christum.—*Conf. Gallic.* xviii : Credimus totam nostram iustitiam positam esse in peccatorum nostrorum remissione, quae sit etiam . . . unica nostra felicitas. Itaque . . . insitâ Jesu Christi obedientiâ acquiescimus, quae quidem nobis imputatur, tum ut tegantur omnia nostra peccata, tum etiam ut gratiam coram Deo nanciscamur.—*Ibid.* xx. : Credimus nos sola fide fieri huius iustitiae participes. . . . Itaque iustitia quam fide obtinemus pendet a gratuitis promissionibus, quibus nos a se diligi Deus declarat et certificatur.—*Conf. Belg.* xxii. : Interim proprie loquendo nequaquam intelligimus ipsam fidem esse quae nos iustificat, ut quae sit duntaxat instrumentum, quo Christum iustitiam nostram apprehendimus.—*Ibid.* xxxiii. : Credimus nostram beatitudinem sitam esse in peccatorum nostrorum propter Jesum Christum remissione atque in ea iustitiam nostram coram Deo contineri.—John 1[12], Gal. 3[26] 4[5].

1. In the treatment of this subject, too, the language of the Confessions cited is not quite consistent, and so the diction of our proposition does not conform to that of every quotation. Some, like us, use the word ' justification ' for the larger conception ; others use for that ' forgiveness of sins,' understanding by that phrase the whole state of blessedness, and accordingly counting justification, if it is to be regarded as something additional, as a special element therein. In this connexion it is evident that forgiveness in itself is just the removal of something negative, and therefore can be no full description of complete blessedness. Indeed, from our point of view, strictly speaking, one relation to God is abolished but no other established, unless indeed an earlier relation had come into existence ; otherwise, though one has forgiven the other, both remain as far apart as ever. The term ' justification,' however, applied to the same experience has, as bearing on inquiry into what happens, a more positive sound, leaving aside for the moment the question of accuracy. It is therefore better fitted either, as in the *Augsburg*

Confession, to describe a positive element accompanying that negative one, or, as is preferred here, to describe the whole, and leave a place for a positive element alongside of forgiveness. This method of description has been chosen because, where sin has to be presumed, an act of justification (however it comes about) must include forgiveness ; at the same time, since justification includes something more than forgiveness, this too has to be specified. This several Confessions express positively, but the others in a rather indeterminate and inconvenient fashion, by 'attaining grace,' 'received into grace '—indeterminate, because the content of the additional factor is not explained ; and inconvenient, because the same expression ' grace,' used everywhere in this connexion for the divine activity itself, is thus made to signify merely its result. Our designation of this positive element is unquestionably more exact, but (even though works on Dogmatics frequently use the terms ' sonship ' or ' adoption ') it is in this connexion so little an accepted credal definition that we need to point back to passages in which its content has been established in the most precise way and in the same connexion. Our designation has, indeed, this drawback, that it is in verbal agreement neither with the ordinary nor with the other and more special expression ; but this difficulty vanishes as soon as the actual interrelations of the subject are understood.

The Roman Church differs entirely from the Protestant in its use of the expression ' justification ' : instead of something correlated to conversion, and therefore included in regeneration, it makes ' justification ' mean something more general than these, including both them and sanctification. If we recall how, on the other hand, the existence of faith is placed anterior to conversion, we can perceive how the two things go together : faith and justification are kept as far apart as possible, in order the more easily to show man's justification to be dependent on his sanctification. But even apart from this, it cannot be advisable virtually to abolish the difference between the divine work on man and the divine work in man. The previous life void of divine influence is what is here given in experience, and we are faced by the task of rightly distinguishing the turning-point which is the source of everything later from the results that flow from it.

2. For the self-consciousness at rest in contemplation, justification is the same thing that conversion is for the self-consciousness passing into movement of will ; an analogy is therefore to be

expected between the two aspects of both. Repentance, as the self-consciousness moved by the consciousness of sin, comes to rest in forgiveness in the same way as the faith which from its birth is active through love is in thought the consciousness of being a child of God, and as this itself is identical with the consciousness of living fellowship with Christ. That this is not to be interpreted as meaning that forgiveness could precede faith is stated in the theorem itself : it means simply that forgiveness, like repentance, denotes the end of the old state ; as also being a child of God, like faith, expresses the character of the new. Each, of course, like both elements of conversion, is dependent on the whole activity of Christ, but directly and for itself expresses merely the relation of the man to God. In the common life of sinfulness the individual as a human being has no other relation to God except (in view of His holiness and justice) a consciousness of being guilty before Him and meriting punishment. It is obvious that this consciousness must cease as soon as, through and along with faith, living fellowship with Christ begins.[1] If we ask how this happens, the easiest answer certainly is that the longer and more uninterruptedly we are under the sway of Christ, the sooner do we forget sin, because it no longer emerges ; and if sin does not come into consciousness, neither does the sense of guilt and of deserving punishment. Yet, for one thing, this would be to place the change in our relation to God at the end of the process of sanctification, during which the sense of deserving punishment and therefore the lack of blessedness would continue. And besides, the forgetting of guilt is not the consciousness of forgiveness ; for even if this last is no more than the abolishing of a previous consciousness, it is also a real consciousness in which the memory of sin is an essential factor.

If, however, justification and conversion are simultaneous, forgiveness must be our present possession, even while sin and the consciousness of it are also present. But if the relation of sin to the holiness and justice of God is to cease, it and the consciousness of it must be transformed. Now, one who has let himself be taken up into living fellowship with Christ is, in so far as he has been thus appropriated, a new man ; and both are one and the same consciousness. Sin in the new man is no longer active ; it is only the after-effect of the old man. The new man thus no longer takes sin to be his own ; he indeed labours against it as something foreign to him. The consciousness of guilt is thus abolished. His penal

[1] Cf. § 107, 1.

desert must vanish with this ; while for the rest, there lies in living fellowship with Christ, immediately and not just as a vague some- thing in the future, a readiness for and a right to fellowship with the sufferings of Christ, which make it impossible for him to keep regarding social and still less natural evils as punishment,[1] or to go on fearing future punishment—impossible, for he is at the same time received into the fellowship of the kingly office of Christ. Thus, owing to faith, the consciousness of sin will become the conscious- ness of forgiveness of sin. And in regard to the second element of conversion, Christ cannot live in us without His relation to His Father being formed in us also and making us sharers in His son- ship ; this is the power to be children of God that flows from Him, and it includes the guarantee of sanctification. For it is the children's right to be brought up to a free, active share in the home- life ; and it is the law of childhood that through the shared life the likeness of the father develops in the child.

The two elements are therefore inseparable. Divine adoption would be nothing without forgiveness, for to deserve punishment begets fear, and fear slavery. And forgiveness without adoption would not fix a settled relation to God. The two, however, in their indissoluble connexion, constitute that complete transformation of the relation to God which, as bound up with the putting off the old man, is forgiveness, and as bound up with the putting on the new man is adoption. The two are so mutually conditioned that either can be regarded as first in order. One can say if one likes that the feeling of the old life must first be wiped out before the new life can begin to take shape ; but just as well that only in the new life is found the right and the power to throw off the old. It is equally true to assert that after a man is forgiven he is made a child of God, and that after he is received among God's children he obtains the forgiveness of sins.

3. This exposition of the matter is indeed readily liable to the misconstruction that each man justifies himself, although in point of fact it traces everything back to the influence of Christ. But truly, deriving justification entirely as it does from conversion, it would appear to ascribe both justification and conversion wholly to Christ and so to harmonize completely with the view that the two elements of regeneration are related to one another as sharing respectively in the perfection and in the blessedness of Christ, and are thus referred entirely to Him. That is a position for which an

[1] Rom. 8[22. 35-39].

exact confessional basis can be found,[1] although it certainly diverges far from the prevailing fashion of basing justification alone on a divine activity and attributes both forgiveness and adoption in a special way to God.[2] The same thing is demanded by our own method of statement, where justification is described as a change in the relation to God. For in that, of course, an activity of God is implied, and man can be conceived only as passive. In regard to this last point we have already put ourselves in harmony with the prevailing view by not ascribing everything in this connexion to the activity of the convert, even though it be an activity conditioned and evoked by Christ (as if justification were a part of sanctification or its result), but by deriving it entirely from the influence of Christ producing faith in man's living susceptibility. In regard to the first point, however, we have to see how the formula of a divine act of justification stands related to what has been said.

In this connexion it is clear, first, that we cannot conceive this divine activity as independent of the agency of Christ in conversion, as if one might exist without the other. This follows from the position already taken, that justification itself and conversion are interdependent ; just as in the Church formula which declares faith to be the receptive organ for this act of justification, which it could not be if the act were not received.[3] In devotional poetry and prose this connexion is usually set forth in its bearing on the intercession of Christ, as if Christ indicated to God those in whom He had wrought faith and urged Him to give them their share in forgiveness and adoption. This is of course a very poetic manner of putting things, for it is materializing things greatly to imagine Christ pointing out something to God. But neither in this positive nor in the other negative formula is there any dependence of the divine activity on the activity of Christ or its result, not even in the intermediate form of its being motived by Christ. For the decision as to *who* is to attain to conversion and *when* we have already

---

[1] *Conf. Belg.* xx. : Necessarium est enim aut omnia quae ad salutem nostram requiruntur in Jesu Christo non esse, aut si in eo sunt omnia, tum eum, qui fide Jesum possidet, totam salutem habere.

[2] This is also scriptural, if we venture to assume that the expression ' justify,' as here expounded, corresponds to the Pauline δικαιῶσαι; this comes out most strikingly in Rom. 8[33].

[3] Confessional formulæ, too, state this inseparability, though often hesitatingly, and in language the content of which becomes clear only after a careful comparison, e.g. *Expos. simpl.* xv. : Itaque iustificationis beneficium non partimur partim *gratiae Dei vel Christo* partim nobis . . . sed in solidum *gratiae Dei in Christo* per fidem tribuimus.

assigned, not to the realm of grace, making it depend on Christ, but to the realm of power, making it depend on God ; which is the Father's drawing men to the Son.

In the second place, if we would as far as possible avoid figurative language and speak in exact dogmatic terms, we can as little here as elsewhere admit an act in time eventuating at a particular moment or an act directed upon an individual. All that can be individual or temporal is the effect of a divine act or decree, not the act or decree itself. Only in so far as the dogmatic treatment makes its starting-point the self-consciousness of the individual, and therefore in this case the consciousness of an alteration in the relation to God, can we think of the justifying action of God as bearing on the individual. Because everyone connects this alteration with others involved in it, that bearing appears simultaneous with these others ; but only thus far and in this respect is such an individualizing and temporalizing of divine activity permissible. It must never be regarded as something in and for itself, as if the justification of each individual rested on a distinct and separate divine decree—not even though it should be described as determined from all eternity and only passing into reality at a fixed point in time.[1] There is only one eternal and universal decree justifying men for Christ's sake. This decree, moreover, is the same as that which sent Christ on His mission, for otherwise that mission would have been conceived and determined by God without its consequences. And once more, the decree that sent Christ forth is one with the decree creating the human race, for in Christ first human nature is brought to perfection. Indeed, since thought and will, will and action are not to be sundered in God, all this is one divine act designed to alter our relation to God ; its temporal manifestation is seen in the incarnation of Christ from which the whole new creation proceeds, and in which it has its starting-point. Thenceforward the promulgation in time of this divine act is really a continuous one, but in its effects it appears to us in as many points separated and (as it were) strung out from one another, as there are different people whose union with Christ is accomplished.

Turning now to justification in its two elements, we must similarly say that to admit an individual decree of forgiveness and adoption would be to subject God to the antithesis of abstract and concrete, or universal and particular, since the decree of redemption

[1] Cf. Gerhard, iv. p. 147.

is just the universal in its two particular bearings. Besides, the consciousness of guilt and of penal desert being ordained for men by God only in relation to redemption, that is, only as something which everywhere and for everyone vanishes with the entrance of redemption into his life, no special decree or act is necessary for its cessation. All that is needful is that the consciousness of its cessation should arise in the individual. How this happens in connexion with conversion has been shown. Similarly with reference to adoption, it is already implied in the divine decree of redemption or of the new creation of human nature that God is gracious to the human race in His Son ; hence an individual act making the individual an object of the divine love is not necessary. All that is needful is that the consciousness of this relation should arise in the individual ; and this happens in the way already described. Thus we have to posit only one universal justifying divine act bearing on redemption, and this realizes itself gradually in time.

In the third place and finally, we cannot pass over the fact that this exposition seems to conceal one other divergence from the view prevailing in our Church. For in our Church the divine act is regarded as declaratory ; the converted man ' is declared just ' by God ; and in such an exposition no room at all seems to be left for this phrase which indicates the opposition between our own Church and the Roman. But the truth is this. The phrase in question certainly goes back to what is here denied, namely, a multiplicity of divine justifying acts or decrees. For in regard to a single universal decree it is not easy to conceive how it could be declaratory in particular cases. God ordained the Redeemer because through Him sin was to be taken away and men become children of God. But in God thought and will are one. He expresses thought by deed, and through preaching the deed propagates the thought. A special act, therefore, by which God—so we should have to state the matter—declared to Himself what He in another act performs, would be an utterly empty thing. This form of representation, so common in the Old Testament, is simply one of its anthropomorphisms. Looked at more closely, however, any individual declaratory act is in the same case. It cannot as such prevent a recurrence of the consciousness of being concerned in the production of sin, and to that extent would be vain. So also would be a declaration of sonship ; for that is not in itself capable of preventing a man from being conscious of sharing in enmity to

God.   Such an act attains reality only as combined with the influence of Christ in effecting conversion.   But this also being traceable
to the universal divine ordinance, the declaratory act is again
merged in the creative act.   Since, however, with faith there arises
a simultaneous consciousness of forgiveness and of adoption, it is
quite right to say that every act of conversion is for the man himself
a declaration of the universal divine decree to justify for Christ's
sake.   But as regards our relation to the Roman Church, it is only
superficially that our opposition to it seems to lie in this point of
the declaratory character of the divine justifying act, and that
Church will assuredly be very far from accepting the mode in which
this character is here denied.   For we still hold to this, that a man
is justified as soon as faith has been wrought in him ; [1] the interest
of Rome, on the contrary, is to establish that this takes place
afterwards by means of good works.

4. The final point in regard to this distinctively Protestant
doctrine that we are justified by faith—that is, that the application
of the universal divine justifying act to the individual is bound up
with and conditioned by the dawn of faith—is this.   The doctrine
is all the more necessary if justification be conceived as a purely
declaratory act.   Otherwise colour might be lent to the notion that
a man has redemption assigned to him in a method which is arbitrary
—a method, that is, which, as far as he himself is concerned, is
baseless.   Yet even if we do not sunder the effective and the declaratory, it is needful to fix the point when, and the manner how,
the justifying divine act completes itself in man.   On this our
theorem makes these pronouncements.

The first is that although once forgiveness and adoption exist,
the man is the object of divine favour and love, this does not
happen until he lays hold believingly on Christ.[2]   This does not in
the least mean that previously he was the object of divine displeasure and wrath, for there is no such object.   But the word
' overlooked ' [English A.V. ' winked at '], used in another connexion, has here its specific sense, inasmuch as for God the individual
is not previously a personality at all in this reference, but merely
a part of the mass out of which persons come to exist through

---

[1] *Conf. Belg.* xxiv. : Fide utique in Christum iustificamur, et quidem
priusquam bona opera praestiterimus.—*Apol. Conf.* ii. : . . . quod fides
sit ipsa iustitia, qua coram Deo iusti reputamur . . . quia accipit promissionem . . . seu quia sentit quod Christus sit nobis factus a Deo sapientia
iustitia sanctificatio et redemtio.

[2] Atqui extra controversiam est neminem a Deo extra Christum diligi
(Calv., *Institt.* iii. ii. 32).

the continuance of the creative act from which came the Redeemer.[1]

But since faith arises only through the agency of Christ, it is clearly implied in our theorem that no natural constitution of man, nothing that takes shape in him independently of the whole series of gracious workings mediated by Christ, alters his relation to God, or effects his justification, and that no merit of any kind avails for this. From this it follows immediately that before justification all men are equal before God, despite the inequalities of their sins or their good works ; this is in harmony with the self-consciousness of everyone who finds himself in fellowship with Christ, as he reviews his former share in the common life of sin.

The second point is this. Since, as has been laid down, sharing in the blessedness of Christ is involved in justification, as sharing in His perfection is involved in conversion, and since faith needs no supplement, it follows that faith gives blessedness (saves), and indeed in such wise that the blessedness cannot be increased from any quarter, *i.e.* faith *alone* saves. For anything that could increase the blessedness could have originated it. This blessedness indeed is such that only in the smallest degree does it admit of maxima or minima, but as far as possible is constant. For just as the union of the divine with the human nature in Christ remained the same through all experience and development, so our union with Christ in faith remains always the same.

On the other hand—and this is the third pronouncement—our exposition of the facts certainly does not lead up to the customary formulæ that faith is the *causa instrumentalis*, or the ὄργανον ληπτικόν of justification. These formulæ, liable to many mis-understandings, are not greatly fitted to throw light upon the subject. A productive cause has no place as an essential constituent in the course of the series of activities for which it is employed. Having done its part, it is laid aside. But faith abideth always. A receptive organ, on the other hand, belongs to the sphere of nature ; and the above formula might give the impression that faith is something which everyone has to produce in order that divine grace may become effective ; whereas we bring with us nothing except our living susceptibility, which is the real receptive organ. It is perhaps this formula that has betrayed many theologians into

---

[1] Sola gratia redemtos discernit a perditis, quos in unam perditionis concreverat massam ab origine ducta causa communis (Augustin., *Enchir.* xxix.).

maintaining the position that faith must be our own work, and that only when this work has been accomplished can the operation of divine grace begin.

Second Doctrine : Sanctification

§ 110. *In living fellowship with Christ the natural powers of the regenerate are put at His disposal, whereby there is produced a life akin to His perfection and blessedness ; and this is the state of Sanctification.*

1. The retention of the term ' sanctification ' is justified because it is scriptural. But as it depends on a rather indefinite concept of the holy, a concept which divergent interpretations and usages have made yet more intricate, a still further exposition is necessary if it is to be used in Dogmatics. The first etymological consideration that has to be taken into account is the Old Testament use of the word for everything separated from ordinary social life and devoted to some use relating to God. This relation to God, however, makes no difference in any activity due to an impulse proceeding from Christ ; for since it is produced by the absolutely powerful God-consciousness of Christ, it of itself includes severance from participation in the common sinful life. And fellowship being essential to human nature, this of itself supplies a basis for an active tendency to a new common life ; just as, owing to its Old Testament use noted above, the expression carries with it the priestly dignity of all Christians and represents the new common life as a spiritual temple. So that the state of sanctification too may be regarded as service in this temple. This close connexion with characteristically Christian ideas makes the retention of the old term in the vocabulary of Dogmatics all the more desirable in view of the temptation at this point to snatch at expressions which tend to obscure what is peculiarly Christian in the spirit of the new life, and make it harder to distinguish the Christian development from a gradual attainment of perfection along purely natural lines.

The second consideration is the connexion of the term with holiness as a Divine attribute ; for of course we hold by the interpretation of this given above.[1] It is, however, also clear that the regenerate man, through the manner of life that we are now going to describe in more detail, develops a conscience also in others, in

[1] Cf. § 83.

proportion as all his activities diverge from what happens in the common sinful life.

In both its aspects, however, we cannot call this condition holiness—that is, being holy—but sanctification, which means becoming holy, sanctifying oneself ; which we call sanctification, because it is a striving for holiness. If the meaning were being holy, it would imply that a complete transformation had occurred at the moment of regeneration, every link with the sinful common life entirely ceasing, and the whole nature being completely and instantaneously penetrated by the life of Christ and brought under His sway. This change would then be all a part of regeneration, and there would be no doctrine to state about what later develops out of it.

Sanctification, then, being understood to be progressive—so that the content of time-experience becomes from the turning-point of regeneration ever further removed from what preceded that crisis, and ever approximates more to pure harmony with the impulse issuing from Christ, and therefore to indistinguishability from Christ Himself—we have the two points of view from which sanctification has to be considered.

2. First then, if we compare the state of one who is in process of being sanctified with what existed before regeneration, it is preferable to dwell not on points of difference from the moments in which the mastery of sinfulness was earlier manifested, but rather on the difference from those moments which previously came under preparatory grace. These preparatory workings we cannot limit to approximations to repentance and faith in thought and emotion ; they are also to be seen in action ; for it is contrary to nature that lively thoughts and strong feelings should have no influence on concurrent actions—stronger or weaker, of course, in proportion to their affinity. Indeed, it is possible that with the frequent repetition of similar influences, the active effects occur more and more easily and become habits. In each separate case, however, the impulse to the alteration of action comes from without and remains effective only for so long as the momentary emotion endures ; it is not in a position to reproduce itself from within, as witness the common feeling of having under external compulsion done something quite foreign to one's nature. Such actions are not the doer's own ; they belong to an external life that is showing its power within him. Deeds therefore which resemble those of the state of sanctification, but are not rooted in the regeneration of the doer, are properly

deeds of the Christian common life exercising its power over the individual. It is thus also with habits formed in the same way, as is best seen by reference to the illustration used in Scripture about strangers and fellow-citizens.[1] The latter out of the inner power of their common indwelling characteristic spirit establish law and custom among themselves, and thus their acts are wholly in character. Strangers have no part in the formation of either ; they have no formative power in themselves and merely accommodate themselves to custom, acting in many ways according to it even when no demand has been made on them. But if they return to their own country where these foreign influences no longer surround them, they divest themselves with the utmost ease of every adopted habit. It is therefore not the form, and still less the numerical value of separate actions or series of actions that differentiates the state of sanctification from the condition before regeneration. It is the fact that unwillingness to remain in the common life in which sin is ever being propagated has become a power of repulsion, constantly at work in the form of an essential tendency of being, while in itself this is but the consequence of having surrendered to the receptive influence of Christ ; a surrender which throughout the entire sphere of spontaneous activity has consolidated itself as a steadfast willingness to be controlled by Him.

This is still the only tenable distinction if, conversely, we look back on the old life from the standpoint of the new. That strength of the God-consciousness is not original ; it is a gift which becomes ours only after sin has developed its power ; and what has emerged in time can be removed in time only by its opposite. Hence not merely is approximation to the goal delayed by the fact that what have become habitual and therefore often and easily provoked sins have to be countered by the aforesaid power of repulsion, but inasmuch as the sinfulness of each has a ground in existence prior to him and external to him, his sin cannot be perfectly blotted out, but remains always something in process of disappearance. In so far as it has not yet disappeared, it may make itself visible, and acts will occur within the state of sanctification similar to those common before regeneration, where what emerges is the power of the sinful common life, whereas the traces of preparatory grace lie deeply hidden. Nay more ; since even in sanctification growth does not take place without a preliminary struggle between the old man and the new, this struggle cannot at any point in its whole

[1] Eph. 2[19].

course be viewed as an even advance to increase in the power of the one and decrease in the power of the other. By the influence of the sinful common life around us our own sinfulness is constantly being stirred up again. In itself it might be steadily limited by the growth of the new man, but this cannot equally be said of the reinforcements it receives from without. At least in view of the variegated changes in this sphere, where in the most irregular and unforeseen ways the individual life is held in grip, more firmly or more slackly, by the common sinful life, it could only be explained by a special miracle, and not by the ordinary course of divine grace among men, if in that struggle there were not special moments when the power of sin came out more strongly than in the earlier moments. Even after regeneration, then, many and varied conditions appear, among others repentance, and this by no means always merely in the form of slight compunction for trifles. But this repentance is distinguished from every previous repentance by the fixed inward resolution to be no longer under the power of sin, and is to be conceived as a vanishing quantity in the same way as the repentance which, so long as even in obedience some opposition to the impulses proceeding from Christ makes itself felt, accompanies all actions which appear as fruits of this obedience, yet also show traces of opposition. Even if these intermittent evidences of the continued presence of sin make particular instants, as compared with others, seem relapses, none the less a settled consciousness remains that the longer the series of such fluctuations observed, the greater is the advance seen to be on the whole, and that the certainty of faith as an understanding of what union with Christ means and as a delight in that union is always increasing, so that in the powers put at Christ's disposal sin can never win fresh ground, while all the time it is being dislodged from its former positions. It is chiefly by this fact, that sin can win no new ground, that the state of sanctification is most definitely distinguished from all that went before.

3. If now, on the other hand, we consider how this condition approximates to likeness to Christ, there has above been drawn a boundary line which it is not given to us to overstep. From the beginning of His incarnation onwards Christ developed in every way naturally yet constantly and uninterruptedly in organic union with the indwelling principle of His life, and in its service. To no other who brings with him a personality that has shared the common life of sinfulness is this vouchsafed. This difference from Christ

must, strictly speaking, be there at every moment, and it will come into actual consciousness in proportion to the clarity of our self-consciousness in relation to the divine—that is, our illumination. For wherever there is imperfection, especially such as not merely represents the form of development in time, but is a real imperfection touching the relation between deed and motive, there will also be a basis for the recollection, and to that extent for an actual realization, of the old life ; and therefore even in moments really involving an advance in likeness to Christ, there will also exist a consciousness of sin.   But this does not prevent union with Christ from being operative in every moment of the state of sanctification ; and thus at every moment that life merits the description given in our proposition.

This is already involved in the analogy suggested—namely, that regeneration may be regarded as the divine act of union with human nature and sanctification as the state constituted by that union.   Just as that act of union would have been an empty illusion had it not produced an enduring state of living union in which the two elements were inseparable, the human nature in all its performances proving itself the instrument of the divine power, so the activity of divine power in Christ that in regeneration flows out from Him and unites individuals to Himself would be nothing at all, would be indistinguishable from the most fleeting and superficial impulses, and as far as possible from being the end of the old life and the beginning of the new, unless that act showed itself operative in every moment in time, making every moment a recapitulation of the first, and, as it were, a being laid hold of afresh by the receptive activity of Christ—every moment thus including in itself a new determination to live not for self but in fellowship with Christ.   Taken together, these two things involve the sinless perfection of Christ and, for the introspective self-consciousness, His blessedness.   To make clear here, too, the limits of the likeness and the difference, we shall have to distinguish a constant and a variable within this growing correspondence between the elements of our life and the impulses proceeding from Christ.   Viewed as a renewal of regeneration every moment is like every other, and is a participation in the perfection and blessedness of Christ ; for without this no reception into fellowship with Him is possible.   This constant is in its one aspect the ever self-renewed willing of the Kingdom of God, on which every single act and resolve of Christ was based.   In its other aspect it is the consciousness of the union of the Divine Essence with human nature through Christ, as was the case in Christ in every detail of His self-consciousness. All this is participation in blessedness, since union with the Supreme Being is absolute satisfaction ; it is equally participation in sinless perfection, for the kingdom of God excludes all sin, yet includes strength for all good. The variable factor, *i.e.* everything else occurring as a particular item in the life of the regenerate, lies within the limits so drawn. Particular actions show in their execution more or less sin, and so do particular purposes. The actual individual self-consciousness bears witness to this in many a moment of sorrow, where the sorrow is assuaged by the simultaneous presence of the constant factor. At other moments the self-consciousness is a joy that passes into humility because its only right to exist is found in what assuages the sorrow lying so near it.

Any further doctrine there is to formulate concerning the state of sanctification must bear upon this antithesis between the element that belongs to the starting-point and the element that belongs to the goal.

First Theorem : The Sins of the Regenerate

§ 111. *Since they are continually being combated, the sins of those in the state of sanctification always carry their forgiveness with them and have no power to annul the divine grace of regeneration.*

1. Taking together the two propositions just laid down, namely, that in the state of sanctification no new sins develop, and that in all moments, in all acts and works, even in the best and likest to Christ, some trace of sin exists belonging to the former state,[1] it becomes clear that in the state of sanctification there can be no sin which could make regeneration nugatory. For every sinful act includes a resistance on the part of the new man, albeit not a persistent or successful resistance ; and therefore in such acts, just as much as in those where the old man is overborne, the new man is seen to be active, and therefore still alive. It is, of course, only in moments of defeat that anyone has ever fancied that the state of grace might be lost ; yet in this region there is no definite contrast between defeat and victory, but only a distinction of less or more in which no definite point can be fixed at which the result begins to be

---

[1] *Expos. simpl.* xvi. : Sunt multa praeterea indigna Deo, et imperfecta plurima inveniuntur in operibus etiam sanctorum.—*Conf. Belg.* xxiv. : Nullum enim opus facere possumus, quod non est carnis vitio pollutum.

fatal.   If we do seek to establish such a contrast, pronouncing this a sinful act and that a good work, we are merely naming it by its preponderating quality.   In some cases, indeed, the difference seems almost infinite ; yet if the sin be the deed of a regenerate man, it cannot be the same sin as a sin ever so like it in the unregenerate ; if only for this reason, that in it as in his good works a constant element is present.   Everyone who observes himself or others will note acts which fluctuate between the two descriptions, and cases in which it is adventitious circumstances that tip the balance one way or the other, making the same action at one time a good work though on the point of becoming a sin, and at another time a sin instead of a good work.   The state of grace cannot possibly be lost in the first case and not in the second.   The principle we here go by, namely, that in the state of sanctification no new sin can develop, seems rather indefinite.   No action is quite identical with any previous action, and it is not every sin that is a novelty.   The labelling, therefore, of any given action as novel seems to depend on a rather arbitrary estimate of the degree in which it is to be regarded as akin or similar to previous actions—a point of which, strictly speaking, a man can judge only for himself.   This, and no more, can be laid down in general terms.   Taking regeneration in the sense we have given it, and assuming that only subsequent to it a sense-function develops which previously was latent, or that relations are formed so entirely new that they awaken an echo in those elements of our being in which sin previously resided, everyone must confess that it is inconceivable that such a function or such relations should develop in sinful fashion.   And in the same way, if in an individual we conceive of any function or relation whatsoever which by personal idiosyncrasy or the influence of training and social morality, was kept so constantly pure even before regeneration that no sin ever arose out of it, it is unthinkable that after regeneration sin should effect an entrance at that point.   What follows is clear enough.   In every case where sin appears to have entered we must say either that the sin is not really new, but belongs to a former period and has simply been revived ; or else that regeneration has not been of a right and true kind, inasmuch as sinfulness has borne new fruit.

Also from another point of view we must reject the proposition contradictory of ours.   The assertion that a regenerate man, though a new man, might by an act lose the grace of regeneration stands in the closest connexion with the idea already rejected, that our first parent could by an act lose the characteristics he still had while acting. If the reply be made that grace is not lost by the act of the new man, but by his not acting, this again conflicts with the assumption that regeneration is the beginning of the life of Christ in us, a life which necessarily is action. In fact, it is evident, just as before, that however such a destructive action might be conceived, the grace of regeneration would have to have been lost previously. Indeed, loyalty to the concept of regeneration permits us another analogy. It would be through the co-operation of the very impulses proceeding from Christ that a man would have to proclaim his severance from living fellowship with Christ, just as, in the case of the Evil Spirit, it was through the very powers that made him most akin to God that he broke away from that relation —the same result following in each case.

Finally, if we return to the problem of how we are definitely to differentiate the condition of sanctification (whether it can be lost or not) from the condition obtaining within the common life of sinfulness (though under the influence of preparatory grace), the problem forces us to make a distinction between the work of divine grace on men and in and through men. If the latter be not a purely momentary thing, ever ebbing again, and equivalent to no more than inspiration, it goes without saying that it must be continuous ; for if even this work of grace could be imagined as ceasing, its duration, whether long or short, would always make it a mere inspiration. The proposition contradictory of ours, therefore, must choose between a self-effected alteration of man's own nature, and a voluntary self-withdrawal of divine grace previous to the decisive action, just as before the fall of man a withdrawal is supposed to have taken place of an extraordinary, restraining divine grace. It seems impossible, therefore, that the doctrine opposed to ours can in this conceptual form be derived from the self-consciousness of one who is conscious of divine grace. For even if we concede that a moment of regeneration is not capable of being definitely isolated in perceptible self-consciousness, and also that the assurance of a form of life antagonistic to the former condition does not at once supervene, still we must agree that in actual experience the manifestations of the new life become ever more continuous, and that confidence in the endurance of this living union with Christ thus becomes more and more a feature of the perceptible self-consciousness, for in spite of all fluctuations an increasing sway of the life of Christ over the flesh marks out the state of sanctification

This natural confidence answering to the fact of regeneration can be expressed in thought only by the first half of our theorem, and not by its contradictory.

2. Even though they are backed by teachers of repute, and have made their way into more than one confessional document, the opposing formulæ, that faith may be lost,[1] that justification may be lost, and that grace may be lost,[2] have the less claim on our acceptance that other credal statements clearly expressing the confidence of our theorem are (in part explicitly, in part by implication) on our side.[3]

If we compare these differing statements with one another, certain facts emerge. First, the concept of falling away and the fallen, and the intrusion of a reference to baptism show that the formulæ opposed to ours are connected with old ecclesiastical decisions which rightly stood out against a harsh desire to exclude certain people. But those falling away, lapsing outwardly from the faith and forsaking the Church, had not necessarily lost faith inwardly : they abjured only outwardly through fear : that is to say, it was merely in courage they were imperfect. Nor were the

---

[1] *Epit. artic.* iv. : Credimus . . . cum dicitur renatos bene operari libero et spontaneo spiritu, id non ita accipiendum esse, quod . . . nihilominus tamen fidem retineat (scil. homo renatus) etiamsi in peccatis ex proposito perseveret.—*Ibid.* : reprobamus dogma illud, quod fides in Christum non amittatur . . . etiamsi (homo) sciens volensque peccet.

[2] Melanchth., *loc.* pp. 124 and 276 : Necesse est autem discernere peccata quae in renatis in hac vita manent ab illis peccatis, propter quae amittuntur gratia et fides . . . est igitur actuale mortale in labente post reconciliationem actio interior vel exterior pugnans cum lege Dei facta contra conscientiam—nec potest stare cum malo proposito contra conscientiam fides.—*Augs. Conf.* xii. : '. . . that those who have sinned after baptism can always, if they are converted, receive forgiveness. . . . Hereby those are repudiated who teach that such as have once become religious can never fall away.'—*Declar. Thorun.* xi. p. 421 : Quasi statuamus semel iustificatos Dei gratiam eiusve certitudinem . . . non posse amittere quamvis in peccatis pro lubitu voluentur. Cum contra potius doceamus, ipsos etiam renatos quoties in peccata contra conscientiam recidunt, in iisque aliquamdiu perseverant, nec fidem vivam nec Dei gratiam iustificantem nedum eius certitudinem . . . pro illo tempore retinere, etc.—Reinh., *Dogm.*, § 127, is careful to take the main proposition, ipsum tamen iustificationis decretum in Deo mutabile non est, along with that (*ibid.* 2.) that a man can be justified more than once in his life. For as often as he receives faith once more after the occurrence of a moral lapse the decretum iustificans related to this faith must again take place in God. See § 128 : . . . iustificatio . . . neglecta fide iterum potest amitti.

[3] *Expos. simpl.* xvi. : Eadem (fides) retinet nos in officio.—*Conf. Gall.* xxi. : . . . credimus fidem electis dari, ut non semel tantum in rectam viam introducantur, quin potius ut in ea ad extremum usque pergant.—*Sol. decl.*, p. 802 : Deus proposuit se iustificatos etiam in multiplici et varia ipsorum infirmitate . . . defensurum . . . et si lapsi fuerint, manum suppositurum ut ad vitam conserventur.—Augustine's sentence is relevant at this point : Ego autem id esse dico peccatum ad mortem, fidem quae per dilectionem operatur deserere usque ad mortem (*De corr. et grat.* 35).

baptized all regenerate then any more than now. Such, therefore, as forsook Christianity, to enjoy perhaps more sensual freedom, had not been completely laid hold of and were not yet possessed of genuine faith and justification. Secondly, as soon as this same concept ' falling away ' is applied to our present circumstances in the same sense that it involves loss of faith or justification, the question what sort of sin it is that occasions this loss is answered in very different ways. To sin with knowledge and with will, to sin deliberately, and to continue in deliberate sin, are widely different.[1] Taking the two extremes, the first belongs to that fluctuating less or more found in everyone who is in the state of sanctification, where even the imperfection of a good work is often enough known and willed ; the second, deliberate continuance in a knowing and com- plete resistance, is obviously a case where regeneration has been only apparent. Thirdly, it is beyond doubt that if the doctrine of the inadmissibility of justifying divine grace (or, better expressed, the absolute trustworthiness of such grace) has not become an accepted dogma of the Church, this is entirely due to the controversy with the Roman Church and the polemic against fanatical sects ; as indeed every dogmatic proposition which cannot be made good by analysis of the Christian self-consciousness must have its basis either in speculation or in some similarly external ground. This is clear enough for the further reason that it also covers the case of one continuing in sin deliberately. The fanatical caricature of this doctrine, which rests solely on an inward certainty of feeling, and enlarges the thesis by inverting it and giving it the form that what- ever the regenerate man does is right or at least permissible, is quite familiar, but finds no support in the formula here adopted. So, too, the inference that the Roman Church seeks to draw from the doctrine of justification by faith is amply guarded against by our presupposi- tion that the regenerate continuously struggles against sin. As for the wanton abuse of the doctrine, there is just as much excuse for it in the doctrine that one can always be converted again if one falls from grace as in the doctrine that the sins which may be committed by a regenerate man do not annul his state of grace. It is, however, much more in accord with our line of argument to meet the objec- tion in view by saying that one who seeks such a subterfuge does not really want to struggle against sin and is therefore not regenerate; this whole doctrine has nothing whatever to do with his case. No ground therefore remains for seeking to improve upon the simple

[1] See above, § 74.

unforced utterance of the evangelical Christian self-consciousness by a preamble made up of additions untenable in themselves and confusing in their effect.

3. Neither is the declaration that in the state of sanctification sins always carry their forgiveness with them intended to mean that the regenerate man is conscious of forgiveness while he is sinning, or that he sins in and with this consciousness ; the sin must come to consciousness as an accomplished fact and as accompanied by repentance ; for forgiveness and repentance are mutually dependent. But this is certain, that resistance, even if not fortunate and victorious, is a presage of repentance, and hence too of the consciousness of forgiveness. The real meaning is simply that what is true of the concept of justification as a whole is true of this particular part of it. The gracious forgiveness of sins is not an individual decree or act bearing on the single life, nor is it merely declaratory ; it is one that emancipates from the sphere of guilt and penal desert, and one that is general—being fulfilled, indeed, at some point of time for each individual, but being then really fulfilled, and needing no repetition. For the divine omniscience cannot in the act of forgiving sins regard them as altogether blotted out at the moment of regeneration, but only as gradually vanishing. If conversion be this turning-point, yet so that sin none the less reappears later, then even subsequent to it there must in consciousness be a relation to this act, though naturally an altered relation. In the life under the dominion of common sinfulness, sin is common guilt, and sins are not reckoned separately to individuals ; each has his share in the common guilt and nothing is separately forgiven him. In the state of sanctification the converse is the case. Redemption is possible only in the form of a common life, and sin has its basis, strictly speaking, not in this common life, but only in the individual, in so far as he still has something in him of the old common life of sin. His is therefore not a guilt appertaining to the common life but to him as an individual, and it is so reckoned. It is only an apparent contradiction that sins are reckoned to him, and are yet always forgiven ; not only because forgiveness itself is always a kind of reckoning, but because it is the only kind of reckoning that enters here. Sins are reckoned personally to the natural person who has passed out of the sinful common life into the new life, and indeed more personally to him than to one who still belongs to the old common life ; they are not reckoned to the new man who, identifying himself with the whole through the feeling of com-

munity, does not carry in himself the sense of guilt. They are forgiven him because they can be reckoned only to the old man that he no longer is. Hence also he has the consciousness of forgiveness as soon as he is conscious of himself as being within the new common life. For in virtue of his willing the Kingdom of God and repudiating sin the continuity of the new life has not been interrupted, having always produced simultaneously some degree of resistance to sin. It is self-evident that this consciousness, in whatever degree it may be felt, cannot be simultaneous with sinning, that the repudiation of sin can make itself felt only after the event, and that the consciousness of forgiveness presupposes regret.

4. Since in dealing with the subject one can hardly avoid diverging into Christian Ethics, less might be said here about the struggle with sin itself, were it not that in this connexion too misunderstandings have arisen. It has now been made quite clear that in the state of sanctification the danger each is in of falling into sin comes from those departments of the sensuous life which before regeneration had exercised most power, and has its seat in those relations where habits in accordance with inclination were most easily formed. This sphere, within which lie the enticements which always are hardest to resist entirely, is the sphere of temptation for the individual. Now in everyone the activity of the life of Christ, issuing from His will for the Kingdom of God, defines itself by the demands that meet him in virtue of his position within the common life. That will takes shape in certain fixed aims ; and these come to constitute a continuous will as the law of Christian morality begins to embrace the whole of life. Hence the sphere of temptation must lie within this sphere of vocation, taking that word in its widest sense. There can be no struggle against our own sin other than the struggle against the sin we actually encounter in the course of our activity in the Kingdom of God ; and any action taken against such sin is part of this activity. The struggle therefore consists simply in this, that we seek to reject or conquer the temptations that arise in the course of this activity; and this formula must cover the whole campaign against whatever sins are possible within the varying course of the state of sanctification. Otherwise two differing yet parallel demands would arise, neither of which at any given moment could be fulfilled without infringing on the other. Both points can be made clear, as follows. The right use of divine forgiveness is conditioned in every case by the struggle against sin ; but the right use of divine adoption by which, within the state

of sanctification, even after sin, that is to say at every moment (for there is always some sin remaining), one can still say he is a child of God, is conditioned by the liveliness and activity of faith.   And since forgiveness and adoption are one and the same, what conditions each must also be one and the same.   There is therefore no such thing as a struggle at random against possible future sins, which could only mean the suppression or weakening of sensuous powers developed in a natural way, and injury to them as instruments of the spirit.   Nor are there exercises in repentance consisting of special acts which do not arise out of our business in the Kingdom of God.   Still less is there room for an arbitrary flight from the sphere of temptation which would be at the same time a flight from the sphere of duty ; no such step could issue from our being taken up into living fellowship with Christ.   Fellowship with Him is always a fellowship with His mission to the world, and this such a withdrawal would contradict.   What remains as the one right course, is resistance to the temptations that actually occur.

Second Theorem : The Good Works of the Regenerate

§ 112. *The good works of the regenerate are natural effects of faith, and as such are objects of divine good pleasure.*

Apol. Conf. iii. : Deinde docemus, quomodo Deo placeat, si quid fit, videlicet non quia legi satisfacimus, sed quia sumus in Christo.—*Artic. Smalc.* xiii. : Hanc fidem sequuntur bona opera.   Et quod in illis pollutum et imperfectum est, pro peccato et defectu non censetur, idque etiam propter Christum : atque ita totus homo, cum quoad personam suam tum quoad opera sua iustus et sanctus est. . . . Dicimus praeterea, ubi non sequuntur bona opera, ibi fidem esse falsam.—*Expos. simpl.* xvi. : Docemus enim vere bona opera enasci ex viva fide . . . et a fidelibus fieri secundum voluntatem vel regulam verbi Dei. . . . Etenim non probantur Deo opera et nostro arbitrio delecti cultus, . . . placent vero approbanturque a Deo quae a nobis fiunt per fidem, quia illi placent Deo propter fidem in Christum, quia faciunt opera bona . . . docemus Deum bona operantibus amplam dare mercedem. . . . Referimus tamen hanc mercedem non ad meritum hominis accipientis.—*Conf. Mylhus.* viii. : . . . quamvis haec (fides) per opera caritatis se sine intermissione exerceat . . . attamen iustitiam et satisfactionem pro peccatis nostris non tribuimus operibus quae fidei fructus sunt.—*Conf. Belg.* xxiv. : Atque haec opera, quae a bona fidei radice proficiscuntur, coram Deo bona eique accepta sunt. . . . Facimus igitur bona quidem opera, sed neutiquam ut iis promereamur. . . . Interim tamen non negamus Deum bona opera remunerari. —*Conf. Angl.* xiv. : Opera, quae supererogationis appellant, non possunt sine arrogantia et impietate praedicari.

1. The discussions, so common in our confessional documents and in all older expositions of doctrine, of the idea that good works

are not necessary for justification, we must regard as irrelevant to the subject ; for if even the first point in the doctrine of regeneration be conceded, the idea is such as could occur to no one.   Justification and conversion are mutually conditioned ; hence as conversion cannot be conditioned by good works, neither is justification.   And it would be odd to put the further question whether eternal life and blessedness are conditioned by good works.   Both begin along with faith, for both are included in what we have seen to be the constant element existing in the soul from the moment of regeneration onwards.   We cannot argue this particular point with anyone who dissents ; we should first have to refute him on other points. Anyone who holds that good works are necessary to blessedness, because for him faith is mere knowledge, is using a different vocabulary from ours, or holding an entirely different doctrine of redemption.

The most remarkable misconception, however, is that which, in the course of this controversy, has led to the extravagant position that good works are injurious to salvation—a position only half-heartedly surrendered, as if there might be something in it, if only the proposition were defined more closely and with more propriety,[1] so as to avoid all offence.   The fact is, that works which would be injurious if a man put his trust in them would not be good works at all in our sense.   Anyone who does truly good works has blessedness already in his faith, and therefore cannot find himself wanting first to rely upon his works.

On the other hand, the positive statement that good works are the natural effect of faith is so closely bound up with all that has been said above that it needs no explanation.   Allowing ourselves to be taken up into living fellowship with Christ, we are laid hold of by the union of the divine with the human nature in His Person, and consent to this becomes a constant and active will to maintain and extend this union.   Anything this will produces is a good work, were it only an incipient resistance to sin.   Thus it is a needless anxiety that wants to deny that faith is conserved or retained by good works.[2]   If we imagine the retention of faith as if its implanting were something transitory (which it really is not, any more than

---

[1] *Epit. Artic.* iv. : Repudiamus . . . *nudam* hanc offendiculi plenam . . . phrasin, bona opera noxia esse ad salutem.   See also what immediately follows.

[2] *Ibid.* : Credimus fidem in nobis conservari aut retineri non per opera, sed tantum per Spiritum Dei.   The latter remark is not yet relevant, but is quite true.   All the same, the Holy Spirit has no other way of giving strength to faith than by activity in works.

any act of recognition), then we can only conceive the life of faith
as a series of moments in which faith is always the same and unaltered. But it is impossible to conceive two moments of faith
thus separated from one another without the first producing a
good work before the second has come into existence. Hence the
retention of faith, if for the moment we speak of such a thing, is
always mediated by good works. The right thing to say is this,
that our union with Christ in faith is, though not as completely, yet
quite as essentially, an active obedience as His life was an active
obedience of the human nature to the indwelling being of God
within Him ; and our reception into living fellowship with Him
is the fruitful germ of all good works in the same way as the act of
uniting was in His case the germ of all redeeming activity. This
may also be expressed by saying that the regenerate cannot but do
good works in virtue of faith ; and it is surely a vain misunderstanding thereupon to interject the question : Are good works
also free ? To ask that involves the assumption that the weakest
will, though the will most easily forced to change, is the most
free, and that the hero of faith, who does not know how to describe
his condition better than by saying that he ' can do no other,' is
not free. The whole living susceptibility which is the condition of
men in conversion is clearly a free condition ; so is the will for the
Kingdom of God arising from conversion, for there is no will without
freedom. To be continuously and receptively open to the influence
of Christ, and continuously active in will for His Kingdom, is the
life-process of the new man.

2. Connected with this is the question how far the good works
of the regenerate man are his own in such a sense that they can be
reckoned to him. We shall disregard to begin with the part of the
question which concerns the possibility of reward, and first answer
that which concerns the authorship of good works. If we recall
at this point the fact that there is no redemption which does not
establish a new common life to which everyone appropriating
redemption essentially belongs, two questions arise : How far do
the good works belong to the individual doing them or to Christ ?
And how far to the community or to the individual ? In regard
to the first question it is self-evident that in virtue of the living
fellowship existing between them, what belongs to Christ in a good
work cannot be separated from what belongs to the individual ;
for this would be to dissolve the fellowship. A formula, however,
has to be found which will bring out the participation of both.

Now conversion is the beginning of sanctification, and in it Christ alone is active, the individual being merely in a state of living susceptibility ; yet in conversion the new life comes into being. Hence every moment of active faith must be ascribed to Christ in so far as the analogy with its commencement holds good, that is, in so far as in that moment new life comes into being or is enhanced ; in short, in so far as it contains progress. For if we could ourselves make the new life grow, we could make it begin. But as in that turning-point the new man came into being, and the will for the Kingdom of God thus arising is our own will, every moment in the activity of faith is to be ascribed to us and is our work, in so far as it is an expression of this implanted will. To call the divine grace in sanctification co-operative grace on this account is an incorrect expression, even apart from its unhappy suggestion that grace is thus assigned a secondary place in the authorship of good works. For the fact is not that divine grace is working along with what is a good work of our own, but that divine grace has here been at work from the beginning, and what is its own it effects by itself. The expression, however, intends to make out a third kind of grace in addition to preparatory and effectual grace, and especially to indicate that the regenerate man has become spontaneously active. This intention is undoubtedly right, but since this third kind is no less effectual than the second, a different word would describe it better than co-operative. Now while this formula obviously applies primarily only to the determination of the will (for in the execution of the act imperfection and sin are always present, and they cannot therefore be ascribed to Christ), it has already been allowed that even in particular resolves something impure may mingle ; hence we shall have to confine it to whatever in a good work is of the nature of progress. If, however, we consider the relation of the individual to the Christian common life, everything shows as absolutely common ; and it would be a misconceived interest to try to define the participation of each in the common activity.

3. From all this it is very easy to understand in what sense good works are the object of divine good-pleasure. The actual deeds, as they come into view, cannot be so, for they are at the same time good works and sins. The object of good-pleasure is only that element in them which is an activity of faith and an expression of our living fellowship with Christ. Thus it is only the love in our good works that is pleasing to God, this being, in the will for the

Kingdom of God, at once love to men and love to Christ and love to God ; while at the same time it is Christ's love working in and through us. Now, since what is sometimes there and sometimes not cannot be an object of divine good-pleasure, this latter must rest especially on the element that remains constant through all moments in the state of sanctification, while also it draws to itself and assimilates what is changing.   It is therefore quite right to say that it is really only the person, and the person only as God regards him in Christ, that is the object of divine good-pleasure ; the works are so regarded merely for the person's sake.   This consciousness, necessarily involved in the will for the Kingdom of God, is the blessedness which accompanies that will.

In this light, the question whether God rewards good works appears very superfluous.   What is our own feeling ?   If sonship is involved in regeneration, and blessedness in sonship, can the regenerate man desire or obtain a further reward ? He already possesses the implicit guarantee for every advance in sanctification.   Nor can he desire any ; for inward spirit and reward cannot really be related to each other ; and besides, the works are sin too, and merit no reward.   This is why it is rightly held that the state of grace leaves no room for reward.   It is quite improper to give the name ' reward ' to a widening of one's circle of influence, or, what is the same thing, an enhancement of one's powers ; that merely offers us a further opportunity of doing things for which a reward is given.   As a matter of fact, in all the citations from Confessions which admit the idea of reward, one has the feeling that they are only half convinced.   There is all the less reason for conceding the point that the idea of reward can be no motive to progress in sanctification.

4. Although we have already made a distinction in the activities of faith between what is an expression of our actual condition, and what constitutes an advance, this cannot be stretched to mean that there are two kinds of good works—those that spring from existing powers, and those that increase power.   There are not two kinds.   If there were, we should be entangled in an interminable and insoluble struggle.   We should have to try at every moment to do some work of each kind, and yet one of the new kinds would always have to be postponed to the other.   It can be shown, rather, that in this sphere there can be no actions specially aimed at enhancing our powers.   With faith the will for the Kingdom of God has come into existence.   This creates for every believer,

in view of his individual situation in the world, challenges to activity in the Kingdom of God, answering to the powers at his command and his knowledge of the conditions by which he is surrounded. The sum-total of these relations constitutes his sphere of vocation, the idea of which is intimately bound up with his will for the Kingdom of God : and all the good works of each individual must lie within this sphere ; nothing outside vocation can be a good work. At certain periods of life and in certain relations, acts directed towards the discipline and the enhancement of power are part of a man's vocation, and are justified on that score ; but real discipline and enhancement of power is found in the actual pursuit of one's vocation, as is the case with all finite spiritual powers ; and the more we consider the inner meaning of things, the more we shall see that there can be no other way of it. For the power of faith cannot be strengthened by special acts not prompted by Christ, while those which He does prompt belong essentially to vocation, and go to achieve something for the Kingdom of God. Just because there are sinful ways, as well as ways well-pleasing to God, of enhancing spiritual and sensuous powers, we must see to it that everything that may be done for this end is justifiable as an act of vocation. Accordingly, if by means of grace we understand such activities as advance sanctification, and by good works the fruits of sanctification, it follows that we recognize no means of grace but such as are at the same time good works, and that all good works must likewise be means of grace. There are no purely ascetic acts, nor are there arbitrary good works—that is, good works lying outside our vocation. Still less are there any such as, after he had done justice to his vocation, a man might do by way of supplement.

5. If the foregoing is the essence of sanctification, so that all activity in the Kingdom of God and every inward development of personality proceeds from the living power of faith and its action through love, it can hardly be more than an accident of memory if at this point a question crops up as to the necessity and use of law, in whatever sense that term be taken. Something like legislation will always exist in Christian life in order in certain spheres to guide the actions of those who lack insight. This is where civil law and the regulations applying to every kind of art and handicraft come in. Such legislation is a good work in so far as it has its basis in love ; and since it is a proceeding that involves and makes large demands on spiritual powers, it is also a means of grace. But

to law itself we can concede no value in the sphere of sanctification, for love always is, and does, much more than law can be or do. Law does not even suffice to produce the recognition of sin in those who are being sanctified, for in itself it does not pierce behind the outward act to the inward mood and temper. In Christ we have a far more perfect means of recognizing sin. And Paul [1] himself no longer grants even this necessity for law once faith has been revealed. Still less can law hold before us the goal of sanctification. That goal can only be behaviour [2] exhibiting in all its details the strength and purity of inward disposition, and law, as a collection of separate precepts,[3] can never let us see this. Paul therefore cites as works of the Spirit things that cannot be defined or measured by any law, for to call propositions expressive of the inward spirit commandments is a most inaccurate form of language. The two commandments cited [4] by Christ as containing the whole law are not really commands. Nor do even they set forth the goal of sanctification in its full purity, for they exhibit love to God and love to our neighbour as two separate things alongside of each other. As for Christ's one commandment,[5] He really means by calling it so to contrast it with the whole law of commandments : for His is no command ; its real analogy [6] is found in His own redeeming love.

Hence one may justly say that in the Christian Church it is neither necessary nor advisable to begin instruction about sin, and still less about sanctification, with the Decalogue. In either case, this can only lead to imperfect and superficial ideas. Even though one endeavours to import into the Decalogue all kinds of things that are not there, such a method is for one thing an opportune illustration of bad, arbitrary exegesis ; and besides, the same result can be more easily and logically derived from the moral

---

[1] Gal. 3²⁵ 5¹⁸, even though he here speaks of the flesh lusting against the spirit.

[2] Eph. 4¹³, where we are expressly pointed to the standard set by Christ.

[3] νόμος ἐντολῶν ἐν δόγμασι (Eph. 2¹⁵).—*Sol. decl.* vi. : observandum est, quando de bonis operibus agitur, quae *legi Dei* sunt conformia . . . quod hoc loco vocabulum legis unam tantum rem significat : immutabilem scilicet voluntatem Dei, secundum quam homines omnes vitae suae rationes instituere debeant.—In this whole discussion, *de tertio usu legis*, which, contrary to our own view, upholds the notion of law within Christendom, we best see the inexactitude of the idea underlying it, and the sort of confusion it inevitably sets up.

[4] Matt. 22³⁷ᶠᶠ.   [5] John 15¹².

[6] *Conf. Gall.* xxiii. : Credimus omnes legis figuras adventu Jesu Christi sublatas esse, quamvis earum veritas et substantia nobis in eo constat, in quo sunt omnes impletae.

law of reason as developed under the influence of Christianity—
a law which formulates, not acts, but modes of action.[1] Christian
Ethics, however, will answer much better to its true relation to
Dogmatics, and so to its own immediate purpose, if it drops the
imperative mood altogether, and simply gives an all-round description of how men live within the Kingdom of God.

[1] One cannot say with truth of any law: Lex inculcat . . . esse voluntatem
et mandatum Dei ut in nova vita ambulemus. Here obviously the Mosaic Law
is meant.

SECOND SECTION

The Constitution of the World in Relation to Redemption

§ 113. *All that comes to exist in the world through redemption is embraced in the fellowship of believers, within which all regenerate people are always found. This section, therefore, contains the doctrine of the Christian Church.*

1. In reckoning the two expressions—the fellowship of believers and the Christian Church—as equivalent, our proposition seems to be in opposition to the Roman Symbol ; but neither earlier versions of the latter nor the Nicene Creed know anything of using the two side by side yet with a distinction. What is evident is that fellowship may be taken in a narrower or a wider sense. For, if the regenerate find themselves already within it, they must have belonged to it even before regeneration, though obviously in a different sense from actual believers. If this were not so, no accession to or extension of the Church could be imagined except by an absolute breach of continuity—that is, in a way unknown to history. But the truth is that the new life of each individual springs from that of the community, while the life of the community springs from no other individual life than that of the Redeemer. We must therefore hold that the totality of those who live in the state of sanctification is the inner fellowship ; the totality of those on whom preparatory grace is at work is the outer fellowship, from which by regeneration members pass to the inner, and then keep helping to extend the wider circle. It would, however, be quite a novel and merely confusing use of terms to try to assign the two expressions in question respectively to the two forms of fellowship.

Further, no particular form of fellowship is here definitely asserted or excluded ; every form, perfect and imperfect, that has ever been or that may yet appear, is included. This, and this only, is assumed, that wherever regenerate persons are within reach of each other, some kind of fellowship between them is bound to arise. For if they are in contact, their witness to the faith must in part overlap, and must necessarily involve mutual recognition and a common understanding as to their operation within the common area. What was stated at the beginning of our treatment [1] of the consciousness of grace, namely, that it always proceeds from a common life, was meant exclusively in this far-reaching sense ; but now that very statement finds for the first time its full explanation. For if, when regenerate, we did not find ourselves already within a common life, but had to set out to discover or constitute it, that would mean that just the most decisive of all the works of grace was not based on a life in common.

2. The more closely our proposition stands connected with that just cited (§ 87), the more difficult does it seem to make it harmonize with the dictum that our dogmatic propositions should express only what is identical in primitive Christian piety and in our own. For how did men find themselves to be already within the fellowship, who received Christ in faith as the result of His personal influence ? On this point we remark that a collective need for redemption and expectation of it already existed, which was prepared to recognize the contrast between itself and One who came offering help. Thus the outer fellowship arose simultaneously with the public appearance of Christ. The power to form the inner was in Him alone, until gradually the inner took shape from the outer, first of all in the disciples who constantly accompanied Him. As to the question that may be interjected, whether Christ had in fact any intention of founding such a fellowship, it is clear enough that He could not have exercised any activity whatever of an attractive and therefore redemptive kind, without such a fellowship arising. Hence there is not the least need to prove when and how He actually did found it. The self-organizing faculty recognizably present in every spiritual relation belongs to the natural form assumed by the supernatural in Christ ; and the essence of the resulting organization must be explicable, partly by the influence of Christ on individuals who thus become His instruments, and partly by His peculiar dignity, which is to be manifested in this organization over against the world. The above question, however, is explained by inward experiences seemingly due to the immediate influence of Christ unconditioned by the fellowship ; and, from an opposite point of view, by the need to guard against collisions between different fellowships within the same circle—on which account also men sometimes wish to recognize only civil society, but not religious. On this point what is needful has already been said ; [2] also upon the relation to civil

[1] § 87.   [2] §§ 100 and 105.

society of the individuals who are bound up with Christ.[1]   And as no redeeming work can take effect on individuals without a fellow-ship arising, this fellowship cannot consist in anything else than all the factors belonging to the state of sanctification of all under grace.

3. The Christian self-consciousness expressed in our proposition is the general form, determined by our faith in Christ, taken by our fellow-feeling with human things and circumstances.   This becomes all the clearer if we combine with it the corresponding negative expression.   For if, leaving redemption out of account, the world is, relatively to humanity, the place of original perfection of men and things which yet has become the place of sin and evil ; and if, with the appearance of Christ a new thing has entered the world, the antithesis of the old ; it follows that only that part of the world which is united to the Christian Church is for us the place of attained perfection, or of the good, and—relatively to quiescent self-conscious-ness—the place of blessedness.   This is so, not in virtue of the original perfection of human nature and the natural order, though of course it is thus conditioned, but in virtue solely of the sinless perfection and blessedness which has come in with Christ and communicates itself through Him.   With this goes the converse,[2] that the world, so far as it is outside this fellowship of Christ, is always, in spite of that original perfection, the place of evil and sin.   No one, therefore, can be surprised to find at this point the proposition that salvation or blessedness is in the Church alone, and that, since blessedness cannot enter from without, but can be found within the Church only by being brought into existence there, the Church alone saves.   For the rest, it is self-evident that the antithesis between what is realized in the world by redemption and all the rest of the world is acute in proportion to the complete-ness with which the peculiar dignity of Christ and the full content of redemption is apprehended.   It disappears or loses itself in a vague distinction between better and worse only where the contrast be-tween Christ and sinful man is similarly obliterated or toned down.

4. This, too, affords the best proof that our proposition is simply an utterance of the Christian self-consciousness.   For if the Christian Church were in its essential nature an object of outward perception, that perception might be passed on without involving attachment to the fellowship.   But the fact is that those who do not share our faith in Christ do not recognize the Christian fellowship in its antithesis to the world.   Wherever the feeling of need of redemption

---

[1] § 106, 2.   [2] Gal. 1[4], 1 John 5[19].

is entirely suppressed, the Christian Church is misconstrued all round ; and the two attitudes develop *pari passu*. With the first stirrings of preparatory grace in consciousness, there comes a presentiment of the divine origin of the Christian Church ; and with a living faith in Christ awakens also a belief that the Kingdom of God is actually present in the fellowship of believers. On the other hand, an unalterable hostility to the Christian Church is symptomatic of the highest stage of insusceptibility to redemption ; and this hostility hardly admits even of outward reverence for the person of Christ. But faith in the Christian Church as the Kingdom of God not only implies that it will ever endure in antithesis to the world, but also—the fellowship having grown to such dimensions out of small beginnings, and being inconceivable except as ever at work—contains the hope that the Church will increase and the world opposed to it decrease. For the incarnation of Christ means for human nature in general what regeneration is for the individual. And just as sanctification is the progressive domination of the various functions, coming with time to consist less and less of fragmentary details and more and more to be a whole, with all its parts integrally connected and lending mutual support, so too the fellowship organizes itself here also out of the separate redemptive activities and becomes more and more co-operative and interactive. This organization must increasingly overpower the unorganized mass to which it is opposed.

§ 114. *In a comprehensive summary of what our Christian self-consciousness has to say about the fellowship of believers, we must first treat of the origin of the Church, the way in which it takes shape and disengages itself from the world ; then the way in which the Church maintains itself in antithesis to the world ; and finally the abrogation of this antithesis, or the prospect of the Church's consummation.*

1. These three points certainly do not seem to have the same relation to our Christian self-consciousness. The second is the sphere of everyday experience ; our spiritual life proceeds within the limits of this antithesis. In proportion as we know how to distinguish within ourselves between what appertains to the fellowship of believers and what still appertains to the world, our Christian common feeling will rightly separate, in what happens around us, what belongs to the Church and to the world. This all contributes to our propositions concerning the maintenance of the Church

co-existently with the world. Propositions even with the same content would be inadmissible if drawn from other quarters. As in individuals the distinction between what belongs to sin and to grace is
drawn, not from the outward aspect of the act open to perception,
but from the constitution of the inward motives, so affirmations
concerning the Christian Church can be rightly made only by those
who know its inner life through personal participation in it. The
affirmations of our self-consciousness, however, about the consummation of the Church, if indeed there are any, are certainly
only most unreliable ones ; and as to the origin of the Church only
historical evidence can be accepted, with which we cannot deal here.
To begin then with this last point : the Christian fellowship gradually expands as individuals and masses are incorporated into
association with Christ. The general fact has been established that
the new life of the individual arises out of the common life within
the outer circle of which it lies. And this holds good also of the
new life of the first disciples, when as yet the power of the inner
circle was entirely confined to Christ. The origin of the Christian
Church is thus the same thing as happens daily before our eyes.
On the principle that the redeeming activity must lay hold of everything gradually, it is of no consequence that we should establish a
technical rule for the exact how and why of this expansion. Rather,
since at any one moment the redeeming activity is reaching out
from the community to cover a far larger number than are at that
time actually led to conversion, our starting-point must be a right
grasp of the distinction between the converted and all the rest ; to
have this is to understand the beginnings of the Church. Here
certainly we have a self-consciousness which has to be grasped in
thought, namely, the antithesis which is established in our fellow-
feeling and sympathy between the previous inclusion of all in the
common state of sinfulness, and the new differentiation between
those under grace and others. As regards the consummation of the
Church : if we go by personal experience, all that is given in our
self-consciousness is, we must grant, just growth in sanctification,
without any presentiment that an entire harmony of all our
faculties, and the consummation of the individual life as an instrument of Christ's life in us, will, after the old man has been completely
eradicated, finally emerge. In the same way, if we go by corporate
feeling, the Church only confronts us as something growing out of
the world and gradually, of itself, expelling the world—the presentiment of the consummation being always held up by the indestruct-

ible element of sympathy due to the fact that the old man is always born again with each new individual. Thus the consummation of the Church, even as a presentiment, requires as a condition that the propagation of the race should cease : it therefore founders on the rock of our racial consciousness ; and it looks as if everything put forward as Christian doctrine on this point must derive from some other source than the Christian self-consciousness. In that case it would have no right to a definite place in our exposition, but, resting as it must on an objective consciousness, could, in view of its source, come in only in subordinate wise.[1] Yet two points may still be noted in this reference. For one thing, we are far from being in a position fully to realize as a presentiment the alternative conception of an advance asymptotically approaching the consummation in infinite time, an advance always limited by the appearance of new generations ; nor does this conception supply what is lacking in the presentiment of the imperfect sanctification of our own self at the end of life. And in the second place, even if this presentiment cannot in itself furnish any doctrine in our sense, because it is not an isolable moment of self-consciousness, still the admission of it can yield a proof, as the other form of infinite approximation cannot, that we have rightly appreciated what underlies it and the doctrine of the maintenance of the Church, namely, the essential nature of the Kingdom of God. The proof is that the truth of the exposition holds good even in an attempt to consider the Church in itself apart from its antithesis to the world ; to this extent this attempt is necessary and natural.

2. Between these three main divisions of the subject there is an analogous dissimilarity, not to be overlooked, which may be put thus. In discussing the second we find ourselves entirely, and all but exclusively, within the sphere of the redeeming activity of Christ, for this is the actual boundary of the Kingdom of Christ.[2] Yet if we were to conceive the absolute consummation extensively as well as intensively, the dissimilarity between Him and us would be entirely abrogated, and His lordship would cease.[3] This is an additional confirmation of the view that this is not matter for Christian doctrine in the strictest sense of the word. Especially as in the consummation itself no sense of need can be supposed to persist in self-consciousness, so that the consummation can be

---

[1] Cf. our former treatment of the facts of the resurrection and ascension of Christ.
[2] Cf. § 105.   [3] 1 John 3[2].

regarded as specifically Christian only in so far as it remains the consummation of a common life dependent on Christ. And while presumably in this consummation natural changes would be involved which lie outside the sphere of the kingly dominion of Christ and belong to the divine government of the world, yet about this bodily side of the matter—which would be the point at issue—we have here nothing to say. Hence, take it how we will, we find ourselves here at the limit of Christian doctrine, and can say nothing definite without overstepping it. So too with regard to the emergence of the Christian Church, alike at its beginning and all the way along. For while the power of the Divine Word and of the Love that seeks the salvation of men remains always the same in the great inward act of preaching, the difference in its efficacy rests on different conditions of susceptibility ; and this again depends on the circumstances in which the divine government of the world places different persons. This cannot but seem very natural ; for in the passing of either individuals or masses from the world into the Church the divine government of the world plays a part and necessarily in the form of activity. Hence our sympathetic appreciation of the matter would be very incomplete if it did not accept the difference that arises as resulting from the divine government of the world. At this point, however, we must bring in another element, to supplement a defect in our previous exposition. We formerly considered the activity of the Redeemer and its operation in the soul of the individual apart from the life of the community ; and thus later, in the doctrine of sanctification, it was still possible for us to consider the individual merely as a separate being, acting independently in living fellowship with Christ. Now of course it is by the very same act that the individual is regenerated and that he becomes a spontaneously active member of the Christian Church. But this second aspect of the matter we previously ignored : hence we must now discuss that act anew and independently of our earlier exposition, in view of the fact that it forms the basis of the relation of the individual to the larger whole. And here our attention is at once focused on the most definite thing in our whole self-consciousness, where we always distinguish and combine both things— our independent personality in living fellowship with Christ, and our life as an integral constituent of a whole.

From both points of view the doctrine of the Church, in its continuous existence alongside of the world, is the essential kernel of this whole section. Hence it is appropriate to establish this doctrine first, and then to treat the other two subjects more by the way of appendix. In adopting the order natural to an historical review, we shall attain greater vividness and simplify many problems.

FIRST DIVISION : THE ORIGIN OF THE CHURCH

§ 115. *The Christian Church takes shape through the coming together of regenerate individuals to form a system of mutual inter-action and co-operation.*

1. In the light of the practice of the Protestant Church for the strengthening of its fellowship, whether by the reception of the instructed youth of the community and by mission work, or in the transfer of individual members from other Christian communions, our proposition certainly gives right expression to the prevailing sentiment and practical methods. The practical methods are always determined with reference to regeneration ; in each case, naturally, in accordance with the manner in which this conception is understood ; and thus (though in most cases one cannot as yet be certain on the point) the prevailing assumption is that regenera-tion has come about. At least the freer a community is within its own sphere, the more strictly will it insist that those about whose regeneration there are good reasons for misgiving are not to be received as members. This would not be necessary, and indeed would be inexpedient, if those received were only being introduced into a communion where preparatory grace was at work. Now with regeneration there is always imparted a strong will for the Kingdom of God. It must therefore be a conviction common both to receivers and received, that all exert the same kind of activity ; and since, belonging to the same locality, they have the same sphere of influence, every such act raises the problem afresh of ordering this common activity aright. That at the same time a mutual influence is provided for, is due not only to the fact that in each there remains much of the world, against which the common activity of the rest must be brought to bear ; but also to the fact that, as none credits himself with a complete and perfect apprehension of Christ, each individual regards that of others as complementary to his own ; and so a mutual and reciprocal presentation results. From this everything must be derivable that can be represented as an element in the life of the Church.

2. It seems harder, certainly, to apply all this to the original emergence of the fellowship emanating from Christ. But if we

recur to the fact that already, when the activity of Christ began, there was a fellowship of those who waited for the fulfilment of their Messianic hopes, while we certainly do not assert that this was the Christian Church before Christ, yet it was a religious fellowship ; there was an interchange of kindred impulses of the spirit and community in all things relating thereto. Now when several of its members came to recognize Christ, they felt no reason to dissolve their fellowship. But as it had now gained a relation to Christ which could not but create a mutual influence among them in the sense explained, they came at the same time to exercise a combined influence upon their fellow-members who had not yet attained to the recognition of Christ. These latter thus formed the outer circle, receiving from the first the preparatory operations of grace, in contrast to the inner circle from which these operations proceeded all the more forcibly that they were exactly adapted to the situation. This combined influence, however, remained subordinate and fragmentary as long as a common susceptibility to the influence of Christ was the predominant factor in their association. In this respect we may say that although a number of regenerate persons were there, yet as long as Christ's personal activity lasted, the Church remained unconstituted, merely latent in the association of these individuals with Him.

§ 116. *The origin of the Church becomes clear through the two doctrines of Election and Communication of the Holy Spirit.*

1. Were it not for the connexion already established, it might perhaps seem strange to find these two conceptions thus put side by side, for they do not sound as if they were at all related ; and as regards their meaning, the idea of election does not seem any more closely bound up with the communication of the Holy Spirit than with, say, conversion or justification. Now, however, it cannot surprise us. The first conception has to do with what, as was argued, in the origin of the Church, is matter of the divine government of the world, namely, the fact that those who are to form the Church must be separated out from the world. This, then, is how we view the origin of the Church, when we look backwards to the region from which its members come. The second conception has to do with what, in the individual, is the basis of the continuity of the Church's co-operation and interaction. Now since this constitutes the very essence of the Christian Church, this conception gives the view of the Church's origin which looks forward to

the common life so arising. This common life can attain and keep true vital unity, like that of a coherent or so-called moral personality, only through the identity of that which stirs and strives in each and every individual. Through this principle, therefore, communicated to individuals as elect, the whole life and work of the Church must be explicable.

The two conceptions, however, have this in common, that they do not fit the situation in which the effective power of the new life was not as yet communicated to others, but existed solely in Christ ; except in the sense in which it may be said also of Christ that He was elect, and that He possessed the Holy Spirit. Really, however, this is to assume the antithesis between the outer circle, which is the area of the preparatory operations of grace, and the inner circle from which these operations proceed. For those who are drawn within the first circle by the preaching of the gospel are not usually, in the language of the Bible or of the Church, termed ' elect,' unless it is as a result of the arrangements of the divine government of the world that they are thus differentiated from the rest. They are termed ' called,' and the other term is left for those who through regeneration are brought into the inner circle. Similarly, of this inner circle the Holy Spirit is the bond by means of which the influences exerted by individuals upon those in the outer circle form a unity, and their mutual interaction becomes, as it were, an organic system. As to the ' called,' however, we do not regard the Holy Spirit as having yet been communicated to them, or dwelling in and moving them.

2. Now, as regards the term ' election ' as applied first of all to the individual, the real problem is the same. All men for us are in the state of common sinfulness, in which everything is common guilt. All thus are absolutely equal : none has any advantage in reference to the new life communicated by Christ. All are first drawn within the circle of preparatory grace ; but, for one thing, the differences between them which thus arise are not attributable to themselves ; and for another, there is favour shown already in the fact that some are called and others are not. Hence for this discussion we can take both together, election and the calling that precedes and relates to it. Thus everywhere, in the light of the partial success and partial failure of preaching, we can see a preference of some to others introduced by the divine government of the world without any ground for it in the persons themselves ; and this can be followed out, in large things and small, not only

in this sphere but also in others, which, however, lie beyond the scope of our present subject. If we conceive the incarnation of Christ as the beginning of the regenerat'on of the whole human race, then the erection of a permanent pla. for the preaching of the Gospel amongst a people through the instrumentality of the firstfruits from its own midst is the beginning of that people's regeneration. Such a nation, then, has an advantage over those among whom the voice of preaching has had no effect. But we cannot ascribe this to a difference in merit in nations any more than in individuals. In the case of individuals the same thing happens, whether they have come in from outside or have been born within the outer circle of the fellowship. Now we certainly ascribe this to a divine ordinance, as the Redeemer Himself did ; [1] it is equally our part to acquiesce in it, for otherwise we should be (and that, too, in our moral consciousness) in contradiction to our God-consciousness. But we have no reason for doing so except that we rest in the will of God ; about which all that we can say is, that it was not determined by the merits of anyone, so that the issue cannot be regarded in the one event as reward or in the other as punishment. For our feelings, as in the conception of election, everything else remains wholly undefined.

3. After what has been said, the expression ' Holy Spirit ' must be understood to mean the vital unity of the Christian fellowship as a moral personality ; and this, since everything strictly legal has already been excluded, we might denote by the phrase, its *common spirit*. Accordingly, it should not really be necessary again to give the explicit assurance that by the phrase we mean to describe exactly what even in Scripture is called the Holy Spirit and the Spirit of God and the Spirit of Christ, and in our Church doctrine is also presented as the third Person in the Godhead. That we have not here to deal with this last point is at once evident from our arrangement of this whole treatise.

But in the Christian Church, as individual influences no longer proceed directly from Christ, something divine must exist. This something we call accordingly the Being of God in it, and it is this which continues within the Church the communication of the perfection and blessedness of Christ. All this, already indicated in a preliminary way, will be more precisely expounded later. Already it is apparent that the communication of the sinless perfection and blessedness which, as an absolute and continuous willing

[1] John 6⁴⁴.

of the Kingdom of God, is the innermost impulse of the individual, must also be the common spirit of the whole, or there could be no common spirit at all.   Were there any other than this, that impulse would be subordinate to it and thus to what is less perfect than itself ; in every corporate life all that is personal must be subordinated to the common spirit.   On the other hand, if there were no common spirit, the Christian Church would be no true common or corporate life ; yet this is what it has professed to be from the beginning as regards the divine Spirit dwelling in it, and this is how it has been accepted in the self-consciousness of every effective member.   This will for the Kingdom of God is the vital unity of the whole, and its common spirit in each individual ; in virtue of its inwardness, it is in the whole an absolutely powerful God-consciousness, and thus the being of God therein, but conditioned by the being of God in Christ.

First Doctrine : Election

§ 117. *In accordance with the laws of the divine government of the world, so long as the human race continues on earth, all those living at any one time can never be uniformly taken up into the kingdom of God founded by Christ.*

1. By ' uniformly ' here is not meant an equality in the strength of faith or in the degree in which all the natural powers are put at the disposal of the common will : for in that sense the proposition would be quite obvious ; it would occur to no one to desiderate such an equality.   The absence of uniformity refers to the definite distinction between the inner and outer circles of the Christian fellowship.   Now all other fellowships of faith are destined to pass into the Christian fellowship ; and if we assume that those born within the fellowship in due time come under the influence of preparatory grace, a time can be imagined when all whose consciousness has reached the necessary point of development will belong to that outer circle.   But in this there is not involved any share in the perfection and blessedness of Christ.   Hence these are definitely distinguished from the spontaneously active members of the fellowship.   This tallies exactly with the distinction already drawn between calling and election.   Two points are involved here, both to be regarded (the one more definitely, the other also in some measure) as laws of the divine government of the world.   One such law obviously is, that what proceeds from a single point spreads only gradually over the whole area.   Less obvious perhaps

is this, that the state of grace cannot be inborn, but that even
Christian children at birth essentially resemble all other sons of
Adam.   Any difference would be an exception not explicable by
the fundamental fact of Christianity : it would be a new, independent
miracle ; and, besides, it would shatter the conception of race.

2. Even suppose that Christ, when He made a beginning of
preaching the Kingdom of God with a reference to His own Person,
had everywhere found an equal feeling of need for redemption ;
yet in one respect, relatively to His Person, some would have been
prepared by the Baptist, others not ; and in another respect,
relatively to His interpretation of the Kingdom of God, some were
specially wedded to the existing idea, and thus disposed to reject
His, while others were not.   Thus He could not but exert His
influence with the most varied degrees of effectiveness : indeed,
though always within definite limits,[1] He at times moved about
and widened the circle of His preaching, and at other times tarried
in one place to consolidate His work.   Nay, even where He was
asked to depart,[2] that fact must have worked to the unmerited
disadvantages of many who would otherwise have come naturally
to join Him.   But all this is rooted in the divine government of
the world.   And we find the same absence of uniformity in connexion
with the subsequent preaching of apostolic times and on to the
present day.   For the tendency to enlarge the Church outwardly—
a tendency which dwells in the whole body but especially appears
in individuals—is in itself quite uniform, proceeding as it does from
the equality of all in the state of sinfulness ; but in practice it is
subordinated, partly to the social circumstances that must offer
a point of attachment, partly to that secret attraction and repulsion [3]
which equally with these circumstances are subject to the divine
government of the world.   It could not be otherwise if the supernatural in Christ is to become natural, and the Church to take
shape as a natural historical phenomenon.

3. If we consider the propagation of the Church from one
generation to another, here too we find that the regeneration of
individuals is bound up with the natural circumstance (also rooted
in the divine government of the world) that every two successive
generations overlap.   A similar absence of uniformity thus arises,
as each person sooner or later arrives within this inner circle among
different and more or less suitable surroundings and influences.
Thus two things always happen.   Among those living within the

[1] Matt. 15[24].   [2] Matt. 8[34].   [3] Acts 16[6-10].

circle of the Church there are in every period many who do not yet belong to it ; and of these it will be possible to say that they might already have been members of the Church if their path in life had been otherwise guided. Of course in any given nation a long series of generations, living on the whole in the state of sanctification, has an influence on those that follow, as natural tendencies to passion are mitigated ; yet this never is more than an improved form of general sinfulness, and at some point self-knowledge and penitence must enter. Yet we grant that if an early and corresponding recognition of the Redeemer also ensues, a time can be imagined in which (although the birth of body and of spirit never coincide in time, and nature and grace never cease to be distinguishable) the development of living faith is as nearly as possible coincident with the first development of moral ideas and sentiments. Such a time is the nearest possible approximation to the human development of Christ. In such a situation, each will attain far earlier to the possession and enjoyment of his appropriate share in the higher life. Yet even so differences will remain, such that some will as yet have failed to attain to enjoyment though their companions of the same age have long possessed it.

4. While we denote this ordinance by the phrase ' divine election,' because we hold firmly that its final ground lies in the divine good-pleasure, this does not hinder us from inquiring by what this divine good-pleasure is determined. Especially as we are not in a position to say that God makes no distinctions, but that some human wills place hindrances in the way ; for at first the will itself develops gradually, not without being influenced by external relations, until it reaches a greater or smaller degree of excitability. Paul long ago broke ground in this inquiry,[1] and tried to formulate the law by which the apostolic Church to begin with filled up with those who previously were heathen, while the great majority of the Jewish people remained outside. The demand for such an investigation has become still more pressing since whole peoples have accepted Christianity, of whom a considerable proportion at least attained regeneration, while on the other hand many a member of nations long Christian remained provisionally excluded from that inner circle. There is besides the fact that the end of life is appointed so differently for different people. To many born in the Christian Church who have already experienced many operations of preparatory grace, it comes before these im-

[1] Rom. 10 and 11.

pressions can be gathered up and intensified in regeneration so as to constitute the beginning of a spiritual life. Many are called away, their length of life divinely fixed, from places where the gospel has only just begun to be heard. Thus obviously it is the divine government of the world which appoints that many—whether many or few really make no difference, since their attitude to the proffer of divine grace is in any case the same—die unregenerate simply because the course of their life is run. We cannot say, then, that God has definitely not willed this ; for it has its basis in the relation between the order of nature dependent on Him and His decree of redemption through Christ, which to us is equally matter of inward certainty. We cannot therefore resist the conclusion that if God had not willed this definitely and unconditionally, He would either have established a different order of nature for human life, or a different way of salvation for the human spirit. His ordinance being of such a nature, we are of course called upon to accept even this divine will as consciously as possible and without inward dissent.

§ 118. *While Christian sympathy is not disquieted by the earlier and later adoption of one and another individual into the fellowship of redemption, yet on the other hand there does remain an insoluble discord if, on the assumption of survival after death, we are to think of a part of the human race as entirely excluded from this fellowship.*[1]

1. Regarding ourselves as members of the Church over against the world, with these two elements in our self-consciousness, the consciousness of sin and the consciousness of grace, we find that in virtue of the latter, in which we are given perfect certainty of the divine decree for our blessedness, we stand opposed to all those in whom this consciousness has not yet developed. On the other hand, in virtue of the consciousness of sin we are on exactly the same footing as they ; for the consciousness of forgiveness belongs to the other element, and yet keeps ever present to our minds that original something which belongs to the consciousness of a nature in which all share. If therefore that equal natural incapacity out of which, in everyone, the consciousness of the need for redemption may spring, is in one case reinforced, but in another left to itself, in one case absorbed into the revelation of the divine decree

---

[1] Once for all in connexion with this doctrine I refer the reader to my treatise on ' Election.'

of pardon, but in another not so absorbed—this non-uniformity within the same human race (no section of which is definitely distinguished from any other in respect of the divine activity of Christ) is of such a kind that to accept it we must either again reduce our God-consciousness to a mere idiosyncrasy, or else attach much less value to the difference between those blessed by grace and others, almost making it a merely accidental more or less. Otherwise the blessedness springing from the consciousness of grace would of necessity be swallowed up in the sympathetic feeling of unblessedness that accompanies humiliation.

All this takes on a quite different aspect as soon as we venture to hold that at each particular point this antithesis is merely a vanishing one, so that everyone still outside this fellowship will some time or another be laid hold of by the divine operations of grace and brought within it. In that case there is no longer a cleavage in our race-consciousness ; the merely gradual passage of individuals into the full enjoyment of redemption is for our race-consciousness just what the gradual progress of sanctification is for our personal self-consciousness, namely, the natural form necessarily taken by the divine activity as it works itself out historically and, as we have seen, the inevitable condition of all activity in time of the Word made flesh.

Any possible objection to this is met by the two following considerations. The *first* is an application we make of the proposition stated above, namely, that the incarnation of Christ is analogous to the regeneration of the whole race considered as a unity. No one can say that it would have been better for the whole race if Christ had been born sooner, and the new spiritual common life sooner begun. It would certainly have been better had it been possible for this new life to emerge in the same purity and power at an earlier date. But when we read that ' when the fulness of the time was come ' Christ was born,[1] this means that the divine fore-ordination concerning the whole human race and the special determination of the point in time when the Redeemer should be manifested are so much a single indivisible revelation of divine omnipotence that the spiritual life conditioned by this determination of time is certainly also the absolutely greatest, and gives expression to the entire idea of the essential nature of humanity. Now the same thing can be said of the individual. Each man, when his time is fully come, is regenerated ; and then his new life,

[1] Gal. 4⁴.

conditioned by this fixation of time, is, however late its appearance, an absolute maximum, and fully expresses the entire idea
of his personality, dependent as this is on its position within the
race as a whole.   In harmony with this belief, therefore, we cannot
imagine, even of an individual, that it would have been better for
him to have been regenerated earlier.   Nor is there any reason to
fear that this will lead to slackness in witnessing to Christ, or under-
mine training and teaching, on the ground that it is useless to press
the gospel on people before their time is come.   This has been
clearly shown by Augustine,[1] and no such application of the doctrine
will readily be made seriously by anyone who is truly being sanctified, that is to say, it will not be entertained by anyone who is
capable of bearing witness or taking part in teaching and training.
For one thing, such a person is moved by an inner impulse [2] irrespectively of any distinct result he may anticipate ; and for another,
he is well aware that the gracious operations of the Spirit that issue
from every regenerate person are a *sine qua non* of the regeneration
of each when his time is fully come.

The *second* consideration is an application of the truth that in
regeneration each person becomes a new creature.   If that is so,
sympathetic concern about a regeneration that occurred too late is
meaningless, for there is nothing originally present to think about ;
just as it would be a waste of pity, on the assumption of a creation
of the world in time, to sigh that it was not created sooner.   And
even if someone inclined to say that for him the earlier period is not
a void but a horror, yet this horror vanishes in the certainty of the
forgiveness of sins just as completely whether that period was long
or short.   And although such a regret may occasionally be felt on
the ground that the new life cannot now endure so long as if it had
developed sooner, this too is a mere delusion, revealing a lack of
acquaintance with the nature of the new life.   For that life is in
itself eternal, and gains no increment by the duration of time.   No
one who is maturely sanctified has such feelings ; they belong to a
morbid condition.   Only beginners can be troubled by such after-
pains, and when peace comes they die away of themselves ; so that
there is no reason why we should take account of them in the
sphere of doctrine.   Rather must the earliest to be regenerated and
the latest each count himself of the same worth as the other, even
though in the one case it happened in the morning of childhood,
and in the other only after a long course of experience.   For while

---

[1] Throughout in his *De correptione et gratia*.   [2] 2 Cor. 5[14. 10].

the one represents a more exact model of the original union of the Divine with human personality, the other gives a better picture of the ultimate penetration of the entire human nature by the redeeming power of Christ, involving as that power does the total effective influence of all those previously regenerated. Every appearance of difference must more and more vanish as a common feeling and common spirit gets the upper hand in both, leaving each to appropriate all that is the other's. There is no ground to fear that this will occasion any indifference towards the operations of preparatory grace, or lead men to put off repentance and conversion to the indefinite future. Anyone desiring to take this course is not putting off conversion because of anything in Christian doctrine, but because even yet he wants to have a share in the common life of sin more than in the Kingdom of God. To withhold this doctrine from such a man is no help to him ; we must find what will awaken his longing for the Kingdom of God.

Summing up, we may conclude that if only everyone who has lagged behind us is some time or another taken up into living fellowship with Christ, our sympathetic concern can accept the fact with perfect satisfaction without any contradiction arising between it and our God-consciousness.

2. It is self-evident, however, that these considerations are no longer applicable, once we come to think of a portion of our race as destined to be entirely shut out from this fellowship and the higher state dependent thereon. Nor can the idea be admitted (here we are strictly in accord with all that we have just been saying) that we may make a distinction according as we do or do not assume a future life. For if this life as such is eternal, the possession and the deprivation of it cannot be thrown into greater contrast by raising the question of its endless or insignificant duration, if it be the case that one does attain the blessedness in which alone life's value lies, and another does not. Assuming this for the moment, the discord can be resolved only in one of the two following ways. We may justify the concurrent existence of such equality and inequality between ourselves and others and try to trace it back to a law ; and this would show the opposition indicated to be an illusion. Or we may explain as an illusion one of the two—either the original equality, or the inequality due to the divine assignment.

As regards the first point, two arguments may be tried. To begin with, if equality is the original appointed plan for human nature, but inequality of the kind noted just as much results from the plan, contradiction between the two can only be stated in the form of some censure of the appointed plan ; which is meaningless, for unless we were men we should not be at all.   But the inequality that first arises through the intervention of Christ cannot have its seat in the human nature underlying the common life of sinfulness, unless, contrary to our assumptions, we go back to Pelagian principles, and admit either powers of attraction in one class of people or powers of repulsion in the other.   And apart from this, we should still be thrown back upon an inequality in the distribution of endowments that can have its basis only in the divine good-pleasure.   Conversely, if the equality is held to have the same basis as the inequality, namely, the divine plan of salvation, this means that in respect of redemption God has put all men under sin, although only for some does redemption accrue.   In that case, the reception of the one and the exclusion of the other has its ground in such divine arbitrariness, that we must rightly describe the ordinance as sheer caprice.   And even if the concurrent existence of the equality and inequality can be thus made conceivable, yet those who, to our advantage, are rejected, are and inevitably remain objects of sympathy ; and the more our race-consciousness equals our personal consciousness, this sympathy extinguishes the blessedness belonging to the latter, for it is a fellow-feeling with misery. An escape from this difficulty and a faultless solution of it have been thought to lie in the hypothesis that the plan of salvation, which is the ground both of the equality of incapacity and the inequality of help received, is intended to bring home to one class the divine mercy and to the other the divine justice,[1] so that within the human race there might be given a complete divine manifestation in both respects : justice toward the lost and mercy toward the saved. Against this, however, it may be pointed out that the solution does not cover the special case in which divine justice also would be completely manifested if all that is possible through redemption were actually realized ; for then it would show itself compensatory toward Christ, but punitive toward all as long as they belonged to the common life of sinfulness.   We cannot, however, concede in general that the revelation of divine attributes is pieced-out or

---

[1] *Conf. Gallic.* xii. : Credimus ex hac corruptione . . . deum alios quidem eripere, quos . . . in Jesu Christo elegit : alios vero in ea corruptione et damnatione relinquere, in quibus iustitiam suam demonstret, sicut in aliis divitias misericordiae suae declaret.—*Conf. Belg.* xvi. : Credimus . . . deum se . . . demonstrasse . . . misericordem et iustum. Misericordem quidem eos . . . servando, quos . . . elegit . . . iustum vero reliquos in . . . perditione . . . relinquendo.

partial ; for then they would be limited, and God would be an unlimited Being with limited attributes. Justice and mercy must not
exclude one another. Mercy in the case of the same people must
show itself as justice. And in thought this is incompatible with
the permanent exclusion of some from the communicated blessedness of Christ.

Thus all that remains is the second line of thought, namely, that
one of the two, either the equality or the inequality of the two
sections of mankind, should be explained as an illusion. But the
inequality between those taken up into living fellowship with Christ
and those excluded from it cannot possibly be regarded as an illusion
without sacrificing the essential content of our Christian consciousness. It is otherwise with regard to the equality which we find in
the consciousness of sin. This would be an illusion if there were
really an original inequality in men, that is, if from the very beginning
there were a cleavage in humanity. For once we realize this, the
contradiction vanishes, those originally not on the same footing as
ourselves not being possible objects of our sympathy, and the unity
of human nature as hitherto understood being a delusion. But if
it is then supposed that only in the one class and not in the other
is there a sensitiveness and susceptibility for divine grace, or that
only in the one class and not in the other is there an invincible
opposition to divine grace, we land in assumptions leading to
Manicheanism which are just as much opposed to our interpretation
as the Pelagian assumptions above referred to. Indeed, redemption
itself then takes on a quite different form. For Christ would then
really have come only to develop and bring to light an already
existing disparity ; His real function becomes that of judge, and
what may be called redemption is merely the form of one side of
this function. There is thus no way of resolving this discord if on
the ground of our Christian consciousness we must accept the fact
that part of our race is utterly excluded. If our proposition indicates that the discord would be greater on the assumption prevailing
throughout the Christian Church of personal survival after death
than if we could adopt the opposite view, the reason is simply this.
In the present life, while we do recognize the state of grace as a
communication of the perfection and blessedness of Christ, it is this
merely in innermost principle : for if, in anyone under grace, his
total self-consciousness in time be considered, it is always found to
include also a consciousness of sin. The inequality is therefore not
present for others, because in the only thing that is open to their

observation, namely, the temporal consciousness, they recognize merely a distinction of less and more, and of this they think less, the less they have been captured by the operations of preparatory grace.   On the other hand, when we take the life beyond into account, we have then to conceive of a complete development of blessedness and woe, which means that the antithesis is stretched to its utmost ; and the more even now we are pre-occupied with the anticipation of the future life the deeper must our sympathy be with a future of woe, and therefore the harsher the discord.

3. There is a certain affinity between the thought of this last paragraph and two other attempts to solve the problem.   One, while admitting the survival of those who attain to the communica-tion of Christ's blessedness, holds that the excluded perish utterly at death, so that they are only to be considered as physically like children who die ere it is theirs to enjoy the light of day.   This indeed lessens the inequality, for a brief unhappiness offers a smaller contrast than an endless woe.   But apart from the point that this makes redemption primarily the cause of immortality, thus attri-buting to it a physical effect foreign to its nature and definition (since otherwise here too we should have a fundamental cleavage in human nature), still there remains the particularizing character of a redemption which can only secure for some both blessedness and immortality, but not for all.   The other attempt seeks to lessen the inequality on a different side, conceding that after the present life even the unregenerate may attain, by a faithful use of the natural light that was given them, to a certain perfection and happiness, if only a subordinate degree.   They would only be excluded from a higher stage.[1]   But in that case one cannot see why they should not stay, or receive a place, within the sphere of preparatory grace, and why this grace should not sooner or later reach its goal.   Other-wise redemption remains particularized in this case also, and we are once more confronted (in a new form) by a divine caprice that makes perfect harmony impossible.

In the light of these explanations, the following theorems of Church doctrine have now to be more closely defined and reviewed.

[1] Cf. Reinhard, *Dogmatik*, § 116, 3.

First Theorem : Predestination

§ 119. *The election of those who are justified is a divine predestination to salvation in Christ.*

Conf. Saxon., Twest., p. 157 : Utrumque certissimum sit agentem poenitentiam propter filium Dei gratis fide accipere remissionem peccatorum et iustificationem et hunc esse haeredem vitae aeternae.—*Ibid.*, p. 162 : Vult deus intelligi, genus humanum a deo conditum esse . . . non ad aeternum exitium, sed ut colligat sibi in genere humano ecclesiam, cui in omni aeternitate communicet suam sapientiam bonitatem et laetitiam.—*Expos. simpl.* x. : Deus ab aeterno praedestinavit vel elegit libere . . . sanctos quos vult salvos facere in Christo . . . Ergo non sine medio, sed in Christo . . . nos elegit deus, ut qui jam sunt in Christo insiti per fidem, illi ipsi etiam sint electi, reprobi vero qui sunt extra Christum.—*Conf. Angl.* xvii. : Praedestinatio ad vitam est aeternum dei propositum, quo . . . constanter decrevit, eos quos in Christo elegit . . . per Christum ad aeternam salutem adducere.—*Sol. decl.* xi. : Praedestinatio pertinet tantum ad filios dei, qui ad aeternam vitam consequendam electi et ordinati sunt.—*Conf. March.* : '. . . that God the Almighty . . . has chosen and ordained to eternal life all who thus steadfastly believe on Christ. . . . Thus too has God according to His strict justice from eternity passed over all who do not believe in Christ, and prepared for them the eternal fire of hell.'

1. Let us consider the self-consciousness we possess as regenerate persons in this aspect. From the very beginning of our progress in sanctification, it is one with our feeling of absolute dependence, and is bound up with that feeling not only in so far as we are conscious of our activity in the Kingdom of God as an activity divinely produced by means of Christ's mission, but also in so far as the course of each man's progress is one with the position assigned him in the general context of human relationships. The natural expression for this fact is to say that the ordinance according to which redemption realizes itself in each life is one and the same thing with the carrying out of the divine government of the world in respect of that person. This holds not only for the period subsequent to regeneration, but also for the previous period spent under the influences of preparatory grace (which equally belongs to the realization of his redemption), and therefore also to the moment of regeneration which binds these two periods together. The self-consciousness that thus expresses itself is, however, not a personal and merely individual consciousness, but the common feeling of all who find themselves within the circle of Christ's influence. It is therefore correctly extended to all who may be approaching the point of being drawn into this circle. If then the very same thing holds good of them at the moment of their regeneration, it follows

that the individual's being drawn, each in his turn, into the fellowship of Christ is simply the result of the fact that the justifying
divine activity is in manifestation determined by, and forms part
of, the general government of the world.   It would be contrary to
this if anyone were to assert that his conversion and sanctification
would have taken place in the same way and at the same time, even
if his course in life had lain in a quite different environment.   How
our proposition is in harmony with the consciousness of freedom
has already been shown,[1] and in that inference it might also have
been stated thus : that the manner and the time of each individual's regeneration is determined by what is peculiar to his own
inner life, that is, his freedom, and by his relations to the natural
and historical development of justifying divine grace, that is, his
place in the world.   Primarily, then, the kingdom of grace or of
the Son is absolutely one in origin with the kingdom of omniscient
omnipotence, or of the Father : [2] and since the whole government
of the world is, like the world itself, eternal in God, nothing happens
in the kingdom of grace without divine fore-ordination.   This
therefore is given from the start in and through the self-consciousness of those under grace : and whether they choose to say that
their state is a work of divine grace in Christ, or that it is a consequence of divine fore-ordination, the one statement in thought
implies the other.

2. But as regards those we find outside the fellowship of Christ
—they cannot so affect us as to give us reasonable cause to make
any statement about them in this connexion.   We are indeed
aware that the preaching of Christ which continually sounds forth
from the Church is a living and not unfruitful influence : we see
the operations of preparatory grace thus beginning in individuals :
we see these individuals going on to become members of the Church
whose advancing sanctification leaves no doubt as to their justification ; thus in their case also the divine fore-ordination is revealed.
But about those in whom these operations have not appeared we
have no ground for anything more than this negative statement,
describing simply their relations, up to that point, to the Kingdom
of God and the operations of grace issuing therefrom.[3]   As regards
divine fore-ordination, this involves only what has been already

[1] § 4, § 46, § 49.
[2] *Sol. decl.* xi. : Pater enim trahit hominem virtute spiritus sui juxta
ordinem a se decretum et institutum.
[3] So in Acts 2[41] and 13[48] it is certainly not meant that of those who did not
then believe, none could possibly become believers at some later time.

explained,[1] namely, that there are always some in whom as yet it
has not attained its aim—that is, the initiation of blessedness in
Christ.   But by this path we can never arrive at the idea that for
them, or some of them, there is a fore-ordination of an opposite
kind.   That ' many are called and few are chosen '[2] holds true
at every particular turn in the preaching of the Kingdom of God,
and at every time, which means at the present time ; and so one
has always a right to say that the majority are *not yet* to be regarded
as chosen—not, that is to say, at the present time.   For naturally
at any particular moment the majority are being held in reserve
for some later moment ; this is in accordance with the order of the
divine decree, since in every process of development in time there
is necessarily a successiveness even of what is originally simultaneous.   Only in this limited sense, therefore—that is, only at each
point where we can make a comparison between those laid hold of
by sanctification and those not yet laid hold of—ought we to say
that God omits or passes over some, and that He rejects those He
passes over, and hence that election always and only appears with
reprobation as its foil.[3]   From the position we take, the term ' pass
over ' is the most fitting ; it merely negatives a definite act, not as
if those passed over were outside all divine activity and all divine
decree, but this activity (by reason of the total divine order) takes
shape so entirely in remote inner and outer preparations that they
appear to us to be passed over.   Those not yet included are for us
just this undefined element.   Not possessing spiritual personality,
they are sunk in the mass of the sinful common life, and as long as
in their case the divine fore-ordination does not come to light, they
are just where the whole Church was to begin with.   On this
account we can never cease to regard them as objects of the same
divine activity that gathered the Church together, and as embraced
along with us all under the same divine fore-ordination.   And
since we have denied the possibility of any relapse from fellowship
with Christ into the common life of sin, whereby that fellowship
were wholly abjured, and have declared this an illusion, it follows
that no divine fore-ordination can be admitted as a result of
which the individual would be lost to fellowship with Christ.
Thus we may reasonably persist in holding this single divine

---

[1] Cf. § 117.   [2] Matt. 22[14].

[3] . . . quando ipsa electio, nisi reprobationi opposita, non staret (Calv.,
Instit. III. xxiii. 1).   Only he does not take it in our limited sense, but rather
says roundly that this limitation, for which the reason is given above, is
brought in *inscite nimis et pueriliter*.

fore-ordination to blessedness, by which the origin of the Church is ordered.

3. It is therefore only as it were in an appendix, not here strictly relevant, that we can deal with the other idea of there being a two-fold fore-ordination—on the one hand to blessedness, on the other to damnation.[1] The only point of attachment for it in the foregoing discussion is the possibility of death intervening in some individual case before fore-ordination has fulfilled itself. Suppose an individual in whom noteworthy influences of preparatory grace are to be seen, but about whom it may be equally certain that he is not yet in the state of sanctification ; then it is very natural to think that it is in virtue of a divine ordinance that he did not attain to fellowship with Christ and the enjoyment of blessedness. If, however, we proceed on the definite assumption that all belonging to the human race are eventually taken up into living fellowship with Christ, there is nothing for it but this single divine fore-ordination. We infer from it that for such an one this fore-ordination has not been fulfilled during his lifetime, but not by any means that a different fore-ordination is being fulfilled by his death ; rather, the state in which he dies is only an intermediate state. Such is the faith in Christ which ascribes to Him a claim and power over the whole human race, without at the same time needing to admit any blind divine preference, and in which there is encountered no contradiction between the end in view in the divine plan of salvation and the result accomplished by the divine government of the world. But as soon as people proceed on the opposite assumption (as is obviously done in our Confessions),[2] namely, that death is the end of the divine gracious working, the proposition given above ceases to be a fitting statement ; and, if everything is to be neat and logical, we must admit a fore-ordination by which some are predestined to damnation, as others to blessedness. If, however, even on this assumption, it is still urged that the fore-ordination only holds of those who are saved, the others being simply passed over or left where they are, we must reply that, if the only conceivable meaning of fore-ordination is a divine decree that

---

[1] Calv., *Institt.* III. xxi. 5 : Praedestinationem qua deus alios in spem vitae adoptat, alios adiudicat aeternae morti, nemo . . . simpliciter negare audet.—Non enim pari conditione creantur omnes, sed aliis vita aeterna aliis damnatio aeterna praeordinatur. Itaque prout in alterutrum finem quisque conditus est, ita vel ad vitam vel ad mortem praedestinatum dicimus.

[2] So, too, Melanchthon, *loc. d. praed.*, when he says : Deus volens non perire totum genus humanum *semper* propter filium . . . vocat . . . et recipit assentientes, means by this only the time ante novissimum diem.

conducts man to his very end,[1] this is an impossible view at least without forced artificiality. Similarly when, identifying fore-ordination with election, some deny that there is any fore-ordination in respect of the wicked, but merely foreknowledge [2]—as if a foreknown passing-over were not also a fore-ordination. For if it be asserted that the individual persons elected are fore-ordained,[3] it follows, if the rest are merely covered by foreknowledge, that in respect of them there is no divine will at all. And even if it be ever so strongly argued that electing fore-ordination is not to be considered as something wholly abstract, but as taking place in Christ, it none the less follows, if in Christ some cannot be elect but merely passed over, that the universality of redemption must be limited in proportion. To sum up, the only possible conclusion is that if—on the presupposition that for those who die outside fellowship with Christ there is no further possibility of entrance into it—it is yet desired to assert that the excluded are simply passed over, they must then be regarded as not having any exist-ence at all. Now this is quite right if the whole proposition be taken as dealing with the sphere of the new creation, for in that sphere the excluded persons are not to be found. But then on that view even the elect are not there to begin with, but only after each comes to be in his own time and according to his own fore-ordina-tion ; and the expression ' fore-ordination ' cannot then be applied to real individuals. Indeed, the proposition would have to run as follows. *There is a single divine fore-ordination, according to which the totality of the new creation is called into being out of the general mass of the human race.*[4] In itself this formula is equally adapted to all assumptions—to that according to which the non-elect perish at death, to our own, and to that with which we are now dealing. All that our assumption adds to it is this, that the totality of the new creation is equal to the general mass ; what the first adds is that the general mass eventually becomes equal to the totality of

[1] Praedestinationem vocamus aeternum dei decretum, quo apud se constitutum habuit quid de *unoquoque* homine fieri vellet (Calv., *Institt.* III. xxiii. 5.

[2] *Sol. decl.* xi. : Aeterna vero electio seu praedestinatio dei ad salutem non simul ad bonos et ad malos pertinet,—and all that follows.

[3] *Sol. decl.* xi. : Et quidem deus illo suo consilio non tantum in genere salutem suorum procuravit, verum etiam omnes et singulas personas electorum . . . ad salutem elegit.

[4] At this point the Augustinian formula already cited is entirely apposite : Sola gratia redemtos discernit a perditis, quos in unam perditionis concreverat massam ab origine ducta causa communis (*Enchir.* xxix.).' To suit our pur-pose, we have to alter this only slightly, as follows : Praedestinatio discernit redemtos a communi perditionis massa.

the new creation ; the last, on the other hand, lets the general mass remain the more extensive.   But in harmony with this one must also say of the redeeming power of Christ that it suffices to save from common ruin the totality of the new creation contained in the human race.   And a composite formula is always unsound which gives foreknowledge a wider compass than fore-ordination, for no such disparity can exist.   God always predetermines the condition just as He foresees that which is conditioned ; and it follows that if He foresees what is conditioned, namely, the lostness of men, and (speaking very humanly) does not alter what conditions it, namely, the particular constitution of the individual in its relation to his position in the course of the spread of the gospel, then He has also fore-ordained what is conditioned.   If the one conception be applied to individuals of both sections of mankind, so must the other.   In one section individuals are both foreknown and fore-ordained as elements of the mass out of which the children of the Kingdom are to be formed.   In the other they are foreknown and fore-ordained as the new creatures that are to be formed out of the mass.   Hence the formula suggested as a way out of the difficulty would still deviate from the Confessions of both divisions of the Protestant Church.   For, as both definitely agree in excluding one section of the human race, so they agree also in referring the expression ' fore-ordination ' to the individual in his whole actuality ; and if the matter is to end there, the logicality of Calvin's formula incontestably ought to be preferred.   The assumption on which it rests has certainly become more and more generally accepted in the Church, but whether it is a necessary or optional assumption is a point to be discussed only when we come to treat of the consummation of the Church, and not here, where we are dealing with its origin.

SECOND THEOREM : THE GROUNDS OF ELECTION

§ 120. *Election, viewed as influencing the divine government of the world, is grounded in the faith of the elect, foreseen by God : viewed as rooted in the divine government of the world, it is solely determined by the divine good-pleasure.*

Canon. Dordr., Art. ix. : Eadem haec electio facta est non ex praevisa fide.—Art. x. : Causa vero huius gratuitae electionis est solum Dei beneplacitum.—*Conf. March.* : ' That God . . . purely of grace . . . has ordained to eternal life and elected all who thus steadfastly believe in Christ, His own know and understand right well.'   Note that (thanks to Prince

Sigismund) it is repudiated as Pelagian that God has elected some, simply on account of the faith He foresaw.—*Colloq. Lips.*, p. 404 (Brandb. and Hess.) : 'That God . . . in Jesus Christ . . . has elected some whom He . . . leads to faith in Christ and renews and preserves in the same to the end.'—(Kursax) : 'That God had chosen from eternity those whom He saw . . . would believe in Christ and continue in faith to their end . . . and that He found no cause or occasion for this choice in the elect themselves.'

1. The antithesis set up here relatively to election applies quite generally to all free actions. Every such action contributes something to the further course of the divine government of the world ; for everything within range of it would be more or less different if *it* were different. At the same time every act is also in its determined place in time and space the result of the divine government of the world in its course up to that point. The consideration of election from this point of view, however, rests on the fact that the Kingdom of God and the divine procedure in its harvesting and propagation is represented as a special divine activity by itself, apart from the divine government of the world in general, and that then (all men on account of sin being originally equal in respect of redemption) the question arises why one is chosen and not another. We have the same title and reason to raise this question, whether the view that all are elect is adopted or not ; though in the first case a more exact expression would be : ' Why is one already, and another not yet regenerated ? ' Now looking back upon what was formerly said about the supernatural becoming natural, this can only be decided in the light of nature ; and all we can say is that if any one is regenerated, it can be then inferred that in his case the preaching of the gospel at its maximum of power and the maximum of his susceptibility must have coincided in time. But the answer gives no satisfaction, for this again depends on conditions that are under divine control. And if at this point the question is again raised why circumstances were so controlled that one was regenerated and another not, we must either seek the ground for the determination absolutely at the beginning, before there was anything at all, which means holding firmly to belief in a divine good-pleasure ; or else we must seek it at the end, in the final result, which means that we hold firmly to a divine foreknowledge. Obviously, however, these two are not separable. For there is no foreknowledge in God that is not connected with a divine good-pleasure ;[1] and just as little is there a good-pleasure in any particular thing apart from its entire con-

[1] Cf. § 55, 1.

text, which in the case of everything temporal necessarily includes foreknowledge. In the credal passages quoted, however, and in other similar passages, there is on this point a remarkable hesitation. Good-pleasure and foreknowledge are contrasted; yet what has been excluded is almost always brought in again by way of some cautious formula. The form of our proposition is meant to do away with this uncertainty and confusion.

2. If the moments of regeneration are chiefly to be regarded as extending the union of the divine with the human nature, and the justifying divine activity as the temporal and particularized continuation of the general act of union begun in the incarnation of Christ, we must admit that the divine procedure will follow the same rule in the one case as in the other. Therefore if the question be ventured, why then for this union with human nature there was chosen precisely Jesus of Nazareth, or rather (since it was only through this union that He became what He was) why exactly this and no other person-creating act of human nature was chosen, at exactly this time—the question must be capable of being answered in a quite analogous way. If we recall that this act was itself a becoming natural of the supernatural, and if we remember the kind of effects that were to proceed from it, we cannot answer in any other way than this : that time and place were chosen as the absolutely best, that is as yielding the maximum operative effect. Now to answer the question thus is obviously to postulate foreseen faith as the ground of individual election. For by the same rule they must be chosen, and the time of their conversion determined, so as to make their share in the furtherance of the work of redemption the greatest possible. In the same way, if we take a large view of election not merely as the determination of the order in which individuals are regenerated, but as the election of nations to have the gospel firmly rooted in their midst, this too will be determined in just such a way as to attain the extensive and intensive maximum for the whole course of the historical development. But everything that the individual or a community can do by word or deed for the extension of the Kingdom of God, being a continuation of, and therefore included in, the prophetic activity of Christ, may be summed up in the terms ' proclamation ' or ' preaching.' And preaching, in this meaning and compass, springs from,[1] and is the natural utterance of, faith. It is thus quite the same thing whether we say that the divine election is

---

[1] Rom. 10^{17}, 2 Cor. 4^{13}.

determined through the foreseen efficaciousness of preaching, or through the foreseen occurrence of the maximum power of faith.

It is true all the same that in the common use of the formula this moment of regeneration is what is least prominent, and what is stressed is the permanence and steadiness of faith rather than its active power.   But the inadequacy of the formula taken in this restricted sense must strike everyone.   On this reading it does not get right back to the idea of the Kingdom of God, or to the origin of the Church, which, according to the Scripture passage [1] that forms the basis of most discussions of the subject, is the natural point at which the question arises.   In fact, an entirely atomistic view of the work of redemption underlies the whole position, if it is always and only the individual as such that is spoken of ; and no such limitation can possibly yield a right view.   This becomes very clear if along with this formula we take two others which are supposed to explain and support it.   First, it follows from the formula that if some are not elected at all, they are those in whom effectual grace would not in any case have had firm root.   But it is also said of them that God has determined to harden and reject those who persist in repelling His word.[2]   If the combination of these formulæ is to lead anywhere, it must be possible to prove a difference between the natural aversion which is the ground of non-election and the antipathy caused by God which is its result.   The impossibility of this makes the formula useless, whether as a canon for the investigation of Christian history, or for conducting fruitful self-examination.   On the other hand, if, after stating that God elects those whom He sees to be such as will continue in faith, it be also said that He has determined to strengthen and confirm those whom He elects, it is equally impossible to define a difference and boundary line between the former merely foreseen steadfastness, and the latter, which is imparted by God Himself.   If, however, it is the intention of the formula to avoid every imputation of Pelagianism, and therefore to reckon the former too as divinely effected (there being no foreknowledge in God that is not operative), the final conclusion is that God has elected only those whom He has also determined to strengthen in faith.   Now this is an altogether empty formula, unless one is conceiving faith as also including its operative effect.   The same holds good of the more modest formula that

[1] Rom. 10 and 11.
[2] *Sol. decl.* xi. : In codem suo consilio decrevit, quod eos qui per verbum vocati illud repudiant . . . et obstinati in illa contumacia perseverant, indurare reprobare et aeternae damnatione devovere velit.

regard to faith cannot be excluded from the divine decree of election.[1]

No one, however, will desire to stretch the application of our first formula so far as to insist on our proving that the maximum fruit of redemption could have been secured only by just exactly the course of election which as a matter of fact has gone to edify the Church. No proof is possible, for there is no alternative with which the comparison can be made. Hence what we have in this formula is faith speaking about what is fundamental to the conception of history and to true self-scrutiny.

3. The answer, however, which has just been given in reference to what can be regarded as divine election in the incarnation of Christ may also be traced back to the second formula of our proposition. For if we say that that point was chosen from which the maximum of efficacy could develop, it may also be said that that point only had this peculiarity because the general situation had become just what it was. But this situation divine guidance might have made different, and then a different point would have had this peculiarity. Christ therefore was determined as He was, only because, and in so far as, everything as a whole was determined in a certain way; and conversely, everything as a whole was only so determined, because, and in so far as, Christ was determined in a certain way. To say this is obviously to take our stand upon the divine good-pleasure, and to say that the determination in both cases is what it is simply through the divine good-pleasure. Indeed, whenever we form an inclusive idea of natural causality as a self-enclosed whole and go back to its basis in the divine causality, we can reach no ground of determination for the latter except the divine good-pleasure. Just as the whole world was so ordered by God that He could say it was all very good, that is, in accordance with His good-pleasure, and as the individual is in this regard not separable from his connexion with the rest of being—so, viewing the Kingdom of God as a self-enclosed whole, we can only say that, as it is, it is simply determined through the divine good-pleasure. And everything appertaining to it is so determined—Christ as He actually is, and the whole actual inward manifold of the human race in space and time, out of which through Christ the Kingdom of God is formed. There is, of course, nothing to hinder it being also said that the order in which the relationship

[1] Dicimus fidei intuitum decreto electionis esse includendum (Gerh., iv. p. 207).

to Christ comes to be realized in each individual case conforms to that manifold, and is determined by it ; but in that case it must also be possible to say, conversely, that the manifold of the human race conforms to that order, and is determined with relation to it so that, within it, redemption through Christ develops on precisely this scale and in this order.   Both statements are equally true, and at the same time, because standing in contrast, they are equally false.   Summing up everything, therefore, all that can rightly be said is that both, in their relation to one another, and also each by itself, are in the above sense ordered according to the divine good-pleasure.   It has been well-pleasing to God that human nature should show itself in this determined multiplicity of thus deter-mined individual beings ; and no other ground for it can be given. For every other explanation would involve conditioning assump-tions ; and these in turn would always themselves be conditioned by the all-embracing divine good-pleasure.   Similarly it has been His good-pleasure to make the dispensation of human affairs perfect through Christ.   He might from the very beginning have arranged the whole march of the human race differently ; only it would then have been a different human race, for when once one thing is fixed, everything else is fixed along with it in just one way.   Every attempted logical proof of the necessity of redemption in this form assumes something the necessity of which itself requires similar proof.   For the religious there is no path of escape from this circle of necessities, each leading back to and conditioned by the others, except by way of this one all-inclusive divine good-pleasure.   Ac-cordingly, all that remains to us is the task of linking up at every point this divine good-pleasure (which is necessarily implicit in our God-consciousness) with what we perceive of the actual course of the work of redemption, and of resting trustfully upon it, however we may be moved by what happens.   Indeed, faith in Christ is itself nothing else than sharing in this divine good-pleasure which abides on Christ and the salvation grounded in Him ; and the con-sciousness of divine grace, or the peace of God in the redeemed heart, is nothing else than just this quiet acceptance of the divine good-pleasure in respect of the arrangement of events which led to oneself being taken up into the sphere of redemption.   Just as in the world in general we meet with the most manifold gradation of life, from the lowest and most imperfect forms up to the highest and most perfect, and cannot doubt but that this very multiplicity is the richest fulfilment, in time and space, of the divine good-

pleasure ; and as such gradations also occur within the sphere of
human nature : so within the sphere of spiritual life resulting from
redemption we shall readily expect all that lies between the greatest
and the least, and find peace in regarding all this abundance, linked
up in living fellowship, as the object of the divine good-pleasure.

4. We have already seen how these grounds of election are
arrived at, and how they seem to be in opposition to one another
because they have opposite points of departure. The previous
exposition will have removed this apparent contradiction, as our
proposition requires, by exhibiting it in formulæ which have an
equivalent content, but merely are construed from different angles,
so that in accepting the one there is no necessity to reject the
other. But it is only possible to show them thus to be in agreement,
if both are freed from untenable elements attracted in large measure
by their very opposition. What has to be detached from the first
is any appearance of the divine decree being dependent on what
would obviously be a human kind of foreknowledge on the part of
God, the object of which would then be independent of the divine
decree, whereas in fact that decree must be guided by His foreknowledge. For if a determination of the divine decree by faith
foreseen be opposed to a determination by the free divine good-
pleasure, the inference is hardly to be avoided that faith is grounded,
independently of the divine influence, in the free will of man ; and
this semblance of Pelagianism cannot be removed by any kind of
artificial qualifications, so as to leave the formula any definite
content at all. As against this, what we say is that faith foreseen
determines the divine decree in so far as it has been the divine
good-pleasure to allow to issue from this point such an activity in
behalf of the Kingdom of God as is conditioned by precisely this
strength and timeousness of faith. The other formula, to the effect
that the divine good-pleasure draws on one person and leaves another
behind, if set up in contrast to the first, seems only too easily to
imply favouritism to the one and repression of the other ; and this
in such wise that on such a beginning the end must follow, no matter
what may happen in between. There is thus an appearance of
divine caprice in an unconditioned divine decree concerning individuals, as though it meant an urgent support of the one person
with irresistible aid and a predetermined abandonment of the
other ; and this is so difficult to guard against without the whole
formula falling to pieces, that the simplest plan is just to accept
it. As against this, our exposition knows of no unconditioned divine

decree regarding the individual, for all individuals are mutually conditioned ; it knows only a single unconditioned decree by which the whole, as an undivided system, is what it is in virtue of the divine good-pleasure. Not at all as if the individual has somehow some kind of existence apart from this divine decree, which then simply does or does not save him. On the contrary, each individual comes into existence only because and in so far as an element of just such a kind, and of such active powers, is given a place in the whole, in accordance with the divine good-pleasure. Each, therefore, is fashioned in readiness to become a member of the Christian fellowship, because he is foreseen as a believer. If now we view our two formulas in combination, they contain two rules by which these disadvantageous inferences are made impossible. The first is that no individual becomes anything whatever for himself, alone and apart from his place in the whole, in consequence of a special divine decree relating to him. In the second place, viewed as part of the general context of things, everything, and in particular the way in which redemption is realized, is the perfect manifestation at once of the divine good-pleasure and of the divine omnipotence.

Postscript to this Doctrine.—From the point at which we have arrived let us return once more to the assumption that a section of the human race remains shut out for ever from the sphere of redemption, or (to express it as it touches most closely the proper content of our doctrines) that the Christian Church only arises out of the human race in such wise that a section of mankind is for ever lost to it. On the one hand, it cannot be denied that at this point a perfect acquiescence in the divine good-pleasure is hard to attain, for racial and personal consciousness are here affected by contrary emotions, and the resulting inevitable and ever-renewed sadness is such as to prevent an unalloyed communication of the blessedness of Christ. And another problem arises, namely, how so to conceive the matter that human nature shall still remain identical in all. Of course if in Manichæan fashion we are prepared to make a cleavage in human nature, that sadness must die out, since the others are no longer our fellows in the old sense. On the other hand, unless our Christian self-consciousness is to be essentially modified, the almost equally insoluble problem arises how so to conceive this as that nevertheless Christ is still sent not only to, but also for, the whole human race. This is only the case if it be admitted that at some time or another some trace of His activity actually makes itself felt in everyone. But it is easy to see that the difficulty is of a

very different sort according as we are dealing with those who have
already experienced the influences of the Christian Church, or
with those who have remained outside all connexion with it.   It
may therefore be advisable to make a corresponding distinction
within the assumption itself.   As regards the former class no
incapacity for redemption must in any sense be ascribed to them ;
rather, as often as some operation of preparatory grace has been
vouchsafed to them up to the point of communication, they have
already and by that very fact become instruments for spreading the
Kingdom of God ; for every such communication bears witness to
the grace of God in Christ.   But the less we are in a position instantly
to mark a man's transition to the state of sanctification, and must
be careful to recognize the possibility of an imperceptible occurrence
of regeneration no less than of a sudden one, the more we are compelled to recognize, with regard to all who already belong outwardly
to the Christian fellowship, the wisdom of the caution that we
should not lightly reckon anyone among the rejected ; [1] so that
there is no conceivable case to which the assumption we are discussing can be confidently applied.   As regards those outside the
Church, it is an essential of our faith that every nation will sooner
or later become Christian, as indeed this was Paul's hope for his
own people, which had so often obstinately refused the divine
grace.   In so far therefore as we view the individual in his national
idiosyncrasy, reckoning the spirit he thus shares an essential element
in his personality, to that extent we may say that he bears within
himself this predetermination to blessedness.   This holds good the
more as he himself possesses more of those qualities of the common
spirit to which, in his race, the acceptance of faith can attach itself,
and the less as he possesses more of those qualities on which the
race's procrastinating resistance depends.   This more and less,
obviously corresponding to the faith foreseen, means for us of
course simply this : that the same people, if alive at the time when
the gospel first appeared among their nation, would have been laid
hold of by it, one man at the very outset, another at some later stage.
None the less, from the fact that out of these circumstances we can
only construct a formula which expresses nothing real, it does not
follow that it could have no other significance in the divine fore-
ordination (even without our having on this account to take refuge
in the *scientia media* of God) : for in those individuals these qualities

---

[1] *Expos. simpl.* x. : Bene sperandum tamen est de omnibus, neque temere
eprobis quisquam est adnumerandus.

are real. Rather, if all in this fashion are included in the divine
fore-ordination to blessedness, then the high-priestly dignity of
Christ for the first time comes out in its whole efficacy—an efficacy
which implies that God regards all men only in Christ. This very
point can be applied also to the previously considered case. So
that at least this result clearly emerges, that if we take the universality of redemption in its whole range (which cannot really be
conceived without this high-priestly dignity of Christ and all its
consequences), then we must also take fore-ordination to blessedness quite universally ; and that limits can be imposed on neither
without curtailing the other.

SECOND DOCTRINE : THE COMMUNICATION OF THE HOLY SPIRIT

§ 121. *All who are living in the state of sanctification feel an inward
impulse to become more and more one in their common
co-operative activity and reciprocal influence, and are
conscious of this as the common Spirit of the new corporate
life founded by Christ.*

1. This fact itself is expressed in the most definite way in all
the scriptural accounts of the first planting of the Christian Church ;
and the favourable impression made on non-Christians is always
represented as due to this unity ; [1] and this quality of fellowship is
brought into the closest connexion with the new life of every individual. Indeed, all informing pictures of the Christian fellowship
agree in describing every individual as an integral constituent of
the whole, and attributing everything to one spirit moving in, and
animating, the whole.[2] And if adherents of the twofold separatist
tendency already frequently censured, the naturalistic and the
fanatical or visionary, should wish to object that this properly
holds good only of the first period of the Christian Church and is
by no means essential to it, but must more and more die out, since
every reason for thus holding together drops away when once the
new life is firmly established and can perfect itself out of the common
source in each individual by himself, they may be answered as
follows.

In the first place, that which can cease or fall into the background
through the gradual strengthening of individuals is only one element
in one half of what our proposition affirms ; it is only that element

---

[1] Acts 1[13ff.] 2[42ff.] 4[32ff.] 5[12-14] 9[31].
[2] Rom. 12[3-6], 1 Cor. 12[4ff.], Eph. 2[17-22] 4[16], 1 Pet. 2[5-10].

of the reciprocal influence which comes under the analogy [1] of teaching and learning, or of imparting and receiving. For if any-one is properly taught of God he does not require someone else to teach him.   This element in fellowship is also, in one particular respect, always on the way to cessation [2]—if, that is, one is always in contact with the same people.   But as new persons are always arriving, this element in fellowship also runs on ; those who were previously receivers now imparting, as givers, to later comers. And this mutual influence has a further element, namely, a reciprocity of impartation and comprehension among equals. This is based on the fact that, owing to varied personal idiosyncrasies, the new life itself is something different in every case ; and every-one, just as he would fain take Christ wholly to himself, strives also to take to himself as far as possible all that Christ has effected ; and thus again each is moved by Christ (as he personally conceives Him) to manifest the power of Christ working in him, which indeed is what happens in all the good works of the regenerate.   Still less does the other element, the co-operative activity, ever tend to cease. On the contrary, it is bound to be facilitated and to expand in proportion as the new life gains strength in each.   And obviously, in proportion as the will for the Kingdom of God originated simul-taneously with living faith in Christ is more definitely formed within each and develops into a system of purposes, so will each necessarily appropriate the help of all kindred forces.   And thus, through this interweaving of what is co-operative and what is reciprocal, and in virtue of the identity of the new life in all, there arises a disposition to a common work or undertaking—a work that can be carried forward approximatingly towards its goal only by means of the conjunction of every power and activity ; a work which would by no means cease though the whole human race were received into the fellowship of redemption, because it ever remains as in itself an infinite and ever-changing exemplification of what is common in the individual and what is individual in the common. For this is the essential thing in the life of a people ; and it is as a people, or a household of God,[3] that Christians have always wished to be regarded.

In the second place, there are, it is true, in this regard two opposite kinds of human association : those which of themselves tend to come to an end, and within which therefore no increasing unity is striven for ; and those which seek to persist, in which

---

[1] John 6⁴⁵.   [2] Eph. 4¹¹⁻¹³.   [3] Eph. 2¹⁹ Tit. 2¹⁴, 1 Pet. 2⁹.

therefore the mitigation of differences must be an object, and unity must be held fast. The former are always merely accidental. Partly they are those which by their very nature can be given neither definite form nor definite limits, as in all associations within a free society, though even there under certain circumstances something like a common spirit comes to exist ; partly they are those formed solely in connexion with some particular joint-undertaking without any inward unity of spirit, in such a way that each is left free to seek his own personal ends. It may be there are even religious fellowships approaching this in character ; of the Christian fellowship it certainly does not hold true. For what each recognizes in the other is a common love to Christ ; and this supplies a unifying principle that is uninterruptedly at work.

2. If now we denote this striving for unity by the expression ' common spirit,' we mean by this exactly what we mean in any earthly system of government, namely, the common bent found in all who constitute together a moral personality, to seek the advancement of this whole ; and this is at the same time the characteristic love found in each for every other. Hence up to this point no objection can easily be made to our proposition. But if one compares its content as there explained with the heading, and rightly infers thence that this common spirit is meant as the Holy Spirit, and the communication of it as the communication of the Holy Spirit, then the suspicion may easily arise that the expression Holy Spirit ' is being taken in an entirely different sense from that given it in Scripture. But the thought-forms that have arisen owing to the place of the Holy Spirit in the doctrine of the Trinity (partly to explain it, partly to refute it, as, for example, when the Holy Spirit is represented as a separate higher Being, indeed, but only a created one) ought none of them to be taken as equivalent to New Testament statements, which as a matter of fact represent the Holy Spirit to us as always and only in believers. He is promised to the whole community,[1] and where an original communication of the Spirit is spoken of, it comes by a single act to a multitude of people,[2] who *eo ipso* become an organic whole, who are urged on to like activity and stand in for each other. In all, however, He is represented as being one and the same, the various effects produced by Him in various people being distinguished from Himself as His gifts.[3] And this is not meant as if merely to indicate an advantage or superiority which some individuals possess ; which would natur-

[1] John 16[7ff.], Acts 1[4, 5].   [2] John 20[22, 23], Acts 2[4].   [3] 1 Cor. 12[4].

ally mean that the Spirit was a particular quality of the personality of each, resembling and generically the same as the quality of anyone else's ; which is how we conceive the matter in the case of special talents and perfections. No : on the one hand the Spirit is represented as a true unity through which the multitude of Christians also become a unity and the many individual personalities become a true common life or moral personality ; and, on the other hand, the Spirit is not assigned to people as it were in a random and unconnected fashion—a phenomenon here one moment and gone the next. The presence of the Spirit rather is the condition of anyone's sharing in the common life ; [1] for, only when this common spirit of the whole begins to show itself at work in a given person can it be known that he is a constituent part of the whole ; [2] just as if anyone joins himself to the whole, it can be taken as certain that he will receive a communication of the Holy Spirit.[3] Now in the sphere of thought there has always been controversy over questions of this kind, as to how far what exists in many is still one, or whether and in what degree it can be rightly said that an idea or a motion of the will common to many is one, or is something particular in each. Here we do not have to decide such differences of opinion, whether on their own account or because we had prematurely represented one view or the other as incompatible with this element of the Christian faith. We prefer not to enter on this field at all, but merely to lay down two points as expressions of our Christian self-consciousness. The first is that the unity of the Spirit is to be understood in the same sense as the unity which everyone attributes to the characteristic form taken by human nature in a nation ; even those who ascribe being only to the separate individual may still say that each man's personality is the national character modified by the original basis of his own nature. Similarly, we say that the new life of each is an activity of this common spirit manifested in the same fashion in all others, an activity conditioned by the state in which regeneration finds him ; and the Christian Church is one through this one Spirit in the same way that a nation is one through the national character common to and identical in all. The second point is that this common spirit is also one, because in all derived from one and the same source, namely, Christ ; for everyone is conscious of the communication of the Spirit as being connected in the closest fashion with the rise of faith in him, and everyone recognizes that the same is true for all

---

[1] 1 Cor. 12³, Rom. 8⁹.   [2] Acts 10⁴⁷, 19².   [3] Acts 2³⁸.

the others. For faith only comes by preaching, and preaching always goes back to Christ's commission and is therefore derived from Him. And as in Christ Himself everything proceeds from the Divine within Him, so also does this communication, which becomes in everyone the power of the new life, a power not different in each, but the same in all.

3. Another possible objection is this. Starting from the point that all other religious fellowships are destined to lose themselves in Christianity, and hence that all nations are destined to pass over into the Christian fellowship, the common spirit of the Christian Church would then be the common spirit of the human race. Now by analogy with the common spirit of a nation such a thing as this latter must exist, and we do not know how to describe it otherwise than by the expressions, racial consciousness, or love of humanity as a species. But in that case the race is one in the same sense as the Church is one, and as there cannot be two living unities for the same whole, what we wish to denote by the expression ' Holy Spirit ' would be exactly the same thing as the racial consciousness. This would mean either that the latter was something supernatural, which no one would desire to maintain, or that the former must be natural, and if derived from Christ, then from the human in Him. This would make the communication of the Holy Spirit nothing more than the awakening by Christ of a pure racial consciousness. For the subject about to be dealt with, this is the most logical form of the view which regards the awakening and expansion of a universal love to men as the proper and essential fruit of the appearance of Christ. To us, however, not only is it certain that our participation in the Holy Spirit really belongs to the things which we are conscious of having had imparted to us by Christ, but also that in Christ everything derives from the absolute and exclusive power of His God-consciousness. And if on the other hand we take into account our self-consciousness as still betraying our participation in the common life of sinfulness, we find in it such a variety of interests belonging to the merely individual though also enlarged personality that the pure racial consciousness cannot prevail as a practical motive any more than could a law of morality couched in different terms ; it merely serves as a barrier against personal and social selfishness. Of course it was first through Christ (as Founder of a society which is capable of embracing all men, and which, while attaching individuals to itself, looks simply to the fact of their being human) that the racial consciousness, along with the

God-consciousness and with the same object in view, has become a powerful practical motive. But just for this reason, this power is no mere natural principle that would have developed of itself out of human nature as human nature would have remained without Christ. On the contrary, we recognize it for the most authentic expression of the Holy Spirit as a consciousness of the need to be redeemed that is alike in all, and of the capacity, alike in all, to be taken up into living fellowship with Christ ; and the universal love of humanity we know only as one and the same thing with the will for the Kingdom of God in its widest compass. It is only in this sense that for us the common spirit of the Christian Church, and every Christian's universal love for men as a love alike for those who have already become citizens of the Kingdom of God and for those to whom this experience is yet to come, are the same One Holy Spirit.

§ 122. *Only after the departure of Christ from earth was it possible for the Holy Spirit, as this common spirit, to be fully communicated and received.*

1. Let us compare this proposition with what is most often taught on this point and is stated not only when the subject is dealt with in presence of a congregation, but predominantly in the public teaching given, where the procession of the Holy Spirit is indeed set forth in the doctrine of the Trinity as timeless and eternal, but the outpouring of the Spirit, as the beginning of His activity within the Christian Church, is connected with the event of Pentecost. The first point needing defence is this, that as has at least been indicated in our argument, the Holy Spirit must already have been at work, even though incompletely. Now it certainly is true that Christ Himself makes His going away a condition of the sending of the Spirit ; [1] but it is equally true that He Himself communicated the Spirit to them before His final departure from earth,[2] and indeed that He even assumed that the Spirit had been already present with them ; for whatever is a divine revelation in the soul relatively to Christ [3] is also a work of the Spirit. Now these various statements are not easily to be harmonized, unless what Christ is said to have expected at His Ascension in Jerusalem [4] was simply a complete filling with the Spirit. If now we start from the position that the Holy Spirit is the inmost vital power of the Christian Church as a whole, we must go back to the two most elemental aspects of life,

[1] John 16[7].   [2] John 20[22].   [3] Matt. 16[17].   [4] Acts 1[4. 5. 8].

the living susceptibility and the free spontaneous activity ; for these together, in their reciprocal relations, are that by which life is constituted—life being the more complete and the more fully developed, the larger the sphere covered by each of the two, and the more exact their mutual correspondence. In company with Christ the susceptibility of the disciples developed, and in their steady apprehension of what He offered to them there was laid the foundation of their future effectiveness as workers for the Kingdom of God. Hence, as they related their apprehension entirely to the Kingdom of God preached by Christ, each recognized this susceptibility in the others as the very same thing, grounded and upheld in the same way in them all. There came to be among them a fellowship in apprehension, and as face to face with Christ each was able to represent the rest in question and answer,[1] this susceptibility revealed itself as an essential factor in the common spirit. In this sense the right apprehension of Christ is itself ascribed to the Holy Spirit.[2] On the other hand, they had at that time no really spontaneous activity of their own. What Christ suggested to them in that line was practice, not performance proper, and just for that reason it was not free activity, but one that needed on each occasion a new special impetus. One step in the transition towards complete spontaneity is shown in the communication of the Spirit, just referred to, in the forty days after the Resurrection. For the right binding and loosing of sin is in the main just an expression of a fully formed susceptibility for what relates to the Kingdom of God. This expression, however, is inconceivable except as having a reaction on those whose sins are bound or loosed ; it therefore marks a transition to free spontaneous activity ; and obviously the susceptibility reveals itself most distinctly as the common spirit in expressions which presumably are unanimous.

2. The common spirit was, however, as yet incomplete ; hence during the personal presence of Christ there can have been no completely common life representing at that time the Kingdom of God. And this, as a matter of fact, was the case. For the more a common life depends on an individual life, the less is it an existence in common. In part it is so far not equipped for permanent identity amid the changes of death and birth ; in part a common life ought to be one whole, but not an individual person. The more all depend on one, each receiving his impetus from him, the more all are merely his tools or members, and the whole is just the enlargement of this

---

[1] Matt. 16¹⁶, John 14⁸⁺ ⁹⋅ ¹¹ff⋅.   [2] I Cor. 12³.

one personality. Or if we consider the multiplicity of individual lives, the whole is really more like a household or a school than an existence in common. The ancients viewed the State in which all are unconditionally subject to the will of an individual, as an enlarged household, where various living tools move at the command of one master ; and school for us means a spiritual life in common which entirely depends on the thinking power and art of making disciples possessed by an individual, who puts a common stamp on them all. In this sense, of course, Christ's life in company with His disciples was both a household and a school. But a house is scattered on the master's death, and if its members are not caught up in some new bond, they disperse. So, too, in a school, if no other common motive comes to replace the original thirst for learning and personal attachment, no further progress takes place after the master's death, and the previous bond of union gradually dissolves. We find the disciples in the mood thus to disperse after Christ's death, and up to the time of His Ascension their life together was so much interrupted and decreased as to become quite formless. But even when Christ was alive it could not but be that each felt mainly dependent on Him, and sought to receive from Him ; no one of them all considered himself ripe for free spontaneous activity in the Kingdom of God yet to be formed.

3. If we do not wish to insist that the Holy Spirit is a divine communication of a quite specific kind, which though conditioned by Christ is yet not thus homogeneous with His earlier influence, it is certainly possible to argue that the distinction here sought to be drawn is untenable. For according to our own statements, in the living fellowship of the regenerate with Christ everything derives from Him, which means that, strictly speaking, there is to be found in every Christian only susceptibility, not spontaneous activity. And hence, it may be said, the life in common is no more now than then a common existence ; for the spontaneous activity then as now was wholly in Christ, and believers' life together even yet is just the mutual impartation of what each has received from Christ. But to this it must be rejoined that when formerly we studied the way redemption is realized in the case solely of the individual by himself, that was an incomplete view of the matter, and at the moment we safeguarded ourselves by a reference to what we are now considering. We said that *ab initio* preparatory operations of grace arising out of the common existence reach everyone. The statement that everything in the regenerate derives from Christ

held good of the communication of His sinless perfection, which simply consists in a pure will directed to the Kingdom of God ; in particular aims and purposes this is no longer present.   If therefore we ask how our particular aims arise out of that pure will, the answer is that it happens only in the common life.   They no longer come to anyone directly from Christ ; no one is given a special command by Christ, as was the case with the disciples.   But as no isolated individual can achieve anything in the Kingdom of God, so no one can really form any purpose but one in which he foresees that he will have the support of others and of which the germ is therefore already present in others.   And again, through every such common movement only so much progress will actually be made as has a true common consciousness behind it.   Here therefore there is more in the individual than susceptibility, and his really spontaneous energetic activity is more than the activity of Christ merely passing through him.   But the common spirit expressed in this spontaneous activity is only the Holy Spirit in so far as the activity it induces is a prolongation of Christ's own activity.   And no more than in Christ's lifetime is the individual's susceptibility open merely to what proceeds directly from Christ ; it is also a susceptibility to the spontaneous activity of others.

If now we wish to apply here the general canon that everything essentially connected with our participation in redemption must be the same in us as in the first disciples, we shall say that as long as all spontaneous activity was in Christ alone, but in them mere susceptibility, the Kingdom of God in the narrower sense was confined to Christ alone—the disciples representing only the outer circle of the preparatory workings of grace, where there is nothing but susceptibility.   And just as then in the disciples, so now in everyone the reminiscent apprehension of Christ must grow into a spontaneous imitation of Him.   This common spontaneous activity —which indwells all and in each is kept right by the influence of all, and prolongs the personal action of Christ—in its unity and identity we have full right to call the common spirit of the Christian Church ; it corresponds to all that Christ promised by the Holy Spirit and to everything that is represented as the Spirit's working. Taking everything together, we are thus able to say how it was that after Christ's departure the disciples' common apprehension of Christ changed into a spontaneous prolongation of His fellowship-forming activity, and how it was only through this activity so related to the fixed apprehension of Christ becoming the imperishable common spirit, that the Christian Church arose. So, too, everyone within the circle of preparatory grace, who through the influence of Christian life upon him and in the activity of others flowing through him, possesses this Christian common spirit merely in the form of susceptibility, must, when through faith the rule of the Kingdom of God has been established in his life, refashion his attitude to the apprehension of Christ accepted within the common life into a spontaneous activity of this kind ; and this is the communication of the divine Spirit. If now the justifying divine activity be conceived under the form of particular divine actions, we should have to say that now this communication is in each case, as it were, the latest element or stage of this activity ; in the lifetime of Christ this final act was, so to speak, put off until after His departure from the earth. But as we do not admit the reality of any individual and temporal divine acts, we are not compelled to adopt any such paradoxical formula ; and we shall state the parallel between the first disciples and ourselves equally well if we say that already, even when Christ was with them, and just because they were taken up into living fellowship with Him, they had the principle of the new life, and had it not merely as susceptibility but also as spontaneous activity ; although as long as Christ was with them it took the form exclusively of a continuous desire to receive from Him, and therefore only afterwards could become truly common and manifest itself as Holy Spirit. It is these aspects that are described with more precision in the following theorems.

§ 123. *First Theorem.—The Holy Spirit is the union of the Divine Essence with human nature in the form of the common Spirit animating the life in common of believers.*

1. When in connexion with the doctrines of Christ we were discussing the union in Him of the divine with the human, we put entirely aside the question whether or not this divine, apart from its union with human nature, was something special, as being the second Person in the Godhead, and something relatively distinct in the Divine Essence. So here too, in proposing a similar formula for the Holy Spirit, we must (although the Trinity is now completely before us) in the same way leave this consideration out of account. What we have to treat here is simply this relation between the highest Essence and human nature, in so far as in its operations it meets us within our Christian self-consciousness. Since these operations are fully expounded only in the next division, and the

content of the following section has already been prescribed for us, a summary view of these relations in the doctrine of the Trinity can only be given at the close of our whole exposition. But in advance we must here make a different point. Our discussion is not in the least meant to embrace all the passages in our Holy Scriptures where this expression occurs, or all the ways in which it is used in dogmatic works. Here we have only to do with the Holy Spirit in the Christian Church, and do not raise the question whether, as used apart from this relation, the expression means the same thing or not. But this is equivalent to saying that the Holy Spirit here discussed is not the same as the Spirit to whom a participation in the creation of the material world is ascribed,[1] or the Spirit whose indwelling is the cause of all sorts of extraordinary talents,[2] or even the Spirit mentioned in connexion with the incarnation of Christ, at least so far as a physical effect is there ascribed to Him,[3] even though, strictly speaking, a connexion with the Christian Church does exist here. Indeed, we even put aside the common way of speaking of the Holy Spirit as already active in the prophets before the appearance of Christ,[4] so as not to feel compelled to identify the common spirit of the Jewish theocracy and that of the Christian Church. And here, however much the letter of Scripture may seem to contradict us, the spirit of the New Testament is on our side. In Christ's promises of the Holy Spirit of truth [5] there is nowhere the slightest whisper that this Something had been present earlier and had vanished only temporarily, or indeed that He is anything at all except as He is for the disciples of Christ. Otherwise the disciples would obviously have been prophets, and Christ could hardly have said that prophecy ended with John.[6]

2. If now (provisionally leaving on one side what we have established in the two last propositions) we return to the point that in the Church from the beginning, and therefore already in the New Testament, all the powers at work in the Christian Church— and not merely the miraculous gifts, which in this connexion are quite accidental—are traced to the Holy Spirit ; [7] and if we ask what is thus supposed to have been present from the very start, the following admissions have to be made.

First, these powers are not to be found outside of the Christian Church, and hence they neither arise from the general constitution

---

[1] Gen. 1[2], Ps. 33[6] ; cf. Augustin., *de Gen. ad litt.* cap. 4.
[2] Ex. 31[2-5].   [3] Matt. 1[18], Luke 1[35].
[4] Isa. 34[16] 61[1], Mic. 3[8].   [5] John 14[16. 17] 16[7ff].
[6] Matt. 11[13], Luke 16[16].   [7] 1 Cor. 12, Eph. 1[17], 2 Tim. 1[7].

of human nature (which would make Christ superfluous) nor from any other divine arrangement.[1] Second, this Spirit is not something supernatural and mysterious though not immediately divine, a higher yet created essence putting itself in secret ways into relation with men. The Church has properly rejected this in the same way and on the same grounds as all representations of Christ with an Arian bias. For as in Christ, too, the human would be no more human if we had to conceive it united with a higher nature in one person, so our own life and the life of other believers would no longer seem to be humanly interconnected if we had to conceive our consciousness and action as determined by the influence of a superhuman nature. Third, the Holy Spirit is not something that, although divine, is not united with the human nature, but only somehow influences it from without. For whatever enters us from without does so only through the senses and never becomes more than an occasion for our action. What action is to follow on this occasion is determined from within, and only this, and not the former region of the senses, is the sphere of the Holy Spirit. That occasions are given us from without does not preclude the unity of our self-consciousness and self-determination. But this unity would at once be dissolved if determinations were given from without. And if there are passages in Scripture largely influenced by prophetic language that in terms seem clearly to assert such an external influence,[2] these have the letter of other passages quite as definitely against them.[3] There is indeed no way of imagining how the Spirit's gifts could be within us,[4] and He Himself remain without, or how He is to influence us from without except through human speech and significant action—which just means that He is already within, and influencing, someone else. And the man *on* whom the Spirit works is not thereby made a participator in the Spirit. Only one *in* whom and *through* whom He works[5] has received the Spirit. Thus in everyone He brings His gifts to pass, and we are not conscious of the gifts as inward, but the power that effects them as outward : what we do is to distinguish him *on* whom the Holy Spirit is still at work, as thus being one in whom no gift is yet produced, from one within the state of sanctification, *in* whom the Holy Spirit is producing gifts.[6] Thus, as Scripture also says, we are conscious both of the Spirit and of His gifts as some-

---

[1] Gal. 3^{2-5}.   [2] Acts 1^5 2^3 $8^{29.39}$ $10^{19.44}$.
[3] Mark 13^{11}, Rom. $8^{9.11}$, 1 Cor. 6^{19}, Gal. 4^6, Jas. 4^5.
[4] 1 Cor. 12^7.   [5] Acts 10^{44-47}.   [6] Gal. 5^{22}, Eph. 5^9.

thing inward ; of the gifts as being different in different individuals, but of the Spirit being one in different people in spite of the difference of gifts. This explains the testimony of the first possessors of the Holy Spirit, who describe Him as a specific divine efficacious working in believers, though not one to be separated from the recognition of the being of God in Christ. The two things are strictly interdependent. For if in the Person of Christ nothing divine had entered into human nature, while there were something divine in the gifts of the Holy Spirit, then this divine element could not proceed from Christ, but would have to be communicated individually in some utterly miraculous fashion. In that case, however, it would always be thus communicable, although, on account of the absolute arbitrariness of the proceeding, no such supposed possessor of the Spirit would be able to make any claim whatever to be recognized as such by others. Thus all reciprocal influence and co-operative activity would be abolished, and every-one who had the Spirit would have Him all by himself ; an idea that the Church repudiated from the very first as contradicting its self-consciousness. If, on the other hand, something divine did really enter human nature through Christ, but did not remain in human nature on earth after the disappearance of His Person, then nothing could remain in human nature of that which in Christ was dependent on the being of God in Him ; and so there would be no communication of the sinless perfection and untroubled blessedness of Christ.

3. That the testimony of the first disciples agrees with what has been stated in the two last propositions concerning our con-sciousness is clear ; and all that remains is to justify by means of both of them the language of the proposition we are now dis-cussing. Now if the Holy Spirit is an effective spiritual power in the souls of believers, we must either represent Him as bound up with their human nature, or we shall have to surrender the unity of their being, if on the one hand they are such that in them human nature shows itself in operation, and on the other, such that in them the Holy Spirit is acting in separation from human nature. To adopt such a view would produce so entire a dualism within human life that it could never be maintained. The theory of a definite activity of the Holy Spirit has indeed been carried to this extreme, not, however, when this supposed activity was still taking place, but only long after it had ceased. All that remains to explain is the fact that this union is realized in the form of a

common spirit. Now everything (even in human nature viewed apart from redemption) that as spiritual power is absolutely the same in all individuals of a race and is incapable of any individualizing modification, and above all, reason, we regard as something not varied according to the individual, but as in all and in each the same. Now if we separate the Spirit from the gifts, which are of course individually modified and personal, then the Spirit is, in all who share in Him, one and the same, without being increased when the participants multiply, or being diminished when they grow fewer, and without being anything whatever in one that He is not in another ; except that, still being the same, He shows Himself stronger in one, and it may be weaker in another. He is, however, not only one in all in so far as His life and work in one cannot be distinguished from His life and work in another, but as already explained, because, as no one can attain the new life except in and through the fellowship, he has his share in the Holy Spirit, not in his personal self-consciousness viewed by itself, but only in so far as he is conscious of his being part of this whole—that is, he shares the Spirit as a common consciousness. Hence also the union of the divine with the human nature in believers is not a person-forming union, otherwise it would be indistinguishable from the union of the natures in Christ, and the distinction between Redeemer and redeemed would be lost. If we consider the individual as existing in an inborn and hereditary common life, no such distinction obtains there, as the formula stated above shows.[1] But if the reference be to the common life into which the individual only enters after his personality has reached a certain point of development, it cannot in that case be said that the personality is simply the common spirit taking a specific form, though more and more it comes to be just that. If we could isolate the new life of the individual that begins with regeneration and construct it by itself, then we should certainly be able to describe it as a life absolutely determined by the Holy Spirit, and the new creature would simply be the Holy Spirit Himself in conscious possession of this specific complex of natural human powers. But as a matter of fact, the new life is not a self-identical whole and does not uniformly penetrate the entire organism of the personality. On the contrary, the person, the continuous unity of self-consciousness, is a mingled separation and union of the divine and the human ; and even if someone were actually to reach the point of having the

[1] § 121, 2.

new life diffuse itself over his entire essence, yet the portion of his life spent before his regeneration would still form part of his personality. Finally, the divine activity constituting the new life in the individual is common spirit for this additional reason, that it is in each without regard to personal peculiarities, provided only he belongs to the fellowship through the influence of which his regeneration was conditioned, and out of which, by preaching in the widest sense of the word, this new life was transmitted to him, exactly as it took shape in the disciples through the power of the self-communicating life of Christ ; partly, too, because it only takes possession of the individual with a view to fellowship, and moulds him solely for one end—in order that, and in the manner that, it may best work through him for the whole.

§ 124. *Second Theorem.—Every regenerate person partakes of the Holy Spirit, so that there is no living fellowship with Christ without an indwelling of the Holy Spirit, and vice versa.*

1. Up to this point the question as to how redemption is realized in the human soul has been answered by saying that it happens through being taken up into living fellowship with Christ. Now the demand is made that everyone must partake of the Holy Spirit. This, however, is not at all to be understood as meaning that the experience is actually in two parts, and that some new and special thing happens to a regenerate person when he becomes a partaker in the Holy Spirit. Neither in fact nor in point of time are the two things to be distinguished, but in strictness we must say that everyone, as regenerate, also receives a share in the Holy Spirit. For being taken up into living fellowship with Christ includes at the same time being conscious both of our sonship with God and of the Lordship of Christ ; and both in Scripture are ascribed to the indwelling of the Holy Spirit.[1] We therefore cannot imagine how one could exist were the other absent. If, to indulge in a flight of fancy, we suppose that we could find ourselves placed in a similar common life representative of the Kingdom of God, and led by the Holy Spirit as its common spirit, with only this difference that we knew nothing of any such Founder as Christ is ; yet we should not, when contrasting that condition and the sinful common life, be able to derive the first from the second ; and at the same time, since in all the members of that common life sin, while not willed, is yet present, we should have to hold that the

[1] 1 Cor. 12³, Gal. 4⁶.

sinful common life is not something grounded within itself (that is to say, something such as it was in its first origin), for otherwise it must have been capable of originating in the same way also at other points. This, we remark in passing, is also the reason why those who start from so imperfect and partial a divine revelation always so easily recognize one another, even in their hostility. So long, therefore, as we do not admit that other similar kingdoms of God may arise independently of the Christian Church at other times or places, we are compelled to accept for it a single origin outside of the common life of sin, from which the divine communication found within it is derived. Membership in this common life therefore means at the same time being set within the sphere of operation of the sole Founder. Thus we find expressed the belief that such an outpouring of the Spirit would only have been possible after the appearance of the Son of God, and on the basis of His personal influence ; and this carries with it the implication that our participation in that Spirit and our own bond with the living influence of Christ are one and the same thing.

On the other side, the same thing holds good. If we begin with Christ and hold to the proposition that the union of the Divine with His human personality was at the same time an enrichment of human nature as a whole, it follows not only in general that even after His departure this union must continue, but also (since this continuation is to proceed from the union itself) that wherever it exists there must be a bond with Christ, and *vice versa*. And since after the departure of Christ the enlarged range of connexion with Him can only proceed from the fellowship of believers, these three facts—being drawn by that union into the fellowship of believers, having a share in the Holy Spirit, and being drawn into living fellowship with Christ—must simply mean one and the same thing.

2. In this connexion it is very natural to ask what is the relation between the two expressions used by the same apostle, that Christ liveth in us, and that we are led by the Spirit.[1] When the same Apostle says that those who are led by the Spirit are God's children, either he is contradicting (and that no one can believe) him who says that those who have received Christ are God's children, or else here too these two things, the life of Christ in us and the leading of the Holy Spirit in us, are one, both within that third thing, being children of God. Either there are two different kinds of children of God (which we should all deny as much as Paul or John), or else

[1] Gal. 2^{20}, Rom. 8^{14}.

these two things are the same. If we are to answer the question from the connexion in which the expressions are used in the Church, we notice to begin with that the second is peculiar and characteristic in a higher degree than the first, and has therefore obtained a larger place in the language of the Schools and in the usage of devotional religion which attributes special value to what is easily understood. On the other hand, the first is very far from prominent in the language of the Schools, and has won a special place in the devotional vocabulary usually known as 'mystical.' Now, if we consider that the Holy Spirit is also called the Spirit of Christ, it follows at once that we say more particularly in one context that the Spirit of Another lives in us, and in a different context that the Other Himself lives in us, without intending to mean anything different by the two phrases. Indeed, in any case nothing different could be meant. If we add the thought of the union of the Divine and the human in Christ, obviously the human can be in us only as a rightly apprehended picture or representation, but the Divine as a powerful impulse, even although in us it does not, as in Him, exclusively determine our whole personality, but only works in and along with His rightly apprehended picture, which again can only take shape in our minds in the measure of truth and perfection in which the Divine glorifies it before our thought. But just this is the work of the Holy Spirit—to bring Christ into memory and glorify Him in us. Thus however they are regarded, the two things are one and the same.

The same result is reached if we compare the content of the two expressions with reference to the effects they indicate. If we conceive ourselves as perfectly within the living fellowship of Christ, then all our actions can be regarded as His. But the Holy Spirit also, when leading us through the knowledge of Christ into all truth, cannot possibly lead us to any other actions than those in which Christ can be recognized ; the fruits of the Spirit are therefore nothing but the virtues of Christ. To recognize in our souls any leading of the divine Spirit which could not be brought into connexion with what Christ's words and life have conveyed to us as His way of acting, is to open the door to every sort of visionary fanaticism that the Protestant Church from the very start has most steadily opposed. The leading of the Holy Spirit is never other than a divine incitement to realize the standard of what Christ, in virtue of the being of God in Him, humanly was and did. And the life of Christ in us is nothing but activity in behalf of the Kingdom of God which embraces men all together in the grasp of the love flowing from Him ; that is, it is the power of the Christian common spirit.

From this it is also clear how, if to believe in Christ and to have Christ living in one are the same thing, it may be said on the one hand that the Holy Spirit produces faith, and on the other hand that the Holy Spirit comes through faith.[1] For through the activity of those who already have a share in the Spirit, He effects faith in others who are brought by them to recognize what is divine and saving in Christ ; in these, thereby, the Holy Spirit becomes the moving principle. And so, since the Divine Essence was bound up with the human person of Christ, but is now (His directly personal influence having ceased) no longer personally operative in any individual, but henceforward manifests itself actively in the fellowship of believers as their common spirit, this is just the way in which the work of redemption is continued and extended in the Church.

3. If then in content the two aforesaid expressions mean the same thing, we must not censure either those Christians who prefer to describe their experiences in the sphere of grace as the immediate being and life of Christ within them, nor those who rather (and almost exclusively) find the explanation of their new life in the indwelling of the Spirit of God. Dogmatic terminology is bound not only to keep both forms, but also to point out the appropriate way of using each, so as to indicate the dangers of a one-sided use ; and this in order that the former, believing themselves to enjoy the immediate influence of Christ, may not break away from the fellowship, or the latter fancy that the Spirit active in the fellowship could carry them on when severed from Christ or lead them beyond Him.

It is difficult, however, to leave this subject without raising the question whether the outpouring of the Spirit is to be conceived as a new divine revelation, and one which, although conditioned by the incarnation of Christ, yet in its characteristic nature is equally original, or whether it is not rather a fact not merely dependent on the appearance of Christ, but its natural consequence. In the latter case the appearance of Christ would be, in the sense already indicated, the one and only supernatural foundation of Christianity ; and following on this the whole further development of the spiritual life would issue naturally from that one source. In the former case, the original outpouring of the Spirit would be a second miracle of the same kind, and equally essential. The question is, of course, not one for Dogmatics in the narrowest sense,

[1] 1 Cor. 14[3], Gal. 3[5, 14].

since we cannot decide it from our Christian self-consciousness ; for to-day the communication of the Holy Spirit to the individual presents itself to each as a natural effect of the presence and activity of the Spirit in the whole formed by the Christian fellowship. But this implies that the acceptance of the former view would have to be based on quite irrefutable testimony. Now the phenomena of Pentecost [1] of course bear distinctly enough the mark of the miraculous. But, for one thing, later communications of the Spirit through preaching (and this is quite analogous to our present situation) are described in exactly the same way and with emphasis on the identity of the phenomena ; [2] so that in this case the miraculous does not belong to the essence of the matter, and we can argue thence that it did not at Pentecost either. On the other hand, it is difficult to assert that the Pentecostal outpouring was the first communication of the Spirit to the disciples, for we are told that already on an earlier occasion Christ had communicated the Spirit to them,[3] and neither the language used nor the treatment of it in the creeds permits us to regard it as a mere promise. On every account, therefore, we do well here to regard the miraculous as not of the essence of the matter but as belonging to the circumstances of the time, and leave the whole question to exegesis. But apart from these accompanying phenomena, the communication of the Spirit cannot be any more or less a miracle in one case than in another ; and in this connexion it may be said that while the gradual dissemination of the Spirit may be in no case a miracle, if regarded as the effect of the living power of the Church, and was no miracle when effected by the living power of Christ, it always is a miracle if regarded as a sudden leap from partially aroused susceptibility into a common and coherent spontaneous activity. As such it broke forth on the day of Pentecost, bearing in token of this originality the miraculous in its train ; and even to-day, in similar cases, the more conversion appears to be something sudden, the more are we inclined to regard anomalous accompanying circumstances as miraculous in character.

§ 125. *Third Theorem.—The Christian Church, animated by the Holy Spirit, is in its purity and integrity the perfect image of the Redeemer, and each regenerate individual is an indispensable constituent of this fellowship.*

1. Fixing our attention on the Redeemer in the maturity of His human life, we see in the totality of His powers an organism

---

[1] Acts 2²ᵇ·.   [2] Acts 10⁴⁷ 11¹⁵.   [3] John 20²².

adequate to the impulses proceeding from the being of God within Him. The individual as regenerate can never in this respect be regarded even as an image of Him, because the condition of varied sinfulness in which divine grace found him does not permit of an exact correspondence in the relationship of his psychical capacities to the impulses of the Spirit. But if the Christian Church is a true common life, a unified or, as we say, a moral personality though not indeed an inherited or natural one, it cannot on this latter account be the same as a personality arising from the person-forming activity of Nature, for in the two cases growth and decay are related in very different fashion ; but none the less it can and must be an image of such a personality. For since the Divine Essence is one and everywhere self-identical, then, even if its mode of being in the individual, Christ, and in the common life is not the same, it follows that the impulses proceeding from it must be the same in both cases. Hence the modes both of comprehension and of action are the same in the Church as in the Redeemer, because there are present in every member, and therefore in the whole, the very same powers which in Christ's case were taken up into unity with the divine principle. Such an aggregate of human powers in a certain sense exists in every organized mass of people, where the most important contrasts which human life offers are ordinarily found side by side. In the primitive Church, too, in spite of its limited size, the same truth was exemplified by the fact that it very quickly spread among Jews and pagans, and thus included what in this respect was the most significant contrast of all, with the result that thus every further development through the inclusion of minor contrasts was prepared for and introduced. If, however, we are seeking the image in its true perfection, we must regard the Church in its absolute purity and integrity. Manifestly we see its purity only if what we view as an element of the Church is not the entire life of regenerate individuals, even subsequently to regeneration, but only that in their life which constitutes its good works, and not that which belongs to its sins. It follows at once that the absolute integrity of the Church is only to be seen in the totality of the human race. For just as in the first pair (viewed as the common ancestors of all) there can be imagined no distinct differences of temperament or constitution simply because it was from them that all differences, whether climatic or more individual, were to develop, and therefore their perfect image is found only in the fundamental types of all human races taken

together, and of all the tribes into which they are subdivided—
which tribes again are completely represented only by the totality
of all the individual beings belonging to them—so too is it in regard
to Christ as the actually given spiritual archetype and original.
If we recall our explanations regarding His sinless perfection on the
one hand and the basis of the sinfulness of all others on the other
hand, it follows that each individual is not merely in each of his
individual characteristics an imperfect image ; even considered as
a whole he is an image of a one-sided and partial kind, which requires
to be supplemented on every side. From this it follows of itself
that the perfect image of Christ is only to be found in the sum-total
of all the forms of spiritual life based on the varieties of natural
foundation ; for it is only so that one-sided tendencies fully supplement each other, and the imperfections compatible with one are
cancelled by the others. We reach the same result if we regard the
work of Christ rather than His Person, and in that relation view the
Church as an organic body, equipped for a sum-total of activities
in which the perfection of each vital function is conditioned by the
integrity of the various members.[1] For various functions can be
properly apportioned only if the apportionment is based on a
variety of gifts, and this again, if it is to arise in a natural way,
presumes a variety present in the personal living unity. In this
way the two facts harmonize well, that the Church is called the
body of Christ, ruled by the Head,[2] and that the more it becomes
externally complete and inwardly perfect, the more it is also said
to become the image of Christ.[3]

2. From this there now follows the second half of our proposition. In reference to this last point it can indeed be said without
hesitation that everything any single person contributes by his
activity to the maintenance and growth of the whole can only be
replaced by the concurrence of several others, else Christ would
have been wrong in saying of each that he was all the same an
unprofitable servant.[4] Yet, in reference to what was said earlier,
in spite of all his imperfection and one-sidedness every individual,
as a subordinate unit in the whole, is a part irreplaceable by any
other. For even in the sphere of the new man there are several
fundamental forms, corresponding to what are national peculiarities in the natural man ; and each of these fundamental types
includes a multitude of subordinate varieties which we can neither
count nor measure, but which nevertheless our Christian senti-

[1] 1 Cor. 12.   [2] Eph. 1²³, Col. 1¹⁹.   [3] Eph. 4¹³, 1 John 3².   [4] Luke 17¹⁰.

ment (just as in the natural sphere our race-consciousness does) compels us to regard as integral and each a whole by itself. And for this we find a justification not only in the Biblical figures already cited, but also in the recognition we are commanded to give all such peculiarities, without limit or exception.[1] Accordingly, we must say also of the development of the Christian fellowship in time that nothing would happen in the Church as it does, unless each individual were what he is. With this is connected the fact that everything in it is common action and common work, there-fore common merit and common guilt ; not manifested in indivi-duals, however, in quite the same ways. Accordingly, the Church only gradually attains to be the perfect image of Christ, and the divine ordinance seen in the gradual addition of individual members and the widening compass of the whole can be expressed in the formula that the advance comes about in such a way that not only is the whole, at every particular moment viewed by itself, as complete and inclusive as possible, but also each moment contains within itself a basis for the largest possible integration in the moment succeeding. At the same time this is only grasped by faith and can never be proved by experience.

Postscript to this Division.—The immediately foregoing dis-cussion concludes our treatment of the many points that have emerged, some of them indirectly related to the previous doctrine, others directly ; a parallel having been shown to exist between the relations of the doctrine of regeneration to the present doctrine and to the preceding one, there can be nothing strange in our thus grouping them together under one Division. Rather it must appear quite natural that the elect are elected to receive the communica-tion of the Spirit. At the same time, this discussion forms the transition to the next Division. In the present Division, we could mention no more than the communication of the Holy Spirit ; in the next, since the Church can be preserved only by the same principle to which it owes its origin and renewal, the continuous operation of the Holy Spirit will be described as we deal with the fundamental features of the Church's life. What will then be set forth will be identical with the content of the doctrine of sanctifica-tion in the same sense that the subject-matter just treated of is identical with the content of the doctrine of regeneration.

[1] I Cor. 12^{19-26}.

§ 126. *The fellowship of believers, animated by the Holy Spirit,
remains ever self-identical in its attitude to Christ and to
this Spirit, but in its relation to the world it is subject to
change and variation.*

1. If the fellowship of believers, as an historical body within
the human race, is to exist and persist in continuous activity, it
must unite in itself two things—a self-identical element, whereby
it remains the same amid change, and a mutable element, in which
the identity finds expression. If we consider it merely in its coexistence with the rest of contemporary human life, summarily
described in Scripture as ' the world,' we might apparently say
that the Church can just as well be known by its difference from
the world as the world can by its difference from the Church. And
certainly amongst believers there are not wanting those who think
that they and their like are recognizable chiefly from the fact that
they are not what the world is. This, however, is a view inclining
equally to separatism and to legalistic righteousness. For the
sinful common life, with the exception of the feeling of need surviving in the mass of men (a feeling which constitutes the Church's
elemental claim upon the world and strictly is characteristic of
the Church itself), is really nullity and a purely negative thing ; as
has been made sufficiently clear by our whole account of sin.[1]
Hence it is quite true that the world, as being formless and confused, can be recognized by believers from the fact that it is excluded from a share in the being of the Church. But the converse
does not hold. The usage of Scripture in entitling ' world ' that
part of the human race which is not yet Church is very natural,
for the whole human race had been so described, and this particular
part only remained what the whole had always been ; unfortun-
ately, however, it may easily give rise to the impression that the
world in this sense is as much a whole as the Church is. Whereas,
in fact, it is only an aggregate of individual elements which in many
respects are antagonistic to each other, and which unite only in
accidental and temporary ways. This erroneous impression is
only heightened when the Church, as it confronts the world, is
constantly described as a ' little flock '—that is, as also being on
its side an aggregate, and one of no importance. It would therefore be best that this use of the term ' world ' should disappear

[1] §§ 65 ff.

from the devotional field and be kept for the field of Dogmatics, where its true significance can be more easily defined and conserved.

The self-identity of the Christian Church, however, can cover no more than the fact that the mode in which the divine exists in the human ever remains the same, and that the goal also remains the same to which the Church throughout all its movements is seeking to approximate. In Christ also the union of the divine with the human was ever the same ; and, since in His case there can be no question of approximation, the adaptation of what in Him underwent human development to the divine impulse in Him was the same too ; but all else was determined in accordance with the laws of the temporal by His position in the world. Similarly, the relation of the Holy Spirit to the Church as its common spirit remains the same, and the Church is ever self-identical as the *locus* of the Spirit in the human race, as also in this further respect that it is always to the same likeness of Christ that the Church is striving to be conformed.

Turning to the mutable, however, we note that even in Christ, though strife and conflict were absent, this element was not as such determined by the divine in Him—the divine being incapable of any temporal determination—but by the human nature conjoined to it. So, too, in the case of the Church, the mutable as such is not determined by the Holy Spirit but by human nature, on which and through which the Spirit works. Now if we apply the term ' world ' to human nature in the whole extent in which it is not determined by the Holy Spirit, we may also say that everything mutable in the Church is as such determined by the world, but not uniformly. For whatever has been or is gradually being realized in man through the Holy Spirit is as it is because the world, operated on by the Holy Spirit, was as it was. In all gifts of the Spirit there is recognizable a definite basis in human nature, causing it inevitably to take the form it does, and throughout the entire development of the new man the kind and the degree of progress depends on the development of nature in the person concerned and on the character of his environment. Similarly, the form which the Christian fellowship takes in a particular nation depends on that nation's peculiar characteristics, for otherwise no reason could be found in the Holy Spirit why it should impress on the Christian fellowship different forms in different places. All this has its ground of determination in the world owing to the law that Christianity must develop as a force in history, and the world as it appears in Christianity is the world as it has been seized upon and permeated by the Holy Spirit. On the other hand, everything that exists within the Church because it is found in those through whom the Holy Spirit works, yet is not due to the Spirit's action, is determined by the world as opposed to the Spirit, and represents the encroachment of the world upon the Church's sphere. This includes not merely what may in a stricter sense be called the sins of the regenerate, but also every hampering and distorting influence which their sinfulness opposes to the Holy Spirit's action, as well as all mistaken and perverse elements that may find their way into the religious consciousness. Now it is true that all such things are in process of disappearing, but they constantly revive as often as the Holy Spirit takes possession of a new field ; just as both things, the signs of having been apprehended by the Spirit and of resistance thereto, are equally found in the sphere of the preparatory operations of grace. The same is true of such differences in the Christian fellowship as are due to the diversities of human nature. Not only is what arises thence, in consequence of the sinfulness persisting in the Church, destined to disappear, but the closer the fellowship is the more will each seek what is his neighbour's and take it up into his own life, with the natural result that differences are correspondingly lessened. But while this happens more or less in each generation, the next is none the less confronted by an undiminished task.

2. If the self-identical element in the Christian Church be considered simply by itself, as something which in a way may be regarded as a manifold, it forms the subject of the disciplines of Christian Dogmatics and Christian Ethics. For if we wish to exhibit that likeness of Christ to which we are ever more striving to approximate, we find it in the outlines of the Christian life laid down in the latter discipline, including as one of its integral parts the development of the Christian consciousness. And if we wish to exhibit the self-identity of the Christian Church as the *locus* of the Holy Spirit, we must present it as inclusive of the truth into which the Holy Spirit alone can lead. Both, however, can only be presented with differences of time and space ; so that all we can say is that in these disciplines and their adjuncts what we are really trying to express is this self-identical element, yet for this purpose we have only these variable means of expression. The same, however, holds true of all aspects of Christian life, in so far as they are based on the truth taught by the Spirit and contain features of Christ's likeness. But the totality of these aspects is just the historical reality of the

Christian Church throughout its whole career, and to this we should have to resort for material if we wished to exhibit the changing and mutable element ; and this we cannot do without at the same time bringing in what is unchanging and self-identical.   This is the more evident because the efforts which give rise to these varying forms of Dogmatics and Ethics are all themselves a minor part of the Church's history.   Thus neither element can be exhibited apart from the other.   If the attempt were made to set forth the self-identical and invariable element in Christianity in complete abstraction from the historical, it would scarcely be distinguishable from the undertaking of people who imagine that they are expounding Christianity when in point of fact what they offer is pure speculation.   And if anyone tried to present solely the variable in Christian history in complete abstraction from the self-identical, his aim would apparently be the same as that of people who, penetrating no further than the outer husk of things, permit us to see in the history of the Church nothing but the complex and pernicious play of blinded passion.

The two aspects or elements, then, cannot be exhibited apart from each other without making the real nature of the Church unrecognizable ; on the other hand, we cannot here treat of both together in the way just indicated.   Consequently, in the doctrine of the Church in its coexistence with the world, we can only state first those chief activities through the continuous exercise of which the temporal development of this whole really becomes the development of the Christian Church, and which thus form its essential and invariable features.   Thereafter we shall treat of those characteristics of the fellowship whereby during its coexistence with the world it is distinguishable from that which it can only become even in appearance after this hampering antithesis between Church and world has passed away, but which—as being the same under both forms—inwardly viewed it already is.   The former invariable element is due to the fact that the Church can only persist and reach its perfection through that to which it owes its very existence ; the latter variable element, however, being conditioned by the world, is chiefly traceable to the material which the world offers to the instreaming influence of the principle by which the Church is constituted.   This division of the subject, therefore, falls into two halves—one of which comprises the essential and (in spite of its coexistence with the world) immutable features of the Church, while the other sets forth the mutable element which belongs to the Church in virtue of its coexistence with the world.

FIRST HALF: THE ESSENTIAL AND INVARIABLE FEATURES OF
THE CHURCH

§ 127. *The Christian fellowship, in spite of the mutability inseparable
from its coexistence with the world, is, nevertheless, always
and everywhere self-identical, inasmuch, first, as the witness
to Christ remains in it ever the same, and this is found in*
Holy Scripture *and in the* Ministry of the Word of God ;
*inasmuch, secondly, as the formation and maintenance of
living fellowship with Christ rests upon the same ordinances
of Christ, and these are* Baptism *and the* Lord's Supper ;
*inasmuch, finally, as the reciprocal influence of the whole
on the individual, and of individuals on the whole, is always
uniformly ordered, and this is seen in the* Power of the Keys
and in Prayer in the Name of Jesus.

1. To begin with, we must put aside the objection which asks
how the unity and identity of the Church can rest upon these
features, every one of which is a subject of controversy, several of
which indeed have assumed such different forms in different parts
of Christendom as to give rise to special and mutually exclusive
communions, while others are totally rejected by particular communions which still claim to be recognized as Christian. In the
first place, this is merely a very direct confirmation of what was
said above, namely, that it is impossible to exhibit either of the
two elements wholly apart from the other. Nay, if we go by what
was indicated in the Introduction regarding the relations between
Catholicism and Protestantism, it will seem entirely natural that on
almost all these subjects Evangelical teaching must find itself in
opposition to Roman. The same is true of several smaller communions which in essence certainly are Protestant, and which in
their antagonism to the Roman Church leave us far behind. But
here we must distinguish between what is inward and what is outward. For no Christian communion will admit that any such body
can exist apart from witness to Christ, in the sense that what is
essential in such witness must everywhere be the same, any more
than it could exist without a continuous living fellowship with
Christ, implying a bond between the changing generations due to

586

their sharing the newly arisen life.   Further, wherever it is possible
to speak of a perfect fellowship resting upon a common spirit, we
must also assume a reciprocal influence of the whole and individuals
on each other.   In part, therefore, differences only concern the way
in which the outward is conformed to the inward ; in part they
consist in varying ideas as to the necessity and exact character of
the connexion which must always exist between the inward and an
outward possessing some particular form or other.   With regard
to these differences, the most important point is this, that we should
judge correctly whether they are rooted in the spatial and temporal
variations found in man's spiritual nature, or are to be viewed as
defects, because due to encroachments of the world upon the
Church.   The latter sort are to be resisted the more stoutly in proportion as such encroachments invade the innermost sanctuary of
the Church ; the former cancel each other where there is mutual
recognition.

2. Thereafter some explanations will have to be given of the
relationships in which the Church institutions named above are
placed in our statement, and the way in which they are combined.
If we start from the principle that our Christianity ought to be the
same as that of the Apostles, our Christianity too must be generated
by the personal influences of Christ, for spiritual states depend on
the mode of their origination.   These influences, however, cannot
now emanate from Him directly, for in that case they could not
be recognized with such certainty as having emanated from Him
supernaturally as to need no confirmatory proof of their identity
with those felt by the Apostles, to which, as we have them in the
New Testament representations of Christ's personality, we have
always to return.   Apart from these influences no activity for the
Kingdom of God could have been evoked even in the disciples by
the imparting of the Holy Spirit ; hence the influence of these representations of Christ will always be an indispensable pre-condition
of the Holy Spirit being imparted. This principle, it is true,
scarcely appears to cover the whole of the New Testament, nor need
all that is taught on the subject be developed from it.   But leaving
this last point to be dealt with later, on the former it may be said
that for the purpose stated not even the fixed written letter of the
New Testament appears to be necessary ; the further possibility of
oral propagation must be admitted, for no more can be guaranteed
than the unimpaired identity of the tradition.   And so far we can
agree that the actual form in which the personality of Christ is set

before us does not belong unconditionally to the *esse* but rather to the *bene esse* of the Church. As regards the larger and not strictly evangelistic part of the New Testament writings, they furnish proof on the one hand that the Church-forming self-activity which He promised to men really flowed from the impressions left by Christ Himself and from the witness He bade the disciples give ; and in this sense they are the source of what we now possess. On the other hand, they form a supplement to those direct utterances of Christ ; for we can argue back from the ordinances and actions of the disciples to teachings and injunctions of Christ as their source. Scripture, however, as we actually have it—each single book and the whole collection as a treasure preserved for all later generations of the Church—is invariably a work of the Holy Spirit as the common spirit of the Church, and is only one special instance of the witness to Christ described in general terms in the paragraph we are ex- pounding. For oral and written teaching and narrative concerning Christ were originally the same, and only differed by accident. Scripture now stands by itself, for its preservation unchanged guarantees in a special manner the identity of our witness to Christ with that originally given. Yet it would be a mere lifeless posses- sion if this preservation were not an ever-renewed self-activity of the Church, which reveals itself also in living witness to Christ that either goes back to Scripture or harmonizes with Scripture in meaning and spirit. And this witness alone, taken universally as the duty and calling of every member of the Church—and viewed provision- ally apart from definite forms of any kind—is what is understood here by the phrase ' the Ministry of the Word of God.' But taken in this general sense and thus related to each other, these two first features of the Church are essential ; for otherwise faith could only be evoked by direct influences [of Christ], in which case we could look for no identity and could have no guarantee of truth. This Ministry, however, by no means acts only on the outside world ; in its operation within the Church equally it is an organic structure, traceable to Christ Himself, for the communication of life and power.

For the same reason, namely, that we have nothing more to expect from unmediated personal influences of Christ, the linking- up of living fellowship with Christ, and its renewal, must come from the Church and be traceable to its actions ; but only to such actions as must also be regarded as activities of Christ—lest Christ should be thought to play a merely passive rôle, and be overshadowed by the Church. And this communal character is the peculiarity of both sacraments. For although baptism as originally instituted was not the first beginning of contact between the Church and the individual, yet it is only through baptism that all that precedes receives such confirmation as thereby to inaugurate a continuous and conscious living fellowship with Christ. And while the Lord's Supper is not the only means of maintaining living fellowship with Christ—and provisionally we are not regarding it here as an isolable action which even in isolation has a specific effect—yet we take it as being the highest of its kind, and subsume under it every other enjoyment of Christ as either an approximation to it or a prolongation of it. Hence we here keep more to this underlying idea than to outward forms in which the idea is realized.

In like manner, the entire influence of the whole fellowship on the individual is concentrated in the forgiveness of sin. For in view of the relationship obtaining between the sins of the regenerate and their good works, these last can be recognized only in the measure in which the sin still clinging to them is removed. But good works are at once the fruit and the seed of the gifts of the Spirit developing in each life, so that the forgiveness of sin first assigns them their place in the fellowship of believers. Finally, as regards Prayer in the Name of Jesus, representing as it does the influence of individuals on the whole, apart from which a whole animated by a common spirit and in that sense self-contained could manifest no progress—there can be no Prayer in the Name of Jesus except in connexion with the things of His Kingdom. Hence its efficacy, promised by Christ even to the smallest gathering of individuals, secures their influence upon the whole. If we regard such prayer as representing all influences of the kind, this rests on the assumption, self-evident to every Christian, that prayer necessarily includes and presupposes personal activity in bringing about what is prayed for. Thus without the two last-named features, there could be in the common life neither order nor progress and success.

3. That we have here given a complete view of the elements on which the unity and identity of the Christian Church rest in every time and place is best seen if we recur to the relation of the Church to Christ. On the one hand, as the organism of Christ—which is what Scripture means by calling it His Body—it is related to Christ as the outward to the inward, so that in its essential activities it must also be a reflection of the activities of Christ. And since the effects produced by it are simply the gradual realization

of redemption in the world, its activities must likewise be a continuation of the activities of Christ Himself. These we have reduced to the scheme of the Threefold Office ; and in the same way it must be possible to show that the three offices of Christ are reflected and carried on in the essential activities of the Church as stated above.

Prayer in the Name of Jesus, embracing as it does the full vocational activity of each individual Christian, is a reflection of Christ's kingly activity, both as it is in itself and as concerns the relation between His rule and that of the Father. It is the latter, inasmuch as it concludes with the reverently submissive utterance of the thoughts of each regarding the extension of the Kingdom of God or the assaults of the world. It is the former, inasmuch as it comprehends all purposes flowing from the energies of the God-consciousness. And in the Power of the Keys there is attached to the forgiveness of sins, rightly understood, all that has to do with Church order and the estimate of persons in the Church which flows from the common consciousness. Thus we have here the continuation of that kingly activity of Christ which began with His choice of the disciples and His giving of ordinances for the fellowship that was to be.

Further, since the prophetic activity of Christ consists in His self-presentation and His invitation to enter the Kingdom of God, the Holy Scriptures are the permanent reflection of His prophetic activity, inasmuch as in their composition and preservation, regarded as the work of the Church, they form the most direct exhibition of Christ. The Ministry of the Word we cannot but regard as also a continuation of His prophetic work, for it essentially consists in the applied presentation of Christ and invitation in His name.

If, finally, the essential element in Christ's priestly office—to distinguish this as clearly as possible from the prophetic and kingly offices—lies supremely in this, that He mediates the fellowship of men with God, there will be no difficulty in acknowledging that both sacraments have a relation thereto. In this sense, that baptism owing to its more symbolical character is related more as a reflection, the Lord's Supper owing to its more real content as a continuation.

This arrangement also shows that everything essentially belonging to Christ's activity has its reflection and continuation in the Church, for the first three features pertain to His redemptive, the other three to His reconciling, activity. Nor in our Evangelical interpretation of Christianity shall we have to indicate any other feature of the Church which could claim to stand on the same level as these institutions.   On the contrary, we shall neither place tradition beside Scripture nor subordinate the Ministry of the Word to any kind of symbolical rites ; we shall neither acquiesce in the multiplication of sacraments nor by attributing magical effects to them destroy the analogy they bear to the other features of the Church ; we shall neither limit Prayer in the Name of Jesus by invocation of the saints nor permit any special representation of Christ—whether individual or collegial—to usurp the place of the Power of the Keys.

First Doctrine : Holy Scripture

§ 128. *The authority of Holy Scripture cannot be the foundation of faith in Christ ; rather must the latter be presupposed before a peculiar authority can be granted to Holy Scripture.*

1. The polemical first part of this proposition is solely due to the fact that what we here deny is actually asserted.   Possibly as a matter of fact it is more widely held than definitely stated, for all text-books and Confessions which put the doctrine of Scripture as the source of Christian faith in the foreground seem distinctly to favour this view.   Hence it is necessary thoroughly to expose the underlying misconception.   If faith in Jesus as the Christ or as the Son of God and the Redeemer of men is to be based on the authority of Scripture, the question arises how this authority itself is to be based ; for obviously the thing must be so done as to impress the conviction on unbelieving hearts, so that they too may by this path come to faith in the Redeemer.   Now if we have no point of departure but ordinary reason, the divine authority of Scripture to begin with must admit of being proved on grounds of reason alone ; and as against this two points must be kept in mind.   First, this always involves a critical and scientific use of the understanding of which not all are capable ; on this theory, therefore, only those so gifted can attain to faith in an original and genuine way, while all others would merely have faith at second-hand and on the authority of the experts.   Now even in the sphere of faith we might accept such a graded distinction if we were speaking of insight into doctrine or a correct judgment upon different doctrinal interpretations ; but to accept it with regard to the possession of genuinely saving faith is incongruous with that equality of all Christians which the Evangelical Church proclaims, and would, as in the Church

of Rome, demand from the laity an unqualified and submissive trust in those who alone have access to the grounds of faith. For the right to the Word of God, which we grant to all Christian people, and the zeal with which we seek to maintain it in vital circulation, has nothing to do with the idea that each individual ought to be able to prove that the books of Scripture contain a divine revelation. Secondly, if such proof could be given and if faith could be established in this fashion—if, that is to say, faith, given a certain degree of culture, could be implanted by argument—then on such terms faith might exist in people who feel absolutely no need of redemption, that is quite apart from repentance and change of mind ; which means that, having originated in this way, it would not be genuine, living faith at all. In other words, a conviction of this kind, gained through demonstrative proof, would in itself have no value, for of itself it would not result in true living fellowship with Christ. But where the need of redemption is really felt, the faith that makes alive may spring even from a message about Christ which is in no way bound up with the conviction that the books of Scripture possess a special character, but may rest on any other sort of witness that is accompanied by real perception of Christ's spiritual power—may rest, that is, simply on oral tradition.

2. With respect to the grounds of faith, then, we can admit no distinction between different classes. And no more can we admit a distinction between different periods of time ; the grounds of faith must be the same for us as for the first Christians. If it be said that in their case, from the Apostles onward, their grounds of faith sprang from their belief in Scripture, that is, in the Old Testament and especially in the prophecies of Christ it contains, we need only add to what was said above on this point that although the Apostles, at the outset of their connexion with Jesus, do describe Him as the Figure whom the prophets foretold, it is impossible to take this as meaning that they had been led to faith in Him by the study of these prophecies and by the comparison of their contents with what they saw and heard in Jesus. On the contrary, it was a direct impression which awakened faith in souls prepared by the testimony of the Baptist, and their description of Jesus was only an expression of this faith combined with their faith in the prophets. Even in their preaching they took the same line. There they first express their faith communicatively by recurring to Jesus' words and deeds ; then they adduce prophetic testimonies in confirmation,

And just as their faith sprang from Christ's preaching of Himself, so in the case of others faith sprang from the preaching of Christ by the Apostles and many more. The New Testament writings are such a preaching come down to us, hence faith springs from them too ; but in no sense conditionally on the acceptance of a special doctrine about these writings, as having had their origin in special divine revelation or inspiration. On the contrary, faith might arise in the same way though no more survived than testimonies of which it had to be admitted that, in addition to Christ's essential witness to Himself and the original preaching of His disciples, they also contained much in detail that had been misinterpreted, or inaccurately grasped, or set in a wrong light owing to confusions of memory.

Thus, in order to attain to faith, we need no such doctrine of Scripture, and the attempt to force unbelievers into faith by means of it has had no success. It follows that, just as the Apostles already had faith before they arrived at that condition of mind, other than faith itself, in which they were able to take a share in producing the New Testament, in our case too faith must preexist before, by reading the New Testament, we are led to postulate a special condition of the apostolic mind in which its books were written, and a resulting special character of the books themselves. A doctrine of this kind can only be made credible to those who already are believers.

3. Hence throughout the whole of the foregoing exposition of faith we have assumed no more than faith itself, present in a feeling of need (in whatever source that feeling may have originated), and Scripture we have adduced only as expressing the same faith in detail ; and it is only now that for the first time we are treating of Scripture in its natural connexion with the Christian Church and considering the question of its difference from other books. None the less, the old method, whether used in Confessions or in text-books, of placing the doctrine of Scripture first is not wholly censurable, if by Scripture proof of doctrine nothing more be meant than showing that a proposition so proved gives expression to an original and authentic element in Christian piety, and if precautions be taken to avoid the impression that a doctrine must belong to Christianity because it is contained in Scripture, whereas in point of fact it is only contained in Scripture because it belongs to Christianity. Were we to rest content with the former position, Dogmatic Theology would continue to be a mere aggregate

of detached propositions, the inner connexion of which was left obscure. Either, its relation to the common faith of the Church would then be what has already been indicated ; true and complete certainty of faith would only exist where there was ability to prove the divinity of Scripture, while all who lacked this degree of scientific culture would believe simply on authority ; and thus piety would spring from, and depend on, science. Or, where the laity break away and base their faith on their experience, rejoicing in its vitality, the scientific exposition of faith would become something which, for the fellowship of the Church, is empty and worthless. Hence for the purpose of our argument it was important to get its true aim quite clear, independently of Scripture ; and only to bring in the doctrine of Scripture at a point where its proper authority can be plainly seen to rest on the relation between the self-identical and the mutable and in its true connexion with the other essential features of the Church.

§ 129. *The Holy Scriptures of the New Testament are, on the one hand, the first member in the series, ever since continued, of presentations of the Christian Faith ; on the other hand, they are the norm for all succeeding presentations.*

1. That the Holy Scriptures are the first member in the series in question implies that the succeeding members are homogeneous with the first ; and this holds true alike of form and content. The New Testament writings are usually divided into historical and doctrinal books ; this, however, is really correct only if the division is based not on the subject-matter preponderant in each case, but on the outward form. In the historical books the discourses of Christ and the Apostles form a very important part, and the apostolic letters with few exceptions are only intelligible in so far as either they contain historical elements or we can form from them a picture of the historical situation. Whether we retain this division or discard it and look more at the form of particular elements in these books, we can only say that all that has approved itself in the way of oral presentation of Christian piety in later ages of the Church has kept within the lines of these original forms,or is attached to them as an explanatory accompaniment. Even religious poetry, in the lyrical form which alone is genuinely churchly, has its germ in the New Testament ; on the other hand, all explanatory and systematizing works, which as presentations of Christian piety have less originality and independence, are only aids to the under-

standing of the original testimonies or compilations drawn from them.

As regards content, however, the general rule is first of all to be applied that in every kind of fellowship the individual element approves itself only in so far as it gives expression to the common spirit. Here too, accordingly, everything of the kind which persists in influence alongside of Holy Scripture we must regard as homogeneous with Scripture ; while nothing that does not persist can be given a place in the series.

2. But if in the historical development of the Christian Church redemption is being ever more completely realized in time, and the Holy Spirit is thus pervading the whole ever more perfectly, it looks as if the first of this or any other series cannot be the norm for all succeeding members ; for in any such development each later member must be more perfect than the preceding. There is truth in this, but only when we are comparing two whole phases of the development, each in its entirety. If we consider the Church during the Apostolic Age as a unity, its thinking as a whole cannot supply a norm for that of later ages. For owing to its naturally most unequal distribution of the divine Spirit, as well as to the further fact that not everyone was equally productive in religious ideas even in the measure of his participation in the common spirit, it was very easily possible (since Jewish and pagan views and maxims were still uneradicated and their antagonism to the Christian spirit could only be recognized gradually) that expositions of religion might be produced which, strictly speaking, were rather Judaism or paganism coloured by Christianity than Christianity itself, *i.e.* were, if considered as Christian, in the highest degree impure. Contemporary with all this very imperfect material, however, were the presentations given in preaching by the immediate disciples of Christ. In their case, the danger of an unconsciously debasing influence from their previous Jewish forms of thought and life on the presentation of Christianity by word and act was averted, in proportion as they had stood near to Christ, by the purifying influence of their living memory of Christ as a whole. Thereby every idea which had attained that clearness in consciousness which must precede oral exposition, was at once forced to betray any antagonism it might have to the spirit of Christ's life and teaching. This holds good, in the first place, of their narratives of Christ's words and deeds, which fixed the standard that was to have the widest purifying influence. But it

also holds pre-eminently of all that the Apostles taught and ordained
for Christian churches, as acting in Christ's name ; though it must
not be forgotten that even when acting merely as individuals, each
of them found not only his complement but his corrective in one
of the other Apostles.[1] Thus in the Apostolic Age what is most
perfect and what is most imperfect stood side by side as *canonical*
and *apocryphal* (both these words taken in the sense indicated by
the discussion above)—two extremes which can never reappear in
the same form in any later age.   Church presentations of Christianity could not but diverge ever more widely from the apocryphal,
since the influence of foreign elements on the Church decreased—
even though in matters of detail there were ever new accretions
from the realm of Judaism—in proportion as the bulk of Christians
came to be born and nurtured in the bosom of the Church.   On the
other hand, the Church could never again reproduce the canonical,
for the living intuition of Christ was never again able to ward off
all debasing influences in the same direct fashion, but only deriva-
tively through the Scriptures and hence in dependence on them.
If then we take both together—canonical and apocryphal—the
Apostolic Age itself comes under the general rule ; the influence of
the canonical evidently becomes surer and wider as the apocryphal
disappears even in outlying parts of the Church ; thus viewed as a
whole, the later presentation is also the more perfect.   On the other
hand, if we take the canonical by itself, it has an authority normative
for all later times.   Such authority we do not ascribe uniformly
to every part of our Holy Scriptures, but only in proportion as the
writers attained to the condition just described, so that casual
expressions and what are merely side-thoughts do not possess the
same degree of normativeness as belongs to whatever may at each
point be the main subject.   Nor is it meant that every later presentation must be uniformly derived from the Canon or be germin-
ally contained in it from the first.   For since the Spirit was poured
out on all flesh, no age can be without its own originality in Christian
thinking.   Yet, on the one hand, nothing can be regarded as a pure
product of the Christian Spirit except so far as it can be shown to
be in harmony with the original products ; on the other, no later
product possesses equal authority with the original writings
when it is a question of guaranteeing the Christian character
of some particular presentation or of exposing its unchristian
elements.

[1] Cf. Gal. 2[11ff.].

§ 130. *First Theorem.*—*The individual books of the New Testament are inspired by the Holy Spirit, and the collection of them took place under the guidance of the Holy Spirit.*

Conf. Helv. i. : Scriptura canonica, verbum Dei Spiritu s. tradita et . . . mundo proposita, etc.—*Conf. Gall.* v. : Credimus verbum his libris comprehensum ab uno Deo esse profectum.—*Conf. Scot.* xviii. : Spiritus dei per quem s. scripturae litteris sunt mandatae.—*Conf. Belg.* iii. : Confitemur sanctos Dei viros divino afflatos spiritu locutos esse. Postea vero Deus . . . servis suis mandavit, ut sua illa oracula scriptis consignarent.—*Decl. Thor.* : Profitemur . . . nos amplecti sacras canonicas . . . scripturas . . . instinctu spiritus s. primitus scriptas, etc.

1. It is not easy to assign exact limits of meaning to the ecclesiastical term ' inspiration ' in general, and here we merely wish to make some preliminary observations before entering on a special discussion of the subject. The word θεόπνευστος, which is used of the Old Testament writings,[1] and which historically constitutes the most definite basis of usage, may very easily lead to a conception of the Holy Spirit as occupying a relation to the writer which has special reference to the act of writing but is otherwise non-existent. This suggestion attaches less to the phrase ὑπὸ πνεύματος ἁγίου φερόμενοι.[2] Here the interpretation that these men were always so ' moved,' speaking and writing in what was thus a permanent state, is in itself quite as natural as one to the effect that they were only ' moved ' to speak and write. Since the ecclesiastical term is not strictly scriptural and is, besides, figurative, it is necessary to define it by relation to cognate terms, which also describe ways of arriving at ideas. Here on the one side what is known by inspiration along with what is learnt stands over against what is excogitated, the latter being that which proceeds entirely from a man's own activity as contrasted with what is due to influence coming from without. On the other side, again, stands what is known by inspiration in contrast to what is learnt ; the latter is derived from external communication, while the former, being as it is original in the eyes of others, depends for its emergence solely on inward communication. Hence the presentation of what has been learnt may approximate to any extent to the merely mechanical, whereas in the forthcoming of what is known by inspiration there may be manifested the whole freedom of personal productivity.

The general custom of calling Holy Scripture as such ' Revelation,' however, leads frequently to the two ideas being treated as

[1] 2 Tim. 3[16].   [2] 2 Pet. 1[21].

interchangeable, which cannot fail to produce confusion. For if this is taken to mean that the sacred writers, being under inspiration, were informed of the content of what they wrote in a special divine manner, there is no foundation for any such statement, whether we consider the act of composing a sacred book itself or the excitation of thought preceding or underlying it. All that they teach derives from Christ ; hence in Christ Himself must be the original divine bestowal of all that the Holy Scriptures contain—not, however, in isolated particulars, by way of inspiration, but as a single indivisible bestowal of knowledge out of which the particulars evolve organically. Thus the speaking and writing of the Apostles as moved by the Spirit was simply a communication drawn from the divine revelation in Christ.

Our paragraph, however, ascribes to the Holy Spirit not merely the composition of the individual books, but also their collection to form the New Testament Canon, and in referring to the latter point it employs a different expression. This distinction is primarily due to the fact that we regard the composition of a book as the voluntary act of an individual, whereas the formation of the Canon is the result of a many-sided collaboration and controversy within the Church ; so that it becomes impossible to ascribe uniformly to the Holy Spirit all the factors contributing thereto. These two expressions will not be interpreted by everyone precisely in our sense ; some will be content to assert merely a guiding influence of the Spirit even in the matter of composition ; others will hold that even in the collection of the books the influence of the Spirit amounted to inspiration.

2. If now we go back to the conception of the Holy Spirit as the common spirit of the Church, and hence the source of all spiritual gifts and good works, it follows that all thinking, so far as it pertains to the Kingdom of God, must be traced back to and inspired by the Spirit. This holds good of the thinking of the Apostolic Age as inclusive of the two opposites—the apocryphal and the canonical ; in this sense, that in the former only isolated traces of connexion with the common life of Christians derive from the Spirit, while in the latter His activity is merely more closely delimited by the individual in whom He is working, with scarcely any weakening or alteration ; yet so that in no case the difference between the individual and Christ is cancelled. While the interval between the apocryphal and the canonical is filled by gradual stages, the action of the Spirit is most profound and concen-

trated within the circle of those singled out by Peter, with the assent of the whole community,[1] as men who had companied with Christ from shortly after the start of His public life.   For the individual members of this apostolic class, as we may call it, were so much regarded as being on an equality with each other that without offence to conscience the number of the original Apostles could be filled up from among them by simple lot ; their steadfastness was a guarantee alike of the purity of their zeal and of their full understanding.   But even within their circle no one can miss the important difference between aspects of personality that affect merely the private life of individuals and such as could be employed in the control of Christian affairs.   It is with reference to the former that even in Apostles human nature most easily betrays itself, while in the latter sphere there could not but be a keener intention to let the Spirit of the whole exert an exclusive rule.   Hence what is here spoken or done can be described as inspired in a much stricter and more definite sense.   On the other hand, we should recklessly break up the unity of life characteristic of these apostolic men if, in order to bring out emphatically the inspiration of the Holy Scriptures, we were to assert that they were less animated and moved by the Holy Spirit in other parts of their apostolic office than in the act of writing, or in the composition of writings (also concerned with the service of the churches) which were not destined to be included in the Canon ; or again that they enjoyed His aid very much more in the public addresses or parts of addresses which were eventually preserved in the Acts of the Apostles than at any other time ; or that this difference, with or without their knowledge, was to be explained by the fact that over and above their immediate purpose these writings were meant to have a bearing on all subsequent ages.   Thus the peculiar inspiration of the Apostles is not something that belongs exclusively to the books of the New Testament.   These books only share in it ; and inspiration in this narrower sense, conditioned as it is by the purity and completeness of the apostolic grasp of Christianity, covers the whole of the official apostolic activity thence derived.

If we consider the inspiration of Scripture in this context as a special portion of the official life of the Apostles which in general was guided by inspiration, we shall hardly need to raise all those

---

[1] Acts 1[21ff.]; cf. John 15[27].   Paul does not belong to this circle, and if the Church has never regarded him as the inferior of the other Apostles in respect of inspiration, it thereby ascribes to him the same prerogatives as to them, although in a sense he had acquired them in a different way.

difficult questions about the extent of inspiration which so long have been answered solely in a manner that removed the whole subject from the domain of experiential insight. Nothing but an utterly dead scholasticism could try to draw lines of demarcation anywhere on the pathway lying between the first impulse to write and the actually written word, or wish to represent the written word in its bare externality as a special product of inspiration. The natural standard here is the analogy of the doctrine of Christ's Person ; at least, if we start with the fact that in the vocational life of the Apostles the whole activity of the common spirit ruling in the Church approximated as closely as possible to the person-forming union of the Divine Essence with human nature which constituted the Person of Christ (this without prejudice to the specific difference that obtains between the two modes of union), and that only in the light of this standard can what is outward in the actions of the Apostles be regarded as partially different in origin from the inward it was meant to express. This being assumed, it at once follows that we must reject the suggestion that in virtue of their divine inspiration the sacred books demand a hermeneutical and critical treatment different from one guided by the rules which obtain elsewhere. This at the same time disposes of all other difficulties.

3. If the inspiration of Scripture be thus traced to the influence of the Holy Spirit on the official activities of the Apostles, it might easily appear as though this held good merely for the doctrinal but not for the historical books, since what is in question in the latter case is not the communication of the writer's own thoughts ; everything depends rather on the sifting and arrangement of exact recollections. But for one thing the thoughts of the Apostles were to be no more than developments of what Christ had said, and these sayings, being elicited by special circumstances, could only be fully understood in their historical context. And this clearly means that a pure and complete apprehension of the various aspects of Christ's life is an essential precondition of the Apostles' official action as a whole. At the same time it is impossible to conceive of any incident in Christ's public life as wholly unaccompanied by quickening and instructive speech ; all His actions were presenta-tions of Himself, and as such were fruitful for His proclamation of the Kingdom of God. Yet these incidents could be interpreted in very different ways ; they could be so interpreted by some observers that the resulting natural impression helped them to

recognize Christ's divine dignity ; by others they could be interpreted so perversely as to yield an impression which was apocryphal
and distorted and could even be used as proof against His Messianic
position.   Thus the correctest view of the facts of Christ's life—
traceable in a certain sense directly to the divine Spirit—we naturally find in just that circle of people who had followed Christ's
public life with the growing confidence that in Him they had found
the Promised One, so that in the same circle both things are inseparably united—the right view of Christ and the right development of His teaching and precepts.   For the same reason it was
afterwards a matter of the utmost importance for the whole Church
to ascertain and select the right memories of Christ's life, asking
how each supposed memory agreed with the view of the Kingdom
of God He had brought.   Hence we must conceive the memory of
the Apostles subserviently to this general aim as also under the
influence of the Holy Spirit ; nor can we in this respect make any
distinction between the apostolic teachings and the evangelical
narratives ; indeed, we find the Apostles themselves narrating
both orally and in writing.   Even though their teaching arose out
of definite official relationships, that is to say, out of their vocational
action in the narrower sense, yet narration too sprang from an
effort to promote the good of the whole Church, *i.e.* from their
vocational action in the wider sense.   This has no bearing on the
question whether evangelistic narration was a special Church
function, whether co-ordinate with or subordinate to the preaching
of the Apostles.   But the reproduction of memories, be it oral or
written, can never quite be separated from historical composition,
as may be seen from the narration even of one isolated fact ; and
the effort to exhibit the Redeemer in His habit as He lived is also
the work of the Spirit of truth, and only so far as it is so can such
narrative have a place in Holy Scripture.   If, on the other hand,
we consider that what happened first was the communication of
just such isolated narratives, their collection in wholes like our
Gospels following later, we must concede both possibilities—that
the narrator presents only what he himself had experienced in this
or that connexion, and that with his personal experiences he mingles
what he has heard credibly from others ; nay more, that one who
himself had had no experience in the matter might yet, moved
by the same impulse and the same Spirit, put together material
which he had derived from the pure and original knowledge of
others as fruitfully as an original witness could have done.   If

what was principally needed was the right selection and arrangement of historical facts already to hand, the influence of the Holy
Spirit in and throughout such work is entirely analogous to His
influence in the selection of individual books for the Canon.

4. Lastly, we have to consider the part taken by the Holy
Spirit in the collection of these books. Here the first difference
which must strike everyone is this, that although all the particular
books in the collection belong to the Apostolic Age, the actual
collection of them certainly does not ; we cannot therefore have
had handed down to us any strictly apostolic indication of what is
canonical and normative. In discriminating, therefore, we can
hardly use any analogy but this, that we should conceive of the
Spirit as ruling and guiding in the thought-world of the whole
Christian body just as each individual does in his own. Every man
knows how to distinguish his own noteworthy thoughts, and how
so to preserve them that he can count on bringing them up later
in his mind : the rest he puts aside partly for later elaboration ;
others he simply disregards and leaves it a matter merely of accident
whether they ever again present themselves to his mind or not.
Indeed, he may occasionally reject some of his ideas entirely, either
just when they occur or later. Similarly, the faithful preservation
of the apostolic writings is the work of the Spirit of God acknowledging His own products ; He distinguishes what is to remain
unchangeable from what has in many respects undergone transformation in the later development of Christian doctrine. On the
other hand, He rejects the apocryphal in part immediately on its
appearance, and partly He ensures that both this sort of product
and the taste for it shall gradually disappear from the Church.
The one apparent difficulty is this, that in history certain books
underwent varying vicissitudes ; at first they were accepted as
canonical and later were rejected as uncanonical, or *vice versa.*
But for one thing what changed here was not the judgment of the
whole Church ; rather a book which had been accepted in one
region and rejected in another was later universally accepted or
universally rejected. And much might well be thought worthy of
rejection for the Church organized as a great unity or in combination
with the other books, which was acceptable or the reverse in isolated
communities and judged merely by its own influence. On the
other hand, this proves no more than that Holy Scripture *as a
collection* came into existence only gradually and by approximation.
The same influence reveals itself even yet in the Church's careful

estimate of the different grades of normative authority to be conceded to particular portions of Scripture, as also in decisions regarding all sorts of *lacunæ* and interpolations ; so that the judgment of
the Church is only approximating ever more closely to a complete
expulsion of the apocryphal and the pure preservation of the
canonical.   The influence directly stimulating this approximation
·guides also the whole course of procedure, and that influence is
simply the Holy Spirit ruling in the Church.   But all vacillations
of judgment, everything that makes approximation more difficult,
can have no other source than the influence which is exerted on the
Church by the world.

Hence if it is sought to distinguish in this connexion between
points that have been decided once for all and others which the
Church might yet take up, we cannot be too cautious.   As history
shows, the sense for the truly apostolic is a gift of the Spirit that is
gradually increasing in the Church ; hence at an early stage much
may, through the mistakes of individuals, have crept into the
sacred books which a later age can recognize as uncanonical and
definitely prove to be so.   But even as regards the collection as a
whole, the mere fact that ever since it has existed in the Church
as a collection, and has always retained its identity as such, is no
guarantee that its limits have been irrevocably fixed.   Its fixation
(which we have the less right to regard as an absolute miracle or an
altogether isolated work of the Holy Spirit that we are not entirely
ignorant of how it came about) must rather be viewed as but one
incident in a process which can only be fully vindicated through
its ever-renewed confirmation as the Church perseveres in its task of
inquiry, but otherwise is liable to correction.   Hence even though
the Canon is fixed in many Confessions of our Church,[1] this ought
not to prevent further unrestricted investigation of the matter ;
critical inquiry must ever anew test the individual writings of
Scripture with a view to decide whether they rightly keep their
place in the sacred collection.   Doubt of the genuine can only
issue in ever greater certainty.   Even the fact that writings undeniably apostolic and others approximately so have perished is no
argument to the contrary, for we are entitled to believe that nothing
essential to the preservation and well-being of the Church has thus
been lost.   We are at least equally entitled to believe that it can
only promote the welfare of the Church if Holy Scripture be distinguished clearly from what does not belong to it.

[1] *Conf. Gall.* iii. ; *Conf. Angl.* vi. ; *Conf. Belg.* iv.

§ 131. *Second Theorem.—As regards their origin the New Testament Scriptures are authentic, and as a norm for Christian Doctrine they are sufficient.*

Art. Smalc. ii. : Regulam autem aliam habemus, ut videlicet verbum Dei condat articulos fidei et praeterea nemo, ne angelus quidem.—*Conf. Gall.* iv. : Hos libros agnoscimus esse canonicos, id est, ut fidei nostrae normam et regulam habemus, idque non tantum ex communi ecclesiae consensu, sed etiam multo magis ex testimonio et intrinseca Spiritus sancti persuasione.— *Expos. simpl.* i. : Credimus . . . scripturas canonicas . . . ipsum verum esse verbum Dei, et auctoritatem sufficientem ex semetipsis non ex hominibus habere. . . . Et in hac scriptura . . . habet . . . ecclesia plenissime exposita, quaecunque pertinent cum ad salvificam fidem tum ad vitam Deo placentem recte informandam.—*Conf. Angl.* vi. : Scriptura sacra continet omnia quae ad salutem sunt necessaria, ita ut quicquid in ea nec legitur, neque inde probari potest, non sit a quoquam exigendum ut tamquam articulus fidei credatur.—*Conf. Belg.* vii. : Credimus sacram hanc scripturam Dei voluntatem perfecte complecti, et quodcunque . . . credi necesse est, in illa sufficienter edoceri. . . . Idcirco toto animo reiicimus quicquid cum certissima hac regula non convenit.—*Conf. March.* ii. : 'At the beginning . . . they confess that they hold . . . the true infallible and solely saving Word of God as it . . . is contained in the Holy Bible, which is and ought to be the one standard for all believers . . . which is perfect and sufficient for salvation and for the decision of all religious controversy, and abides for ever.'

1. From the foregoing explanation it follows that the authoritative character of Scripture does not in the least depend on each book having been written by the particular person to whom it is ascribed. A book might, owing to a later judgment, be wrongly attributed to a certain author in all the surviving MSS., and in this sense be unauthentic, and yet it might belong to the circle where alone we can expect to find canonical writings and hence would none the less remain an integral part of Holy Scripture. Nay more, at its very first appearance a writing (owing to a fiction permitted by the author's moral sense and sanctioned by the feeling of his contemporaries) might have borne in its title the name of someone other than its real author, and yet a book of this character might be an authentic part of the Bible. It is only if such a self-description were positively intended to mislead that the book could not be recognized as fitted to supplement the normative presentation of Christianity. Hence even if many of the doubts that have been raised as to the correct statement of authors' names should be confirmed, we should have no right, much less would it be our duty, to expel those books from the Canon.

There is, however, no way of forming a list of authors to whom particular books must belong in order to be canonical, or of indicating a class of persons all of whose productions would have a right to canonicity. On the contrary, if even now writings should be discovered which were attributable with the highest degree of human certainty to an immediate disciple of Christ or even to an Apostle, we should not without more ado incorporate them in the New Testament, but at most attach them to it as an appendix. Not even the early Church—especially as it is unable to prove apostolic sanction for the separate books [1]—can bind us by its decisions, even had such decisions about the Canon been unanimous ; hence the first part of our theorem can scarcely be taken as expressing anything more precise than what is indicated in the confessional statements quoted above, namely, that we trust universal Christian experience as the testimony of the Holy Spirit that the Canon we have received from Church tradition has not by deceit or ignorance had introduced into it such constituent parts as belong to either an apocryphal or an heretically suspect zone of Christianity, to which such pre-eminent dignity could not be ascribed without danger. But in saying so we concede that not all the books of the New Testament are equally fitted, by content and form, to vindicate their place in the Canon.

Since, however, this fixation of the Canon was arrived at only gradually, and we know besides that the imperfections and errors present in the Church could only gradually be brought to light and removed by the action of the Holy Spirit, we must show our trust by practising the greatest freedom as well as the strictest conscientiousness in our treatment of the Canon. This means, first, that all inquiries intended to ascertain the authors of the books we have, and the genuineness or the reverse of particular passages, must pursue an unhampered course, and that no doubts which may arise should either be accepted by unfriendly prejudice or rejected without scrutiny. Not only is this a part of a complete knowledge of Scripture ; it is not without influence on the interpretation and the use of individual passages. It means, secondly, that we refuse to be perverted from the purest hermeneutical methods, as would be the case if we knowingly preferred to put an artificial interpretation on a passage rather than construe it in a sense suggestive of a less pure view of Christian faith. Under no other circumstances

---

[1] The accounts given by Irenæus, iii. 1, and Eusebius, H.E. ii. 15, iii. 24, 39, v. 8, and elsewhere, are bound, as time goes on, to be less and less regarded as based on trustworthy information.

could we take the credit of being as actively engaged (though within a smaller field of controversial questions and with better equipment and a more cultivated sense) in the discrimination of Scripture as those were who first made the decisive selection of Holy Scripture out of the whole mass of early Christian writings.

2. To understand the second half of our paragraph in its whole range, we must first go back to the influence originally exerted by the writings of the New Testament. The doctrinal books were meant to bear upon the actual circumstances of Christian people, so that the utterances of the Apostles went to form both the dominant ideas and the purposes of believers ; the historical books were meant simply to rehearse the similarly influential words and deeds of Christ and the Apostles. Hence they must become the regulative type for our religious thinking, from which it is not of its own motion to depart. And when Holy Scripture is described as ' sufficient ' in this regard, what is meant is that through our use of Scripture the Holy Spirit can lead us into all truth, as it led the Apostles and others who enjoyed Christ's direct teaching. So that if one day there should exist in the Church a complete reflection of Christ's living knowledge of God, we may with perfect justice regard this as the fruit of Scripture, without any addition of foreign elements having had to come in. Of course the effects of what was due to the previous action of Scripture are here reckoned to the account of Scripture itself. Thus it is as representing each individual's personal understanding of Scripture that, in the measure of his command of thought and speech, his true expressions of Christian piety take shape. And the interpretation of Christian faith which validates itself in each age as having been evoked by Scripture is the development, suited to that moment, of the genuine original interpretation of Christ and His work, and constitutes the common Christian orthodoxy for that time and place.

To this constitutive influence of Scripture, the second or critical influence—and when we speak of the normative place of Scripture, it is often this alone we have in view—is related in a merely subordinate way ; almost, so to speak, as its shadow. True, we can imagine thinking which is independent of the action of the Holy Spirit through Scripture and yet is religious in its content as well as Christian in its original roots, yet the results of which are trivial and infertile, or erroneous and all but heretical. All such thinking, originating as it does in the immature or confused state of mind of those who receive and develop it, must be tested by Scripture, and

can only prove that at least it means to be Christian by seeking to
base itself on Scripture and so acknowledging the test. But clearly
this critical aspect of the normative use of Scripture must decrease
as the productive increases, and as the perfected understanding of
Scripture renders its misinterpretation more difficult.

As regards the scientific expression of Christian faith in Dogmatic
proper, it is no doubt undertaken solely by persons of a scientific
turn ; but they are always persons who desire to be instruments of
the Spirit that acts in and through Scripture, in systematizing what
is fragmentary in scriptural expressions and in harmonizing different
presentations—the original ones and those directed against Judaism
and Paganism—with each other, and in supplementing one by
another. Here too, therefore, the productive, normative power of
Scripture is shown, although in itself Scripture scarcely even suggests
the distinction between a more popular and a more scientific terminology. On the other hand, strong suspicion cannot but be felt
of a Dogmatic which, after pursuing its own line all along, objects
to anything more than a critical use of Scripture for the purpose of
proving that certain isolated details in its structure can be paralleled
from the Bible and that no part of the system contradicts the
language of Scripture properly understood. Only, it ought not to
be demanded even in the former case that each individual dogmatic
locus must be represented in Scripture by a passage specially
devoted to it.

3. If we take strictly the phrase that Scripture as norm is
sufficient, it follows that Scripture can contain nothing superfluous.
What is superfluous is confusing and hence of no more than negative
value ; also it tempts the mind into comparisons that lead nowhere.
But Scripture does contain much that is little more than repetition,
indeed frequent repetition, of what is said elsewhere, and this
appearance of superfluity is all the more curious when contrasted
with the lack of it in a dogmatic system apparently just as incomplete. This, however, is to be expected from the nature of the
case, for Scripture did not come into existence all at once ; and in
this regard our paragraph gives expression to the conviction, which
is fundamental to the right use of Scripture and is ever anew confirmed by a sound hermeneutical method, that repetitions in the
historical books are all the better guarantee of the authenticity of
tradition, while quite possibly they may supplement each other.
The same holds of repeated discussions of the same topics in the
doctrinal books. For, even assuming that in different passages the

writer was not dealing with different situations and relationships, the identity of the Spirit in varied circumstances and individuals is thereby attested all the more powerfully.

§ 132. *Postscript to this Doctrine.—The Old Testament Scriptures owe their place in our Bible partly to the appeals the New Testament Scriptures make to them, partly to the historical connexion of Christian worship with the Jewish Synagogue; but the Old Testament Scriptures do not on that account share the normative dignity or the inspiration of the New.*

1. Our exposition of this doctrine diverges from custom in this respect, that in the two theorems the New Testament writings alone were treated of ; and this postscript has to justify this divergence and give it clear expression. Intentionally, however, it is announced as a postscript, because it is merely polemical and therefore will have lost its relevance as soon as the difference between the two Testaments is generally recognized. That time is as yet apparently distant, and in a Church system it would be correspondingly hazardous to include, as a theorem proper, a proposition of so dissentient a character. Especially as the same view is dominant outside the Schools ; very often, and sometimes even by emphatic preference, Old Testament passages are made the basis of Christian exhortation, and the New Testament seemingly is allowed an influence merely proportional to its size. This is done from opposite motives alike by people who attach less value to the distinctive features of Christianity and by those who recognize it alone and exclusively as charged with redemptive power. It is only to the latter that we seek to justify our position ; the former are outside our province.

2. As regards the inspiration of the Old Testament writings, we must first of all distinguish between the Law and the Prophets. If the Apostle is right in representing the Law as, although a divine ordinance, yet something that came in between the promise to Abraham's seed and its fulfilment,[1] and in asserting further that the Law lacks the power of the Spirit from which the Christian life must flow,[2] then it cannot well be maintained that the Law was inspired by the same Spirit of which the same Apostle says that it is no longer communicated through the Law and its works,[3] but God sends it into our hearts only through our connexion with Christ. Similarly, nowhere and in no sense does Christ represent

---

[1] Gal. 3[19].   [2] Rom. 7[6ff.] and 8[3].   [3] Gal. 3[2].

the sending of the Spirit, with whose witness He combines the witness of the disciples,[1] as the return of what had been there already and had merely disappeared for a while. But on the Law there depend all the historical books subsequent to its being given. For if Messianic prophecy as that which has most affinity with Christianity be confronted with the Law as that which has least, no one will venture to hold that what the Jewish historical books contain is the history of Messianic prophecy rather than of the Law. Nay, even in the prophetic books most of the contents relate to the legal dispensation and the circumstances of the people as such, and the Spirit in which they originate is simply the spirit of the people ; it is therefore not the Christian Spirit, which as One Spirit was to break down the wall of partition between this people and all others. So that only Messianic prophecy would remain as capable of sharing in inspiration in our sense. But if we consider that it is only at isolated moments that the prophets rise to inspiration, and that it is only in this reference that the Spirit moving and animating them is called holy,[2] our conclusion surely must be that this title is merely given in an inexact sense, to indicate that this common spirit, bound up as it was with a conscious need of redemption, and revealing itself in the premonition of a more inward and spiritual Reign of God, carried in itself, and could kindle and sustain even outside itself, the highest receptivity for the Holy Spirit.

Let us inquire, secondly, as to the normative dignity of the Old Testament, first of all in the productive sense. Here it cannot on the whole be denied that the religious sense of Evangelical Christians recognizes in the main a great difference between the two Testaments. Even the noblest Psalms always contain something which Christian piety is unable to appropriate as a perfectly pure expression of itself, so that it is only after deluding ourselves by unconscious additions and subtractions that we can suppose we are able to gather a Christian doctrine of God out of the Prophets and the Psalms. On the other hand, a strong inclination to the use of Old Testament texts in expressing pious feeling is almost invariably accompanied by a legalistic style of thought or a slavish worship of the letter. Lastly, as regards the critical aspect of the normative use of Scripture, probably there are few Christian doctrines which at a certain period it was not attempted to prove by Old Testament passages. But how was it really possible that in an age merely of premonition any truth connected with the doctrine of redemption

[1] John 14[26] and 15[26, 27].   [2] 2 Pet. 1[21].

through Christ could have been set forth so clearly that it could be used with advantage side by side with what was said by Christ Himself, and, after the completion of His redeeming work, by His disciples ? Or if it be thought that inspiration does make this possible, would not in consequence an entirely different reception of the Saviour and the form in which He preached the Kingdom of God have been prepared for among the Bible-reading part of His nation ? The effect is in no sort of keeping with the cause to which it is ascribed. Further, the history of Christian theology shows only too clearly on the one hand how gravely this effort to find our Christian faith in the Old Testament has injured our practice of the exegetical art, and how on the other it has submerged the later development of doctrine and the controversies regarding its more exact definition under a flood of useless complications. Thus a thoroughgoing improvement is only to be looked for when we utterly discard Old Testament proofs for specifically Christian doctrines, preferring to put aside what chiefly rests on such support.

3. But if a practice which has so long been prevalent in the Church is to be reformed, it is necessary to show how the practice arose. There are two grounds on which this external equating of both Testaments rests. In the first place, not only did Christ Himself and the Apostles give instruction on portions of the Old Testament that had been read aloud, but the same custom was perpetuated in Christian public gatherings, before the New Testament Canon had been formed and even later. But from this it by no means follows that a similar homiletical use of the Old as well as of the New Testament ought still to be continued, or that we must put it down to the corruption of the Church that the Old Testament is not so much read by Christians of our time as the New. On the contrary, the ecclesiastical status of the Old Testament was due to its historical connexions, so that its gradual retirement into the background lies in the nature of the case ; and these historical connexions are very far from vouching adequately for the normative dignity or the inspiration of the books of the Old Testament. The Pauline passages which testify to the value of the Old Testament [1] relate chiefly to the usage above described ; and the freedom with which the Apostle employs it is in perfect agreement with our contention, so that we might well call him as a witness in support of the position that Old Testament proofs are no longer required.

The second ground is that Christ and the Apostles themselves

---

[1] Rom. 15[4], 1 Cor. 10[11], 2 Tim. 3[16].

refer to the books of the Old Testament as divine authorities favourable to Christianity.   But from this it does not in the least follow that for our faith we still need these earlier premonitions, since we have actual experience ; and the New Testament approves of men ceasing to believe on the ground of such witness when once they have gained immediate certainty through their own perception.[1] Only, for that very reason historical fidelity and completeness of view demand that what Christ and His first preachers appealed to should be preserved.   This, however, scarcely covers more than the prophetic books and the Psalms ;   which would justify the practice of adding these to the New Testament as an appendix. But in the time of Christ these books did not exist separately, but only as parts of the sacred collection ;   they are often cited exclusively in that character ; certain quotations, moreover, occur from other books.   Hence, although for us the Old Testament cannot be an indivisible whole as it was for the Jews, there can be no objection to its being added in its entirety to the New Testament.   None the less, the real meaning of the facts would be clearer if the Old Testament followed the New as an appendix, for the present relative position of the two makes the demand, not obscurely, that we must first work our way through the whole of the Old Testament if we are to approach the New by the right avenue.

SECOND DOCTRINE : THE MINISTRY OF THE WORD OF GOD

§ 133. *Those members of the Christian fellowship who maintain chiefly the attitude of spontaneity perform by self-communication the Ministry of God's Word for those who maintain chiefly the attitude of receptivity ; and this Ministry is partly an indeterminate and occasional ministry, partly formal and prescribed.*

1. The assumption, true for every corporate fellowship, that the common spirit is unequally distributed, we have already [2] made for the fellowship of the Christian Church.   This distinction between strength and weakness, between purity and impurity in the presentation and grasp of truth (each of these antitheses viewed in itself and also in combination with the other) can be seen in the early Church ; and in each province of the Church it is most clearly marked at the beginning and gradually diminishes.   Yet in every part of the Church it will long remain important enough as an inequality of

[1] John 4[42].   [2] § 129, 2,

persons. And even if it had wholly ceased to exist as such, none the less in each individual so much of inequality of feeling and mood remains that at one moment he finds himself spontaneously active and at another only stimulated receptively. The suggested antithesis, then, is always present, and the problem thus raised has to be solved. For those who are even momentarily weak and impure only belong to the fellowship in so far as they have a receptive capacity to be purified and strengthened, and the fellowship can retain them only as there are those within it who spontaneously supply to them purification and strengthening. This must here be considered—apart from the distinction of an outer and an inner circle within the Church [1]—as a distinction even among the regenerate themselves.

That the relation of the spontaneously active to the receptive is a communication from the former to the latter, and that every such communication is a service and supply of the Word of God, may be shown as follows. There can be no self-communication except through self-presentation acting by way of stimulus ; the imitatively received movement of the self-presented person becomes in the receptively stimulated person a force that evokes the same movement. If this produces a purifying or strengthening, it can only be an effect such as is found in all similar cases where one common spirit works in each of many—an effect of the Holy Spirit working in each of many Christians. And as the Spirit, taking all from Christ, is ever the same Spirit as inspired the Scriptures, no expression of the individual can evoke a similar effect except in so far as it is analogous to Scripture and hence can justify itself as scriptural. Thus with equal justice it may be said that every self-communication that makes for salvation is certainly also scriptural, and every scriptural one is also edifying. For no true Christian can wish to retain anything in his inner life, and at work there, in which he does not recognize Christ ; so, too, no one can wish, in his self-communication within the Christian fellowship, to commend and disseminate himself and his own things, but rather Christ alone and whatever of Christ lives in him. Similarly, no one can wish to take up anything into his life for self-advancement, save as he takes it from Christ. Hence with every communicative and stimulating activity within the Christian fellowship is bound up self-knowledge (to call it self-denial would be inaccurate), to the effect that the communicated gifts are not to

[1] Cf. § 115, 2 and § 116, 1.

be ascribed to the person communicating them, or to any private divine revelation of his own. Everything must be traceable to the view of Christ given in Scripture, so that the individual can only act as the recollecting and developing organ of Scripture ; otherwise unchristian personal claims and separatist influences would break the fellowship in pieces. So, too, a genuinely Christian receptivity will disdain to take the words and acts of any mere individual as example, or to receive them as truth. And this critical attitude, to avoid being deceived, will not hesitate to make distinctions even within what is scriptural ; as in a case where some particular point can be defended by a single Biblical passage, but is out of harmony with the spirit of the whole.

2. If now we consider this influence of the stronger on the weaker, we can see that it embraces the whole Christian life. Even the acts of individuals, in so far as expressive of the same Spirit, are an offering to others of the Word of God ; as follows indeed from what was said above [1] regarding Christ's prophetic office, on which this Ministry depends. Hence the distinction stated at the close of our paragraph is important. All the personal influences just indicated, occurring separately in individual lives, often unintended in part and in part unsought, are the indeterminate and relatively fortuitous ministry of which we cannot speak here, because it belongs to Christian Ethics. But although we have here to do exclusively with the formal and ordered Ministry, the other had to be mentioned ; for the Evangelical conception of the ordered Ministry has its firmest basis in the fact that in all essential respects it is homogeneous with that which is more general and indeterminate. This view, which forbids any sharp distinction between those who discharge the ordered Ministry and other Christians, we find in Scripture itself. When Paul enumerates the different gifts and offices, he mixes both kinds together indistinguishably.[2] So, too, many persons were called by Christ into His discipleship in a more indefinite fashion as contrasted with the definite relationship in which the Twelve stood to Him, or the Seventy-and-two who were sent out on a definite Ministry. In the early Church, too, the Ministry of the Apostles was an ordered one, for they kept to a definite number [3] and acted upon common decisions. The same is true of the office of deacons at first in Jerusalem [4] and on the same model in other churches. But the polemical effort of Stephen in defence of Christianity was no part

[1] § 103.   [2] 1 Cor. 12[8-10. 28-30].   [3] Acts 1[17].   [4] Acts 6[2].

of the definite Ministry assigned to him ; he was acting *ad extra* simply as an individual. So, too, the general and indeterminate ministry within the churches was recommended to, and demanded of, all suited for it.[1]   Indeed, the distinction lies in the nature of the case ; not that higher and special qualities necessarily belong to the regular Ministry : but if even in civil society the common life cannot be wholly resolved into definite functions assigned to each by the society as a whole, much less is this compatible, in the fellowship of the Church, with religious influence and communication. For, on the one hand, the Holy Spirit can never be inactive, and therefore can never be tied in its activities to definite times ; rather it moves each believer to do whatever comes to hand. On the other hand, even so spiritual a society cannot be regarded as wellordered unless there be a division of labour ; otherwise none of the different gifts could attain to its maximum of activity. Especially as the division can be made with more ease and certainty in proportion as the One Spirit guides in completer harmony the judgments of different minds.

§ 134. *First Theorem.—There is in the Christian Church a public Ministry of the Word, as a definite office committed to men under fixed forms ; and from this proceeds all organization of the Church.*

Conf. Aug. v. : ' For the obtaining of this faith, the ministry of teaching the Gospel . . . was instituted by God ; even as by the Word and Sacraments, as by instruments, the Holy Spirit is given ; who worketh faith, where and when He pleaseth.' xiv. ' Concerning Church Government they teach that no man should publicly in the Church teach or preach or administer the Sacraments without a regular call.'—*Conf. Saxon.* (p. 196 Tw.) : Agimus autem gratias Deo . . . quod . . . conservavit publicum ministerium et honestos congressus, qui ipse etiam distinxit quaedam tempora.—*Expos. simpl.* xviii. : Deus ad colligendam vel constituendam sibi ecclesiam eandemque gubernandam et conservandam semper usus est ministris. . . . Nemo autem honorem ministerii ecclesiastici usurpare sibi . . . debet. Vocentur et eligantur electione ecclesiastica et legitima ministri ecclesiae. . . . Eligantur autem . . . homines idonei, etc.—*Conf. Helv.* xv. : Atque hanc ob causam ministros ecclesiae cooperarios esse Dei fatemur, per quos ille cognitionem sui et peccatorum remissionem administret, homines ad se convertat erigat consoletur . . . ita tamen ut efficaciam in his omnem Deo, ministerium ministris adscribamus.—*Conf. Gall.* xxix. : Credimus veram ecclesiam gubernari debere ea disciplina, quam Dominus noster Jesus Christus sancivit, ita videlicet ut in ea sint pastores presbyteri et diaconi, ut doctrinae puritas retineatur, vitia cohibeantur, pauperibus consulatur et sacri coetus habeantur.—*Conf. Angl.* xxiii. : Non licet cuiquam sumere sibi munus publice praedicandi . . . nisi prius fuerit legitime vocatus et missus.

---

[1] Eph. 4^{29}, 5^{19}.

1. If in our inquiry as to the origin of this public Ministry we go back to the commission given by Christ to the Apostles,[1] we find that this commission was chiefly directed to those without ; for any instance of a Ministry internal to the Church might be taken as coming under the more general and indeterminate ministry.[2] The internal, however, grew out of the external, for the newly converted required steady teaching and admonition ; so that the internal was included in Christ's commission as the natural pro-longation of the external. It was the Apostles themselves, how-ever, who proposed a division of this internal Ministry and left it to the whole body to transfer the ministry of serving tables to others ;[3] thus the teaching office became something entrusted to the Apostles by the community, just as the community had formerly transferred both offices combined to the new member of the Twelve. Thus both offices have been perpetuated in the Church as the main branches of the public Ministry, for it is self-evident that the diaconate can be a Church office only if it be a supplying of the Word ; that is, if it be an expression and manifestation of Christian brotherly love in act. But the triple division, however construed, is arbitrary ; in essence it must reduce to that double division between teaching and serving tables which really rests on the fact that the gifts requisite for the one task are as nearly as possible independent of those which constitute qualifications for the other. Indeed, from the first, women have always taken part in the public service of tables,[4] but have always been excluded from the public discharge of the office of teaching.

2. No individual or small group of individuals can represent Christ : all the more must we regard this transference of offices as deriving solely from the whole body, and the formation of the clergy into a self-contained and self-propagating corporation has no Scriptural basis of any kind. When it is a case of propagation, Scripture signalizes only two points—determination of the qualities requisite for the performance of the task, and selection from among those who are known to be so qualified. Here, then, there remains a wide freedom of choice in assigning different tasks to different people, without infringement of the principle that it is the whole body that organizes the discharge of its functions and distributes these amongst its members. Such distribution is impossible without a definite fixing of objects and an exact delimitation of the

---

[1] Matt. 10[6ff.].
[3] Acts 6[2].
[2] *E.g.* Matt. 18[15-20].
[4] 1 Tim. 5[9, 10], Luke 8[3].

area within which each is to function.   It must be decided what is
transferable and what is not ; we therefore indirectly subsume
the indeterminate ministry under organization, so as to soften the
contrast between the two ; as is also done when temporary associations of more closely related individuals are formed, from time to
time, in the interest of what has not been transferred.   But even
the Ministry of the Word can never be transferred in so exclusive a
sense that self-communication of the same kind could not take place
between individuals apart from the public Ministry ; this would be
to lord it over conscience [1] and quench the Spirit.[2]   From the
transference there arise two sorts of relationship—that of each
needy soul to a variety of communicators as determined by his
peculiar needs and their methods, and that of each communicator
to various receptive souls with reference to some definite need and
within the area assigned to him.   It is—if we think of a great
continuous mass of Christian life—through these two relationships taken together that churches are delimited and separated ;
each as an area in which there are present all the gifts needed for
the promotion of Christian life, and in which all the transferable
tasks are advantageously distributed.   The ramification of Church
offices, as well as the forms under which they are transferred, may
be very different ; and the theory of such matters belongs to
Practical Theology.   Here we need only say in general terms that
they are good in proportion as, on the one hand, the distribution
takes place, and is recognized, as the act of the whole body directly
or indirectly ; and as, on the other, the most spiritual Ministry
of all—namely, the ordered presentation of the Word of God—
keeps its place as the mid-point, from which all radiates out and
to which all is in relation.

3. Without this ordered public Ministry and the constitution of
the churches that goes along with it, Christian communication
would merely be isolated and sporadic in character, and to all
appearance fortuitous.   In fact, however, it would be impossible
to avoid a confusing uncertainty, leading to a fruitless and self-
consuming waste of varied forces, were the receptive soul with his
needs not referred to definite communicators, and conversely were
communicators with their gifts not referred to definite circles of the
receptive.   But even granting that in the power of the Spirit each
gifted person were doing everything possible to employ his gifts
for the common good, and similarly that each needy soul had dis-

[1] 2 Cor. 1[24].   [2] 1 Thess. 5[19].

cernment enough to try the spirits—in other words, that individuals left nothing undone that might be done, a state of matters only imperfectly realized by the very best distribution of forces—still, everything would rest on the stimulation of personal religious feeling and of individual sympathy. No true common consciousness, no living conviction of the identity of the one Spirit present in all, could arise thus. But without it there could be for us no recognition of the Holy Spirit in ourselves or any proper consciousness of the nature of our vital fellowship with Christ ; to ensure that, we must be conscious of ourselves as members of His Body. Hence nothing but an utterly superficial view of Christianity will find it possible to reduce Christian fellowship to the area of domestic life and to silent, private relationships devoid of publicity. On the contrary, public gatherings for common confession and common edification are the principal thing, and the transference to certain persons of predominance and leadership in these gatherings is merely a side-issue. Indeed, so far as this point is concerned, a Church fellowship can be quite in the evangelical spirit which knows nothing of such transference, and concedes to every Christian the right of leadership.

§ 135. *Second Theorem.—The public worship and service of the Church is in all its parts bound to the Word of God.*

1. Even the isolated and informal communications of Christian people must, in so far as what they communicate is due to the Holy Spirit, be explanations and active manifestations of the Word of God. If the same is to be true of the public Ministry, not in the same fashion merely, but in a fashion peculiar to itself, it must be owing to the fact that this characteristic of being bound to the Word of God definitely enters into the form of public communication. As regards doctrine, this is secured in part directly by the individual expositions of religious truth being so arranged throughout as evidently to be interpretations of particular passages of Scripture ; partly indirectly through the Creed, which is a brief compendium of doctrine based on Scripture, and which (assuming its scriptural character) ought to be controllingly present to every mind ; by which, too, it ought always to be possible to have the doctrine tested. Both securities, however, must inevitably degenerate into empty forms, easily circumvented, unless the free and informal communication prevailing in the same circle of persons is itself scriptural. If it is not, the Creed will usually assert itself as the

authentic sense of Scripture, so as to prevent any still wider divergence therefrom ; but the result is an unevangelical worship of the letter, and the deeper penetration of Scripture is made impossible.

The same scriptural character is required of Christian poetry if its creations (although originally meant only for the individual) are to pass into public Church use. It comes out in one way in the psalmodic type of Christian verse, which, attaching itself as it does more or less loosely to paraphrastic translations of the Psalms in the style of the earliest Christian hymns, treats of particular passages and situations in Scripture. It comes out differently in the confessional type, which points back to the ecumenical Creeds and clothes the sum of common doctrine in poetic harmonies. The more Christian poetry departs from these two basal forms and represents purely individual aspects of the religious life, the more its influence is confined to small coteries.

Under the conception of public Ministry we have subsumed everything that is the act of the Christian body as such, and the demand for scripturalness must cover such acts too. Hence these active public communications also are seen to be bound to the Word of God ; in part directly, since particular admonitions rest on definite exhortations contained in Scripture and seek to realize them, or are attached to scriptural models ; in part indirectly, through the fixing of Church rules which, derived like the Creed from Scripture, seek to establish an order of Christian life in relation to public worship and service—an order to which all public active communication must be conformed, and from which it can be known which actions of the individual the Church acknowledges as its own, and which it does not.

2. Thus we can see how Confessions or Symbols and Church rules or Canons arise in the Church, not so much as standards by which to test the varied presentations of faith in word and act, as rather the more certainly to secure that the individual shall conform to the original utterances of the Spirit. But it by no means follows that in every age it is possible for them to correspond as perfectly to this ideal as in the period of their formation. That this is not the case is a consequence of the simple fact that they are always the work of the whole Church—using that word as embracing the antithesis used above—not merely of the spontaneous and communicative but also (at least indirectly) of the needy and receptive : and this not merely in the sense that while they originate

with the communicative they yet owe their influence solely to the freely given recognition of the needy, but also because a diffused knowledge of the spiritual state of the needy—in other words, the special circumstances of the moment—was one motive in their production. Hence from the nature of the case every product of the kind falls short of its ideal, the reason being that the progress of the Church is faltering and that at every moment the effects of reactionary tendencies are a part of the situation. They have validity for us only with the reservation that their scriptural character must always be liable to scrutiny. Hence the public worship and service of the Church must always have attached to it a highly developed organization designed to keep up the expert interpretation of Scripture and to bring it to perfection by ceaseless industry. This need not mean that everywhere and in every age those who are charged with the public Ministry must form a special class within the Christian fellowship. On the contrary, our two theorems show that the ecclesiastical distinction, strongly marked as it may be in particular cases, between those who discharge the public Ministry and those to whom they minister is always subordinate on the one hand to the unity and identity of the Spirit in both, on the other to the fact that both are directly dependent on Scripture. This, as also the unfailing affinity between activities which are sporadic and informal and those officially assigned and ordered, means that the antithesis between the two types of member is an ever-decreasing one. If we further consider that on its critical side the normative use of Scripture must one day cease, the antithesis of the two types, in so far as personal, is lost in a direct assurance, common to both, as to the scriptural character both of the accepted doctrines and the canons of practice.

Third Doctrine : Baptism

§ 136. *Baptism as an action of the Church signifies simply the act of will by which the Church receives the individual into its fellowship ; but inasmuch as the effectual promise of Christ rests upon it, it is at the same time the channel of the divine justifying activity, through which the individual is received into the living fellowship of Christ.*

1. We have already [1] put the case for what is essential in this paragraph, namely, that the reception of an individual into the

[1] § 114, 2.

Christian fellowship and his justification or regeneration must be one and the same act. Otherwise, if reception into the Church were solely an act of the Church, then, since the act in question cannot be conceived as taking place without the Holy Spirit, the Supreme Being in preparing His union with human nature under the form of the common Spirit, would be in a state of passivity. But the outpouring of the Holy Spirit is conditioned by Christ,[1] and rests on His promise ; the same must therefore hold good of the impartation of the Spirit to the individual, even if (as is essential to the unity of the Church) the Spirit comes to all from Christ in the same manner. Thus the Church is relieved of a great uncertainty by the fact that Christ Himself enjoined baptism as the act of reception into the Church. For now every such reception is an act of Christ Himself, if performed in the manner He enjoined and according to His command. Hence the Church can neither depart from this form of reception through baptism nor, on the other hand, doubt that in every case where the command of Christ is properly carried out, His promise will be fulfilled that with such reception the salvation of the person received begins. The latter would be to doubt the redeeming power of Christ Himself ; the former would be an audacious notion which could not possibly be derived from the Holy Spirit, for the Spirit takes all from Christ.

This fixes it that baptism must be retained by the Church in the form in which it received it. But it is impossible either to obtain or to give any information as to whether, or how, the outward form of the act is connected with its inward content and purpose. On that point we can only say that if Christ had enjoined an utterly different outward rite for the same purpose, we should regard it as equally sacred and expect from it the same results. Only so much is certain, that if Christ had specially instituted something that was altogether new, it would be incumbent on us in that case to seek for a relationship of the closest possible kind between the outward rite and the alleged inward result ; for it is only under the severest compulsion that we could bring ourselves to suppose that any institution of Christ was purely arbitrary. It is otherwise inasmuch as He attached His institution to something already in existence, and since baptism was already historically conditioned by its connexion with the preaching of John. This historical basis is perfectly sufficient, without our being tempted to develop the symbolism universally recognized in that sphere further than is done in Scrip-

[1] § 124, 3.

ture, or to regard the symbolism as so essential as to justify the
position that the act itself is only complete and can only secure its
purpose when even outwardly it is so performed as perfectly to
bring out its importance.

2. In spite of this undeniable connexion between the baptism of
Christ and that of John, we can scarcely hold that the two are precisely the same without in some degree lessening the importance of
the former.[1]　Even if in John's baptism the idea of the Kingdom
of God as coming through redemption was fundamental, yet prior
to his recognition of Jesus in the act of baptizing Him the person
of the Redeemer was undetermined alike for John and for those
whom he baptized.　Hence we should at least have to distinguish
between his baptism before and after this incident, in the sense that
the former, to equal Christian baptism, needed supplementing.
This distinction, however, could only be important if John later had
baptized in Jesus' name, which, all things considered, we have more
reason to deny than to assert.[2]　Thus it can scarcely be conceded
that the baptism of John can have been either reception into the
Christian Church or a bath of regeneration ; in other words, it could
only be construed as being identical with Christian baptism if we
regarded both as equally ineffectual,[3] or if, virtually abrogating the
distinction between the old covenant and the new, we held that
John, without any definite relation to Christ, was able to give
precisely what Christ gave.

On the other hand, not only is it impossible to maintain that for
those baptized by John the recognition of Jesus as the Christ was
an insufficient additional step, and a new baptism indispensable,
but it is not even clear that so long as the Redeemer lived, baptism
was invariably essential for entering into fellowship with Him.　It
rather appears that when by word He imparted forgiveness to someone, and called him to follow Him, this acceptance was itself the
act of Christ, and baptism would have been no more than an utterly
meaningless supplement.　Indeed, it is impossible to hold that even
the Apostles had received the baptism of John, not to say all the
disciples of Christ, especially those from Galilee ; still less that
Christ Himself baptized any single person on whom it would then
have been incumbent to baptize others.[4]　Hence we must apply

---

[1] See Gerhard, *Loc.* ix. p. 101 f.　　[2] Cf. John 3[22ff.] and Acts 19[3-5].
[3] As Zwingli does, *de ver. relig.* p. 208 : Quid vero distent Joannis baptismus et Christi multa tum olim tum nunc est quaestio, sed inutilis plane, nam
discrimen omnino nullum est. . . . Nihil efficiebat Joannis tinctio . . . nihil
efficit Christi tinctio, etc.　　　　　[4] John 4[2].

at this point the distinction between the Church as it still awaited institution and the Church as it already existed, and it is no matter for surprise if many of the Christians who had not been won by the already existing Church were unbaptized. The personal choice of Christ as an act of His will must have been completely sufficient of itself to secure both the blessings which our paragraph ascribes to baptism—namely, the application of the divine decree of redemption to the individual, and the placing of the individual in fellowship with all who already believe. This makes it as clear as possible that baptism as Christ's universal ordinance has taken the place of His particular personal choice.

3. Suppose we hold to this point of view and conceive each act of baptism, if it is to have this effect, as a decision of the whole Church, to which through the action of the Holy Spirit in its fulness there attaches the highest canonical authority ; so that the Church could baptize no one who was not as mature and as ready actually to begin a new spiritual life in fellowship with Christ as everyone chosen by Christ Himself must have been. There would in that case be no occasion to raise questions as to the possibility that baptism and regeneration might be separated from each other ; we could assert without more ado that everyone is regenerated in baptism, and only so. For since the Holy Spirit was bestowed on the whole body of disciples, it might be held that the divine activity in regeneration and justification was so exclusively attached to the administration of baptism that everyone whom in baptism the Church presents to God not only is acknowledged by Him, subsequently as it were, but in and with baptism itself is given a share in the Holy Spirit and divine sonship. In fact, however, this is not the case ; baptism is only granted and administered by a relatively self-contained part of the Church, in a transitional phase of its development, for none of whose particular actions therefore any such canonical perfection can be claimed. Hence no particular act of baptism can do more than approximate more or less to perfect correctness. And if we add that the moment of the individual's regeneration cannot humanly be exactly determined and still less exactly foreseen, it will appear that the supposed incorrectness in the administration of baptism is traceable to the fact that the Church does not approach the baptism of a catechumen in quite the same way as the soul of the catechumen himself (though all is mediated through the activities of the Church) moves on to regeneration. And thus, what on the formal view of the Church's action

would be an absolutely simple process now falls apart into two series of events, with two different terminations. Now if it were demonstrable that the series of the Church's actions which lead up to regeneration were, just because derived less personally and more directly from the power of the Word of God, more closely representative than the other series of the influence of the whole body, and that accordingly what would be most perfect in this imperfect state of things would be that the administration of baptism should always be attached to the rightly discerned moment of regeneration, yet it is undeniably in the nature of the case that the inclination of the Church to baptize will sometimes run ahead of the inward workings of the Spirit for regeneration and sometimes lag behind them, according as those whose office it is to baptize lean to one estimate or the other of the catechumen's inward state. Hence—as if to mitigate our dissatisfaction with this imperfect state of things—already in the Apostolic Age we find both forms of variation : the impartation of the Spirit before baptism and of baptism before the Spirit ; it is obvious, besides, that the distance between the one and the other may be greater now than it was then. In every case, however, where the decisive gracious workings of the Spirit precede, there is a peremptory summons to let baptism follow immediately as reception into the fellowship ; and, conversely, the priority of baptism is only justified by the assured faith, based on the living activity of the Church, that the regeneration of the person received will now result from the influence of the whole body. Thus taken as a whole, the number of the baptized and of the regenerate should always be identical ; yet, owing to the above-mentioned variations, though in an ever-diminishing ratio to the whole as the Church becomes more perfect, there will always be some regenerate persons who are not yet baptized but who might well have claimed to be received earlier into the Church ; similarly there will be baptized persons who are not yet regenerate but in the most active way are being commended to divine grace for regeneration by the prayers of the Church. Hence the relation of the two elements is always at bottom essentially the same, and both must be conceived as absolutely correlative, however they may now and then diverge in time.

4. It is easy to see from this how widely opinions about the worth and effects of baptism may differ without our being justified in stigmatizing as unchristian those that diverge farthest on the one side or the other. If we start with the fact that, in the actual state

of the Church, baptism and regeneration do not always coincide, it is only giving emphatic expression to this fact if we say that even if they did coincide it would be an accident, and that a man is by no means regenerate simply because he has had baptism administered to him. The same position to which, when rightly understood, there is nothing to object, may also be expressed by saying that baptism of itself produces no inward result, but is only an external sign of entrance into the Church.[1]   This also is true ; but only if the external particular action, the exact moment of which is for the most part externally conditioned either by general regulations for public worship or by special circumstances, be viewed as quite independent of the activity of the Spirit in the Church. In other words the statement is true, but only as indicating the imperfection of the Church in the matter of baptism ; but if taken as a complete and general description of baptism, it is false. Without the action of the Spirit, baptism with water is certainly no more than an external rite which Christ Himself declares to be insufficient ;[2] but, as was the case with its first administration in the Church proper on the first day of Pentecost, so ever after baptism is meant to be evoked by the action of the Spirit and bound up therewith in the closest possible way. If, however, on the ground that baptism by itself does not produce regeneration, which alone matters, this position be further extended to mean either that baptism is superfluous and were best omitted, or at least that there is no better reason for retaining it than a laudable reverence for ancient institutions, such a view as this last would so entirely reverse the relationship indicated above between the baptism of John and Christian baptism that the latter would seem to be no more than an appendix to the former—an appendix always more meaningless, too, as time went on. But the former view, that baptism is superfluous, by destroying all connexion between the influences of the Christian fellowship (and on these influences baptism sets the crown) and the inward development of the individual up to regeneration, or at least by refusing it any outward expression, really destroys the Church itself, at least as an external institution ; and in all outward respects the Christian fellowship takes on as shadowy and all but fortuitous an aspect as in the case of the Society of Friends. Still, even this

---

[1] Zwingli, *l.c.* p. 220 : Externa vero res est quum tinguntur . . . ac verae rei signum ac ceremonia. . . . Sic sunt ceremoniae exteriora signa, quae accipientem aliis probant, eum se ad novam vitam obligavisse, etc.

[2] And that, as is shown by the connexion in which John 3[2] occurs, even when it is a confession of repentance.

view cannot be called absolutely unchristian ; for it disparages
baptism as no more than outward in order to exalt the sole worth
of what is inward, namely, regeneration.[1]

On the other hand, if we start from the fact that regeneration
and entrance into the fellowship of believers are essentially bound
up together and reciprocally conditioned—the more so that it is
from this fellowship that all the influences of the Spirit which produce
regeneration are derived—the most natural and most original statement of this is to say that one and the same series of Church actions
terminates in both things—baptism and regeneration. Now this
certainly is also true ; but, as has been shown, it is true only as
describing a certain ideal perfection of the Church, which is not at
any single point really *given*, and cannot really be manifested in any
single action. From this a further inference may be drawn. It
may be held that the one termination and goal must be conditioned
by the other ; but that baptism cannot be conditioned by regeneration (for as regeneration is only recognizable in the facts of the new
life, this would presuppose that the influence of the Church acted on
the individual prior to his being received into it, which is absurd),
therefore regeneration must be conditioned by baptism. Also since
the earlier inward states of the individual preparatory to regeneration are evoked by earlier influences and actions of the Church,
regeneration itself can only be evoked by the last action of the
Church in the series, namely, baptism. This reasoning also is true
and accurate if taken in a purely spiritual sense, and if even in the
case of baptism as the final item in the series regard is paid solely
to an inward reality which is not bound up with any particular
moment of time—I mean the self-expanding movement of the
Church, which can only attain its goal through the regeneration of
new members. If we consider further that the inner fact of regeneration does not become fully certain in time to a man's own
consciousness except through his progressive sanctification,[2] and
that for a while it may often be imperilled by whatever interrupts
or hinders sanctification, it must be admitted in this reference also
that regeneration, as an inner possession, is conditioned by baptism.
The personal self-consciousness, if uncertain and vacillating, may be

---

[1] The attitude to the Church which this view represents is revealed in the
classical passage in Robert Barclay's *Apolog. Theol.* xii. p. 269 : Ea hac in re
sicut in plerisque aliis inter nos et adversarios stat differentia, quod frequenter
nedum formam et umbram substantiae et virtuti praeponunt, sed umbram
saepe opposite ad substantiam stabiliunt.

[2] Cf. § 108, 3.

strengthened and confirmed by the common consciousness of the Church expressed in baptism and hallowed by prayer in the name of Christ.[1] The statement, however, is false if taken in a temporal sense and related to the outward action, all the more if this action be conceived in abstraction from the motives on which it is based, as well as from their antecendent influence. For then what emerges is the monstrous position that God must necessarily justify the man to whom the Church grants baptism, however little ground there may be for that in his inward condition. Such distortions of the truth we cannot all the same describe as absolutely unchristian, though they come very near to magic and therefore are censurable and dangerous and have done most to provoke the above-cited assertions, which are one-sided in the opposite sense. For the power thus ascribed to the Church is after all traced back to Christ Himself, and the fruit of baptism is represented as being not merely the remission of sin but also living union with Christ.

In the following paragraphs we shall develop what can be put forward as Church doctrine within these limits, allowing for the necessary margin of freedom.

§ 137. *First Theorem.—Baptism bestowed according to the institution of Christ confers, along with citizenship in the Christian Church, salvation also as conditioned by the divine grace in regeneration.*

Conf. Aug. ix. : De baptismo docent quod sit necessarius ad salutem, quodque per baptismum offeratur gratia dei.—*Art. Smalc.* v. : Baptismus nihil est aliud quam verbum dei cum mersione in aquam secundum ipsius institutionem et mandatum. . . . Quare non sentimus cum Thoma qui dicit deum spiritualem virtutem aquae contulisse . . . quae peccatum per aquam abluat. Non etiam facimus cum Scoto, qui docet baptismo ablui peccatum . . . et hanc ablutionem fieri tantum per Dei voluntatem, et minime per verbum et aquam.—*Conf. Saxon* : Ego baptizo te, id est ego testificor hac mersione te ablui a peccatis et recipi iam a vero deo . . . quem agnoscis . . . et certo statuis tibi tribui beneficia, quae in evangelio promisit, te esse membrum ecclesiae dei.—Luth. *Catech. maj.* : Sola fides personam dignam facit, ut hanc salutarem et divinam aquam utiliter suscipiat. . . . Eo enim quod te aqua perfundi sinis baptismum nondum percepisti aut servasti ut inde aliquod emolumenti ad te redeat. . . . Deinde hoc quoque dicimus non summam vim in hoc sitam esse, num ille qui baptizetur credat necne ; per hoc enim baptismo nihil detrahitur.—*Expos. simpl.* xix. : In baptismo enim signum est elementum aquae, ablutioque illa visibilis quae fit per ministrum. Res autem significata est regeneratio vel ablutio a peccatis. Baptizari in

---

[1] Ita baptismus intuendus est et nobis fructuosus faciendus, ut in hoc freti corroboremur et confirmemur, quoties peccatis aut conscientiâ gravamur. Luther, *Catech. maj.*

nomine Christi est inscribi initiari et *recipi* . . . in haereditatem filiorum Dei
. . . et *donari* varia dei gratia ad vitam novam.—*Conf. Gallic.* xxxv. :
Baptismus nobis *testificandae* nostrae adoptioni datus, quoniam in eo
inserimur Christi corpori, ut eius sanguine abluti, simul etiam ipsius spiritu
, . . renovemur . . .—*Conf. Belg.* xxxiv. : Mandavit ut omnes qui sui sunt
. . . baptizentur, ut eo significet, quod sicuti aqua in nos infusa . . . sordes
abluit, sic et sanguis Christi per Spir. s. idem praestat interne in anima,
adspergens eam et a peccatis suis eam mundans, nosque ex filiis irae in filios
dei regenerans.—*Colloq. Lips.*, p. 400 : ' Although the grace of God doth not
work salvation through baptism *ex opere operato* . . . or through the mere
outward washing; yet is it done in virtue of the word of institution and
promise by means of baptism.'

1. In the statements of the two Protestant Churches there is
òbvious a certain vacillation of opinion, so that if we compare the
different passages it is not easy to decide whether in baptism something is given and communicated from the one side and acquired
on the other, or whether something is merely indicated and attested
or offered. Of this vacillation our paragraph shows no trace ; it
places itself on the side of those who ascribe most to baptism ;
hence the greater the effect attributed to baptism, the more important it is to determine how much belongs to the institution of
Christ to which such an effect is attached. Here we may first of
all distinguish between the action itself and the intention with which
it is performed : the first by itself alone is only the external side of
baptism, the second the internal ; and since the alleged effect is
something purely spiritual and inward, this means that the external
action simply by itself cannot produce the effect, and the connexion
between the two is mediated solely by the intention on which the
whole is based. According to the words of Christ Himself [1] and the
interpretation of them in act given by His disciples,[2] this effect is
reception into the fellowship of disciples ; for only within this
fellowship is that ' teaching them to hold ' all that Christ commanded
to be found which differs from the evocation of faith or ' making
disciples.' Only, the effect of the action does not depend on the
intention being pure and unmixed, or on its always being definitely
present to the mind of the person by whom baptism is administered.[3]
For the action is not the action of any single individual ; the individual only performs it in virtue of the authority therefor which
he has received from the Church, and thus as an action of the
Church. But the intention of the Church in bestowing this authority
can have been none other than the right and true intention indicated

[1] Matt. 28[19. 20].   [2] Acts 2[41. 47].
[3] Here the canon is applicable : Licet uti sacramentis quae per malos
administrantur. *Conf. Aug.* vii. and elsewhere.

above. On this assumption, it is a general principle for all ages during which the Church may continue to be divided into a number of relatively antagonistic communions, that baptism which anyone of them causes to be administered is valid not only for the administering Church itself but for all Churches whatsoever, because in baptizing they all have the intention to receive into the Christian Church. Nay, even supposing some one Church were to add to the action something having a special relevance to its own party interest, the other Churches might certainly correct this necessarily improper addition, and deny its value, but they would not on that account challenge the validity of the action as a whole, provided the institution of baptism was not itself challenged. This principle is rightly taken to cover heretical parties also ; for they regard themselves as the true Christians, and their intention always is to receive those baptized into Christendom. It is true, in doing so they likewise intend to propagate their heresy ; but all the orthodox Church need do is to counteract such heresy strongly in the minds of the persons baptized, without having on that account to destroy the original common Christian foundation that has been laid.

As regards the action itself, what ought principally to be noted in the descriptions given of it in the passages cited is this, that not only does the water not have any importance in itself apart from the action, but even the external action, be it complete or partial immersion—and to the latter type belongs every kind of laving or sprinkling with water—is connected with the intention solely through the accession of the Word of God ; without this the action would be incomplete. Obvious as this may be, we would not thereby assert that in His institution Christ gave command that specific words should be pronounced during the outward action, and that a baptism therefore is invalid which is lacking in the words meant to be uttered uniformly, always and everywhere. What we do hold is that along with the action there must go a presentation of the Word of God on which discipleship rests, and this in point of fact is the Word of Father, Son, and Spirit ; and through appeal to this Word, as of equally sacred significance for baptizer and baptized, baptism has its higher significance conserved, for that appeal expresses the intention of the Church and the assenting wish of the catechumen. The utterance of the regular formula, however, can only be described as an ancient Church tradition ; the only general rule we can state is this, that as no man performs baptism except by the authority of the Church, he ought to perform it in a manner

consonant with his authority. Hence it cannot be right to make
the validity of baptism administered by different religious parties
depend on their keeping the formula unchanged, as though in
baptism the formula were the substantial thing.[1] Such a demand
would certainly bring us into conflict with baptism as performed
by Christ's disciples during His lifetime, for they cannot at that
time have baptized in the name of the Holy Spirit.[2] Nay, it will
probably never be possible to make out whether later, from Pentecost onwards, the Apostles themselves used the formula, or felt
that Christ's teaching enjoined them to use it. Occasion has been
found in hypothetical cases of extreme urgency, such as could never
really occur, to raise the question whether in such a case something
else might not be substituted for water ; but it might also be asked
whether, if a case arose in which for the sake of the baptized person
signs had to be substituted for words, such signs would be valid as
reproducing not the words themselves but only their meaning,
whereas spoken words differing from the formula but the same in
meaning would be invalid. What, however, is much the most essential
point in the relation to the Word of God that goes to constitute
baptism, is just that the Word must be known to the baptized
person and acknowledged by him. For obviously this implies that
his being made a disciple, which can only take place through the
power of the Word, preceded baptism ; this is the practice which
everywhere we find observed by the Apostles, so far as our information goes. Indeed, apart from this the action cannot be regarded
as complete. For just as it is only through the accession of the
Word to the external rite that the Church expresses her intention,
so, too, it is only through his appropriation of the Word that the
baptized person's assent to this intention is expressed.

2. From what has now been said regarding the nature of the
action, and especially from the fact that the baptized person is
asked to give a confession of the Word joined to the action, it follows
very clearly that the baptized person's faith is a precondition of the
action really being what it is intended to be. So much lies before
us in Christ's two sayings about baptism.[3] For even if in the first
saying we seek to combine ' making disciples ' and baptizing as
closely as possible, what we there have is a later elaboration which
only reached its final stage in the second saying, and which from the
outset could only represent an approximation to faith ; and even in

[1] Cf. Gerhard, *Loc. Theol.* ix. p. 90.   [2] John 4^2 ; cf. 7^{39}.
[3] Matt. $28^{19. \ 20}$ and Mark 16^{16}.

baptism this approximation could only be fully realized if the baptized person were prepared to make confession of the Word that accompanies baptism. Similarly, the faith which in the other passage Christ makes an antecedent of baptism must be the very faith of which we have been speaking all along. Peter, indeed, seems to demand merely repentance, not faith, before baptism ; [1] still, it was repentance for the part which his hearers, as members of the Jewish nation, had had in the rejection of Christ, a repentance which had only been rendered possible through the acknowledgment of Christ and adoption of His cause which they owed to Peter's address ; and this of itself must involve faith. Peter brings in this demand at the close of his sermon ; he must therefore have started with the same assumption as Paul,[2] and been convinced that his preaching had already produced faith in every case where this was a possibility. Similarly, our thought of the Church, as constantly engaged in preaching, must be that it ought to conclude preaching by baptism, but not interrupt preaching to baptize. Now in the quoted credal passages it is also stated that baptism is proper and complete even without faith, and it tallies with this that other thinkers represent faith as the fruit and consequence of baptism. But against both views we must enter a protest. Baptism is received wrongly if it be received without faith, and it is wrongly given so. True, the ordinance loses none of its significance, whether considered as originally an institution of Christ or in its more definite form as an ordinance of the Church ; but this is so only because the Church can never have laid down that it is a matter of indifference whether those baptized are believers or not. For the same reason, baptism as an act of the mere individual has never been such that the Church could approve of it and regard it quite as its own ; in any case such acts of baptism fall under the head of imperfect Church administration. But if this only means that even in such cases baptism need not be repeated, the point is one which requires to be stated more emphatically, lest we should seem to be ignoring what are manifest imperfections. Baptism, that is to say, is ineffectual only when it is imparted prematurely, before the work of preaching is complete and has awakened faith. It is different with the assertion that faith springs from baptism as its fruit.[3] This is obviously in contradiction to the whole practice of the Apostles

---

[1] Acts 2[38].　　　　　　　　　　　　　　　　[2] Rom. 10[17].

[3] See Gerhard, *Loc. Theol.* ix. p. 152, where the statement is made that baptism kindles faith in the heart of the person baptized, but not the slightest proof is given of the connexion between the two things.

and the whole experience of the Church as it grew in consequence of mass-baptism ; nay, even in the individual case, where one who is still an unbeliever has been baptized too early, the Church does not rely on baptism alone but carries on the work of preaching in the full sense of the word ; and if in these circumstances faith arises later, no simple Christian mind will ascribe this to the wrongly administered baptism, but to what subsequently to baptism has been done by the Church.

As regards complete baptism, which implies the existing faith of the person baptized, what we say is that it effects salvation, but only along with citizenship in the Christian Church ; that is to say, only in so far as it mediates reception into the fellowship. To this it might be objected that if baptism presupposes faith, then salvation precedes baptism, for we ourselves have explained faith as the appropriation of the perfection and blessedness of Christ ; [1] and a study of this objection is peculiarly fitted to cast light on the whole problem. It goes back to the relation of this Section to the second Division of the previous Section. Faith as an inward state of the individual is the appropriation just described, but the influence of the appropriated perfection of Christ and the enjoyment of His appropriated blessedness become real only within the fellowship of believers ; hence the man in whom faith develops also has the desire to enter the fellowship. In this sense baptism as direct reception into the fellowship of believers is also named the seal of divine grace,[2] because the real enjoyment of grace is thereby guaranteed. Hence all such persons can be regarded as seeking baptism which then the Church grants, just as conversely in other cases the Church offers it and those who have become believers receive it. In the same way we called baptism the channel of God's justifying action, because it is only within the fellowship that an individual can come to have the forgiveness of sins, which is essentially conditioned by the influence of the new communal life, and divine sonship, which is essentially conditioned by fellow-citizenship with the saints. If we want to separate in word what is inseparable in fact, we may on the one hand say that where faith is, conversion must have been ; and where complete regeneration is, there too is justification. Hence if faith was there before baptism, all that is ordinarily represented as the fruit of baptism was there also thus baptism would really effect nothing, but only attest and point to what had been effected already ; and thus the one class of credal passages

---

[1] See § 108.　　　　[2] *Heidelb. Catech.*, Quest. 69–72.

can take the form they do without in the least impairing the true force of baptism. On the other hand, it may be said that even if faith is not yet present at the time of baptism, yet it will arise not merely *after* baptism but—baptism being the first item in the whole series of influences which the Church brings to bear on the baptized —*through* baptism. Thus every sort of connexion between personal spiritual life and the perfection and blessedness of Christ would arise out of baptism ; the more so that if (to suppose the case) a regenerate person remained unbaptized and hence was not received into the Christian fellowship, we should have to admit that he could have no real share in the perfection and blessedness of Christ because he had neither come under Christ's fellowship-forming action nor shared in His blessedness as mediated through the communal consciousness. This, it is true, would hold good in a still greater degree if it were the personal desire of the person in question to remain outside the fellowship, and in a less degree if it were only through an ecclesiastical oversight that, although regenerate, he was not yet baptized. Hence the other set of our credal passages is able to ascribe to baptism both faith and all that flows from faith without giving to its mode of operation the least colour of magic. The meaning is not that the outward performance works even in the faintest degree *ex opere operato*, whether by itself or in conjunction with the utterance of certain words (the utterance would itself in that case be no more than an outward performance), but that it works solely in union with the Word which ordains baptism for the Church and along with the Church, and which is uninterruptedly active in the Church throughout its whole extent. And as our paragraph only asserts the efficacy of baptism in connexion with divine grace in regeneration, and thus links up the act of the Church with what is going on in the individual soul, magical conceptions are very definitely barred out. But it distinctly ascribes a saving efficacy to baptism, as the conferring of Christian citizenship, and this is a rejection of the view according to which baptism is a merely external act. Thus our paragraph lends itself to both readings of the credal phrases, which otherwise mutually impute responsibility for one or other of the misconceptions we have been discussing.

4. Hence we may say that everything that is taught about the efficacy of baptism is perfectly clear if we only assume a correct and sound administration of the sacrament ; in that case there is absolutely no reason to ascribe to it magical effects or to depress it into a merely outward usage. It is only the assumption of a wrong

administration that raises difficult questions : that is, if our aim is
to formulate doctrines which shall be equally valid for both cases.
For then one party sets up a principle which obviously isolates the
outward aspect, namely, that the effects of divine grace ought not
to be made dependent on any external act ; [1] the other urges the
principle, plainly favourable to magic, that no state of human consciousness can make inoperative divine promises which have been
attached to an external act ; [2] both without sufficiently remember-
ing that God is not a God of disorder in the assemblies of His people.
Hence everything depends on a sound rule of administration.
Against the Donatists it is rightly taught that the validity of
baptism does not depend on the state of heart in him who performs
it ; but the same cannot be said equally regarding the saving virtue
of baptism.   If the person baptizing is not a pure organ of the
Church in judging of the inward state of the person baptized, the
saving virtue of baptism must be impaired in every case.   Every
such baptism, however, is an act of sin ; and the oftener it occurs,
the more imperfect the Church is.   ·Hence the first rule is that not
only the decision when baptism should take place, but its administration too, ought to rest in the hands of the ministers of the Word in
the strict sense ; [3] for obviously the person who must have the
most vivid conviction of the faith evoked in the candidate for
baptism is also the best organ of the Church in performing the act
itself.   And for the same reason baptism is not put at the mercy of
some one hour of exalted feeling ; it is only performed as a well-
considered act at a prearranged time, no exception being permissible
except under special circumstances.   The rule to follow will always
be this, that the administration must be conditioned by the sympathy
of the Church (for of those operations of the divine Spirit on the
soul which may be trusted to evoke faith there can scarcely be
knowledge proper), and that when such sympathy is absent, it is
best to wait for the recognizable tokens of faith.

§ 138. *Second Theorem.*—*Infant Baptism is a complete Baptism
only when the profession of faith which comes after further
instruction is regarded as the act which consummates it.*

   Conf. Aug. ix. : docent . . . quod pueri sint baptizandi, qui per baptismum oblati deo recipiantur in gratiam Dei.   Damnant Anabaptistas, qui
improbant baptismum puerorum et affirmant pueros sine baptismo salvos

---

[1] Zwingli, *de ver. relig.*, p. 200: Nam hac ratione libertas divini spiritus
alligata esset, qui dividit singulis ut vult.
[2] *Catech. Rom.* ii. *de bapt.* 58.
[3] *Expos. simpl.* xx. : Baptismus autem pertinet ad officia ecclesiastica.

fieri.—*Art. Smalc.* v. : . . . docemus infantes esse baptizandos. Pertinent enim ad promissam redemtionem per Christum factam ; et ecclesia debet illis baptismum et promissionis illius annunciationem.—*Expos. simpl.* xx. : Cur non per sanctum baptisma initiarentur, qui sunt peculium et in ecclesia Dei.—*Conf. Gallic.* xxxv. : Praeterea quamvis baptismus sit fidei et re-sipiscentiae sacramentum, tamen cum una cum parentibus posteritatem etiam illorum in ecclesia Deus recenseat, affirmamus infantes sanctis paren-tibus natos esse ex Christi auctoritate baptizandos.—*Conf. Belg.* xxxiv. : . . . quos (infantes) baptizandos et foederis signo obsignandos esse credimus. Quin etiam revera Christus non minus sanguinem suum profudit ut fidelium infantes quam ut adultos ablueret, ideoque signum seu sacramentum ejus quod Christus pro eis praestitit, suscipere debent.—*Decl. Thorun.*, p. 429 : . . . Quamvis necessitatem illam adeo absolutam non esse statuamus, ut quicunque sine baptismo ex hac vita excesserit sive infans sive adultus . . . propterea necessario damnandus sit.

1. Thus far we have treated of baptism in general, without even considering the difference between the original institution and the present almost universal practice of the Christian Church, though certainly with the intention that the propositions laid down should not be limited in their application to the baptism of adults but be valid for every baptism that means to be genuinely Chris-tian. Hence we insisted on at least incipient faith and (in line with former paragraphs [1] and therefore necessary) repentance also as preconditions of baptism. With this the practice of the Apostolic Age completely agrees, as far as we know ; for every trace of infant baptism which people have professed to find in the New Testament must first be inserted there. Similarly, in the absence of definite information it is difficult to explain how such a diver-gence from the original institution could arise and could prevail over so wide an area. It might be difficult to specify *one* sufficient reason for the change, but there might well be a multiplicity of reasons which, taken together, were able to win over Christian feeling. First, the desire to be able to include among those who die in the Lord those Christian children who had died before the age of instruction.[2] Next, to make the Christian community more definitely responsible for the children of Christian parents in cases where the parents might not themselves be in a position to imple-ment the obligations of the congregation. And finally, in order to separate off Christian children from Jewish and pagan youth. These may from the first have been the strongest motives. When, how-ever, it became an established custom to regard children who had re-ceived baptism as for that reason members of the Church, it was felt as being in itself a source of comfort that in this act there should be

---

[1] Those referring to regeneration, §§ 107–109.   [2] 1 Thess. 4[16].

expressed a firm confidence that children born of Christian parents
would not miss the nurturing care of the Holy Spirit. Our credal
passages, however, view infant baptism entirely apart from history
and undertake to vindicate it in and for itself, but they do so
ineffectively and on grounds that are mutually destructive. If the
children are already God's possession, they have no need of baptism
in order to be thus offered to God and received by Him to grace ;
and conversely, if they need baptism for this, the justification of
its being administered to them cannot lie in the fact that already
they are God's possession. Similarly it needed to be specially
proved (for it does not prove itself) that God reckons offspring
along with parents as forming part of the Church ; also a certain
qualification—which is not mentioned—needs to be attached to
the principle that we ought to baptize children because Christ
shed His blood for them also. On these grounds we should have to
baptize all men whatsoever, as we could lay hold of them. The
missing qualification of this last position rests ultimately on the
peculiar situation of the children of Christian parents, as the special
justification of the former position does also ; hence it can be seen
that our paragraph is an effort to supply these defects and at the
same time to solve the contradictions first alluded to. For while,
if we take it in close connexion with the previous paragraph, it
gives an inadequate explanation of infant baptism, which here is
administered in the absence of repentance and faith in those
baptized, yet it tacitly admits that infant baptism cannot produce
in those baptized the effects of which repentance and faith are
the necessary conditions. And just as we cannot suppose that
before baptism children are subject to misery due to a consciousness of sin which is growing into penitence, we cannot after
baptism ascribe to them blessedness due to a dawning sense of
divine sonship. Hence there need be no talk of proving that even
in such children faith can be produced by baptism. Our paragraph
shows, nevertheless, why there is occasion to administer baptism in
this form, namely, because in the case of such children we have
reason to count upon their future faith and their confession of it.
With this is bound up the question how far we may consider them
as reckoned by God part of the Church ; the answer being that it
is part of Church order to bring them, as the outer circle most
intimately entrusted to us, into direct relation to the Word of
God, and to maintain them therein until faith awakens. It is from
this point of view that the contradictions referred to are most

easily resolved.   For we only wish to avoid saying that we baptize children because they are already in the Church and in order to commend them to divine grace ; we baptize them rather because already they are marked out for it by their natural connexion with the Christian order in which God has placed them, and with a view to bringing them into the Church.   The full truth of both aspects is expressed by saying that for us personal confession of faith is the goal of infant baptism, a goal which it must reach, and by reaching which it has to vindicate itself.   On the other hand, it is certain that where this point is not carefully attended to, the ecclesiastical custom of baptizing infants is largely responsible for the fact that some people attribute magical powers to baptism, while others disparage it as a purely external custom.

2. Clearly then this sort of baptism merely by itself, while a bond between the individual and the Kingdom of God, does not straightway imply the possession and enjoyment of salvation but only a normal preparatory operation of the Holy Spirit.   Hence any such act taken by itself is in no sense to be equated with baptism according to Christ's original institution, where a personal confession of faith is included in the act itself.   Yet this defect does not render the act invalid, as though it were positively wrong ; and the Anabaptist assertion that, in the case of persons baptized so, baptism must be repeated, has rightly been felt to give offence. On such terms no baptism at all would be secure except such as in the early Church—and it was certainly not a laudable custom— was administered shortly before death ; for there can be no surer sign of real regeneration than steady progress in Christian sanctifica- tion.   Thus infant baptism is the same as any other baptism which has erroneously been imparted prior to the full faith of the person baptized and yet is valid ; only, its proper efficacy is sus- pended until the person baptized has really become a believer. Our paragraph, however, has still to vindicate itself on the point that we made these imperfect baptisms in detail a reproach to the Church, whereas we now are seeking to find a legitimate place for them as a whole.   But this is one of those cases in which conscious divergence must be judged more leniently than unconscious.   The latter is at all events overhasty, and on the other hand, it repre- sents as a believing Christian one who as yet is not so ; the former, on the contrary, is a Church rule, and by its forward reference to the personal profession of faith it definitely marks off those baptized in this way from those who already believe.   It is there-

fore unjust to infant baptism when confirmation—which for us is simply the depositing and acceptance of a personal profession of faith, and thus supplies a lack in baptism—is regarded as non-essential ; for it is only as combined with confirmation that infant baptism answers to Christ's institution. Hence our paragraph, by making confirmation a part of the administration of baptism, lays it as a duty on the Church to give confirmation very close attention, in order that, so far as the Church can secure it, the later rite may approve itself the true and worthy consummation of infant baptism. It is equally unjust when confirmation is torn away from this context and represented as a sacrament by itself. Whatever we ought to think otherwise of the importance and benefit of confirmation, to isolate it is to render infant baptism incomplete and ineffectual.

Still, we cannot affirm the necessary character of a baptism thus divided into two parts, as is done when the Anabaptists or Baptists are condemned on the ground that they believe that children dying unbaptized may be saved. In this matter we take sides unhesitatingly with the last credal passage quoted above. It is certainly the case that as soon as large numbers of children born of Christian parents had to be nurtured in the Christian Church, a situation emerged which previously had been unknown ; and it seems as if it were in the highest degree natural to mark this by a symbolic act, the more so that nearly everywhere just such acts are performed to indicate that the newly-born do not belong exclusively to their parents, but corporately to the whole fellowship. Besides, nothing was more natural than to select baptism for this purpose. Hence it would have been quite intelligible if, to recover touch with Christ's institution, infant baptism had been abolished at the Reformation ; and this we might do even yet, without thereby losing continuity with a fellowship in whose history there was a period when nothing prevailed except infant baptism—provided only we did not declare infant baptism to be invalid. And we might equally well give up the practice altogether without doing our children any injury. For it is only if we ascribe magical powers to baptism that we can believe that it confers a claim relating to the life after death, quite irrespectively of its influence on this life. Hence no one who does not believe in such magical powers can suppose that there is any difference between children who have been baptized but die before renewing their baptismal covenant, and children who pass out of time without any baptism at all. It would therefore be a natural thing to leave it to each Evangelical household to decide whether it will present its children for baptism in the ordinary way or only when they make a personal profession of faith ; and we ought to make it known that in regard to this point we cancel the sentence of condemnation passed on the Anabaptists, and that on our side we are prepared to enter into Church fellowship with the Baptists of to-day, if only they will not pronounce our infant baptism absolutely invalid, even when supplemented by confirmation. On this point it should easily be possible to reach an understanding.

FOURTH DOCTRINE : THE LORD'S SUPPER

§ 139. *Christians in partaking of the Lord's Supper experience a peculiar strengthening of the spiritual life; for therein, according to the institution of Christ, His body and blood are administered to them.*

1. Our paragraphs ought in every case to contain simply the expression of our Christian consciousness ; hence at this point we must start with the experience we ourselves have of this sacramental action, and (proving that we do not regard the experience as a purely personal thing) expect all believers to have. Only thereafter can we take up the further question how this experience first originated. The two questions hang together only in this respect, that the experience would not repeat itself perpetually, or at least the interpretation and treatment of the subject would have taken a quite different line, if there had not been some need which thus found satisfaction. To keep touch with the previous Doctrine, the subject of the present one would be utterly devoid of content if the salvation beginning with rightly administered baptism were so conferred that automatically it sustained itself unimpaired and adequately secured its own growth. The analogy of all life, however, argues the contrary ; and it lies in the indissoluble bond between entrance into the living fellowship of Christ and entrance into the fellowship of believers that each of these two must be supported by the other. But just for that reason the mode in which the Church coexists with the world, as well as the hampering influence of the world on the Church, demands that this fellowship should periodically be nourished and strengthened ; and it is the satisfaction of this need that believers seek in the sacrament of the altar. If now we provisionally regard the fellowship of believers with each other and the fellowship of each individual

with Christ as being each of them separate and by itself, the latter fellowship will be fortified against the influences of the world by every moment of devout self-recollection in the believer's life, during which on the one hand he closes his heart to worldly influences and on the other presents Christ to himself, out of Scripture—for it is always out of Scripture, directly or indirectly, that the thing is done.   Over and above this, the fellowship of believers with each other is strengthened by every energetic and affecting manifestation of Christian love in any sphere of the common life.   But each of these kinds of fellowship should influence the other ;   therefore between lonely contemplation and common active life there lies that intermediate sphere which we describe by the general term, public worship.   This, viewed on one side, is simply the common life itself, withdrawing from outward activity to communicative representation of what is inward ; viewed on the other side it is simply contemplation itself, moving out of privacy and expanding into the communal.   Here, therefore, the two kinds of fellowship unite—that of believers with each other and that of each soul with Christ ; and hence it is clear that everything that takes place here must have effects on both ; while at the same time every effect one kind of fellowship has on the other seems necessarily to emanate from this intermediate sphere and to pass through it.   It is to this sphere that the Lord's Supper too belongs ; for Christ instituted it as a communal act, which, while it is a presenting of Himself, is certainly a strengthening of both kinds of fellowship.   For this reason, in the Church it is invariably celebrated in gatherings of the congregation : every other sort of celebration is an exceptional case, which ought also to be representative of the congregation assembled together.

But as it is only through trust in what other people profess as their experience that the individual can come to have the same experience as his own, we are led back by an unbroken tradition to the beginnings of the Church, and to the Supper itself as Christ held it with His disciples.   Now from of old the essential thing has been held to be the bestowal of Christ's body and blood, and elsewhere He makes participation in His flesh and blood essential for having life.   These two, accordingly, are the principal points which have first to be discussed—namely, how the Supper as the bestowal of Christ's body and blood is related to the purely spiritual participation, and how the Supper as an element in public worship is distinguished from other parts thereof.

2. To begin with the second point, it is pretty clear that Christen-dom as a whole in its public teaching and practice has from of old regarded the Supper as the climax of public worship.[1] The rounded whole of our united experience in public worship would seem to us incomplete unless at definite points—and most often at the highest and holiest points—the Supper held its place as the most intimate bond of all. Similarly we should feel it to be a morbid thing—whether in the case of individuals or of entire congregations—if any other element of worship were to have attri-buted to it a greater power of sustaining and heightening blessed-ness than the Supper has. But we cannot rest satisfied with this ; we must inquire as to the specific difference between what has come to be practised in the Church (even though it were with an unerring sense for the common good) and what Christ has thus ordained ; and the difference appears to be this. In all other elements of public worship the aforesaid twofold effect on the fellowship of believers with each other and on the fellowship of each with Christ respectively is unequal ; and for that reason they seem one-sided. The more markedly an individual stands out and draws others to himself, or the more powerfully a common mood of feeling finds expression and is heightened by being communicated to others, the intenser is the reaction on the common life. But what the effect on the fellowship of each soul with Christ will be depends on the personal spontaneity with which each brings that which has been publicly represented and expressed to bear on his relation to Christ and inwardly digests it. Each of the two kinds of effect, that is, depends on something else ; hence one may be strong while the other is weak. In the Supper, on the other hand, it is impossible for the two to be separated or distinguished ; the Supper rests on nothing that is individual or peculiar, which might turn the effect to one side or the other ; nor does the distri-buting minister exert any personal force on the receivers, or the receivers individually exert any special and inward spontaneity. Rather it is simply the whole redeeming love of Christ to which we are pointed there ; and as the distributing minister is nothing more than the organ of Christ's institution, the receivers uniformly find themselves simply in a state of completely open receptivity for Christ's influence. Without the special interposition of any in-dividual, therefore, every effect flows directly and undividedly from the Word of institution in which the redeeming and fellowship-

[1] Cf. *Conf. Saxon.*, pp. 170 f.

forming love of Christ is not only represented but made newly active, and in trustful obedience to which the sacramental action is ever anew performed.   It is in this undivided and exclusive immediacy and in the resulting freedom of its effects from dependence on changing personal moods and circumstances, that the Supper differs from all other elements of public worship.

As regards the second point, it is clear that in the discourse,[1] where Christ recommends as essential the eating of His flesh and the drinking of His blood, He had in mind neither the Supper nor any other definite act.   He wished rather to indicate in how profound a sense He Himself must become our being and well-being ; and clearly, if we compare His words here with that other saying that we must be related to Him as the branch to the vine,[2] there is no difference between the two except this—that the latter lays stress more on the continuity of the relationship, the former on its periodical renewal.   Nor can anyone doubt that the same expression may be used to denote the periodically recurring effect of the Supper ; and not merely the effect which it has on the fellowship of the individual with Christ, as a repeated nourishing of personal spiritual life out of the fulness of Christ's life, but the effect which it is also bound to exert on our fellowship with each other.   For, as it is a simultaneous act of many, and has the same effect in all, the consciousness of benefit in each is accompanied by a sympathetic sense that the same thing is happening to others ; and as each knows that the others are being united more closely with Christ, he feels himself more closely united with them.   This is not in any sense an exclusive relation to each other of those who are communicating at any one time ; as explained above, each represents to the others the whole congregation.   But while indisputably the spiritual participation in the flesh of Christ referred to above can take place more generally in a variety of ways, the Lord's Supper is distinct from all else in this respect that in it the same result is bound up with this definite action, blessed and hallowed by the word of Christ.   In itself this is not something unintelligible to believers or requiring special explanation, all the more that it follows the analogy of all important memorial rites ; and deeply as the external side of the action, in its actual form, appeals to us by its varied significance, we yet can easily concede that if it had pleased Christ to give His ordinance a different form we should

[1] John 6⁵² ⁵⁶.   [2] John 15⁴ ⁶.

nevertheless expect from it the same result, and that that outward form would soon have come to possess a like suggestiveness of meaning. Hence anything that is obscure and, in the degree in which it is explained, more or less unintelligible is to be found solely in the terms used by Christ in relating the outward action to the effect as above described.

3. With a view to more exact discussion of this, assuming (as our paragraph does) that the effect of the action depends on the action being in harmony with Christ's institution, we must first clear up our minds on the point, what precisely such harmony implies. Even if different parties did not protest that the Supper as celebrated by others than themselves was no Supper at all, the variety of eucharistic practice within the Church sufficiently declares that on this point no agreement has so far been reached. It is not difficult, however, to show that such agreement is impossible. As regards both the action and the elements used there are a material and a formal identity which, owing to changed modes of life, cannot be attained together, but only one at the cost of the other ; and in such a situation it is virtually impossible that all should make their choice on the same principle. In general it may be said that insistence on material identity betrays an imperfect inward state, and a truly spiritual Christianity without troubling about the matter would be content if only the rite were so arranged as to represent the original action in its essential features. On the one hand, the historical unity and continuity of the ordinance would be endangered, and there would be no limit to the arbitrary variations introduced, if we were to be wholly indifferent to material identity. On the other, the representation of the original action may be made to depend on quite different points. Hence the problem to be solved can hardly be stated otherwise than by saying that we ought to try for just so much of each sort of identity as can be obtained without sacrifice on the other side. Thus in regard to the elements, we ask that in the Supper there should be eaten what, as used, can rightly be called bread, but not that it should be prepared from the ordinary materials or in the ordinary way ; on the other hand, that in what is drunk there should be wine of the grape, but not the common drink of this place or that, even supposing the common drink to be something different from wine. In regard to the action, we consider it essential that all the communicants should eat and drink in the same way, and that bread and wine should be distributed and received, also that the action

as a common meal should follow upon a devotional address and common prayer. But that it should take place in the evening and be merely the conclusion of another more complete meal, in itself of a worshipping character, so that what is partaken of in the Supper is only what remains over from the former meal—this, it would seem, we cannot insist on, for under present conditions it is unattainable. Indeed, if, still keeping to the last point, it were held that the Supper had such a close relation to the Jewish feast of the Passover that no representation of the impression originally made could be attained unless the Passover too were represented in all its original significance, it would be easy to infer that in that case the Supper can never again be what in Christ's institution it was, and therefore cannot really have been ordained by Him for the Church as an independent and never-ending institution. This objection is so natural that it may yet easily make itself more audible in the Evangelical Church than has hitherto been the case, and it of course raises the question on what in this matter our faith really rests. It can hardly be maintained that the intention to institute a permanent rite is revealed with perfect clearness in the words of Christ, as they have actually been preserved. On the contrary, some of the narratives contain no such injunction ; [1] in others it is only indistinctly expressed ; [2] and as the Apostles deduced no such command from Christ's words at the foot-washing,[3] they could (it is said) have had no more right to make of the Supper a perpetual and universal institution.[4] But as it is obvious that they did the one and did not do the other, we may well keep to the procedure they actually enjoined, without having to decide whether Christ expressly gave them still other injunctions touching the Supper,[5] or whether they deduced such injunctions from His words, or whether it was simply by their direct impressions of the case or by the accompanying circumstances that they were led to take different courses in regard to the Supper and in regard to the foot-washing. In the last of these cases we should not be able to view the Supper as in quite the same sense directly instituted by Christ, but we should still have to hold that the Apostles acted in His sense—unless, indeed, we are going to give up their canonical authority in a matter which touches the very heart and core of their vocation.

[1] Matt. 26²⁶⁻²⁸ and Mark 14²²⁻²⁴. [2] Luke 22¹⁹⁺ ²⁰ and 1 Cor. 11²⁴⁺ ²⁵.
[3] John 13¹⁴⁺ ¹⁵. [4] Cf. R. Barclay, *Apol. Th.* xiii.
[5] Cf. 1 Cor. 11²³.

§ 140. *With regard to the connexion between the bread and wine and the body and blood of Christ in the Lord's Supper, the Evangelical (Protestant) Church takes up an attitude of definite opposition only, on the one hand, to those who regard this connexion as independent of the act of participation, and, on the other hand, to those who, regardless of this connexion, would not admit any conjunction between participation in the bread and wine and spiritual participation in the flesh and blood of Christ.*

Augs. Conf., Art. 10 : ' On the Lord's Supper accordingly it is taught that the true body and blood of Christ is veritably present in the Supper under the form of bread and wine, and is there distributed and received.'—*Apol. Conf.* iv. : Quod in coena domini vere et substantialiter adsint corpus et sanguis Christi, et vere exhibeantur cum illis rebus, quae videntur, pane et vino his qui sacramentum accipiunt. . . . Cum enim Paulus dicat panem esse participationem corporis domini, sequeretur panem non esse participationem corporis sed tantum spiritus Christi, si non adesset vere corpus domini.—*Art. Smalc.* vi. : De sacramento altaris sentimus panem et vinum in coena esse verum corpus et sanguinem Christi, et non tantum dari et sumi a piis sed etiam ab impiis Christianis.—*Expos. simpl.* xix. : In coena domini signum est panis et vinum sumtum ex communi usu cibi et potus, res autem significata est ipsum traditum domini corpus, et sanguis eius effusus pro nobis, vel communio corporis et sanguinis domini.—*Ibid.* xxi. : Foris offertur a ministro panis, et audiuntur voces domini, etc., ergo accipiunt fideles et edunt, etc. : intus interim opera Christi per spiritum sanctum percipiunt etiam carnem et sanguinem domini et pascuntur his in vitam aeternam.—*Conf. Gallic.* xxxviii. : Dicimus itaque . . . panem illum et vinum illud, quod nobis in coena datur, vere nobis fieri spirituale alimentum, quatenus videlicet velut oculis nostris spectandum praebent carnem Christi nostrum cibum esse et eiusdem sanguinem nobis esse potum.—Itaque fanaticos illos omnes reiicimus qui haec signa et symbola repudiant.—*Conf. Anglic.* xxviii. : Panis et vini transsubstantiatio in Eucharistia ex sacris litteris probari non potest, sed apertis scripturae verbis adversatur. . . . Corpus Christi datur accipitur et manducatur in coena tantum coelesti et spirituali ratione. Medium autem, quo corpus Christi accipitur et manducatur in coena, fides est.

1. If the question in view here were a merely exegetical one, Dogmatic might await the close of hermeneutical discussion, and then accept the result just as it does other propositions which are not dogmatic in the full sense because what they contain is not statements about our immediate self-consciousness but facts which we receive on testimony. It is only as a fact in this sense that we could accept the conclusions of exegesis on the meaning of the words, ' This is My body,' etc. But the question is far from being purely exegetical. The language of the different narratives is not uniform ; hence (this belongs to historical criticism) we must first

of all ascertain what kind of expressions Christ can have used, from which these reports may have arisen ; only then will the time have come for inquiring into the sense of Christ's *ipsissima verba* as thus ascertained. Here we may start from very different points of view, and it is improbable that we shall be able to fix Christ's original language in a way to satisfy everyone. Also we are specially bound in dealing with the different views valid within the Evangelical Church to set forth the conviction, fundamental to the Union [of the Lutheran and Reformed Churches], that these differences are not such as to prevent common participation in the Supper. Hence we must endeavour to settle points of controversy as well as may be, and then set forth the principles on which we, so to speak, abolish the differences prevalent within our Church ; whereas we should still retain, on the one hand, the points of difference with the Catholic Church brought out in the credal passages quoted above, and, on the other, with communions and individual thinkers who deny all reality to the sacrament.

Now, to fix the points of controversy, since the differences are all due to the words of Christ just cited, and we can only recur here to what has already been made out in the previous paragraph, the question arises how the meaning of His words bears first on participation in the bread and wine, and next, on the strengthening of spiritual life expected from that ; a second question is, how far insight into the meaning of these words is requisite to the completeness of the action, and hence how far agreement in their interpretation is requisite to its communal character. To the last of these questions we can only reply by saying that the interpretation of Christ's words is essential just in so far as the expected result— namely, the strengthening of spiritual life—depends on it ; and agreement is only beneficial if differences have to be reconciled which might hinder the common performance of the rite. Regarding the first question we can only say—whether the difficult words uttered by the Redeemer be referred more to the bodily action or to the spiritual effect—that any explanation of them which can establish its own exegetical validity may be accepted as sound, provided it does not endanger for the believer the bond between the action and its effect.

2. The first kind of antagonism stated in our paragraph is that to the Catholic Church. It is on the whole wrong to look for this chiefly in the doctrine of transubstantiation. For the real issue it is an unimportant point of difference whether the body and blood

of Christ are partaken of corporeally along with the bread and wine, or the body and blood of Christ are produced in place of bread and wine for corporeal reception.   The only distinction between the two is this, that in the one case bread and wine are also partaken of, while in the other we do not partake of them also ; and for the intended result this is quite immaterial.   And if there had only been a willingness to give up the further notion that this change in the elements persists even apart from the act of reception, or that even what is not partaken of in the Supper undergoes the same change as the rest of the elements, the Saxon Reformers, as may be seen from the third passage quoted above, would have had little to object.   On the other hand, if a disposition had been shown in any quarter to take so physical a view of consubstantiation as that the body and blood of Christ are present in the bread and wine, after the words of Christ have been spoken over them, even when they are not partaken of in the Supper, Luther would have made a serious protest.   Even where he is setting forth his own view in the strongest antagonism to the Reformed doctrine, he nowhere affirms any such presence of the body and blood outside the eucharistic action ; on the other hand, ever since the rise of the doctrine of transubstantiation in the Catholic Church, this assumption of a physical and permanent change has been fundamental in all casuistical discussion.   Essentially, therefore, what, on this side, provoked persistent opposition was every kind of elevation and adoration of the consecrated elements, as well as every pretension thereby to achieve something apart from actual participation ; and similarly, everywhere within the Evangelical Church it would be distinctly denied that partaking of the consecrated elements outside the celebration of the sacrament conduces either to salvation or to judgment.   Hence the chief reason why (apart from its exegetical unsoundness) we reject the theory of the Catholic Church is that, advancing beyond common participation, it seeks by its so conceived union of the elements with the body and blood of Christ to attain quite different ends, and to attach magical spiritual effects to an effect that is bodily.

3. By the second antithesis indicated in our paragraph the Evangelical Church marks itself off from the Sacramentarians— taking that word not, of course, in the sense used by Luther and other theologians in the heat of controversy as applying even to the adherents of the Helvetic and the Gallic Confessions (*their* opinions lie wholly within the limits laid down in our paragraph),

but as denoting those who reject the sacrament. They assert that partaking of the bread and wine indicated by the phrase ' body and blood ' is only a shadowy emblem of that spiritual participation in the body and blood of Christ which is in no sense bound up with any such sacramental action, and that as soon as we have the assurance of this spiritual reality, the merely figurative action is better given up. Now we own that spiritual participation, to which Christ invited men long before the institution of the Supper as to something not merely future, is in no sense bound up by His institution exclusively with the sacrament or confined to it. None the less we confide in Christ's word that in the later institution that invitation is so realized in fact by His power that every believer may count on finding spiritual participation in the sacramental action, and that the action, if it be rightly administered in all respects, gives believers certain and infallible access thereto. Hence, as the most perfect common spiritual participation, the Supper is related to private participation in Christ apart from the Supper as the organized is related to the accidental, just as organized edification in public worship is related to edification which is individual and sporadic. But the opposed view, even when it does not deny that spiritual participation may be found in the sacramental action also, none the less protests that the conjunction of the two things is uncertain and purely fortuitous ; otherwise it would not seek to dissuade men from communicating. And in this it misconceives the value of Christ's institution.

Almost the same thing might be said of those who desire that the Supper should be permanently retained in the Church as Christ commanded, yet abolish its connexion with spiritual participation in the body and blood of Christ, declaring it to be no more than a custom whereby we bear witness, or make a profession of faith.[1] These we oppose, partly because they do not even regard the Supper as the climax of public worship, believing as they do that in the Supper they receive absolutely nothing ;[2] which means that to this gathering of people (which is pre-eminently a gathering in Christ's

---

[1] *Catech. Racov.*, Qu. 334–345. Zwingli is not to be confused with this party. He does call participation in the bread and wine in the Supper merely a thankful remembrance, but at the same time he always assumes a spiritual participation : Cum ad coenam domini cum hac spirituali manducatione venis . . . ac simul cum fratribus panem et vinum, quae jam symbolicum Christi corpus sunt, participas, jam proprie sacramentaliter edis cum scilicet intus idem agis quod foris operaris (*Expos. fid. chr.* Opp. ii. 555).

[2] Apparet coenam domini non eo institutam esse ut aliquid illic sumamus (*Catech. Racov.*, Qu. 338).

name) they would not even apply the general promise given by Christ to all such : partly because on their showing the Supper would not be the same thing in every age. For not only was there no one present at the original institution before whom the disciples could bear witness, but the ancient Church did not admit non-Christians as spectators ; while in their congregational relation-ships, apart from the sacrament, there is no lack of opportunities for Christians to make themselves known to each other as members of the Church.

4. If we leave open to the Evangelical Church the whole inter-vening ground between these two views—the one ascribing a magical value to the sacrament, the other depressing it into a bare sign—the historical reason for this is first of all that at the very beginning of Protestantism two views developed, one of which (within these limits) approximated most to the Catholic view, the other to the Socinian ; while on the other hand both clung to a consciousness of common antagonism to the other two.   In part there were ever-renewed efforts to reconcile their differences ; in part out of these very efforts there arose a third Protestant view intermediate between both. Hence wherever these two views came in contact, the common conviction came in time to prevail that as they all looked for the same result under the same conditions—namely, the presence of true and living faith—each side must believe that the other had the same right as itself to expect this result, since neither could be certain that it was interpreting the connexion between the action and the result (so far as its production is beyond our power) pre-cisely as the Redeemer intended it, while yet each side was eager to conform to the mind of the Redeemer as closely as possible.   This conviction rests simply on a recognition of the exegetical difficulties attaching to the manner in which Christ speaks of His body and blood in offering the bread and wine. One side in interpreting words of such significance will admit nothing but literal explanation, which yet they cannot apply consistently owing to the fact that the reports of Christ's words differ—' this ' in one case having ' blood ' as its predicate, ' cup ' having ' testament ' in the other. So that our Supper and the original Supper cannot be the same if the offered body is literally the same as the body offering it. From this the other side argues that this equating of the bread and the body is only to be taken loosely, the former being a sign of the latter. They have then to explain not merely why in that case a special sign of the blood had to be offered in addition to the sign of the

body, but also whether the disciples (assuming that they were meant to understand Christ's language) were intended to interpret His words analogously to previous words of His own, or rather in the light of the Old Testament rite to which Christ's institution was attached. These problems have not so far all been solved by either side; yet it is possible that new attempts may still be made deserving of a place among the helpful efforts of the Evangelical Church, and that an adequate explanation may at last render all other imperfect ones superfluous. The three views, however, which have stood out from among these imperfect attempts and established their position most firmly may best be exhibited as follows. The first or Lutheran view declares that with the bread and wine Christ conjoined for participation the real presence of His body and blood, but only for the action of bodily partaking in both elements. The second or Zwinglian view declares that Christ conjoined nothing with the bread and wine in themselves ; by His command He merely conjoined spiritual participation in His flesh and blood with the action of partaking in the bread and wine. The third or Calvinistic view declares that while it is true that Christ conjoined something exclusively with the action of eating and drinking, this was not merely spiritual participation, available quite apart from the sacrament ; it was a real presence of His body and blood not to be had anywhere else.[1] The second view recognizes two things only, bodily participation and the spiritual effect, both linked together by the Word. Beyond all question this view is the clearest and the easiest to grasp, for it sets up an exact analogy between the Lord's Supper and baptism, and leaves the real presence of body and blood (which it is scarcely possible to describe) altogether out of account, so that by sacramental participation it can only mean the conjunction of spiritual participation with bodily participation as defined above. But even though we emphasize the words of Zwingli as just quoted, even though many other expressions by which it might be thought he meant to minimize or even abolish the powers of the sacrament be explained in the light of his polemic against Roman doctrine [2]—still this view leaves it unexplained

---

[1] Itaque si per fractionem panis dominus corporis sui participationem vere repraesentat, minime dubium esse debet quin vere praestet atque exhibeat (Calv., *Institt.* IV. xvii. 10). . . . Dico igitur in coenae mysterio per symbola panis et vini Christum vere nobis exhiberi, adeoque corpus et sanguinem eius . . . quo scilicet primum in unum corpus cum ipso coalescamus, deinde participes substantiae eius facti in bonorum omnium communicatione virtutem quoque sentiamus (*ibid.* 11).

[2] Sacramentum vim nullam habere potest ad conscientiam liberandam.

why, if Christ meant no more than this, He made use of these particular expressions. In addition to these two things, both the other views recognize a third thing, namely, a real presence of Christ's body and blood. According to Luther, through a special and secret power of the Word this presence is so conjoined with the elements of bread and wine as to yield what resembles bodily participation ; according to Calvin, it merely is so conjoined with the believer's spiritual participation as to yield a peculiar sacramental intensification thereof, to effect which no other power is required than the power of the divine promise familiar to us all. In both theories this supposed third thing explains why Christ had to use such very peculiar expressions in stating His intention. But, apart from the fact that Luther's view is too near the Roman type not to have encouraged the transference of many superstitious ideas, the mode in which the body of Christ is partaken of along with the bread, as well as the mode in which this sacramental participation differs on the one hand from bodily participation in the symbolic elements, and on the other from spiritual participation in the flesh and blood, is so difficult to make intelligible that while formulæ about it can be composed out of unscripturally devised words, the fact itself can never be made clear. The Calvinistic theory escapes many of these difficulties by holding aloof, alike from the over-intellectual bareness of the Zwinglian view and from the mysterious sensuousness of the Lutheran ; but no more than the latter does it succeed in making it clear that we have an interest in the body and blood of Christ, and no more than the former does it yield any explanation of the kind of relation obtaining between the body and the blood, or the ground of distinction between them. Hence, although this view has had a strong power of attraction, it provides new excuses for vacillating between the charm of symbolism which allures men to seek more in the sacrament than is brought out in the explanation itself, and on the other hand resting satisfied with something more external, on the ground that it is impossible to make out what the peculiar significance of the Supper is. We need not therefore expect that this view will become universally predominant in the Evangelical Church. As a result of the steady unprejudiced work of interpreters we may rather expect yet another view to emerge which will not make ship-

. . . Toto igitur coelo errant qui sacramenta vim habere mundandi putant. . . . Sunt ergo sacramenta signa sive cerimoniae, quibus se homo ecclesiae probat (*De vera et falsa relig.*).

wreck on any of these rocks. Till then it will not be possible to state any common Church doctrine except regarding the effects of the Supper, and all that can be set forth under that head is the contents of the following two paragraphs.

§ 141. *First Theorem.—Participation in the body and blood of Christ in the Lord's Supper conduces in the case of all believers to confirm their fellowship with Christ.*

Luther's *Larger Catech.*, 247 : 'For this reason we go to the sacrament, because we there receive the treasure through and in which we secure forgiveness of sin.'—248 : ' Hence it is well named a food of the soul, which nourishes and strengthens the new man.'—*Expos. simpl.* xxi. : Est ea spiritualis manducatio corporis Christi . . . qua manente in sua essentia corpore et sanguine domini ea nobis communicantur spiritualiter . . . per spiritum s. qui videlicet ea quae per carnem et sanguinem domini pro nobis in mortem tradita parata sunt, ipsam remissionem peccatorum liberationem et vitam aeternam applicat et confert nobis ita ut Christus in nobis vivat.—*Conf. Scot.* xxi. : Sed unio haec et conjunctio quam habemus cum corpore et sanguine Jesu Christi in recto sacramenti usu operatione spiritus sancti efficitur, qui nos vera fide supra omnia quae videntur vehit, et ut vescamur corpore et sanguine Jesu Christi semel pro nobis effusi et fracti efficit.— *Conf. Belg.* xxxv. : Convivium hoc mensa est spiritualis, in qua Christus seipsum nobis cum omnibus bonis suis communicat efficitque ut in illa tam ipsomet quam passionis mortisque ipsius merito fruamur.—*Melanchth.*, *loc. theol.* : Ad hoc igitur prodest manducatio poenitentiam agenti, videlicet ad fidem confirmandam.—*Calv.*, *Institt.* iv. vii. 5 : In hunc modum dominus voluit . . . vera etiam sui communicatione fieri ut vita sua in nos transeat et nostra fiat. . . . *Ibid.* 11 : Per effectum autem redemtionem iustitiam sanctificationem vitamque aeternam . . . intelligo.

1. The one benefit of this participation is stated as being the confirming of our fellowship with Christ ; and this includes the confirming of Christians in their union with each other,[1] for the latter rests so entirely on their union with Christ that the union of an individual with Christ is unthinkable apart from his union with believers. In the credal passages just quoted this is made less prominent than could be wished, owing to the fact that in such discussions the question of the benefit of the sacrament customarily came up only in connexion with the questions we discussed above, where each individual participant is considered only *as* an individual. Hence light on the subject now before us is only to be sought from the enumeration of the benefits won by Christ, or under the all-embracing idea of sanctification. The general expressions for the effects of participation which stand out most clearly are confirmation

---

[1] Cf. 1 Cor. 10^{17} 12^{27}.

in faith, and the nourishment of the new man or the passing over of Christ's life into ours. Essentially both are the same, for living faith in Christ is simply the consciousness of our union with Him. It is usual, however, to emphasize two points specially—namely, that in the Supper we have renewed or confirmed to us the forgiveness of sins, and that we experience a heightening of the powers that make for sanctification. The two things really cannot be separated, and both rest on the fact that owing to the incomplete removal of sin even the new spiritual life has its progress interrupted by tendencies of a partially retrograde kind. For just as regeneration only becomes really firm and sure through our being in the status of sanctification, so, too, when union with Christ has been disturbed by sin, the certainty that the sin has been forgiven can only be made really secure through the feeling of restored and strengthened life. And for this the representation of the whole body of believers natural in the action of the Supper is an important factor. For it cannot but give rise in each individual to a strong excitation of the common Spirit, as well as to a heightened consciousness both of his general and his special vocation within this fellowship ; and this cannot but be accompanied by a new impulse to develop his gifts.

As regards the relation of the Supper to the forgiveness of sins, it must first be observed that in this respect no distinction ought to be drawn between original and actual sin, as if baptism referred only to original sin and the Supper only to actual. Apart from the fact that baptism cannot be completed until a time when actual sin has already issued from original, and that it could not be an index of the beginning of the new life unless in consequence of it actual sin ceased to hinder fellowship in the blessedness of Christ—apart from this, baptism as the seal of regeneration has itself a relation to all actual sins, inasmuch as the sins of the regenerate are always *ipso facto* forgiven.[1] But so it is, too, with the Supper ; just as it is original sin which is perpetually being manifested in the actual sin which obstructs vital fellowship with Christ, so it is the forgiveness of original sin that we ever anew require to have confirmed to us. In the second place, the forgiveness of sins ought not to be divided in two, nor ought the sin-pardoning power of the sacrament of the altar to be regarded as of a special character, as though sins were first forgiven in one way through the justifying action of God in regeneration and then in another way through the special presence

[1] Cf. § 111.

and communicative action of Christ in the sacrament.[1] On the contrary, there is but one and the same sin-pardoning power ; and just as regeneration is nothing but the general and ever-active relation of Christ to the totality of the human race, as that relation first comes in touch with the individual life, so the forgiveness of sins in the Supper is simply this living relationship as it reveals itself at a moment when Christ is presented in common to a number of individual believers.

In this connexion it may appear an enigma (for this does not rest on Christ's institution) why, on their confession of sin, the Church should declare forgiveness to those communicating at any given time, before they have taken the sacrament. As an anticipation, however, this declarative act belongs to the Supper in the same way as, conversely, confirmation belongs to baptism as its subsequent consummation. Hence the practice in the Evangelical Church, which at first obtained here and there,[2] of regarding absolution as a sacrament by itself, was soon given up. The confession of sin has no public ecclesiastical character save in relation to the Supper, and the wish to participate in the Supper cannot be otherwise expressed than through confession, for apart from sin there would be no need to renew our union with Christ. But when the Church proclaims the forgiveness of sin in connexion with such confession, what it really does is first to declare that the man who at this very moment feels the need of renewing his fellowship with Christ is put by the Church on an equal footing with those who already have satisfied that need, and next to give the needy soul thereby an assurance that he will find the satisfaction of his need in the sacrament. Hence every evangelical Christian will probably find that the sense of forgiveness which follows absolution imparted by the Church is no more than a shadow of that which he enjoys in partaking of the Supper itself, for it is there combined with the sense of a new influx of living spiritual power out of Christ's fulness, such as really removes the obstructions of the new life and the lingering effects of sinfulness in general.

2. The consequences of all this for the procedure of the Church

---

[1] *Conf. Saxon.*, p. 173 : Monemus etiam ne existiment propter hoc opus . . . remitti peccata, sed ut fiducia intueantur mortem et meritum filii Dei . . . et statuant propter ipsum nobis peccata remitti.

[2] Melanchth., *loc. theol.* : Numerantur haec sacramenta, baptismus, coena domini, absolutio. The same thing is meant by the order of Articles 8–13 in the *Augsburg Confession*. Hence, too, the *Apology* says : Vere igitur sunt sacramenta baptismus, coena domini, absolutio, quae est sacramentum poenitentiae.

in the sacramental action are as follows. First, the Supper refers
back to baptism, and therefore, as long as infant baptism is maintained, there can be no participation in the Supper before confirmation in the Protestant sense of that word. The communicating of
children, in whom neither the consciousness of sin nor the consciousness of grace can be properly developed, is for that reason a grave
abuse infested with superstition. Secondly, on none of the different
views can participation in the Supper take place without Christ being
presented in the spirit ; hence there can rightly be no eucharistic
action designed for those whose mental condition is defective or
whose consciousness is obscured or on the very point of disappearing.
Thirdly, the Supper was instituted by Christ as a common action ;
hence it should always be held so in the Church. Fourthly and
lastly, the doctrine of the Greek and Roman Churches that the conjunction of the body of Christ with the bread even apart from its
use in the sacrament constitutes a perpetual sacrifice offered to
God,[1] finds no support on our side and is for ever excluded ; even
when allowance is made for the mitigating explanation that this
repetition (as it were) of the sacrifice of Christ upon the cross is
merely a memorial thereof.[2] We know nothing of merits or satis-
factions as intended here.[3] The evasive suggestion that such
sacrifice is not different from but identical with that accomplished
on the cross,[4] has for us no value whatever, for in that case we
should have to separate altogether the sacrifice in the death of
Christ from the obedience in His life,[5] and His original sacrifice
would then be just as arbitrary a transaction and just as magical
as the sacrifice of the Mass. In any case this latter sacrifice would
have to be regarded as supplementary to Christ's original sacrifice ;
the consequence of which would be, for one thing, that apart from
this supplement God would not behold believers in Christ, and thus
justification would be cancelled all over again, in defiance of the
fact that the circumstances which alone could bring this about must
already have been present to God's foreknowledge in His justifying
action. Along with this goes a second consequence, namely, that

---

[1] Ἔκθεσις ὀρθοδ. πίσ. 107. Catech. Rom. ii. 77 : Ut ecclesia perpetuum
sacrificium haberet, quo peccata nostra expiarentur.

[2] Sacrosanctum missae sacrificium esse non solum nudam commemora-
tionem sacrificii quod in cruce factum est, sed vere etiam propitiatorium
sacrificium.

[3] Qui hoc sacrificium offerunt, quo nobiscum communicant, dominicae
passionis fructus merentur et satisfaciunt (ibid. 79).

[4] Unum itaque et idem sacrificium esse fatemur et haberi debet, quod in
missa peragitur et quod in cruce oblatum est (ibid. 53).

[5] Heb. 2[10, 17] 3[2] 5[8].

redemption—not merely as concerns its realization in men, viewed, that is, in its temporal aspect (where the matter is self-evident), but even when taken as the ground of the divine good-pleasure, *i.e.* in its eternal aspect—is only made complete through this supplementary action of the Church. And this means that in part men redeem themselves, for the priestly work of Christ would be insufficient apart from the sacrifice of the Mass. Hence, while there is no longer any need to describe the Mass as idolatrous, we persist in rejecting unconditionally the whole idea of a sacrifice subsequent to the end of all sacrifices ; issuing as it does from a demonstrable misunderstanding, it confuses faith and therefore necessarily encourages superstition, and in particular falsifies the idea of the priesthood of all believers. It is thus that we regard it simply in itself, and irrespectively of the doctrine of transubstantiation, with which, of course, it hangs together.[1]

§ 142. *Second Theorem.—Unworthy participation in the Lord's Supper conduces to judgment for the partaker.*

Apol. Conf. iv. : Christus ait (1 Cor. 11[19]) : illos sibi iudicium manducare qui manducant indigne, ideo pastores non cogunt hos qui non sunt idonei, ut sacramentis utantur.—*Conf. Belg.* xxxv.: Nemo itaque ad hanc mensam se sistere debet, qui prius sese recte non probaverit, ne de hoc pane edens et de hoc poculo bibens iudicium sibi edat et bibat.—*Catech. Heidelb.* lxxxi. : Hypocritae autem et qui non vere resipiscunt, damnationem sibi edunt et bibunt.

1. It is not easy to explain to oneself clearly how this paragraph is to be applied. In the first place, it is difficult to form an exact idea from what quarter the unworthiness indicated could arise ; for one who is not a member of the Church has no access to the sacrament, while every true member of the Church is a partaker all the more worthy that the Supper through Christ's institution so possesses a peculiar and independent power which marks it off from all other expressions and media of piety, that everyone must feel stimulated to the most appropriate mood of feeling. What first suggests itself, however, is this. The Supper was instituted as a common action and is publicly administered by the ministers of the Word, hence by Church order definite times and seasons must be appointed for it. Such order has the look of a summons, and it is possible that individuals—whether from custom merely or to meet the views of others—obey this summons without an inward longing for communion being awakened by any sense of their own spiritual

[1] *Heidelb. Catech.*, Qu. 80 ; *Artic. Smalc.* ii., *de Missa* ; *Expos. simpl.* xxi.

deficiencies. In its origin such participation is unworthy, for it has no connexion with the purpose of the institution ; without a lively sense of personal relationship to Christ there can be no active recollection of Him, as He is represented in the Supper. This will always be lacking whether we conceive the inward state in question as one of dull thoughtlessness not banished even by the action itself, or as the steady presence in consciousness of alien motives, which can hardly fail to be accompanied by a real, even if temporary, disbelief in the power and greatness of the sacrament.

2. If, however, the judgment described as a consequence of this unworthiness be taken as meaning consignment to eternal damnation, then it seems impossible to establish any connexion between the two things. Indeed, assuming that unworthy participation is an actual possibility and is attended by these dangers, and on the other hand that saving spiritual participation in Christ's flesh and blood may be had elsewhere than in the sacrament, it looks as if we might well wish that the sacrament had never been instituted, and that we had been relegated solely to the extra-sacramental participation just referred to. But let us put the idea of eternal damnation provisionally on one side and concentrate on the question of unworthiness. In that case the thoughtlessness which turns so rich an opportunity into a meaningless external performance, and the insincerity which masks unfitting motives by an action so sacred, are a degradation of it which is eminently calculated to induce a condition of unreceptivity and hardening, such as we have every reason to regard as one element in damnation. This entirely justifies the wording of our paragraph. The Supper, that is to say, is seen to be a means of discrimination ; fit and worthy participation in it promotes living fellowship with Christ, while participation of an unworthy kind is always rendering more ineffectual what is the most powerful means by which such fellowship can be strengthened, and thereby is always enhancing the power of hindrances. If now we consider how insuperable thoughtlessness must be, and still more how shameless insincerity must be, if they prove stronger than what is so sacred, and how little faith can keep hold of the Redeemer if what He has instituted can thus be torn away from its purpose, we shall find it quite possible to understand the fearful awe into which the devotional language of the ancient Church falls when treating of this subject. All the more essential is it that the public teaching of the Church should refrain from discouraging pronouncements not necessitated by the facts.

3. It is worth while to look back once again from this point at the distinction between the Lutheran and the Calvinistic view of the Supper, and feel how incapable it is of excusing a breach of Church fellowship.   Neither of the two is at all successful in clearing up the third element which they accept, and which we have indicated by the phrase ' sacramental participation.'   But a reference to our paragraph makes plain how much the distinction between them amounts to.   The Lutheran view insists upon it that as sacramental participation in the body and blood is bound up with participation in the bread and wine, it is shared in by worthy and unworthy communicants alike ;   only that in the one case it conduces to judgment, but in the other to spiritual participation and, thereby, to salvation. The Calvinistic theory, which attaches sacramental participation to spiritual, can only rejoin that in such sacramental participation the unworthy have no share.   If this is the one point of distinction that can be clearly formulated, the difference will become quite negligible, once unworthy participation has disappeared from actual practice. Such difference in doctrine in any case would vanish of itself, as the two Churches approximate to perfection, and is therefore no justification of their separate existence ;   for unworthy participation always is an evidence of imperfection in the Church.   If the action of those who come to the sacrament is in harmony with the common sentiment of the whole body, and if the Church administering the sacrament develops a perfect sympathy between the whole body and the inward state of each member, no one in that case will seek to come to the sacrament unworthily, and the congregation will offer it to none whose participation would be unworthy.   As the Church really advances to a better state, the only cases which tend to recall the difference between the two theories are bound to become fewer in number and gradually to disappear.

APPENDIX TO THE LAST TWO DOCTRINES :   THE NAME
' SACRAMENT '

§ 143. *The Evangelical (Protestant) Church uses the name ' Sacrament'
only for these two institutions, Baptism and the Lord's
Supper, which were instituted by Christ Himself and which
represent His priestly activity.*

1. It is natural enough that a term taken over from a realm wholly foreign to theology should have no exact delimitation. Hence it was only very gradually that the Roman Church reached

its seven sacraments, and it was also by gradual steps that we fixed upon these two. Now the fundamental elements in the meaning of the term ' sacrament ' we must accept very cautiously, for the word, although based on the New Testament representation of a good soldier of Christ, has given prominence to one of its elements which is of most precarious application. Hence we may well wish even more unreservedly than Zwingli did [1] that Church terminology had never adopted the word, and also that it might be found possible to dispense with it. This might be done by way of approximation to the Eastern Church, which has never adopted it, and which instead uses the term ' mysteries '; but anything of the kind will certainly have to wait to a later time. A wish, however, is only rational in so far as it contributes to its own fulfilment ; we have therefore prepared a way here for the change by treating of baptism and the Supper each by itself and without any definite relation to the term ' sacrament,' though as it is familiar we have used it now and then for convenience. The ordinary procedure (to begin with an explanation of this so-called general notion) is always tending to confirm the false idea that it is a strictly dogmatic conception expressive of something that is essential to Christianity, and that it is from the fact that they are exemplifications of this conception that baptism and the Supper derive their special value. That prejudice we may at least claim is not fostered by the treatment adopted here, for even the close relation we have established between baptism and the Supper has been kept quite independent of this traditional term (sacrament), and—like that between the two other pairs of doctrines in this Division—been based solely on a common relation to one of the essential activities of Christ's vocation. So that it has the look of a mere accident that this middle pair of our six doctrines bears a common name, while the other pairs do not.

2. In any case it would be a fruitless proceeding to enter upon an etymological examination of the name, and seek thereby to decide what can and what cannot be subsumed under it. The controversy with the Roman Church, too, is quite an empty one, if it concerns merely the interpretation of the name and does no more than raise the question whether our interpretation is right or theirs, which applies the name to five other ordinances. The controversy has a meaning only if in some vital connexion our opponents are trying to give those five other actions an equal place with these two. In fact, however, there is an obvious dissimilarity among the

[1] *De vera et falsa relig.*, p. 194.

actions and situations which for the Roman Church are embraced under the term ' sacrament,' while the closeness of the connexion between the two to which our Church restricts the term has already been shown. Hence, if the name is still to be used, nothing remains but to fix its meaning in a purely arbitrary way without regard to its original sense, as a communal designation of these two institutions. The usage of the Evangelical Church at first was not fixed either ; not only was absolution received as a third sacrament, but Melanchthon also proposed to make ordination a sacrament as well.[1] Absolution, however, failed to keep its place, and the latter suggestion obtained no support. In general we think it more correct (and it is wholly on this model that our eucharistic service has been formed) to regard the absolution as a part of the communion service, as contrasted with which it has lost its sacramental independence ; and it was equally correct to take confirmation as a part of baptism, once confirmation had had restored to it a definite significance. Baptism, however, was also a consecration to the true priesthood common to all Christians, whereas the Ministry of the Word in the narrower official sense is not common to all ; hence dedication to it is not to be put on the same level as baptism. Marriage was only brought in because Scripture uses of it the term ' mystery,' which the term ' sacrament ' displaced ; but not only has it as a permanent state no similarity to our two ordinances, so that by analogy only consecration to marriage could be called a sacrament but not marriage itself, but in addition it has no place here because as a divine moral institution it has existed from the beginning quite irrespective of the mission of Christ. Finally, as regards the virtue sought to be attributed to extreme unction as a usage of the Apostolic Age, this could only be based upon the efficacy of the Church's prayer in the name of Jesus, and the benediction of marriage could only rank as prayer of the same kind. Clearly enough, then, these other usages are distinct from our two sacraments. What is common to both, let the Church name them as it may, will always be this, that they are continued activities of Christ, enshrined in Church actions and bound up therewith in the closest way. By their instrumentality He exerts His priestly activity on individuals, and sustains and propagates that living fellowship between Him and us in virtue of which alone God sees individuals in Christ.

3. We cannot quite ignore here the connexion between our two

[1] *Loc. theol., de num. sacram.*

sacraments and two Old Testament institutions, namely, circumcision and the Passover ; a connexion which has been emphasized more or less at different times, but which has often been quite wrongly conceived. It is an entirely erroneous idea, for instance, that circumcision and the Passover had any particular relation to each other, as baptism and the Supper have. Circumcision as an Abrahamitic institution had no other relation to the Passover than to other Mosaic institutions. Apart from this, it is going much too far to assert that baptism took the place of circumcision and the Supper that of the Passover. Baptism was instituted quite independently of circumcision ; moreover, circumcision was not put a stop to by baptism but by the preponderance of Gentile Christians over Jewish Christians, as well as by the intermingling of the two. The Supper did indeed attach itself to the Passover, but it was at once separated from it ; while the Passover continued to be celebrated by Jewish Christians without any relation to the Supper. Still, it is not impossible that a closer examination of the original relation between the two might be the very thing to yield a more correct understanding of the difficult expressions used by Christ in instituting the Supper. And a comparison of the two New Testament institutions with those of the Old Testament has the very definite result of bringing out with great clearness the real difference between the old covenant and the new.

FIFTH DOCTRINE : THE POWER OF THE KEYS

§ 144. *By reason of its coexistence with the world there exists in the Church a legislative and an administrative power, which is an essential effluence from the kingly office of Christ.*

1. If the Church were completely self-contained, so that in none of those who belonged to it there survived anything of the world, the soul of each Christian in the whole system of its powers rather being a perfect organ of the Holy Spirit, then always and everywhere all events in the Church would happen of themselves as the Spirit prompted. Owing to the identity of the Spirit in all, everything that happened would show a spontaneous consistency ; there would exist no difference between the general will and that of individuals, and there would nowhere be any occasion for law. If general conceptions were applied to Church affairs, those so applying them would in reality only be formulating the ways in which men actually behaved. This ideal, however, has never been realized

except in Christ Himself ; hence the utterances and impulses of
the Spirit, when resisted, take the form of law and are accepted as
such. This being the case, the analogous activities of Spirit-filled
men also take on a relation to law as well as to the resistance which
law implies, and assume the form of executive power. Not in any
external fashion, as with civil authority (for an external apart from
an internal out of which it springs has not the slightest value
for the Church), but owing simply to the natural predominance of
the common Spirit over persons—a predominance such as every
member of a community feels has won his free assent. Should
there be someone who does not feel this, or who in his own person
is consciously antagonistic to the challenge of the common Spirit,
that fact denotes an anti-church element in his life, and the predominance of the common Spirit must be re-established inwardly
before the person in whose case it was infringed can again be
acknowledged as a true member of the Church. Now this power
of producing without any external means a steady voluntary submission, is the very power exerted by Christ ; and in every case
where men were united to Him this power was manifested precisely
in the fact that impulses coming from Him were recognized as law,
and that His judgments regarding men were felt to be final pronouncements on what is in man—the new community thus becoming
His Kingdom. In this respect, too, the Spirit actualizes in the
Church what is to be received out of Christ's fulness. Or to put
it otherwise, when Christ breathed the Spirit on the community of
His people, He thereby conveyed this power to it—a power which
cannot be conceived apart from this original ruling influence of
Christ, and without which the union of the Divine Essence with
human nature exemplified in the Church must either be much more
or much less than is involved in the conception of a guiding common
Spirit.

2. At first this explanation does not at all seem to lead up to
what is generally understood by the Power of the Keys, for that
spiritual power is ordinarily taken to refer to the expansion and
maintenance of the Church, in the sense that it rests with the
Church to decide who shall and who shall not be received into the
Christian fellowship, and also who shall remain there or be expelled
—a matter so far not even mentioned here, but left to be inferred
by way of appendix to the foregoing. But the two things can
easily be combined, and the path we are now taking is merely that
which enables us better to subsume the whole of Church govern-

ment, as is fitting, under one conception. If we start with the kind
of resistance mentioned above, every case of permanent submission
produced subsequently by the Church's legislative authority is a
new conquest for the common Spirit, which thereby wins a place
for itself in an individual life which previously was, at best, a disputed possession hovering on the border between Church and
world. By every such removal of hesitation through legislative
action, the Church's realm is extended. But it is also through
such action that the first entrance of the individual into the Church
is brought about, for regeneration is the effect of the same cause,
for the first time presenting to men the preponderance of the God-
consciousness as the law of spiritual life. The same is true of the
power which applies this law in particular judgments and pronouncements ; these define the place taken in the community by
each individual as a consequence of his inward state, and determine
whether much or little can be entrusted to him.

Another peculiarity seems to be that we formerly [1] described
the Power of the Keys as a prolongation of Christ's kingly activity,
whereas it is here taken more as an effluence thereof, mediated by
the Spirit. But in this respect there is no more than a slight difference between the institutions treated of in this Division. The
mediation of the Spirit comes in in every case, otherwise these
institutions would not be actions of the Church ; and the actions
are all of them effluences of Christ, for it is always from Christ that
the Spirit draws. It is less easy to describe this power as a prolongation of Christ's activity, for the difference between legislative
and administrative activities essentially relates to the organized
community, while Christ's own activity preceded it. If, then, the
difference has no application to His case, the Power of the Keys as
thus defined cannot in the strictest sense be called a prolongation of
His activity, although it does develop the outline of the common
life as Christ drew it, and that without absorbing alien accretions
from without.

§ 145. *Theorem.—The Power of the Keys is the power in virtue of
which the Church decides what belongs to the Christian life,
and disposes of each individual in the measure of his con-
formity with these decisions.*

Conf. Aug. de abus. vii. : Sentiunt potestatem clavium esse . . . mandatum
Dei praedicandi evangelii, remittendi et retinendi peccata et administrandi
sacramenta.—*Ibid.* : Respondent quod liceat Episcopis seu pastoribus facere

----
[1] § 127.

ordinationes ut res ordine gerantur in ecclesia.—*Expos. simpl.* xiv. : De
clavibus regni Dei . . . simpliciter dicimus omnes ministros legitime vocatos
. . . exercere . . . usum clavium, cum . . . populum . . . increpant inque
disciplina retinent. — *Ibid.* xviii. : Atqui debet interim iusta esse inter
ministros disciplina. Inquirendum enim diligenter in doctrinam et vitam
ministrorum in synodis.—*Conf. Basil.* xvi. : Ipsa pascendi gregis auctoritas,
quae proprie clavium potestas est . . . cunctis aeque inviolabilis esse, et
. . . electis tantum et idoneis administrandum committi debet.—*Conf. Gall.*
xxxii. seq. : Credimus expedire, ut . . . ecclesiae alicuius praefecti inter se
dispiciant qua ratione totum corpus commode regi possit . . . eas tantum
leges admittimus, quae fovendae concordiae et unicuique in obedientia
debita retinendo subserviunt, qua in re sequendum nobis putamus quod
dominus noster . . . de excommunicatione statuit quam quidem approbamus
et una cum suis appendicibus necessariam esse arbitramur. Rom. 16[17].
Cf. *Conf. Belg.* xxxii.—*Conf. Tetrapol.* xiii. : Hi (ministri) claves habent regni
coelorum ligandi et solvendi peccata remittendi et retinendi potestatem, sic
tamen ut nihil nisi ministri Christi sint, cuius hoc ius solius est et proprium
est.—*Conf. Saxon.* : Et ad ministerium haec pertinent . . . exercere iudicia
ecclesiae legitimo modo de iis qui manifestorum criminum in moribus aut
doctrina rei sunt, et contra contumaces sententiam excommunicationis ferre,
et conversos rursus absolvere et recipere. Haec ut rite fiant, etiam con-
sistoria in ecclesiis nostris constituta sunt.

1. The term Office or Power of the Keys, in combination with
the terms ' bind ' and ' loose,' occurs in a discourse of Christ [1] which
bears upon the first part of our paragraph ; the terms ' bind ' and
' loose ' occur in another and related discourse,[2] where, at least
judged by the context, they bear upon our second part ; and this
again is very like a third passage,[3] which probably has to do with
the second part exclusively. To say that this or that shall be bound,
means that it shall be fixed by command and prohibition, while
that is loosed which is exempt from such rule and is left to the
self-determination of each individual [4]—the common feeling of the
whole body taking the same attitude to one who adopts one course
and to another who adopts the opposite, provided only that a good
conscience can be assumed in both cases. Now here we have the
legislative activity of the Church described in the previous paragraph, and its limitations as well. The common feeling of the
body has no occasion to express itself in a determinative way
except when, through the imperfect permeation of the Holy Spirit,
there is not being realized in certain members something which
common feeling demands as an essential manifestation of faith, or
when, in certain lives, there is still going on what, if left uncensured,

---

[1] Matt. 16[19].   [2] Matt. 18[18].   [3] John 20[23].
[4] *Conf. Aug. de abus.* vii. ; Necesse est enim retineri in ecclesiis doctrinam
de libertate christiana.

would tend to injure the Spirit's action in others. But it is equally essential, and equally pertinent to the same legislative activity, that things should be ' loosed ' which presumption or spiritual arrogance might seek to bind. The unity of the Church cannot continue to exist if individuals try to make their personal modes of acting or thinking obligatory, as the only proper expression of the common Spirit. Now if people insist on taking the scriptural passage referred to (and it is the chief Biblical authority for the doctrine) in the literal sense that Christ conferred this power on Peter alone, we should have to carry through that view strictly ; and then, with the death of Peter, the legislative activity of the Church would have come to an end—in so far, that is to say, as it rests on this injunction of Christ. Nobody will doubt that in that case it was bound to reappear ; for otherwise, if we suppose every-thing to have been decided for all time in the first generation, this could only have come about in a supernatural fashion which would destroy the genuinely historical character of events ; and this could never have led up to a free and living development. It follows that if this were the literal sense of Christ's words, the legislative activity of the Church could not be based on them alone. But it would not for that reason cease to be a prolongation of Christ's activity. It would still be an effluence from His will that a com-munity should exist, and without legislative activity its existence is impossible. Peter himself cannot have understood Christ's words in any such sense, for, when general pronouncements became necessary, he did not arrogate to himself alone the right of making them, but brought the questions at issue before the community. Even in the second passage quoted from Scripture, the ecclesiastical activity which applies the law in judgments and represents law executively is ultimately attributed to the community ; hence it goes without saying that even earlier individuals must have worked in the name of the community, and as its organs ; the more so that the Redeemer certainly did not mean to give any irritated person the right to call his brother to account. But once we regard the individual as the organ of the community in dealing with a brother, every sin against the whole body is also done against the individual ; and the natural organ of the whole body in each case is the individual who first has certain knowledge of the facts. If we further bring in the third Scripture passage quoted—and it is always reckoned as bearing on our problem—it may no doubt at first sight be interpreted as meaning that the forgiveness of sins is first

imparted in baptism, and that one whose baptism is postponed
to a later time therefore has his sins longer retained.[1] We have
no desire to exclude this ; clearly the right administration of
baptism (or, as now with us, of confirmation), which is to be expected from the action of the Spirit, also belongs in essence to the
Power of the Keys. But this certainly does not exhaust the
meaning of the passage. The Apostles themselves and the Early
Church after them applied it to persons who had already been
received into the Church ; [2] further, the passage contains the promise
given by Christ with regard to every judgment declaring whether
or not a given person is in that fellowship with Christ in which sin
disappears. Now all regenerate persons are in this fellowship ;
hence their actual sins, which alone could evoke a judgment of the
Church, are already forgiven. If we add the fact that no one
simply as an organ of the Spirit is within the Church, and that
activity within the Church can only take place through powers
which are themselves channels of the Spirit, *i.e.* spiritual gifts (since
there must be sin where there are still vestiges of resistance to the
Spirit's indwelling), it is clear that the Redeemer's promise entails
that the Church will judge rightly on the question what, and how
much or how little, is to be entrusted to the individual member
of the Church, and to what extent his influence on the Church or
his collaboration with it ought to be restricted, if the minimum of
disturbance is to result from his inward state. Thus all that
belongs to the second part of our paragraph we find based on the
words of Christ.

2. If now we survey the credal passages quoted above, we find
that they refer to the same principal points which we have seen to
be constitutive of the Office of the Keys, though not everywhere
expressed quite definitely or distinguished with equal clearness ;
and all that need be added by way of comment is the following.

First, we often find the Ministry of the Word taken as part of
the Office of the Keys. This is obviously the case with regard to
the administration of the sacraments, which is so closely bound up
with the forgiveness of sins ; and what we have already conceded
respecting baptism must hold good also of the Supper, namely, that
its right administration belongs to the Office of the Keys. It is,
however, a mere misunderstanding to say the same of preaching

---

[1] Cf. Matt. 10[14. 15]. For wheresoever the disciples thus withdrew, there
no community arose, and sins were retained in every case.
[2] Acts 8[20-23], 1 Cor. 5[4. 5].

considered by itself ; yet viewed as a special instance of the general principle formulated above, it does belong to the Office of the Keys to determine rightly who is to be admitted to the Ministry of the Word of God—a matter which incontestably must be regarded as one of the most important aspects of the Office.   Assuming this, we cannot 'but judge it natural that with this Ministry nearly everywhere the Church should have combined the administration of both sacraments.

Secondly, many of the credal passages, taken by themselves, appear to suggest that the whole Office of the Keys resides in the whole body of Ministers of the Word.   If it were so and if (the testing and the authorization of ministers of the Word being, as it is, an essential part of the whole Office) the entire body of Church teachers were a self-propagating organism and thus in exclusive possession of the Power of the Keys, then the distinction between the clergy (in this narrower sense) and the laity would be sharpened to such a degree that the difference between us and the Roman Church would entirely disappear.   This, however, cannot be the intention ; for Christ Himself assigns one part of the function to the congregation, and from the very outset the congregation was given a share in the most important tasks of administration.[1] Indeed, the very passage which gives ministers exclusive power to execute the congregation's judgment takes for granted that it is by the congregation that the judgment is pronounced.   As for legislative action, it cannot occur until there has developed in the Church an important distinction or antithesis ; but this distinction is not the same.   It is specially incumbent on those entrusted with preaching to train themselves to be ever more perfect interpreters of the Word of God in Scripture, but it is one thing to explain the words of Christ and the Apostles rightly and quite another to apply them profitably in more or less general forms under very different conditions of life ; so, too, it is in one way that Scripture is applied from the pulpit and in quite another that rules for the life of the congregation under definite circumstances are evolved in a spirit of loyalty to Scripture, even though they often cannot be supported by any particular Scripture passage. Hence the distinction between one who grasps the religious meaning of life's conditions and tasks swiftly and surely enough to tell how the law bears on them, and one who accepts the law as law because he hears in it the sound of his own true inner voice, is a quite

[1] Acts 1[15-23] 6[2-6].

different distinction from that between minister and hearer. Hence in public teaching it is best to avoid giving even an impression that Church legislation and administration ought to belong chiefly to ministers. We must not then overlook those passages which assign the duty of consulting on the government of the whole body to the leaders of congregations, and among the leaders reckon not only elders but deacons, in spite of the fact that they have no part in the teaching office.[1] Thus both legislative action and administrative action derive ultimately from the congregation.

Thirdly, while so much can be gathered from our credal passages, they do not make clear the scope or manner in which this whole Office resides in the congregation, or how the congregation exercises it. In point of fact, it exercises it not merely indirectly, by ordering and distributing the offices to which legislation and judgment are formally assigned (for how could the holders of these offices come to have such abilities and faculties, unless they have previously had some experience of them ?), but each individual as such also exercises a punitive office, in an independent and informal manner, by the judgments he passes upon what goes on in the congregation, and by praise or blame. Not only so : legislative action is exerted by each through everything he does that goes to form public opinion ; and public opinion must always be the living fount of expressly legislative acts, for these acts are simply a definite way of gaining recognition for public opinion in Church affairs. If in this sphere anything be attempted which is not a pure expression of the way in which, at a particular time and place, human nature in union with the divine Spirit is seeking to give actual form to itself and its concerns, then the attempt fails, and the law, which is thus incapable of securing its own recognition, simply reveals an imperfection in the Church. Inevitably the Church is disturbed, and it is only through controversy that agreement (all the more conscious for what has occurred) can be regained, and along with it a less ambiguous state of the whole body.

Fourthly, the direct consequence of the foregoing is nowhere expressed so clearly that we feel dispensed from stating it, although in a sense it takes us back to what we first said regarding our present enterprise—namely, that all legislative acts within the congregation are always subject to revision. For just as there was a time when none of the now prevailing usages could have been made law, because the law would not have been acknowledged, so, too, a time

[1] See § 134.

may come when the law will be acknowledged no longer ; and if it
still struggles to keep up its legal validity, the outcome will be false
appearances, of an injurious kind.   This is by no means to assert
that every enactment publicly made a rule of faith or life is equally
mutable, but only that none should rank as immutable ; for we
may be sure that certain items will always reassert their validity.
If, finally, the right to pronounce excommunication be also reckoned
as part of administrative action, this right must be understood in
a very limited sense.   If this aspect of the Office of the Keys be
traced back to the undivided rule of Christ, it is true that in addition
to choosing Apostles and calling disciples and entrusting tasks
to both, we find Christ pronouncing woes on the Scribes and
Pharisees and on places that had not received Him.   These, however, were persons who had not yet been received into His fellowship ; He needed only to withdraw from them but not to expel
them ; indeed, He Himself did not cast out the prodigal son.
Thus we can have no such thing as complete excommunication,
breaking off all fellowship.   Every condition which might rightly
provoke a judgment excluding from all share in the life of the
Church ought to be regarded as merely temporary, and no judgment
should seek to terminate the influence of the Church on the individual who has once been received into its bosom.

SIXTH DOCTRINE : PRAYER IN THE NAME OF CHRIST

§ 146. *The right prevision which it befits the Church to have of what
will be salutary for it in its coexistence with the world
naturally becomes Prayer.*

   1. The manner in which the Church forms and propagates
itself in history necessarily involves that, owing to the influence
of worldly factors both within (for something of the world still
clings to every member) and without, there will arise within it
more or less marked obstructions and fluctuations.   The same
holds good of its external task of absorbing the world into itself,
for here too it fails to attain to a uniform or an easily discernible
progress.   The common consciousness of this is therefore a consciousness of the imperfection of the Church.   As, however, the
desire fully to attain the ends of Christ's coming lives on in the
Church unbrokenly, the consciousness of the Church's imperfection, closely in touch with this impulse, becomes the consciousness
of a defective state ; and this, being as it is simply the correct self-

knowledge of the Church in relation to its love for the Redeemer, must necessarily in the measure of its purity be regarded as an effect of the divine Spirit.   Now as the consciousness of the Church thus moves to and fro between the present and the future, it enters in a twofold way into combination with the God-consciousness.   In view of the fact that every success attained is due not solely to its own activities but also to the divine government of the world, it becomes thankfulness or resignation for what in the present is the outcome of previous exertions, according as the average result of human effort is surpassed (thankfulness) or unachieved (resignation).   But for that which still remains undecided it becomes prayer—*i.e.* the inner combination with the God-consciousness of a wish for full success.

If we always considered and kept clearly in view the fact that in every case we arrive either at resignation or thankfulness (both of which are inward states in which our share in the perfect blessedness of the Redeemer finds expression, so that in this respect we are perfectly sure of good either way), then the Church, wholly intent on its own activities, would do well to refrain from wishes altogether. And since everything that seems fixed and done with is only a point of transition, so that what at first is accepted with resignation makes itself felt later as a subject for thankfulness and *vice versa*, both resignation and thankfulness ought to disappear—the Church leaving all such transitional stages behind and holding fast exclusively to the irrefragable certainty of ultimate success, and thus through joy in God attaining to perfect peace.   But the mind of man (ever anticipating as it does the temporal development of things) is unable to refrain from painting what is possible in a variety of imaginative pictures and comparing their values for its own projects, or from coming to cling by preference to those from which it expects most advantage ; and as long as this mental activity lasts, it is bound to combine with the God-consciousness and become prayer.   This is always going on, so that we have no cause to regard the injunction to pray without ceasing [1] as hyperbole.   If we did not pray, that could only be due to a disappearance either of our interest in the Kingdom of God, which evokes these ideas of an advantageous but uncertain future, or of our God-consciousness, which keeps present to our mind the absolute powers of the divine world-government.

2. The injunction of the Apostle just mentioned seems rather to

---

[1] 1 Thess. 5[17].

be addressed to the individual, as indeed it is only in this individual mind that the play of fancy over the as yet indeterminate events of the future occurs.   In individuals, however, even correctness of prevision in no way leads to prevision turning into prayer ; differences here are usually due to the importance of the matters at stake. So that it is only in a minor degree that our paragraph is elucidated by what has so far been said.   It will be different if we note carefully the relation of the Church to the individual at this point.   The individual here has in view first of all his own sanctification, and next the activity within the whole body made incumbent on him by the gifts he has already received.   Each of these is a manifold, the separate parts of which it is impossible to promote equally by each act, and very soon there comes home to everyone the experience that while his purposes and hopes may be veering in one direction, there come to him, from the divine government of the world, demands and challenges which bend him in another.   Hence he cannot trust his own presentiment of what is for the moment best for him personally.   No more can the individual from his standpoint reach certainty of judgment as to what is advantageous for the whole body in the actual state of its total task.   True, individuals will differ in this respect ; and only those would rightly be judged fitted to exert a definite influence on the whole body who have developed their capacities on this side into a gift analogous to that of the prophet.   Besides, this presentiment as found in the corporate consciousness might be more sure and certain in those times when the individual still formed a large part of the whole [1] and was able to apprehend it *as* a whole.   So that from Christ onwards (and He must be conceived as having possessed this faculty, humanly considered, in the highest possible perfection) this gift must be regarded as present approximately, but certainty of insight diminishes in proportion as a personal element enters more and more into the individual's premonition of the future. What is true of the individual will also be true of every group of people, whether freely associated or constituted by nature, in proportion as they form a smaller or larger part of the whole, and feel for the others a less or more disinterested love.   Hence, when matters have reached that point, we must say, on the one hand, of the whole body that, as personal consciousness and common consciousness are here no longer distinct but completely one, it forms the most faithful likeness of Christ, and therefore that it is in the whole

[1] Cf. Acts 16[6, 10].

body, revealed as a unity, that the most sure and certain prevision will be found.   On the other hand, the Church is the common home of all those imperfect presentiments which, in their differing imperfections, are so often controversially opposed to each other. It is first of all incumbent on the Church to compare itself with that perfect reflexion of Christ which in its temporal consciousness it is not yet, and to make it its prayer that those of its members may gain an ever larger influence who are the most fully developed organs of the divine Spirit for rightly discovering and introducing whatever may be necessary for the increase and progress of the Kingdom of God.   This is the one presentiment of the Church which it is absolutely right should become prayer, and in which therefore all individuals are at one with the whole body.   In the next place, the Church's duty is first to reconcile the uncertain elements of prevision (so far as they may be discordant) which flow from the imperfect common consciousness of individuals, and then to appease the feeling of uncertainty by turning it into prayer. Both these things are done through the gathering together of individuals for common prayer ; for through the very form of common religious action each individual feels himself drawn away from what is more personal in origin to that which could be the same in all, and is guided by the content and meaning of such common action to that which lays hold on all equally.   Both results are aided by the fact that when a difference emerges between personal presentiments and wishes, each joins in prayer for the others that, through the facts of the divine world-government, they may be led ever more into pure joy in God, whether in the form of resignation or that of thankfulness.   And to this all Church prayers may be reduced.

§ 147. *Theorem.—Every prayer in the name of Jesus—but only such prayer—has the promise of Christ that it is heard.*

Expos. simpl. xxiii. : Oratio fidelium omnis per solum Christi interventum soli deo fundatur ex fide et caritate.—*Conf. Belg.* xxvi. : Proinde secundum mandatum Christi patrem coelestem per unicum mediatorem nostrum invocamus . . . certo persuasi nos ea omnia impetraturos, quae a patre in nomine ipsius petierimus.—*Catech. Heidelb.* cxvii. : . . . huic firmo fundamento innitamur, nos a deo, quamquam indignos propter Christum tamen certo exaudiri.

1. When we use the phrase ' praying in the name of Jesus,' [1] we may have more in mind praying about the concerns of Jesus or

[1] John 16[25, 26].

praying in His sense and spirit ; but in fact the two things cannot really be separated. If we could desire to further men's spiritual welfare otherwise than in His sense, we should have to conceive that welfare otherwise than as He did ; in which case it would not be His concerns that were being thus laid before God in prayer. So far, then, it is true that every prayer is prayer in Jesus' name where the petition (whatever it be) is offered with reference to the Kingdom of God. But the more definite the prayer is, the more necessary it becomes that its object should be conceived of as in agreement with the order according to which Christ rules His Church, so that the person who prays may as such be regarded as a true and acceptable representative of Christ. It follows that none can be true prayer in Jesus' name except that which springs from the self-consciousness of the Church as a whole, *i.e.* such prayer as in its content keeps the whole condition of the Church in view. Prayer of this kind certainly belongs to the common prayer of the Church at any given moment, and that such prayer is heard it is impossible to doubt. If the Church's need has been rightly apprehended, and if the dominating presentiment has arisen out of the Church's whole consciousness of its own inner condition and outward circumstances, then the prayer is charged with the full truth : it represents Christ's knowledge of His spiritual body and defines His ruling activity. Hence, in view of the power received by the Son from the Father, its content cannot but be fulfilled. Every other prayer springing from a less perfect Church consciousness, even though it touch equally Christ's concerns and arise from a sincere endeavour to act in His spirit, can look for fulfilment only in the measure in which it harmonizes with the normative prayer as just described ; indeed, it is only thus far that it ought to claim fulfilment. Such prayer, accordingly, can only gain confidence by subordinating itself to prayer that is normative and seeking to be heard only on that condition. An example of such ' conditional ' prayer (as it is best named) used by Christ [1] is found in more than one book of Scripture ; but it merely concerns times and seasons, and therefore does not conflict with what we said above as to the utterly right character of His presentiments. From it we can see how such prayer may be without sin, including as it does resignation as a corrective of its own uncertainty, and only desiring to be heard in so far as what is asked for could form part of a normative prayer. So understood, our views are in perfectly natural

[1] Matt. 26⁴²ᶠᶠ..

accord with the explanation ordinarily given, for the most part, with respect to conditional prayer, namely, that the man is praying in Jesus' name who only desires to be heard for Christ's sake, or in so far as what is asked for is God's will relatively to the divine purpose in Christ.

2. Still, the objection is constantly put forward that if this explanation really exhausts the matter, then the whole doctrine of the hearing of prayer is a delusion. The objection assumes that we really believe that by prayer we can exert an influence on God, His will and purpose being thereby deflected. Now this conflicts with our primary and basal presupposition that there can be no relation of interaction between creature and Creator ; and a theory of prayer which starts with ideas like those just indicated we can only describe (even though it be held by Christians as devoted as they are believing) as a lapse into magic. True, the promises of Christ [1] are adduced in support ; but either the promises themselves are misunderstood, or the conditions to which the promise is attached are not fully taken account of. For how could one fail to have doubts regarding what—to use the ordinary phrase—can only be called a future accident, unless in another respect he took it to be necessary ? And what can the Christian as such take to be necessary except that without which a regenerate person could not be sustained in the state of sanctification, or the Kingdom of Christ persist and advance ? But this simply means that in this way we are brought back to unconditional prayer. When Christ makes faith the condition of prayer being heard, He does not in the least by faith mean a separate faith that prayer *is* heard, but faith in Himself, in the full sense of the word, therefore faith in the imperishable and supreme value of the Kingdom of God He was founding. In faith so understood all that has here been set forth is embraced. Thus by repelling all magical conceptions of the hearing of prayer, we do the promises of Christ no wrong. For as we do not grant that things, the prayer for which is heard, take place for that reason, even contrary to the original will of God, because prayer has been offered about them, so we do not assert that they would have taken place even had there been no prayer. But between prayer and its fulfilment there exists a connexion due to the fact that both things have one and the same foundation, namely, the nature of the Kingdom of God. In that Kingdom the two are one—prayer as Christian presentiment growing out of the whole action and

[1] Matt. 17[20] and 21[21, 22].

influence of the divine Spirit, and fulfilment as expressive of Christ's
ruling activity in relation to the same object.   Seen thus, fulfilment
would not have come had there been no prayer ; for then the point
would not yet have arrived in the development of the Kingdom of
God on which the fulfilment must follow.   But fulfilment does not
come because prayer was offered (as though prayer could here be
regarded isolatedly as a cause in itself), but because the right
prayer can have no other object than what is in line with the divine
good-pleasure.   Neither would it have come, in virtue of the divine
decree, even had there been no prayer (as though the divine decree
bore upon particulars apart from their natural nexus) ; it comes
because the inward state that gives rise to prayer itself forms
part of the conditions under which it was possible for the result
effectually to emerge.

This view of the case meets another objection to the doctrine
of the hearing of prayer, namely, that it is fitted to depress the
activity of believers, or, to express it more fully, that if we believe
in the hearing of prayer we are certain to separate ' praying ' from
' working ' and substitute prayer for work all through.   Over
against the formula ' pray, and thou needst not work ' is set (if
the hearing of prayer be denied) the other, ' work, and leave no
time for prayer.'   We are bound to reject both views, for, according
to the explanation just given, right prayer only arises when we are
engaged in the activities that go to fulfil our Christian vocation.
Thus every true moment of prayer rests on a moment or element of
action, so that prayer cannot destroy action without being itself
destroyed ;   on the other hand, the presentiment expressed in
such prayer as originates otherwise is bound to be purely arbitrary,
and can carry with it no certainty whatever that it is in harmony
with the ruling activity of Christ.   No more can action destroy
prayer, for action of such a kind could not be directed upon the
Kingdom of God.   The agent is readily satisfied with what he
himself can achieve ; and such action could give no guarantee of
its being under the influence of Christ's rule.

3. In thus interpreting prayer solely by its bearing on the
concerns of the Kingdom of God, we started with the assumption
that prayer in the name of Jesus is the only kind natural to the
Christian.   At the same time, our paragraph does refer to another
kind, familiar to us all from common experience.   Now, to prayer
of this sort we can allow no share in Christ's promise, yet it is so
far suggested by conditional prayer in Jesus' name that it ought

not to be rejected. For human feelings and emotions always exist in combination with the God-consciousness, and in this combination they will always find for themselves a less passionate and more spiritual expression than without it. This sort of prayer (be it the prayer of piety, or of self-love, whether in its nobler or its more inordinate form) is not specifically Christian ; whereas the hearing of prayer is a special promise of the Redeemer to His people. Hence such prayer can only share in the promise in so far as it stands in a close relation to the subject of the promise, *i.e.* in so far as the wishes laid before God can also be regarded as needs of the Church. The prayers of ' piety ' (*pietas*) come nearest to this. For the higher place we give an individual, the more easily we may be seduced to believe that it is a distinct loss for the Kingdom of God that he should be snatched away from his sphere of influence, or hindered in his work. But on closer inspection we shall always be compelled to own that except Christ Himself no individual is indispensable to the Kingdom of God. At a still greater distance stand all wishes relating to our own external welfare or that of others, where too we are less easily deceived. But yet, as long as we have not attained to simple resignation that excludes all wishes, it is natural and wholesome for us even as Christians to combine these wishes with the God-consciousness.[1] It is wholesome for us, however, only as we are led to simple resignation by the feeling that we cannot spread these wishes before God in the name of Jesus. Nay, if this is not the result, the prayer in question would have to be changed, almost in the moment of utterance, into a prayer for resignation ; and this *would* be prayer in Jesus' name. But every such prayer is simply an item in the individual discipline of the soul ; it is therefore best that it should be confined to the circle of personal and domestic life, which is its natural sphere. But public and common Christian prayers ought always to be representative of the pure type of prayer in Jesus' name, without bringing in subjects the connexion of which with the progressive development of the Kingdom of God is doubtful. Otherwise it would be part of the public cure of souls by means of public prayer to turn common wishes, springing from some worldly interest, into prayer for resignation. This is the rule which all public intercessions should follow, and scriptural injunctions on the subject [2] must be interpreted in the light of the promise of Christ here treated as fundamental.

[1] I Pet. 5[7] ; cf. Matt. 6[31, 32].   [2] I Tim. 2[1-4], Phil. 4[6].

§ 148. *The fact that the Church cannot form itself out of the midst of*
the world without the world exercising some influence on the
Church, establishes for the Church itself the antithesis between
the Visible *and the* Invisible *Church.*

1. If every person in the world who has been laid hold of by the
Spirit of Christianity were instantly so to become a possession of
the Spirit that every element in his life was solely determined by his
reception of the Spirit's influence, and he became entirely free from
vestigial traces of his former life, it would certainly mean that the
world might persist alongside of the Church, opposing the Church's
further advance ; and in this way the world might modify the
Church's action and throw it back upon itself. But yet the Church,
as actually existing, would none the less be without any worldly
admixture ; the two would be entirely separate and mutually
exclusive societies. In point of fact, however, regeneration is not
a sudden transformation ; even though delight in God's will has
become the man's proper self,[1] there remains in him everywhere an
activity of the flesh striving against the Spirit ; and thus even in
those who taken together compose the Church, there is always
something that belongs to the world.[2] Hence Church and world
are not spatially or externally separate ; at each point of human life
as we see it, wherever there is Church, because there faith and
fellowship in faith are to be found, there is world as well, because
there exist also sin and fellowship in universal sinfulness. Each
visible part of the Church, accordingly, when more closely examined,
is a mixture of Church and world ; and only if we could isolate
and collect the effects of the divine Spirit in men, should we have
the Church in its purity. Now not merely are these effects certainly
present, inasmuch as the Holy Spirit is only given in this active
union with human nature ; they also form a connected and co-
operative whole. Yet they cannot be exhibited in isolation ; it is
only invisibly that they are contained within the whole complex
as the element in it which opposes the world and separates it from

---

[1] Rom. 7[17. 20], 1 John 1[8-10].   [2] Cf. § 126, 1.

the world. Thus the *invisible* Church is the totality of the effects of the Spirit as a connected whole ; but these effects, as connected with those lingering influences of the collective life of universal sinfulness which are never absent from any life that has been taken possession of by the divine Spirit, constitute the *visible* Church.

2. By the Invisible Church is commonly understood the whole body of those who are regenerate and really have a place within the state of sanctification ; by the Visible Church, all those besides who have heard the gospel and therefore are called, and who confess themselves outwardly members of the Church, or who (as we should prefer to express it) form the outer circle of the Church, inasmuch as they receive preparatory gracious influences through the medium of an externally constituted relationship.[1] But if this externally constituted relationship be taken as consisting in the fact that they have received baptism and call themselves Christians, it must be pointed out that according to Christ's original intention there was not to be any such visible Church, since only those were to be baptized who had repented and were mature enough to receive, in and with baptism, the forgiveness of sins and the bestowal of the Spirit. Thus the called too were to remain outside the Church until both the community and they themselves were at one in the conviction that a living fellowship had been established between Christ and them ; and the outer circle aforesaid was to be composed, not of members of the Church, but of candidates for the Church. It may be urged that this original arrangement cannot now be restored, not merely because of infant baptism, but much more because the nations have been Christianized *en masse* and Christianity has been given civil privileges, and that therefore the arrangement may in a way be regarded as having been altered by Christ Himself. Yet this would not make it any more fitting to describe the fellowship of the regenerate as invisible. Even though the moment of regeneration cannot be fixed, and many Christians may feel uncertainty regarding many other Christians, questioning whether they really are in the state of sanctification ; still, this uncertainty regarding some cannot make the whole invisible. On the contrary, the fellowship or community of those who, just because most firmly settled in the state of sanctification, are most strenuously opposed to the world, cannot but in this sense be the most visible of all.[2] The body, then, which in ordinary usage is known as the invisible Church is for the most part not invisible, and what is

[1] Cf. § 115, 2.   [2] Matt. 5[14].

known as the visible is for the most part not Church. On the
other hand, as we have explained it, the antithesis affirms something true and necessary. Even if it were possible to keep all the
non-regenerate outside the Church, the whole body of the regenerate
would only constitute the visible Church in our sense of the term,
and, because visible, would for that very reason not be pure from
alien admixture. The pure Church cannot everywhere be made
visible ; but it is necessary to treat of it separately as the peculiarly
active element in the other. The institutions dealt with in the
doctrines of the First Half are the principal organs of the invisible
Church, and most of all represent its forces at work within the visible.
Here we treat of those general conditions of the visible Church which,
as perpetually self-renewing consequences of the persistence of the
world within the Church, do most to bring to clear consciousness
the antithesis between the visible Church and the invisible.

§ 149. *The antithesis between the Visible and the Invisible Church may
be comprehended in these two propositions : the former is a
divided church, while the latter is an undivided unity; and the
former is always subject to error, while the latter is infallible.*

1. If we merely recur to what was said above regarding the
sphere and manner in which the sinless perfection of Christ is communicated,[1] we are in a position to assert that what is innermost
in every truly regenerate life is simply the whole truth of redemption;
and it is solely as limited to this domain that we affirm the infallibility of the invisible Church. There is first of all the consciousness
of divine sonship in living fellowship with Christ, a consciousness
which each has for all and all for each ; and to this is essentially
attached the consciousness that in them and for their good there is
being vouchsafed a leading into all truth.[2] But when this innermost consciousness comes to be particularized in definite ideas, it
no longer has the same full truth ; for the individual's ideas are
the outcome of his previous life and are formed out of his previous
thought and interests, and for this reason regeneration cannot be
a sudden transformation of his whole style of thinking. Hence the
outward expression of the inner truth becomes more or less distorted, and of its organized form the Spirit takes possession only
gradually. The same holds true of the bent imparted to the will
by the life of Christ within us ; it is the pure bent of Christ Himself,
against sin and for the dissemination of His life. But when this

[1] Cf. § 88, 3.   [2] John 16[13].

takes shape in particular acts, it comes to be mediated not only through the view taken of a specific situation, but also through the purpose in which the action is pre-formed. Both of these, again, are conditioned by ideas formed during the period when the will was still the slave of sense ; hence they can no longer give pure expression to the new inward impulse. Thus, starting from the point to which the new life attaches itself, the pure and the impure very soon separate, and appear as the visible and the invisible ; for that which passes over into the phenomenal consciousness is *eo ipso* no longer pure. Yet both belong to the Christian fellowship ; for to say that redemption is being realized in anyone, and that he is beginning to form a part of the believing fellowship, are the same thing. Someone may say that he acknowledges the distinction between the pure and the impure as a distinction between the visible and the invisible, but that the invisible is not really a fellowship, because what is absolutely inward is absolutely isolated too, and a fellowship (which only becomes possible through means of self-expression) cannot from its very nature be the pure and the true. This objection certainly has to be admitted inasmuch as the invisible Church is not a fellowship by itself alone, entirely separate from the visible. But even in the ordinary usage of these terms, this is not the case ; there as for us the invisible Church as a fellowship (and in our reading of these matters the conception of fellowship is given greater prominence than ever) is mediated through the visible. But in daily experience everyone will certainly make a distinction between the two. In the one case, reaching over and abstracting from the confused multiplicity of particular acts (our neighbour, too, contemplating us in exactly the same way), we each of us enter into a mutually strengthening and supporting union with the innermost impulses of the other, and thus constitute an element of the invisible Church ; in the other, we enter into a fellowship of these very particular acts and forms of self-expression, so as uniformly to occupy a common area with those who have closest affinity with ourselves and to repel what is alien—and thus constitute an element of the visible Church.

It need not be explained that in the infallibility of the invisible Church we include also its purity, and in the fallibility of the visible also its sin. This is due partly to the fact that particular acts have underlying purposes that determine their range and are themselves subject to the imperfection of the ideas present in the mind, partly to the fact that the development of religious ideas also depends on activities of will, which are affected by the lack of purity in particular resolves.

2. Closely connected with this is the fact that the invisible Church is everywhere essentially one, while the visible is always involved in separation and division. The innermost consciousness and impulses of believers are nothing but the presence and living movements of the Spirit itself ; their fellowship is nothing but the Spirit's knowledge of itself ; and this fellowship must extend wherever the Spirit is the same, *i.e.* over the whole of Christendom. Since it is only an invisible fellowship, it lacks everything that might give it a definite form, and everywhere and always it is simply the direct relationship to one another of all in whom the Spirit dwells and who, meeting and touching as they do in their innermost being, include in their fellowship all like souls. That is to say, it is the common striving of all to recognize everywhere the same Spirit through what is outward, and draw it to themselves. But particular forms of outward expression, ideas no less than acts, which are the channels through which this one fellowship is mediated, are also in themselves the divisive element in the visible fellowship ; not only because, by the laws of physics, attractive force radiating out from the chief controlling points must find its limit somewhere, so that the connexion is broken, but principally because the uniting consciousness of affinity, being bound up with what to our perception are sensible differences between men, takes the form of self-love, thus imposing limit and division.

And here it once more appears, as we have elsewhere shown, that the Christian fellowship as being one cannot possibly impose limits on itself, *i.e.* cannot actively will to have other fellowships alongside of it. That would mean either that the attractive power of Christ stopped at a certain point, His living fellowship thus narrowing itself to a certain circumference, in which case He would not have been inspired and endowed as Saviour of the whole human race ; or the impulse emanating from Him would of necessity be confined in self-love to the fellowship of believers, thus keeping others alongside of them who would not share the same advantages ; and such love could not be identical with the love of Christ.

3. It can, however, be easily shown that in these paragraphs we have stated the whole difference between the visible and the invisible Church. Whether we start from the life of Christ within us or from the action of the Spirit within us, they both issue simply in the twofold fact that everything human in the individual is ap-

propriated by the divine, and then as appropriated enters actively into the communal spiritual life. Now if the still worldly element in the individual has a disturbing influence on this activity, one of these activities must thereby be obstructed and diverted ; indeed, it will be possible everywhere to trace what seems mere negation or omission to what is positively real, namely, an act. But all action within the fellowship is productive of fellowship, which can only continue to exist through actions bearing upon it ; thus whatever disturbs such action must carry with it division. Similarly, if the Spirit present in each is one that leads into all truth, everything in the individual that works disturbingly must be a lapse into untruth. The fact that at this point our paragraph includes in untruth any aberration of the will in sin is justified by the consideration that when we speak of the Church, we have the actions of individuals in view only so far as they take place within the fellowship. And there they can only be disturbing in so far as they are perceived by others and constitute a process ; which again can only be the case when they are adopted as guiding maxims, and maxims that contradict the basal forms of self-expression characteristic of the new life or are asserted as false subsumptions under maxims that are sound—in either case, therefore, in so far as they can be traced to error. On the other hand, isolated sins which spring from no purpose disappear in the life of the fellowship, without leaving a trace. There is no influence arising from the still worldly element within us able to disturb our relationships in the Church, other than those influences which confuse the Spirit— error affecting the Spirit as it leads into truth, and division as it binds and unites. Not only so, these two things are so closely connected that it is only through the presence of either that the other can be detected. Much may appear to be a disturbance of fellowship and yet not be so, unless it is also a defection from truth ; so, too, nothing that seems to be error or sin really is so unless it at the same time disturbs fellowship.

First Doctrine: The Plurality of the Visible Churches in Relation to the Unity of the Invisible

§ 150. *Whensoever separations actually occur in the Christian Church, there can never be lacking an endeavour to unite the separates.*

1. If every worldly element present in individuals is as such disturbing to fellowship, the visible Church always and everywhere

has dispersed within it germs of division.   But each of those germs in itself is infinitely small ; and in the measure in which these elements fall apart or unite to form masses, there will in the latter case appear in the Church more or less division, while in the former nothing more will result than temporary disturbance in restricted circles.   It is obvious that from the outset those elements united most powerfully and became most strongly antagonistic to each other, which sprang from the former religious life of the first Christians as Jews and Gentiles.   Hence even in the age of primitive Christianity, which we can scarcely help regarding as an exception to the general divisive tendencies characteristic of the visible Church, the basis of a separation between Jewish and Gentile Christians existed in so developed a form that only the counter-force of the community-forming principle operating in its primitive strength could delay its actual outbreak.   From this it is clear that the more the uniting Spirit pervades the mass and drives the worldly elements in it apart, the more these elements will lose their divisive force.   Hence this force was never again present, in particular differences that arose in the course of the development of doctrine, with the strength it possessed in the age of heresies and the General Councils.   But, on the other hand, the tendency to division invariably becomes active in proportion as aberrations, which otherwise would fade away of themselves, almost unnoticed, are strengthened by some selfish motive.

2. Yet even in the state of division each part of the visible Church remains a part of the invisible, for in it are found the confession of Christ and therefore also the activity of the Spirit. Hence the impulse from which the division sprang will gradually weaken, and where these different parts of the Church are in contact with each other, the community-forming principle which is the same in all will bring its influence to bear against division, and an impulse towards reunion will arise which of course in the Church as we see it is subject to the same changes and vacillations as its opposite. Indeed, even when this impulse fails entirely to make itself perceptible in history, it is none the less moving sporadically in individuals ; we cannot but assume this if we are right in believing that the Holy Spirit cannot wholly disappear or be banished from any part of the Church, nor can it ever neglect any of its essential functions.

Still, the undeniable experience that apart from this there are frequently also efforts at union which do not originate in the Spirit of the Church, and the success of which cannot therefore be regarded as a gain, reminds us that there may also be divisions which are not due to the worldly elements in the Church, but must ultimately be reckoned among the effects of the Holy Spirit. So that the truth we have established can only be of subordinate importance, and seems to call for further definition. But just as those unions may be only apparent, and the united elements may certainly tend to separate from the whole body in some other fashion, so too that which is in fact only seeking closer union within the great fellowship in a way that will do it no injury, or again that which is really a return to a formerly abandoned fellowship with earlier forms of the Church, may seem to be a division, and yet not be such. Hence it is universally true that the Spirit unites, and that it is the fleshly mind that disunites. But the application of this may be difficult ; and when several communions separated from each other exist side by side in Christendom, it must be left to criticism to decide on which side the disuniting principle is entrenched, and which therefore is responsible for division. This is a question which it will often be as difficult to solve as the question which of two sides in a war has been the aggressor.

§ 151. *First Theorem.—The complete suspension of fellowship between different parts of the Visible Church is unchristian.*

1. What was said in the Introduction [1] about religious fellowship as such, can also be said of Christendom in view of its wide expansion over so great a number of peoples and tongues, namely, that no uniform sort of connexion between its various members is possible, not merely owing to unlike internal affinities and external contacts, but also owing to the unequal distribution of the common Spirit. It is natural that the first of these unlikenesses should be connected with the influence of language and of the whole system of social relationships, and that Christians who speak the same language and belong to the same nation should form a separate communion. But such national and territorial Churches are simply the form in which alone, by the appointed divine order, a larger fellowship is possible ; and they by no means involve a suspension of fellowship with other Christians, for fellowship can exist after as well as before, once the natural conditions for it are present. The same is true of those societies (always strongly marked in external form) of Christian people who, drawn by various affinities, gather

[1] § 6.

specially round those who give a strongly original expression to their individual thought ; for this too can happen without any existing fellowship with other parts of the Church being suspended. It only begins to be suspended when more restricted societies which have originated in the manner just described get into antagonism to each other, and find themselves unable to enjoy their own peculiar life without drawing apart from others and shutting the door upon them. Such a polemical relationship is certainly a suspension of fellowship, and yet only in part. Even though controversy should actually break out over their incompatible peculiarities, it really depends solely on the interest which each side has in the other, and thus is merely the mode in which under the given conditions fellowship can exist between them. Nay, since it is implied in the case that the *lowest common denominator* on which in controversy they fall back is a Christian principle, they cannot fail (if each side is to understand itself and the other) to distinguish the non-controversial region from the controversial, by saying that they maintain a different kind of fellowship in the former region and in the latter. Hence a complete suspension of fellowship only arises when each of the two communions refuses to recognize in the other any element that is identical simply because it is Christian ; that is to say, when all religious communications between the two have ceased, and no sort of Church hospitality obtains between them which would not be shown by either to non-Christians. In that case, all they still have in common is the empty name of Christianity.

2. A complete suspension of fellowship in this sense is unchristian as long as the communion that has been cut off retains its historical connexion with the preaching of the gospel by which it was founded, and does not, itself breaking the connexion, trace the origin of its present form to a different revelation. For as long as in any given communion the acknowledgment of Christ is still found, the action of Christ must be telling there, in however hampered a form ; while, if we cast loose from this, then, since all who have been received into the living fellowship of Christ ought to have fellowship with each other, we are excluding and separating ourselves from the unity of the invisible Church.[1] On this principle, even heretics in the narrower sense (much more, later degenerate forms in which other communions say they find heresy) are still part of

---

[1] Quidam ita perturbant ecclesiae pacem, ut conentur ante tempus separare se a zizania, atque hoc errore excaecati ipsi potius a Christi unitate separentur. August., *de fide et opp.* c. 4.

the Church, and fellowship with them ought not to be completely suspended.   Indeed if, to fix a limiting point, we consider that in the most heretical of all, *e.g.* Manichaeism, elements non-Christian in origin are mingled with Christian, and if, on the other hand, the Indians (say) were ready to acknowledge Jesus as one of their many divine incarnations (which would be merely the introduction of one Christian ingredient in an unchristian whole), we should not own the latter as Christians in any sense,[1] but neither should we describe them as heretics.   Thus for external fellowship we can fix no other limit than this, that we ought not to break completely with any communion which persists in attaching itself to the Christian tradition and on its side cherishes the desire to belong to the Christian Church.

Clearly, too, between all religious bodies of which this holds there is no complete suspension of true Church fellowship ; and so round the whole compass of the field there is exhibited the unity of the Church invisible.   But this all-pervading fellowship consists not merely in the fact that each acknowledges the scriptural baptism of the others, but in this, that all can look back in common to a primitive period of the Church which in the main extends much farther down than Scripture and the Apostolic Age ; that each accords to the others the right to expansion at the cost of the non-Christian world ; and that they accept each other, if not in the fellowship of other forms of Christian work, at all events in the fellowship of this work of extension.

§ 152. *Second Theorem.—All separations in the Church are merely temporary.*

1. If between the separate portions of the Church, fellowship is not completely suspended—if, that is, each separation is relative—we must recognize (if each part is conceived as having a life of its own) that in each there is a twofold movement : at one time the motive of unity is more prominent, at another this weakens and the motive of separation becomes stronger.   This of itself implies the possibility that if a moment of the first kind should coincide with the emergence of a new antithesis within the whole, the previously active motive of separation might merge in the latter, and the particular Church which had hitherto stood by itself thus throw itself wholly on one side of the new antithesis, so becoming an integral part of it, and its previous character passing over with it as a merely subordinate feature.   Or the Church in question may break up

---

[1] It is probably only to *individuals* of this kind that 1 John 4[5] refers.

altogether, some of its members turning to one side of the new
antithesis and some to the other.   In this case, however, the old
antithesis will gradually lose its intensity, having become subordinate to the new one.   And even without this, if any of the other
circumstances change, the interest felt in the old antithesis may so
decline that it no longer retains power to hold a special communion
together.   Or, to assume the best that could be said of such a
particular Church, namely, that it rests on some spiritual peculiarity
which the Spirit appropriates as a special instrument, even such a
case, spatially limited as it is, is one of merely transient validity.
This is a view, however, which it is only possible to take of such
communions as show Christian piety assuming all round an individual form ;   there must be greater transience in proportion as
the unity that forms the core of the particular communion is small
and inadequate.   Hence no special communion ought ever to be
based on the peculiarities of a specially prominent individual,[1] and
no communion has the prospect of long life which seeks to base
itself merely on divergent moral practice in the absence of relatively
different doctrine, or conversely simply on certain peculiar doctrines
in the absence of different ways of life.

To the more fixed divisions belong also those which rest on
physical grounds and are delimited by national affinities or by
language.   And yet for one thing these natural forms are themselves
temporary ;   for another, Christianity more than anything else has
exerted a helpful influence on the inter-communion of languages and
peoples.   Hence inward forces of division often overflow these
limits ;   at one time they bind together the Churches of different
peoples and tongues in a whole of like spirit and form, at another
they sever in opposition elements that naturally belong together.

2. From this it follows of itself that the zeal with which the individual clings to his particular communion can only be genuine, in
the sense that no injury is thereby done to full interest in the all-
combining unity of the Church invisible, if it is kept within certain
limits.   The essential thing is that each should love the special form
of Christianity to which he adheres only as a transient form of the
one abiding Church, though a form that involves a temporary being
of its own.   A love so qualified is very far from indifference, for it
starts with the fact that it is only through his special communion
that each stands in union with the whole Church.   But equally it is
very unlike the partisan assumption, often to be met with when

[1] Cf. 1 Cor. 1[12].

the ardour of ecclesiastical antagonism has risen to a certain point, that antagonism can only be removed by the other side coming over to our side.   The extremes here (which need not now be touched upon) we usually describe by the terms ' indifferentism ' and ' proselytizing.'   But to accept in advance the position that a form already acknowledged to be temporary will one day actually disappear is not indifferentism in the least : that can only be charged on one who is unable to regard his relationship to the communion to which he belongs as more than casual, and is unconscious of having any inward reason for decision one way or the other.   Nor is the effort to commend one's own communion in the strongest way to members of other communions what we call proselytizing in the bad sense, otherwise Christianity as such, and Evangelical Christianity in particular, would have been objectionable from the first. No : nature itself prompts to such efforts whenever in another communion we see an enervation or corruption of Christian piety. Indeed, in the partisan assumption just mentioned, this very fact is accepted generally, and therefore the effort, if organized on this basis, is justified as an effort operating on universal lines ; and for that reason it ought not to be charged upon the members of an opposed communion as unchristian.   Proselytizing of the objectionable type is that which regards the extension of one's own communion as an absolute end, and uses individuals for this purpose as mere means.

SECOND DOCTRINE : THE FALLIBILITY OF THE VISIBLE CHURCH IN RELATION TO THE INFALLIBILITY OF THE INVISIBLE

§ 153. *As in every branch of the Visible Church error is possible, and therefore also in some respects actual, so also there is never lacking in any the corrective power of truth.*

1. Every error, in so far as it is an act of thought completed with knowledge and will yet not in agreement with the object thought of, is sinful in character, and hence must be in general overcome or prevented by the increasing action of the Holy Spirit, not directly, but by the Spirit's counteracting its sinful cause.   Yet here we speak solely of truth and error in the religious sphere. What was said above [1] regarding the absolute purity of impulse must be applied here ; yet error is possible everywhere, alike in the formation of religious ideas and in the religious formation of purposes, and possible on every point.   If a sensuous movement of

[1] § 110, 3.

feeling should pervert a purpose unconsciously, it is possible that
the will, as it bears on religious ideas, may be perverted at the same
time, and error must then enter into every part of the execution
of the purpose. And so long as the view we take of our relations
within the Church may be corrupted in this fashion, no purpose
can be formed wholly without error, so that no real element of life
in its fulness has its being in pure truth ; in every act of the religious
consciousness truth is more or less infected with error. The
formulæ just used reflect the whole circle and compass of error as
it mingles with the action of the Spirit of truth, and at every point
each individual will find the source of falsification in himself ; his
own consciousness will not suffer him to doubt that error is everywhere real, although in particular cases it may be reduced to scarcely
perceptible dimensions.

It is equally certain, however, that even if in this or that quarter
of the Church error has accumulated in mass, yet we cannot suppose
that any part of the Church, organized as a separate whole, could
be wholly devoid of the action of the Spirit of truth. Where acknowledgment of Christ forms the basis of common life, a foundation
is thereby laid for all worship of God in spirit and in truth, even if
corruption of such worship should be the most conspicuous feature
of the body in question. This follows from the simple fact that in
no branch of the visible Church (even though the sacraments were
absent or had to be regarded as absent in consequence of the
abnormal style of their administration) is there lacking the recognition of Scripture or the Ministry of the Word of God. Hence in
every communion there are at least some who rise superior to prevailing errors, and in whom the germs are to be found of a more
precise development of truth.

2. Our statement, however, assumes the presence of error everywhere, if only in a minute degree, and thus appears to contradict
what we formerly asserted about Scripture.[1] For if even Scripture
be so exposed to the possibility of error as in some degree to contain
it, it cannot be the norm of all religious thinking ; for its normative
authority, thus communicated to error, could only spread and confirm it. In that case truth would have to find within the Church
some other firm seat, so as to bring its corrective forces to bear on
the errors contained in Scripture itself. But at the moment we
have to do not with Scripture as it lies before us now, but with its
origin ; and in perfect consistency with what has just been said

[1] §§ 129 and 131.

we can easily make the admission that even in the religious thinking of the Apostles the general possibility of error became a reality
here and there without affecting Scripture, for Scripture precisely
as a collection of all that was freest of error was brought together
under the Spirit's guidance.   Nay, Scripture itself testifies [1] to the
fact that human error occurred as a passing phenomenon even in
the thought of the Apostles, and allows us to surmise from this how
perhaps still oftener the first movements of error may have been
suppressed before their influence could make itself felt.   Hence in
the second place (in order not to sever its natural connexion with the
rest of things) we may well admit as regards Scripture that among
the many peripheral ideas which prevailed at the time yet were not
ultimately given a place in the Bible, but none the less belonged to
the thought-processes of the sacred writers, slight traces of human
error might have been found.   This does not in any way detract
from the normative authority of Scripture, or from the influence of
the Holy Spirit in its composition.

§ 154. *First Theorem.—No presentation of the Christian religion
        issuing from the Visible Church contains pure and perfect
        truth.*

    1. If it be the case that Scripture itself is not such a presenta-
tion issuing from the visible Church, but rather itself constituted
the visible Church, Scripture does not so far come under the scope
of our paragraph.   But the objection might well be raised that the
very principles which our paragraph affirms suggest that error will
be at its minimum in all acts of ordination, and hence in the appointment of those persons in whose hands the duty is placed of purifying
pre-existing ideas for the dissemination of Christian truth.   If each
of these persons, taken by himself, was exposed to error, then in
the discharge of this duty the controlling power of the common
Spirit must have manifested itself in the fact that wrong individual
tendencies in the community cancelled each other out.   This, however, would imply that every such tendency found its exact counter-
weight in some other.   It is true that in the whole body all possible
tendencies exist ; but if the whole be divided by inner differences,
the onesidedness of each part of the whole cannot find its corrective
opposite within itself ; each particular Church may err even in its
official presentations of truth.   But from this it does not follow
that if there was a time when the Church was as yet undivided, the

[1] Acts 10[14] 16[7], Gal. 2[11].

presentations then given were pure and perfect truth. For the tendencies which cancel each other are not all present in the Church at the same time ; ages too can be onesided, in ways that can only be cancelled in a later age. Indeed, if we are bound to hold (and it is a position which alone can justify the existence of the Evangelical Church) that specially inspired individuals may exert on the whole body a reforming influence, and an influence which at first was not official, it at once follows that what has its seat in the official organization of the body is not the reforming power, but the need for reformation. This is a condition of things which may arise any-where and may recur periodically, wherever and as long as the relation between the whole body and individuals varies between preponder-ating spontaneity and receptiveness on the one side or the other.

2. No definition of doctrine, then, even when arrived at with the most perfect community of feeling, can be regarded as irre-formable and valid for all time. This is pre-eminently true of definitions which arose after controversy as presentations put forth by a larger or smaller majority, for controversy more than anything else rouses all those impulses that lead to error. Hence no one can be bound to acknowledge the contents of such presentations as Christian truth except in so far as they are the expression of his own religious consciousness, or commend themselves to him by their scriptural character. On the other hand, the revision of the Church's public doctrine is a task in which every individual is bound to take a share, testing the established ideas and propositions in the measure of his power and the helps at his command ; he has rights in this matter, in the exercise of which he must be left free. Still, through the whole course of this work there runs a natural agree-ment with regard to the principles on which, and the aims with which, error is to be counteracted ; but even this agreement is a thing of gradual formation in each Church, and can only arise when the Church has come to self-consciousness. Hence we must always reflect with satisfaction that as regards the doctrines which had come to be matters of controversy, the incipient Evangelical Church declined to submit to the decisions of a General Council ; but we can no longer approve of its having none the less accepted all the ecumenical Creeds ; for these Creeds are but the product of similar Councils, which besides were due to divisions within the Church, and hence were not pre-eminently fitted for the ascertainment of truth. Similarly, it is a matter for satisfaction that the convictions then held were set forth in brief Confessions for the whole of Chris-

tendom, which was the first thing to give reforming influences acting
on the whole body their assured place ; but it is a matter of regret
that by means of these very documents (as if they had been irre-
formable) an effort was subsequently made to hinder the performance of the very task to which they owed their birth.

§ 155. *Second Theorem.*—*All errors that are generated in the Visible
    Church come to be removed by the truth which never ceases to
    work in it.*

   1. This paragraph is so closely connected with the previous one
that, on the whole, no objection can reasonably be made to it. If,
however grave it be, error is only attached to truth in the way just
described, its influence within each organic part of the whole body
must diminish in proportion as the Holy Spirit takes possession of
the organism of thought ; and error is restrained by two forces,
prevalent in different degrees at different times : in the individual
whose errors are peculiar to himself, it is restrained by the influence
of public thought, which makes its pressure felt on him from every
side, while in the mass of believers it is restrained by the influence
of men of spiritual distinction, spreading clear views ever more
widely. If it be thought, however, that in addition to such error
in the truth, there exists in Christendom also absolute error *from*
the truth, and that different methods must therefore be adopted
for dealing with *it*, the matter really stands thus. Not merely may
certain ideas issue from an imperfect faith in Christ—they may
even be directed against other ideas that reveal a faith more perfect—
yet none the less underlying them may be that truth which in the
Church remains ever the same. On the other hand, conceptions
and maxims which in no sense issue from the Christian consciousness,
and of which accordingly it cannot be said that they constitute
merely error *in* the truth, belong to Christendom only in so far as
those who cherish them have become subject in other ways to the
influence of the Christian Spirit, although as yet they are not
definitely aware of the fact. For where no relation to the Spirit
exists of any kind, there no part of the visible Church exists ; and
in that case the Church has to do with the wrong ideas of individuals
only in so far as they offer a point of attachment for its self-
expanding action. In the first case, however, even where there is
absolutely no Christian truth on which it seems to rest, error is only
a forerunner of such expansion, for it means that already a point
exists from which the Christian consciousness may spread.

2. But of course it is impossible for our paragraph to fix times and seasons ; indeed, in the history of Christendom one can actually mark off important periods in which error grows and gains the upper hand, while truth is forced back.   Yet such phenomena are more calculated to suggest a revision of our judgment on previous apparently favourable conditions than to justify the view (incompatible with belief in the Kingdom of Christ) that the truth had disappeared from the Church or been even partially lost.   It all comes to this, that the progress of truth and the consequent removal of error within the Church visible takes either of two forms—one when the truth gradually destroys the opposed error, the other when the error which unconsciously has clung to the expression of real truth is, with all its effects, cut away from the truth ; while the truth, although seeming to lose in power and influence, is purified and thereby exerts a completer influence.

Irrespectively of this, history often exhibits an apparent diminution of the domain of truth due to apostasy, usually under the pressure of external violence.   But if the apostasy is more than apparent, it means that the Christianity rejected was itself merely apparent ; for there is no conceivable point of contact between violence of any kind and living fellowship with Christ.   Hence the Christian consciousness can never really be repressed in this way, much less wholly exterminated.

§ 156. *Appendix to these two Doctrines.—The assertion that the true Church began with the beginning of the human race and remains one and the same on to the end of it, must not be taken as implying that the Christian Church properly so-called is in itself only part of a larger whole.*

Augsburg Conf. vii. : '. . . that a holy Christian Church must ever be and abide . . . in which the Gospel is purely preached and the holy sacraments are administered in harmony with the Gospel.'—*Apol. Conf.* iv. : At sic discernit Paulus ecclesiam a populo legis, quod ecclesia sit populus spiritualis. . . . In populo legis praeter promissionem de Christo habebat et carnale semen promissiones rerum corporalium. . . . Igitur illi tantum sunt populus juxta evangelium qui hanc promissionem spiritus accipiunt.—*Expos. simpl.* xvii. : Quando autem Deus ab initio salvos voluit fieri homines . . . oportet omnino semper fuisse, nunc esse et ad finem usque seculi futuram esse ecclesiam.—Haec aliter fuit instituta ante legem inter patriarchas, aliter sub Mose per legem, aliter a Christo per evangelium.—Agnoscimus hic tamen diversa fuisse tempora, diversa symbola promissi et exhibiti Messiae.—*Conf. Scot.* v. : Credimus Deum . . . omnibus aetatibus ecclesiam suam ab Adamo usque ad adventum Christi iri carnem vocasse.—*Conf. Belg.* xxvii. : Credimus —unam ecclesiam catholicam. . . . Haec porro ecclesia et ab initio mundi fuit et usque ad eius finem perdurabit.

1. It is not merely the last-quoted Confessions on the Reformed side which definitely assert the unity of the Old Testament and the New Testament Church; the same is the case on the Lutheran side. Some people might infer the opposite from the language of the Augsburg Confession, but the same view as the Reformed is unmistakably expressed in the authentic explanation of that Confession —the *Apology*. Only in the Saxon Confession does Melanchthon appear in a more cautious mood; in his examples there he goes no further back than the birth of Christ. But he really does this intentionally; his inconsistency is only apparent, for, after all, Christ could not have exerted any redeeming influence on Simeon and Hannah and the others there named.[1] But Melanchthon indubitably regards the faith of Simeon and the Messianic faith of earlier times as being of the same type. If this unity of the Church from the beginning were to be understood (as appears from one passage) in the sense that Christ was the same for the third period as Moses was for the second, our divergence from these credal statements would be even greater. But we appeal to what was said above on this subject.[2] The one point we are concerned about is to define more exactly the difference between our paragraph and these credal passages. Both sides start from the position that the Church only exists where there is faith in Christ; the Confessions, however, assert that this Church has been in existence from the beginning of the world, whereas we hold that it only began with the personal action of Christ. The Confessions therefore must assume that faith in Christ existed before His personal action, but we make such faith conditional on, and derive it from, His personal action: this, then, is the first point we have to decide. But along with this goes the fact that, while we both start from the position that faith saves, the Confessions assert that the personal action of Christ is not necessary to effect human salvation, but we hold that the saving love of God did not become effective till Christ appeared; and the question arises whether, in point of fact, we have to choose between these positions, and on what principle in this instance the choice is to be arrived at. Now these paragraphs are not in themselves utterances of our immediate consciousness; also by its negative form our paragraph shows that it has been constructed simply in contrast to positions which we do not share; hence, in the comparison now to be undertaken, we can recognize no other criterion than agreement with what has already been established as the expression of our immediate consciousness.

[1] *Repetit. Conf.* (ed. Twesten), p. 164.   [2] § 12, 2.

2. As regards the first point, we have already shown[1] that the fulfilment of Old Testament prophecies does not constitute them grounds of faith for us, in the sense that we believe in Christ because He was foretold as that which He was later found to be ; this could be no ground of faith in our evangelical sense.   But this certainly does not make it impossible that before Christ appeared, promises as such might have become for men a ground of salvation.   Given an acute sense of sin and of the need of redemption, this yearning might (if a Redeemer were promised) attach itself to the promise, and a presentiment might arise of the salvation of future ages in fellowship with Him—a presentiment which as sympathetic joy might in a sense overcome the feeling of personal unblessedness. Even granting so much, this was no more than a shadow-life, a dim premonition of the Christian Church, not the Christian Church itself.   All we say is that the Church exists wherever there is faith, because faith is the complete appropriation of Christ and is, in addition, of an essentially fellowship-forming character.   In the case in question, it is true, we can in a way admit the appropriation of Christ's blessedness, not however the appropriation of His perfection.   And this faith in the Messianic promises was never anywhere in the Old Testament a fellowship-forming thing ; that the existing fellowship rested on the Law is obvious historical fact. Hence it is no adequate statement of the difference merely to concede that there was one kind of symbols so long as the Messiah was promised and another after He appeared ; on the contrary, faith itself changed in kind, and in the time of the Law true New Testament faith was merely in the future.[2]   Indeed, the position conceded above is incapable of proof, namely, that Messianic promises in the Old Testament really contained the idea of a Redeemer in the sense that we, along with the Protestant Confessions, accept, or that in this sense they offered a Redeemer to the consciousness of sin as we understand it.   But if it is sought not merely to affirm all this, but actually in respect of the perfection of Christ as it works upon us and of the bond of brotherly love to identify faith before Christ appeared with faith as we know it, it will have to be admitted that the hearers of the promise were able to construct the idea of sinless perfection out of extremely imperfect indications, and not merely construct it but put it in action.   And this, of course, leads to the position that the actual appearance of Christ was not necessary for our salvation, and that nothing more

[1] § 14, Postscript.   [2] Cf. Gal. 3[22, 23].

was requisite than that all the time the promise should be kept alive.

3. However little we may agree with this, it looks as if equally inconvenient consequences followed from our own position that men did not attain to salvation before Christ appeared. The inference, however, that the saving love of God only began with the appearance of Christ, we must forthwith qualify (as our principles demand) by saying that it was only the temporal manifestation of that love which then began. Put thus, there can be no objection to its acceptance ; for it simply means that we and the whole human race find ourselves in the same case as even now every individual does who for the first time comes to enjoy redeeming love through becoming regenerate. In the same way, until the appearance of Christ humanity was in a condition of living under preparatory grace—the whole of humanity, and not merely that descending succession of persons through which we are led by the Jewish historical books, from Adam and the patriarchs to the founding of Mosaism. For this preparatory grace was manifested in every place where, and in the measure that, there were to be found the workings of the divine holiness and righteousness ; and from this point of view we obtain that very equality between Jews and Gentiles which Paul took as his starting-point. This harmonizes more closely than may at first sight appear with the mode in which Paul relates Christ's appearance to the promise and the faith of Abraham, when he argues that the preparatory divine grace was not manifested in a special or exclusive fashion in the statutory Law, but pre-eminently in the fact that monotheism should have had a place kept for it ; and action so motived is faith, which can equally well be regarded as obedience. It therefore was reckoned to Abraham for righteousness, because he now became the instrument of preparatory divine grace, and in this relation to future generations could through his faith be an object of the divine favour. In this sense, then, we may also accept a justification for Christ's sake before Christ, analogous to blessedness in sympathy with the future ; and thus scattered rudiments of the Church, although not the Church itself. But if for the position that from the beginning of the human race there has existed a true Church, there be substituted the position merely that from the beginning there has never been any source of salvation for men, or any ground of divine favour towards men, other than Christ—to this there can be no objection.

§ 157. *Since the Church cannot attain to its consummation in the course of human life on earth, the representation of its consummated state is directly useful only as a pattern to which we have to approximate.*

1. The Holy Spirit, as the common vital principle of the Church, is of itself the sufficient reason of this consummation ; but, His action being subject to the laws of temporal life, the consummation can only arrive when all opposition is so completely overcome that in the field of His activity nothing in time remains which is hostile ; when, that is to say, all the influences of the world upon the Church have exhausted themselves. This implies first of all that Christianity has spread over the whole world,[1] in the sense that no other religion survives as an organized fellowship. As long as these antiquated and imperfect forms of religion persist alongside of Christianity, striving to maintain themselves side by side with the Church, their character will be so deeply impressed on their adherents that when these have been captured by Christianity, whether individually or in the mass, they will (even if it be unconsciously) carry over many corrupting elements, which must prove a source of division and error. Now our self-consciousness testifies that in general the origination of faith in the Redeemer is not conditioned by any special circumstance, but depends solely on the common consciousness of sin which can be evoked in all, as well as on the equally universal faculty, due to the sameness of human nature everywhere, of receiving a specific impression from the Redeemer. We therefore cherish the hope that the expansion of Christianity will be accelerated in proportion as the glory of the Redeemer is ever more clearly reflected in the Church itself.[2] It is an undeniable possibility that this might take place in the course of human history ; yet we cannot forget that during all that time the propagation of the species goes on, and that sin develops anew in each generation. Thus even assuming that the power of sin is being ever more widely and thoroughly repressed, and hence more easily broken, the Church is thus ever anew admitting worldly elements. Thus it is always

[1] Rom. 11[25. 26].   [2] Eph. 1[22. 23] 2[21. 22].

involved in the conflict described above, and hence is never per-fected. In this state it is usually designated the *Church militant*, because it has not only to stand on the defensive against the world but must seek to conquer the world. Just for that reason, as conceived in the state of consummation it is called the *Church triumphant*, because all that in this sense was worldly has now been wholly absorbed in it, and no longer exists as its opposite.

2. Strictly speaking, therefore, from our point of view we can have no doctrine of the consummation of the Church, for our Christian consciousness has absolutely nothing to say regarding a condition so entirely outside our ken. We have recognized Christ as the end of prophecy;[1] which implies that even the Church does not acknowledge any gift of the Spirit enabling her to form a prophetic picture of a future on which (since it lies altogether beyond human experience) our action can exert no influence what-ever ; indeed, in the absence of all analogy we could hardly under-stand the picture aright or retain it securely. None the less, these prophetic pictures fill a great place in the Church, and it is incum-bent on us, before pronouncing for their exclusion from this ex-position, to inquire as to their source. In the first place, reference must be made to the New Testament predictions of the consumma-tion of the Church, all of which we certainly must trace back to prophetic utterances of Christ. Now if these are to be treated by the rules of art, and yet not to be made doctrines proper, but only propositions which we receive on testimony, yet which do not stand in so intimate a relation with our faith as do similar propositions regarding the Person of the Redeemer, we shall hardly be able to give them a place in our Dogmatic, or at least only in so far as they concern the Redeemer and our relation to Him. While, however, these propositions are not doctrines of faith, since their content (as transcending our faculties of apprehension) is not a description of our actual consciousness, the matter takes on another aspect if, abstracting from the fact that they transcend our present conditions, we concentrate on the point that they must contain no reference to anything in our present state due to the influences of the world. That these influences may be restrained, in a higher degree than the mere co-operation of individuals could secure, is the constant object of our prayers ; and the consummated Church is accord-ingly the sphere where such prayer is answered in full measure. Hence this idea of the consummation of the Church is rooted

[1] § 103, 3.

in our Christian consciousness as representing the unbroken fellowship of human nature with Christ under conditions wholly unknown and only faintly imaginable, but the only fellowship
which can be conceived as wholly free from all that springs from
the conflict of flesh and spirit.

§ 158. *As the belief in the immutability of the union of the Divine
Essence with human nature in the Person of Christ contains
in itself also the belief in the persistence of human personality, this produces in the Christian the impulse to form
a conception of the state that succeeds death.*

1. The meaning of this paragraph cannot be that belief in the
continued existence of personality after death or (as we usually
express it) the immortality of the soul arose in the way here indicated ; for traces of that belief exist everywhere, and especially
in the times of Christ and the Apostles it was prevalent among the
Jewish people. The only thing the paragraph can mean is that
apart from this connexion the belief could not have been given a
place in our Christian Dogmatic. Indeed, the whole of the preceding argument has been set forth and proved without reference
to this belief, and only one paragraph, that on the ascension of
Christ (which is not directly a doctrine of faith) points in its direction. So that the reader who so far has found his Christian consciousness reflected in our exposition must own—assuming the facts
of Christianity and our acquaintance with them—that faith in the
Redeemer as it is here described may develop out of a sense of sin
calling for redemption, and that from it we might infer the communication of Christ's blessedness at every moment of life, including the last moment of all, even though we had no conception whatever of a life after death. Thus the question naturally arises
whether, and how, this belief would have come to be bound up
with our religious consciousness, had not the Redeemer accepted
and sanctioned it. Only two possibilities are open. Either the
survival of personality would have been ascertained as a truth
through the activities of knowledge, that is by way of objective
consciousness ; or it might have been given us originally in our
immediate self-consciousness, whether vitally bound up with the
God-consciousness which everywhere is fundamental, or independently thereof and by itself. As regards the first, it would
mean that the doctrine of immortality belonged to the higher
natural science, and in that case the certainty of it could only exist

for those who had mastered scientific method, while others got it from them at second hand.   But this evidently is not how matters stand ; it is undeniable that on the scientific plane the belief has always been attacked by some people as vehemently as it has been defended by others.   Indeed, anyone who considers the so-called rational proofs of immortality more closely will scarcely find it possible to believe that the idea itself originated with science. It came from some other source, and what science did was to seek to combine it with other scientific results ; and from the nature of the case any such procedure must always be liable to attack. Hence in the event of Dogmatic wishing to make a further use of the idea of immortality, it is not entitled to adopt these proofs ; still less is it obliged to scrutinize them and supply their defects.   On the contrary, its duty would be to await scientific demonstration of the idea, leaving the matter on one side till this was forthcoming. Otherwise, Dogmatic would be made dependent on a philosophical theory still under dispute.

As regards the second possibility, if belief in immortality were bound up with the God-consciousness in general, it would be a serious error on our part not to have developed it at the outset when dealing with that subject.   This error, however, would have revealed and revenged itself before now, which in point of fact it has not done—a circumstance not calculated to predispose us to believe that the two things are really bound up together.   True, there is an impious denial of immortality which is bound up with the denial of God ; both things go along with a materialistic or atomistic type of thought ; but there is also a surrender of the survival of personality which is of a quite different sort, and which, far from regarding spiritual activity as a mere phenomenon of matter, or making matter superior to spirit, strictly regards spirit as the power which produces living matter and conforms it to itself.   From this point of view it may similarly be affirmed both that the God-consciousness constitutes the essence of every life which in the higher sense is self-conscious or rational, and that while spirit is essentially immortal in such productivity, yet of such productivity the individual soul is only a transient act, and thus essentially perishable ; in which case every ' act ' over and above the definite point reached by evolution and transcending the definite realm of human existence (to which personality belongs) would forfeit all significance.   Between such a surrender of the survival of personality and the predominance of the God-consciousness (even a predominance which insisted on the purest morality and the loftiest spirituality of life) there would be no incongruity whatever.   Added to this is the fact that there certainly is a belief in personal survival which is in harmony with the general spirit of piety, a belief which regards the presence of the God-consciousness in the human soul as explaining why the soul cannot share the general lot of transience ; but there is also a belief which is impious.   For how could this belief have any affinity with the God-consciousness, if it merely issued from an interest in the sense-aspect of life, even were that interest in some degree ennobled and refined ?   And yet this invariably is the case when immortality is postulated for the sake of retribution, on the assumption that no such thing exists as a pure and direct impulse to piety and morality, but both are sought only as means to the attainment of perfect felicity in a world to come.   If then it must be admitted that there is a way of denying the survival of personality in following which we may be more deeply pervaded by the God-consciousness than if we accepted it, we must not continue to assert that this belief and the God-consciousness are bound up together.

2. None the less, it may well be held that belief in the survival of personality is bound up with faith in the Redeemer. The Redeemer ascribes such survival to Himself in everything that He says about His return or reunion with His people ; and (since He can only say these things of Himself as a human person, because only as such could He have fellowship even with His disciples) it follows that in virtue of the identity of human nature in Him and in us, the same must hold good of ourselves.   Self-evident as this may seem, we must nevertheless inquire whether objections can be made, and what these objections are, whether to the correctness of the underlying assumption or the legitimacy of the inference.   Objections of the former kind could only relate to a divergent interpretation of Christ's sayings, and so far they would not be matters for discussion here, but would belong to exegesis.   Here it need only be said that even if in good faith one were to maintain that, in one way or another, the relevant sayings of Christ are all figurative, and not to be interpreted strictly, and that He nowhere claims personal survival, yet faith in Christ as we have here presented it would certainly still be possible.   (For although the surrender of personal survival as just described would then be common to Christ and to ourselves, yet this would not necessarily abolish the specific difference between Him and us.)   None the less, a complete transformation of Chris-

tianity would be the result were such a mode of interpretation to
prevail within the Church and be made fundamental to the Christian
faith.   And this of itself implies that we cannot assume that such
an interpretation could be put forward in good faith.   The case
would not be greatly altered were anyone to impugn the legitimacy
of the inference referred to above on the ground that even if Christ
did ascribe personal survival to Himself, it was an opinion which He
merely took over from current belief without definite personal conviction, making no other use of it than He did of similar opinions in
similar cases ; so that His utterances on the point do not belong to
the type which is so closely bound up with His assurance regarding
His own dignity and destiny that neither of these could really be
believed in if those utterances were rejected.   In fact, it would
scarcely be possible for anyone to hold sincerely that it was without
personal conviction that Christ rejected the view of the Sadducees,
or that His faith in the irresistible progress of His Word did not
depend on His faith in the persistence of His personality.   But if we
cannot deny His firm conviction on the subject, the only further
objection that could be suggested is that the survival of His personality (His belief in which we, in that case, should have to share)
implies nothing for our own ; on the ground that His survival
depends exclusively on what is peculiar to Him, namely, the union
of the Divine Essence with human nature which alone constitutes
His human person, and that therefore we must say that just
because the Redeemer is immortal, all other men are not.   Such an
explanation would be docetic, and none the less docetic that it is
so only in one particular respect.   For the difference between an
immortal and a mortal soul cannot consist, or reveal itself, solely in
the fact that at some time or other one of them really dies ; the
activities and states of each must always and in every respect be
different from those of the other.   Hence, if the soul of the Redeemer
were imperishable, but our souls perishable, it could not justly be
said that as man He was like us in all points, except sin.   For if it
were to be maintained that originally it was the nature of the human
soul to be immortal, but that each soul becomes mortal by the
transmission of sin, this would imply that the whole original work
of God had been destroyed by sin, and its place taken by something
else.   Hence we must put aside a distinction favoured by some, to
the effect that all souls become mortal through sin, and at death
perish with the body, but that through fellowship with Christ believers obtain a share in immortality and pass through death to life

along with Him.   Either this goes back to an assumption which is
Manichean in spirit, namely, that those who do not attain to living
fellowship with Christ could not in any case have become immortal ;
or, if the others are like them in nature, that very nature must have
been made totally different by regeneration.   Nothing remains
therefore but to say that if we take the utterances of the Redeemer
about His eternal personal survival as being imbued with His
perfect truth, as His disciples undeniably did, then all who are of
human race can look forward to survival too.   Even so the Redeemer
continues to be the mediator of immortality, only not exclusively
for those who believe on Him here, but for all, without exception ;
in this sense, that if personal immortality did not belong to human
nature, no union of the Divine Essence with human nature to form
such a personality as that of the Redeemer would have been
possible ; and conversely, that since God had determined to perfect
and redeem human nature through such union, human individuals
must all along have possessed the same immortality as the Redeemer
was conscious of.   Such is the true Christian assurance concerning
this belief ; every other guarantee for it, even were it clearer than
efforts at proof would so far lead us to expect, must remain alien
to the Christian mind, at least until this belief comes to be one of
the ideas constituting the complete and universal body of human
conviction.

3. This belief naturally is accompanied by a desire to form and
keep clear ideas as to the condition of personality after death.   But
it is wholly impossible for us to claim that in this we shall definitely
succeed.   The question as to the conditions of existence after death
(and a knowledge of them must form the basis of any clear conception) is a purely cosmological question ; and space and spatialities
are so closely connected with times and seasons that equally with
these they lie outside the range of those communications which the
Redeemer had to make to us.   Hence all the indications He gives
are either purely figurative,[1] or otherwise so indefinite in tenor that
nothing can be gathered from them more than what for every
Christian is so much the essential thing in every conception he may
form of existence after death, that without it such existence would
be mere perdition—namely, the persistent union of believers with
the Redeemer.   Similarly, what the Apostles say on the subject is
said merely by way of dim presentiment, and with the confession

---

[1] The sayings I refer to are familiar to everyone, and are too numerous to
be cited in detail.

that definite knowledge is lacking.   True, then, as it may be that
each moment of our present life is intrinsically more perfect and
wise the more completely and clearly it embraces both past and
future, we should not seek to determine our purposes by picturing
to ourselves the form of our future life.   Such efforts, which spring
from the interest of our sensuous self-consciousness in the survival
of personality, are always sensuous in character, even when nobler
than those of Judaism and Islam ; and we must carefully guard
ourselves against allowing them an influence (as though they derived
from our Christian faith) which may only too easily injure Christian
faith and life, and thereby spoil for us the present.   Hence, as regards the idea of the future life, what we shall chiefly have to do is
to scrutinize carefully the propositions put forward by others, as
well as the opinions which have become dominant.

§ 159. *The solution of these two problems, to represent the Church in
        its consummation and the state of souls in the future life, is
        attempted in the ecclesiastical doctrines* of the Last Things ;
        *but to these doctrines we cannot ascribe the same value as to
        the doctrines already handled.*

  1. The phrase, ' the Last Things,' which has been somewhat
generally accepted, has a look of strangeness which is more con-
cealed by the word ' Eschatology ' ; for the term ' things '
threatens to carry us quite away from the domain of the inner life,
with which alone we are concerned.   This of itself indicates that
something is being attempted here which cannot be secured by
doctrines proper in our sense of the word.   The terms have this in
common, that if the beginning of a wholly new and ever-enduring
spiritual form of life be represented as from our point of view ' the
last thing,' that endless duration appears merely as the end of a
time-life which, as contrasted therewith, is almost a vanishing
quantity.   This can only be justified by bringing in the idea of
retribution, and that idea accordingly becomes dominant.   On
the other hand, if the same endless duration be regarded as the
further development of the new life begun here, the brief time-life
appears rather as its preparatory and introductory first stage.   The
former view, insisting on the idea of retribution, appeals for support chiefly to those passages in which Christ represents Himself
as one to whom judgment has been committed ; the latter, based
on the idea of development, to passages in which He says that He
is come to save.   Indisputably this latter view is more closely akin

to the premonition of personal survival as that is demonstrably present in the Christian consciousness ; on the other hand, the former is more in harmony with the idea of the consummation of the Church, an idea which, in order to find a point of attachment in our present life as a whole, insists on the exclusion of all that can be called ' world ' even from the Church's environment. Thus doctrines of the Last Things have connexions equally with both these problems ; each doctrine relates to both. If we tried to form a Christian idea of a state subsequent to this life, and it failed to agree with our idea of the consummation of the Church, we could not believe that it really expressed the absolutely final stage ; we should have to suppose that there still remained a further development, in which the Church would be perfected. Conversely, if we viewed the consummation of the Church as arriving within the present course of human affairs, we should have to add something in thought for the state after death, in order to give it a content of its own ; the material for this, however, could not be drawn from our Christian consciousness, for its contents are all of the other kind. Hence it was in the nature of the case that both elements should be thus conjoined—the consummation of the Church (which we cannot regard as possible in this life) being placed in that future life of which we cannot but form a conception, and the idea of that life (based as it must be on fellowship with Christ) being filled out with content from the perfected state of the Church. It must be so, if the new form of life is decisively to transcend the present.

At the same time we are not in a position to exhibit the confluence of the two factors, or to guarantee it. The consummated Church cannot be thought of as analogous to the Church militant ; nor do we know whether into the future life we ought to project the idea of an interdependent common life and work, to which no proper goal can be assigned. On the other hand, if we seek to conceive the future life by analogy with the present, as an ascending development, we cannot but have doubts whether any such development is possible in the consummated Church. Thus the solution of one problem seems never exactly to fit the other. We encounter the same difficulty if we keep to the indications of Scripture. There much is said by way of representing the consummated Church ; but it is not so said that we can affirm with certainty that it ought to be dated subsequently to the end of all earthly things ; [1] and for that reason from of yore many Christians

[1] John 6[53-58], Acts 1[6, 7], Eph. 4.

have actually expected the consummation of the Church here on earth. Other passages are meant rather to describe the life after death,[1] but whether they are also a representation of the consummated Church may be doubted.

2. Hence the following paragraphs, which treat of the Last Things, cannot have ascribed to them at all the same value as the previous doctrines. It is certainly not to be denied that we are conscious of our spiritual life as being the communicated perfection and blessedness of Christ, or that of itself this implies that in every case only the perfect is the originally real, whereas the imperfect owes its being to it ; or that this conviction is likewise faith in the reality of the consummated Church, yet only as an actively motive force within us, which is the really operative element in every aspect or moment of life which promotes the Church. If, however, the distinction (ineradicably bound up with our self-consciousness) between inner principle and outward manifestation be abolished (this active principle being also conceived as somehow attaining to expression in space and time), the position stands on a less firm foundation. Similarly, the equating of all human individuals with Christ implies that the general premonition of the imperishability of spirit, even in individual form, becomes certain for the Christian mind ; but this in no way involves any particular way of conceiving survival. Indeed, we cannot really make a picture of it either in the form of an infinitely progressive development or in that of an unchanging completeness ; to such a task our sensuous imagination is unequal. If, on the other hand, we treat these paragraphs, irrespectively of their source in our self-consciousness, as matters simply to be received on the authority of Scripture, even so they are not comparable to the doctrine of Christ's resurrection ; for what is in question there is statements made by the disciples regarding a fact connected in the closest possible way with their vocation. True, if we had evidence to show how, in ways we could reproduce, Christ formed these two conceptions in His own mind, we should endeavour with perfect confidence to appropriate His thought for ourselves ; for here too we should ascribe to Him nothing less than a perfectly developed human power of premonition, free from all uncertainty due to sin. But the content of these paragraphs cannot be so derived. We nowhere find in His teaching a connected and unambiguous treatment of these subjects, obviously meant to convey definite instruction about them. In

[1] I Cor. 15[23f.], Phil. 3[21].

each particular saying either the subject is doubtful, or the outline drawn is indistinct and the interpretation in a variety of ways uncertain. Hence there is nothing for it but that we should bring up those thought-forms which early became prevalent in the Church and passed over into our Confessions without being submitted to a fresh scrutiny, and should adduce them, under the title of *prophetic doctrines*, merely as the efforts of an insufficiently equipped faculty of premonition, adding reasons for and against. But we give fair warning that in any new forms which these docti ines may assume, the fancy (for to it belongs everything alien to the scope of our present experience which is set forth as object of a possible future experience), if it is to remain Christian, must place itself under the protection of exegesis, and only elaborate the material which exegesis supplies. What it must not do is to let itself become the play-thing of caprice or of alleged new revelations.

3. Under the circumstances, an exact construction of these paragraphs in a closely knit context is not to be thought of. We must be content to assume their sense as generally acknowledged, and let the facts prove that in their regard matters really are as I have indicated. This means exhibiting the two points—personal survival and the consummation of the Church—in their relation to each other, in a picture appealing to the sensuous imagination. Hence, in the first place, the survival of personality, above all, as the abolition of death, is represented under the figure of *the resur-rection of the flesh*. The consummation of the Church, on the other hand, is represented in a twofold manner—first, as conditioned by the fact that no further influence upon the Church can now be exerted by those who form no part of the Church, it is introduced in its character as the separation of believers from unbelievers, by the *Last Judgment*. But as excluding (in contrast to the Church militant) all the activities of sin and all imperfection in believers, it is represented as *eternal blessedness*. Since the survival of per-sonality, and therefore also the resurrection of the flesh, had to be taken as applying to the whole human race, and some mode of existence had to be found for those separated from believers, over against eternal blessedness stands (also introduced by the Last Judgment) the eternal damnation of the unbelieving. It is clear that, as this last pictorial representation is not an anticipation of any object of our future experience, it cannot be given the form of a special doctrine ; all we can do is to treat it as the shadow of eternal blessedness or the darker side of judgment. These separate pictures

fit together into a single imaginative picture, for this reason that the new form of existence is conditional on the *Return of Christ*, to which everything which belongs to the completion of His work must be related.　Hence it seems entirely natural to begin with the Return of Christ, which introduces all the rest ; in this way the other items develop out of it, and in relation to it, in their natural sequence.

First Prophetic Doctrine : The Return of Christ

§ 160. *Since the disciples of Christ could not consider the comforting promises of His Return* [1] *as having been fulfilled by the days of His resurrection, they expected this fulfilment at the end of all earthly things.*[2]　*Now since with this is bound up the separation of the good and the bad, we teach ' a Return of Christ for Judgment.'*

Symb.˝ Roman. : ὅθεν ἔρχεται κρίνειν ζῶντας καὶ νεκρούς.—*Symb. Nic.* : καὶ πάλιν ἐρχόμενον μετὰ δόξης κρῖναι ζῶντας καὶ νεκρούς· οὗ τῆς βασιλείας οὐκ ἔσται τέλος.—It is solely to this point that the *Augsburg Confession* refers, Art. 3. A much fuller statement in *Expos. simpl.* xi.　Ex coelis autem idem ille redibit in judicium, etc.—*Conf. Belg.* xxxvii. : Credimus . . . dominum nostrum Jesum Christum a coelo corporaliter et visibiliter sicut ascendit magna cum gloria et majestate venturum, ut se vivorum atque mortuorum declaret iudicem.

1. From the days immediately subsequent to Christ's resurrection we have no record of His having repeated promises of this kind ; [3] rather He speaks exclusively of His entering into His glory, and refers His disciples to His spiritual presence.[4]　But this could not cause doubt in the disciples' minds, leading them to explain the former promises as having been fulfilled already ; for His words in their context had pointed too clearly to a Return of Christ, in which He would manifest Himself to the whole world. Hence the disciples were so deeply impressed by a definite assurance [5] (although not given them in Christ's name) which interpreted these sayings of His literally, that later, when the destruction of Jerusalem occurred (in distinctly prophesying which Christ had spoken also of His own future), the question was not even raised among Christians whether all those sayings might not be referred to

---

[1] Omitting all the passages which are obviously parabolic, we have the following : Matt. 16[27. 28] 24[20ff.] 25[31ff.], Mark 13[26ff.], Luke 21[27. 28], John 14[3. 18] 16[16].

[2] 2 Cor. 5[1-10], 2 Thess. 1[7-10] 2[8], 2 Tim. 4[1], 1 Pet. 4[5-7. 13], 2 Pet. 3[10ff.].

[3] John 21[22. 23] is surely not sufficiently definite in its terms.

[4] Matt. 28[20], Luke 24[26], John 20[17].　　　[5] Acts 1[11].

Christ's future understood in a non-literal way.   Accordingly, after everything Chiliastic had been purged out, the opinion very early became fixed and almost universally accepted that the Return of Christ would coincide with the close of the present state of the earth.

2. If, however, we consider more carefully such passages as are most generally taken to refer to this subject, and also are most explicit, it turns out either that they excite the suspicion (some owing to the dates they fix, the others on account of their predominantly ethical tone) that they are not to be taken literally, or that, even if we interpret the personal Return literally, still there is much else in the context which cannot be taken literally on any terms, because any interpretation of the kind would destroy the whole unity of the discourse.   Yet, apart from this literal exegesis we have no Biblical warrant for the position that the reunion of believers with Christ (which is the essential content of our belief in personal survival) is conditional on such a personal Return ; indeed, elsewhere He Himself speaks of the first without any mention of the second.[1]   Still less have we Biblical warrant for believing that there is bound up with both a prior universal separation of the good and the bad (of which even Paul says not a word [2]), or for thinking that this event, due to a definite reappearance of Christ, will be accompanied by the termination of our present form of existence.   Thus all that might go to form a definite picture falls asunder ;   and, as the essential content of our paragraph, there remains simply this—that (if we substitute the efficacious activity of Christ for His bodily presence) the consummation of the Church, regarded as the cessation of its wavering growth and development, is possible only through a sudden leap to perfection, and on condition that procreation ceases, as also the coexistence of the good and the bad ; and that, therefore, this leap to perfection must simply be regarded as an act of Christ's kingly power.   This is certainly rooted deeply in Christian faith ; even if it does not of itself emerge as a distinct idea in every mind, yet all feel attracted by it when presented to them.   For in Christ the Divine Essence is permanently united with human nature ; hence human nature cannot be so inseparably restricted to a particular planet as to be involved in that planet's destruction as resulting from cosmic laws.   On the contrary, everything pertaining to it must be capable of being conceived in the light of this union and as an effect of it.

So that in this doctrine everything that is figurative and

---

[1] John 17[24].   [2] 1 Cor. 15[20ff.], 1 Thess. 4[14ff.].

necessarily uncertain in quality flows from our interest in personal survival, whereas everything that can be stated with assurance relates to the consummation of the Church.

SECOND PROPHETIC DOCTRINE: THE RESURRECTION OF THE FLESH

§ 161. *Not only did Christ sanction, by figurative utterances* [1] *and also by His teaching,* [2] *the idea, prevalent among His race, of the resurrection of the dead, but He further in His utterances ascribed this awakening from death to His own agency ; and it is an extension of this His teaching—a perfectly natural extension based on kindred utterances—to say that the general awakening of the dead will in a sudden manner interrupt the usual course of human life on earth.* [3]

1. We are so much aware of the connexion of all our mental activities, even the most inward and profound, with those of the body, that we really cannot form the idea of a finite spiritual life apart from that of a bodily organism.   Indeed, the spirit we only conceive as soul when in the body, so that it is impossible to speak of the soul's immortality in the strict sense apart from bodily life. Since the activity of the spirit as a definite soul ceases at death simultaneously with the bodily life, it is only with bodily life that it can recommence.   Indisputably, however, the idea of the resurrection of the flesh implies something more than this ; it implies such an identity of life that life after resurrection and life before death constitute one and the same personality ; and this formed part especially of the Jewish conception of the matter. [4]   Clearly, too, the soul as an individual entity only persists by itself in the continuity of consciousness, which again appears to us as conditioned by memory ; and memory in its turn is as much bound up with bodily states as any other mental activity.   We cannot then conceive how under absolutely different bodily conditions such a unifying memory could get to work ; yet in its absence the soul itself would not be the same.   But insistence on this appears to bring us back to the position which we rejected above—namely, that the human mind is rigidly restricted to the surface of this globe.   On the one hand, every organism is a product of the planet on which it appears, and dependent on the specific nature of that

[1] Matt. 25[31ff.], John 5[28. 29] 6[40. 54].   [2] Matt. 22[30-32].
[3] I Cor. 15[51. 52], I Thess. 4[13-18].   [4] Luke 20[28-33].

planet ; hence the similarity of the future body to the present would imply a similarity of the two worlds ; but even memory, again, in virtue of its organic aspect is dependent on the near affinity of impressions ; thus, for example, in the present life our memory of a definite period of time grows extremely faint once the whole scene has changed. If we further add that, the greater the excellence of the future life, the less could a definite volition come to the aid of such memory, it must be owned that the more the soul in itself remains the same, the more must the future life be a simple, easily attachable prolongation of the present. But, in that case, the other point of departure for all these eschatological ideas—namely, the consummation of the Church—gets less than justice ; for in such a life as that just described no consummation is possible. Hence the latter interest compels us, if we wish to escape the other extreme, once again to limit more strictly the similarity between the future organism and the present ; and it is on this that the description of the resurrection body as immortal [1] and without sex [2] is based. The first of these qualities, which of itself implies a world of a quite different constitution, completely gets rid of that interest in bodily self-preservation which by experience we know to be so fruitful a seed of strife between flesh and spirit. The second quality, in addition, guards against the entrance into the consummated Church of new souls called into being through procreation ; for we cannot conceive of such souls not being handicapped by natural forces in the development of spirit, *i.e.* we cannot conceive them without sin. But obviously both qualities are inimical to the identity of the soul and the continuity of consciousness. The immortal body will then at every moment and in every function reveal its difference from the mortal ; and the soul in that case will be all the less capable of appropriating the share which the mortal body had in the formation of our present consciousness, and of retaining it in memory. And as regards the second quality, it is impossible to see how, if the relations of sex cease, the organic system on which they rest can be retained ; or, again, how a male and a female soul can as such fail to be different. And thus, if owing to changed organization each soul ceased to be either male or female, no soul would be the same as before. Thus it is clear that in our doctrine both points of departure must be provided for, but that the two really represent different interests ; for the resurrection of the flesh must be conceived in one way if individuals are to remain

---

[1] 1 Cor. 15[42].   [2] Matt. 22[30].

absolutely the same, and in another if one and all they are to be merged in the consummated Church.   Hence the different items cannot be combined in an idea capable of clear representation ; any idea we can form suffers from the indeterminateness peculiar to these doctrines, a characteristic harmonizing with the special name we have given them.

2. The general and simultaneous resurrection of all men implies that those who rise have existed since death in a state different from that which they enter by resurrection ; and upon this implication rests the reality of the idea of a Last Judgment.   It is naturally to this intermediate state, as immediately impending, that our sense-bound interest in the survival of the individual is primarily directed ; and the question arises whether at our point of view we possess any rule by which to guide efforts at explanation, or are at all bound to supervise them.   The first would be the case only if we found something laid down about this state in the New Testament ; but all the passages [1] which might be reckoned in here are either of uncertain doctrinal character or of doubtful meaning.   The second would be necessary if such explanations contained anything inconsistent with our Christian consciousness.   Now, the intermediate state can be conceived of in a purely negative way, as meaning simply that the old life-activities have ceased and the new have not yet begun—and this is the idea of the sleep of the soul.   To this our Christian consciousness can make no distinct objection ; but while thereby, on the one hand, all Christians are made equal (since, alike for those who first fell asleep and for the last, the interval is nil), yet on the other hand, if the waking of the soul is to be conceived as synchronous with the origin of the new body, it is difficult to imagine how recollection of the former state can simultaneously be implanted and retained.   If the intermediate state be conceived as a conscious state, Christian faith certainly will insist that it cannot be a state devoid of fellowship with Christ ; for in that case it would be a lapse from grace which could not be regarded otherwise than as punishment, and would mean the reintroduction of an idea which the Evangelical Church discarded soon after its formation.[2]   But if

---

[1] Luke 16[22ff.] 23[43], 1 Pet. 3[19, 20].

[2] *Art. Smalc.* ii. : Quapropter purgatorium . . . mera diaboli larva est. Pugnat enim cum primo articulo qui docet Christum solum et non hominum opera animas liberare.   Et constat etiam de mortuis nihil nobis divinitus mandatum esse.—*Expos. simpl.* xxvi. : Quod autem quidam tradunt de igne purgatorio, fidei christianae, credo remissionem peccatorum et vitam aeternam purgationique plenae per Christum, et Christi domini sententiis (John 5[24] 13[10]) adversatur.

the intermediate period is to be conceived as one of fellowship with Christ, it must be freed from all resemblance to ancient or even Jewish notions of an impoverished sort of life in the underworld. For all the obstacles to blessed fellowship with Christ, which in this life arise from the sense-world, have fallen away ; the intermediate state, therefore, must be a state of enhanced perfection. But in that case it is difficult not to regard the general resurrection of the dead as superfluous, and reunion with the body as a retrograde step. Indeed, it looks as if in consistency only one way of escape were left open, namely, to suppose that in the intermediate state each in-dividual soul by itself is in fellowship with the Redeemer, but that the fellowship of the blessed with each other, and hence too the activity of individuals, is conditional on the resurrection of the flesh, which therefore is necessary to perfection. Still, even on this supposition, the existence of the Church remains interrupted till the resurrection, as the existence of the individual does on the former supposition ; and so one of the two elements comes to be more en-dangered as the other is better secured. Hence some have taken the simultaneous general resurrection in a merely figurative sense, and have wished to infer from other scriptural passages [1] that for each individual the future life begins immediately after death.[2] But for one thing this means that the soul is already in possession of the new body when it parts from the old, an idea we find widely accepted ; on the other hand, the simultaneous Last Judgment and also (since its alleged purpose has wholly lapsed) the personal Return of Christ must in that case be taken just as figuratively as the simultaneous general resurrection. Thus we cannot help wavering between this more Biblical idea, which represents the action of Christ, in conjunction with great cosmic changes, as suddenly giving existence to the future life and the Church triumphant as a great whole (though at the cost of unbroken continuity), and the less Biblical view which (though in a fashion which compels us to ask for scientific proof, since so much emphasis is laid on exact affinity with the conditions of earthly life) maintains the continuity of personality as strictly as possible, the consummated Church only growing little by little out of the earthly life which goes on alongside of it.

[1] Directly, though not with certainty, from Luke 23[43]; indirectly from Phil. 1[21-24].

[2] *Expos. simpl.* xxvi. : Credimus enim fideles recte a morte corporea migrare ad Christum . . . Credimus item infideles recte praecipitari in tartara.

3. If we now turn to the general resurrection, and the pre-dominant modes of conceiving the subjects treated of in the follow-ing doctrines, there is one more difficulty to be solved.   If saved and unsaved enter upon utterly different states, there is an unanswerable case for holding that the new bodies which they receive cannot be the same in both cases.   The organism must be adapted to the conditions of life which are impending ; and this gives rise to a new difficulty if we seek to conjoin the idea of the general resurrection with that of the Last Judgment.   If both classes equally become different at the resurrection, sentence has already been pronounced upon them before the judgment comes on, and judgment becomes superfluous ; the more so that such a difference in bodies which originate simultaneously could not be produced by the action of identical cosmic forces combined with differences of a purely ethical kind, but only by a directly creative divine fiat.   On the other hand, if those destined to bliss and those destined to perdition are still alike at the resurrection, the resurrection is not an execution of the judgment, and since in one class or the other or in both inward changes must later take place which transform the organism, the reality of the idea of the Last Judgment depends solely on these changes occurring simultaneously, but there is no further need for the simultaneity of the resurrection of the dead and the transforma-tion of the living.

Taking all these considerations together, we find that the various ideas of how the future life is attached to the present are incapable of being made perfectly definite.   As the essential content of the doctrine there remains only this, that the ascension of the risen Redeemer was possible only if all other human individuals too can look forward to a renovation of organic life which has links of attach-ment to our present state ; and further, that the development of the future state must be posited on the one hand as dependent on Christ's divine power and on the other as a cosmic event for which arrangements have been made in the universal divine world-order. The first of these last two ideas is certified as implied in the faith underlying the endeavour to form ideas on this matter ; the second hovers before the mind as indicating a problem we can never completely solve.

THIRD PROPHETIC DOCTRINE : THE LAST JUDGMENT

§ 162. *The idea of the Last Judgment, the elements of which are like-*
wise found in the utterances of Christ, is meant to set forth

the complete separation of the Church from the world, inas-
much as the consummation of the former excludes all in-
fluences of the latter upon it.

1. The main element in the idea of the Last Judgment, namely,
that Christ will utterly separate the believing and the unbelieving
from each other, so that they are consigned to quite different places
and can exert no further influence on each other, does not at all
involve the consummation of the Church.   As has been shown,[1]
the imperfections of the Church are due much less to the influence
of unbelievers mingling with believers in this world than to the
carnal elements still present in the regenerate themselves.   Hence
if at the resurrection believers were the same in soul as at their
departure from this life, they would enter the new life, in spite of the
supposed separation, as persons in whom sin, though in process of
disappearing, was still at work.   Thus the value which in this
respect is attributed to separation rests solely on an incorrect reading of the distinction between the visible and the invisible Church.[2]
But if this distinction, as we have understood it, is to cease with the
beginning of the new life, it follows that at that point the regenerate
themselves must discard those elements of sinfulness and carnality
which still cling to them.   But this is not effected by the outward
separation itself, and it was for this reason that in his own exegetical
fashion Origen [3] sought to interpret one of the relevant passages as
indicating an *inner* separation.   Apart from the fact that to have
all worldly and carnal motives and ideas so abruptly torn away
would so far endanger the continuous identity of personal life, such
an inner separation would simply be completed sanctification ;
and, as all sanctification must flow from vital fellowship with the
Redeemer, the Christian consciousness is unable to recognize itself
in any view from which this is absent.   Indeed, in any such abrupt
cessation of sanctification, not mediated by our own spontaneous
action, we cannot help finding something magical, which, had it
only been applied to each individual earlier, would have made superfluous the whole redemption which depends on living fellowship
with Christ.   Thus it always seems as if one of these two things
excluded the other.   John does appear to offer a mediating idea
which might reconcile the discord ; [4] for if the inner separation is
effected by the perfect knowledge of Christ consequent on His

[1] Cf. § 126, 1.   [2] Cf. § 148, 2.
[3] *Comment. in Matt.* x. 2 (on Matt. 13[36-40]), ed. R., vol. iii. p. 444.
[4] I John 3[2].

Return, it is a work of redemption.   But if considered more closely, this suggestion too breaks down.   If the Return of Christ effects this change only in proportion to each person's receptivity, it still remains that such receptivity is not equally great in all the regenerate when they leave this world.   So that the complete purification of the soul due to the appearance of Christ would not be wrought in each case with equal instantaneousness, but more swiftly in some and more slowly in others.   Hence even this separation would not be simultaneous ; it would only come to be gradual after the new life began.   If, on the other hand, whether the degree of receptivity for the knowledge of Christ be higher or lower is a matter of no importance, the inner separation certainly would be effected abruptly ; but the same change would necessarily be produced in the unbelieving, for Christ appears to them also at His Return, and in them, too, the receptivity in question is present, even in the worst of cases, in some infinitely small degree.   In that case, we should find this growing on our hands into a sudden recovery of all souls for the kingdom of grace, which, while making the separation of persons meaningless, would in itself not be wholly free from an admixture of magic.

2. If now we turn back to the idea of a separation between persons according as they have reached the close of life in a state of belief or unbelief (and it is this idea which has become dominant, because it seems to be approved by Christ's own words), we can hardly deny that it is better fitted to bring about the blessedness of believers in the new life than their perfection.   For if the influences emanating from the unbelievers mingled with believers are received by the regenerate solely in their character as organs of the Holy Spirit, and lead solely to action derived from, and determined by, the Spirit, many perfections will be evoked thereby, such as we find likewise in the Christ's pattern life—perfections which apart from such influences could never have developed.   But it seems to be otherwise as regards blessedness.   The evils due to sin always spread over the entire common and corporate life ; hence even in the next life believers, if involved in the same common life with unbelievers, would have to suffer from the evils these brought with them.   But here too people have not recurred as they should have done to the idea of living fellowship with Christ.   During His sojourn here Christ also partook in the common life shared by sinners, but we do not suppose that, apart from sympathy and bodily pain, He was a sufferer.   Similarly, those united to Him in living fellowship will

experience nothing which tends to hamper their spiritual life and could therefore be felt by them as evil—just as Christ Himself never felt bodily pain and sympathy as evils.   Besides, even bodily pain (if a possibility at all in the life after resurrection) would necessarily be capable of being produced in other ways than through sin, so that separation would be no guarantee against it.   Sympathy, too, would still be inseparably bound up with identity of nature ; so that the blessed would still have sympathy with the others, though wholly separate from them.   Thus the separation contemplated at the Last Judgment remains, even from this point of view, both inadequate and superfluous.   All that might be said is that it takes place for the sake not of the blessed but of the others, whether to ensure that they reap no benefit from what the good might do to alleviate the evils pervading the fellowship of the new world, or lest in that very fellowship they might find means of themselves attaining to communion with Christ.   But either this would mean attributing jealousy to the Supreme Being, an idea against which even the higher paganism protested ; or it must rest solely on that familiar and widespread idea of the divine righteousness which in its one-sidedness looks so like caprice that before we could feel ourselves entitled, not to say obliged, to regard the idea as in harmony with the mind of Christ, it would have to be much less equivocal in its origins, the expression given to it much more decisive, and the Apostles' use of it much more comprehensive.

3. The idea of the Last Judgment, then, we are unable to state in a final form which perfectly satisfies both demands.   None the less, in view of its almost universal prevalence in Christendom, we must try to elicit its essential meaning.   By way of preliminary it may be remarked that in so far as it can be traced to an all but vengeful desire to enhance the misery of unbelievers, and to exclude them from all the redemptive influences of the good, or again so far as there has contributed to its prevalence a fear lest, even after attaining perfected fellowship with Christ, we might be pained by the company of the bad, it springs from an unpurified Christian temper and obscures the essential meaning of the whole conception. It follows that this essential meaning can only be what remains over, when we have completely freed our thought from fear and vengefulness.   This appears to consist in the following two points.   First, once our fellowship with Christ has been perfected, we are so completely freed from evil that even though evil men and evil things be present, both as such are for us non-existent.   Wrong and evil being

thus wholly shut out from the common consciousness of believers, that consciousness can embrace nothing but the untroubled and unimpeded fulness of divine grace ; the Church is really then a wholly self-enclosed body, so that an outlook (and of this we can never rid ourselves here) that dwells upon opposition and contrast will there give place utterly to one for which evil has ceased to exist, because God cannot originate it. Secondly, if we conceive the Church as consummated, but at the same time suppose that there still exists a part of the human race which has not been captured and pervaded by its spirit, such a supposition is possible only on the assumption that the part in question is completely isolated from all influences issuing from the Church, which means shut off from all contact with it. There is indeed one discourse of Christ,[1] at least very closely related to this theme, which clearly implies that every influence (even the faintest) passing from the seats of the blessed to those who during their earthly life have failed to turn to God, touches them to better issues.

FOURTH PROPHETIC DOCTRINE : ETERNAL BLESSEDNESS

§ 163. *From the resurrection of the dead onwards, those who have died in fellowship with Christ will find themselves, through the vision of God, in a state of unchangeable and unclouded blessedness.*

1. The state of believers after their full reinstatement in life may be conceived under two forms, either as a sudden and unvarying possession of the highest, or as a gradual ascent to the highest— an ascent, however, which like the development of Christ Himself must be thought of as without retrogression and without conflict. Both views have their own special difficulties, when we try to fill in the general outline and to shape the mere formula into a clear imaginative picture. As regards the first, we can hardly explain to ourselves how the consummation can be reached by us, or implanted in us, just at the resurrection, without destroying all connexion with our present life ; which would not be the case if this life were gradually forgotten, like our childhood, as we grew by degrees in perfection. Still more, if we are to conceive a perfection incapable of any further increase—and this in a finite being completely severed from all that admitted of cultivation, or required it—then we find it embarrassingly difficult to imagine how this

[1] Luke 16[19-31].

being, now deprived of every object for its activity, could express its perfection. We cannot separate communal life from man's nature as such, still less can the Christian conceive himself apart from such a life ; for the fellowship of believers with each other and that of each with Christ are one and the same thing. Not only so ; a common life, devoid of every object of common activity, a life which therefore must limit itself exclusively to the mutual presentation of the contents of the inner life, can scarcely be thought of as an absolutely perfect state. It is true, we have in our present life an element which is akin to such a state, namely, common worship, and all æsthetic representations of the God-consciousness. But we find it deplorable that for such things pious Christians should neglect their practical obligations ; such a life impresses us as meagre ; hence we cannot bring ourselves to think that the highest perfection of existence can be reduced to such an alternation of giving and receiving empty and aimless representations. Instead, our imagination strains to discover some work which in that life might be entrusted to us. On the given assumptions, however, nothing remains but either the cultivation of some external nature or the oversight of some less perfect spiritual world—both such that occupation with them could not disturb our bliss. But we do not find in Scripture any encouragement to such an idea,[1] nor have we the power to fill out such a formula with real meaning.

It is no easier, supposing we try to imagine that at the resurrection there will begin a perfection which rises up and up to infinity. We can hardly conceive such a thing without inequalities and variations, and, even were it not so, at all events not without such a dissatisfaction with what is present as naturally goes along with the expectation of something better yet to come ; and this after all is a sense of imperfection, and therefore in free beings a sense somehow of guilt. Indeed, progress can scarcely be thought of apart from external relations and conditions of development. But if once we open this sluice, there sweep in at once diversities among those who are the same in kind, the antithesis of the pleasant and the unpleasant, and, as a consequence, everything that characterizes human life here below. In fact, nothing remains (and perhaps on these assumptions it is a position we cannot avoid without inconsistency) but that we should accept the change from life to death as itself an element in that future experience. This makes it clear that what we have conceived in this form is not the consum-

---

[1] Matt. 19[28] and 2 Tim. 2[12] cannot really be taken in that sense.

mation of the Church, but merely a gradually self-amending and self-purifying repetition of the present life. Thus the problem remains unsolved.

2. If now, selecting either form, we inquire as to the real vital content of this future state, and concede at the start that this content, so far as our activity is concerned, is limited to representation ; then, in order to gain a clear imaginative picture, we should have to know what there will be for us to represent there ; *i.e.* what influences will affect us and be taken in by us. To this question the usual answer is to say that eternal life will consist in the vision of God.[1] This we can only take to mean the completest fulness of the most living God-consciousness : the next question is how this will be distinguished from our present God-consciousness. The simplest reply would be that while our God-consciousness now is always a mediated one, inasmuch as we have it only in and with some other element, there it will be unmediated. But this can scarcely be harmonized with the retention of personality. For as self-conscious individuals we can only have the God-consciousness, if it is really to be ours, along with our self-consciousness ; and even if the latter has to be distinguished from the former, this will only be conceivable in one of two ways. Either we merely distinguish our self from our God-consciousness, as the subject in which the God-consciousness dwells, without our self-consciousness having any other content ; and this is an idea which hardly anyone will tolerate. Or our self-consciousness, as being changeable and constantly affected, must differ from the other conceived as something which remains ever the same. Hence, if the individual life is to persist in human nature and even in finite nature as such, our God-consciousness must always remain a mediated one ; and it is exclusively within this sphere that we shall have to seek the distinction between its present and its future form. In that case, nothing remains but that (even here we strive after it, though with a sense of inability to attain) we should have an unimpeded knowledge of God in all and along with all ; and also, so far as finite nature allows it, that we should steadily have knowledge of all that wherein and whereby God makes Himself known ; and this without conflict arising between this desire in us and in any other, or between the steady God-consciousness and consciousness in any other of its aspects. This certainly would be pure and assured vision ;

---

[1] A thought first derived from Matt. 5[8] and 2 Cor. 5[7], but with what justice is disputed.

it would render us completely at home with God.   Only, we can no
more understand how we are to find ourselves at this point just at
the resurrection without thereby imperilling the continuity and
identity of our existence, than we can see how, if we start there at
the point we have attained here, we can ever reach the consummation.   Thus we can take our departure from either point—from
the problem of imagining an unchangeably identical blessedness, or
from that of conceiving an endlessly progressive advance.   But we
really can solve neither problem ; and we therefore always remain
uncertain how the state which is the Church's highest consummation can be gained or possessed in this form by individual
personalities emerging into immortality.

APPENDIX : ON ETERNAL DAMNATION

The figurative sayings of Christ, which have led to a state of
irremediable misery for those who die out of fellowship with
Christ [1] being accepted as the counterpart of eternal bliss, will,
if more closely scrutinized, be found insufficient to support any
such conclusion.   Either these passages cannot without extreme
arbitrariness be separated from others which must allude to some
earlier event,[2] or they are countered by others which forbid us to
think of the definitive victory of evil over one part of the human
race, and from which we must rather infer that before the general
resurrection evil will have been completely overcome.[3]   Still less
can the idea of eternal damnation itself bear close scrutiny,
whether considered in itself or as it is related to eternal bliss.   If
we once agree that eternal damnation cannot mean condemnation
to bodily pains and sufferings, for the simple reason that (if human
nature is not to be utterly destroyed) the alleviating influence of
custom must be allowed for ; and if the sense of ability to bear
what has been inflicted entails some satisfaction, so that what
results on the whole is something less than pure and irremediable
misery—if all this be so, there is scarcely any firm ground on which
we can stand.   If the misery is of a spiritual kind, and if accordingly it consists of the pains of conscience, then the lost are better
by far in their damnation than they were in this life ; yet although
they are better, they are to be more wretched.   We cannot imagine
this ; for even if such a lot were in keeping with divine justice,

---

[1] Matt. 25[46], Mark 9[44], John 5[29].
[2] Cf. Matt. 24[30-31] and John 5[24, 25].
[3] 1 Cor. 15[25, 26].

still there would be no way of preventing the self-approval of the awakened and quickened conscience from supplying a counter-weight to misery. Indeed, we cannot imagine how the awakened conscience, as a living movement of the spirit, could fail to issue in some good. If it be rejoined that what is to be regarded as the source of everlasting torment is not any sharpened feeling for the difference between good and evil, but only the consciousness of self-forfeited bliss, yet such a consciousness could not be living and acute except in so far as bliss could be pictured in the mind ; nor could it be torturing unless a capacity were present to share in the blessed state. But this capacity would itself imply a moral improvement, and the mental picture of bliss would constitute an enjoyment by which the misery was lessened.

If we now consider eternal damnation as it is related to eternal bliss, it is easy to see that once the former exists, the latter can exist no longer. Even if externally the two realms were quite separate, yet so high a degree of bliss is not as such compatible with entire ignorance of others' misery, the more so if the separa-tion itself is the result purely of a general judgment, at which both sides were present, which means conscious each of the other. Now if we attribute to the blessed a knowledge of the state of the damned, it cannot be a knowledge unmixed with sympathy. If the per-fecting of our nature is not to move backwards, sympathy must be such as to embrace the whole human race, and when extended to the damned must of necessity be a disturbing element in bliss, all the more that, unlike similar feelings in this life, it is untouched by hope. For, reflect as we may that if eternal damnation exists at all, it must be just, and that the vision of God embraces also His righteousness, yet even so sympathy persists ; indeed, even in this life we rightly expect a deeper sympathy to be shown to merited than to unmerited suffering. In some form or other personal survival includes memory of our former state, in which it will always happen some of us were associated with some of them in a common life ; and sympathy will be all the stronger because in that earlier time there was a point when we were as little re-generate as they. In the divine government of the world every-thing is inseparably conditioned by everything else ; hence we cannot ignore the fact that the circumstance of our having enjoyed helpful dispensations was due to the very same disposition of things as insured that such help should not reach them. Thus our sym-pathy cannot fail to be attended by the bitter feeling always present when we see a real connexion between our own gain and another's loss.

From whichever side we view it, then, there are great difficulties in thinking that the finite issue of redemption is such that some thereby obtain the highest bliss, while others (on the ordinary view, indeed, the majority of the human race) are lost in irrevocable misery. We ought not to retain such an idea without decisive testimony to the fact that it was to this that Christ Himself looked forward ; and such testimony is wholly lacking. Hence we ought at least to admit the equal rights of the milder view, of which likewise there are traces in Scripture ; [1] the view, namely, that through the power of redemption there will one day be a universal restoration of all souls.

POSTSCRIPT TO THE PROPHETIC DOCTRINES

What seems to emerge from these considerations is this. Both elements—the consummation of the Church and personal survival —can each for itself be taken up with perfect truth in our Christian consciousness ; it is certain, too, that the consummation of the Church can never be manifested in this life, and that the state attained in the next life must bear a different relation to the consummation of the Church from that of our present state. And yet the combination and correlation of these two elements yields no firmly outlined or really lucid idea, nor can any such idea of either the one element or the other be developed out of the intimations of Scripture. If we try to use the idea of the consummation of the Church so as to determine, from its relation to what as yet is unconsummated, the relation of the single life in the next world to the single life here, or the difference between the two, we can reach no fixed conclusion. And if we seek, by means of the idea of the future life, to assign a place to the consummated Church where it will no longer be a productive factor but a product only, again we fail. The one point of view will always tend to merge in what is mythical, *i.e.* in the historical presentation of what is supra-historical ; the other point of view will always approximate to what is visionary, *i.e.* the earthly presentation of what is more than earthly. These were everywhere the forms of prophetic thought, which in its higher import makes no claim to furnish knowledge in the strict sense, but is meant only to give stimulating expression to principles already known.

[1] I Cor. 15[26, 55].

THIRD SECTION

THE DIVINE ATTRIBUTES WHICH RELATE TO REDEMPTION

§ 164. *When we trace to the divine causality our consciousness of fellowship with God, restored through the efficacy of redemption, we posit the planting and extension of the Christian Church as the object of the divine government of the world.*

1. This is the only meaning which can be attached to the conception of the government of the world, as we are able to employ it here. For our Christian consciousness, all other things have existence only as they are related to the efficacy of redemption—either as part of the organization in which the reawakened God-consciousness finds expression, or as so much raw material which this organization is to elaborate. The word 'govern,' however, means to set in motion, and direct, forces whose presence is due to other causes ; hence the term may easily mislead us into thinking even here of a divine direction of earthly forces conceived of as already existing, as also into separating the government of the world from creation in such a way that it comes to look like something that has supervened later or been interjected, and as if from the creation onwards everything could have happened otherwise than in point of fact it did happen. The Christian faith that all things were created for the Redeemer [1] implies on the contrary that by creation all things (whether as prepared for or as overruled) were disposed with a view to the revelation of God in the flesh, and so as to secure the completest possible impartation thereof to the whole of human nature, and thus to form the Kingdom of God. Similarly, the world of nature is not to be considered as going its own way on the strength of the divine preservation, the divine government only exerting influence on it through special isolated acts, so as to bring it into harmony with the kingdom of grace. To us, rather, the two things are absolutely one, and we have the certainty that from the beginning the whole disposition of nature would have been different had it not been that, after sin, redemption through Christ was determined on for the human race.

[1] Col. 1[16].

2. The conception of divine government laid down in our paragraph seems, it is true, to belong to a time when nothing suggested the existence of any other form of spiritual life than that of man, with the exception of angels. The angelic nature, however, glorious as were the descriptions given of it, was placed beneath the human by the first Christians owing to its defective union with the Divine Essence, and put in exclusively subservient relations to men. But even though we assume most willingly that the world forms the richest revelation of God of which it is possible to conceive, though we had become fully persuaded that on every one of the planets organic life is developed up to the level of rationality ; still the subject of angels would be one on which we had nothing to say. Even if our racial consciousness were able to transcend the human and embrace intelligence of every kind, yet such extra-human intelligence does not affect us in such wise as to compel us to expand our ideas of the divine government, so long as we receive no clear impression of how such intelligence operates in time. No such impression is given us, however ; it is therefore only within the compass of our own world that the divine government is known by us—within the sphere, that is, in which redemption makes its power felt. Now the element in our consciousness which becomes the sense of sin does not carry us back directly to the divine causality, so that the conception of the divine preservation of the world derives its full meaning exclusively from the relation obtaining between the divine causality and that element in our consciousness which becomes the sense of grace. Hence we can say, regarding two points formerly made out [1]—both the essence of things in their relations to each other and the order of reciprocal interaction between them—that they exist through God (in so far as they do exist) relatively to the redeeming revelation of God in Christ, by which the human spirit is developed to perfection. Everything in our world, that is to say—human nature in the first place and all other things in direct proportion to the closeness of their connexion with it—would have been disposed otherwise, and the entire course of human and natural events, therefore, would have been different, if the divine purpose had not been set on the union of the Divine Essence with human nature in the Person of Christ, and, as a result thereof, the union of the Divine Essence with the fellowship of believers through the Holy Spirit. And with respect to our conclusion as to the idea of the unity and identity of

[1] Cf. § 46, Postscript, p. 175.

the Church in all ages,[1] we must mark off two periods in the divine
government of the world—one before the union just mentioned was
realized in time and space, when all was merely preparatory and
introductory ; the other subsequent to its being realized, and this
a period of development and fulfilment.

3. In the divine causality there is no division or opposition
anywhere, nor can we regard the government of the world as other
than a unity, directed towards a single goal.   Hence the Church,
or the Kingdom of God in its whole extent as well as in the whole
course of its development, forms the one object of the divine world-
government ; whereas any particular thing is such an object only
in the other and for it.   True, we cannot avoid affirming the independent existence of the particular as an element within this
whole ; but we instantly leave the right track when we assume for
this particular a special divine causality in any way separate from
connexion with the whole, and thus view the particular in question
as the special object or result of divine government, to which other
things therefore are subordinated as means.   As a necessary
correction, rather, we must at once subordinate it to other things ;
each particular thus appearing, simultaneously and equally, as
both conditioning and conditioned, a point at which the threads
of relation cross.   Even the Redeemer, while He does represent
particular disciples at particular junctures of their life as objects of
the divine care, always in doing so has their vocation (*i.e.* their
activity in the Kingdom of God) in view as that on which strictly
the divine care is bent.

Hence for us the usual division of divine Providence into
generalis, specialis, and *specialissima* is nearly useless.   The first is
supposed to cover everything, the second the whole human race,
and the third the saints or the Kingdom of God ; but for us it is
only under the third that everything can be subsumed, for to its
object all else is referred.   In any case, the term ' providence ' is
of foreign origin and was first taken over from heathen authors
into later Jewish writings and adopted later by Church teachers,
not without many disadvantages for the clear exposition of the
authentic Christian faith, a circumstance which would have been
avoided by the use of the scriptural terms ' predestination,' ' fore-
ordination.'   These words express far more clearly the relation of
each single part to the connected whole, and represent the divine
rule of the world as an inwardly coherent order.   They do so in a

[1] Cf. § 156.

way by no means equivalent in meaning to the equally unchristian term ' fate,' which always implies that the particular is determined by the co-operation of all other things without the least respect to what would have issued from the independent existence of the object. Similarly, the term ' providence ' chiefly suggests that the particular is determined without respect to what would naturally have resulted from its coexistence with other things ; and this onesidedness, too, is foreign to the idea of predestination. Scripture itself does not hesitate to admit that even sin is embraced under divine fore-ordination, in spite of its really being contrary to the notion of the Kingdom of God ; it reckons sin, however, as among the preparatory and introductory elements of the divine government of the world ; and we can also recognize as perfectly self-consistent the divine decree that all men should share this earlier state previous to the new creation, so partaking in the powers thereof only by way of *contrast*—a form of experience that runs through the whole of human life. Only, the difficulty which we encountered above of forming the idea of eternal damnation now reappears ; the problem being how to combine this idea with that of a divine government which is a unity in itself and is directed to a single end.

§ 165. *The divine causality presents itself to us in the government of the world as* Love *and as* Wisdom.

1. The one and undivided divine causality cannot without anthropomorphic error be represented in a circle of divine attributes ; hence, to bring clearly to consciousness its nature and its aim we must look for differences which, as being human, depend on some antithesis. Now in all human causality we distinguish between the underlying temper or disposition and the more or less corresponding form in which it is given effect to. By the former, what is innermost in the spontaneously active being as a unity is represented as will stimulated in a particular way ; the latter is traceable rather to the understanding, and shows us the spontaneous activity in relation to its object as a multiplicity. The divine attributes named in the paragraph above are conceived on the lines of this human distinction, thus corresponding to the meaning we have attached to the divine government of the world. Love, that is to say, is the impulse to unite self with neighbour and to will to be in neighbour ; if then the pivot of the divine government is redemption and the foundation of the Kingdom of God, involving

the union of the Divine Essence with human nature, this means that the underlying disposition cannot be conceived otherwise than as love. By wisdom, on the other hand, is understood the right outlining of plans and purposes—these regarded in their manifold characteristics and in the whole round of their reciprocal relations. Hence, since the divine government manifests itself in the self-consistent ordering of the whole sphere of redemption, alongside of the divine love we rightly place wisdom as the art (so to speak) of realizing the divine love perfectly.

2. These two attributes, love and wisdom, are of course separable in human life, and this the more easily that owing to the distinction between understanding and will which is essential to man, it is only in a few persons (and never completely even in them) that disposition and the formation of purposes merge in each other ; either ability of understanding more or less lags behind purity of will, or *vice versa*. No such dualism can be conceived of in the Divine Essence ; hence the two attributes are never separate in any way ; they are so entirely one that each may be regarded as being intrinsically contained in the other. Without ascribing any limitation to God, therefore, we may assert that the divine wisdom is not capable of producing any other disposition of things, or any other ordering of their course, than that in which the divine love is most perfectly realized ; and just as little is the divine love capable of leading to self-impartations other than those in which it itself finds perfect satisfaction, and in which accordingly it presents itself as absolute wisdom. This agreement must be brought out still more clearly in the two doctrines that follow.

FIRST DOCTRINE : THE DIVINE LOVE

§ 166. *The divine love, as the attribute in virtue of which the divine nature imparts itself, is seen in the work of redemption.*

Conf. Basil. v. : Status huius scripturae canonicae totius is est, bene Deum hominum generi velle et eam benevolentiam per Christum Dominum declarasse . . . quae fide sola recipiatur.

1. The two points indicated in the paragraph are not infrequently questioned even in the circles to which we belong. That the Supreme Being imparts Himself, and that this constitutes the very essence of divine love, is a position rejected by many as mystical ; and the second point, that, namely, which restricts to the channel of redemption a divine self-impartation alleged to be

going on everywhere, is rejected as unduly exclusive, and as confining the manifestations of the divine perfection to too narrow a range. Moreover, those who diverge from us in this way are chiefly people who, generally speaking, tend to conceal the distinctive features of Christianity rather than give them prominence. As regards the first point, such thinkers recognize the divine love in all those arrangements of Nature and all those dispositions of human affairs which protect life or further it. And yet, apart from redemption, and taken only in this sense, the divine love must always remain a matter of doubt. Supposing we regard the single life as its object, then, if we are not going to lapse into the grossest particularism, it is impossible from such aids to life to infer the divine love ; they involve restraints upon the lives of others ; so that the presence of love would always imply the presence of its opposite.[1] Indeed, this is true not merely of helps and hindrances to sensible well-being ; it applies also to the spiritual development of the single life ; in very many respects favour to one involves the neglect of others. But if we put the single life aside and rather consider humanity—that is to say, our racial consciousness—then (since in this case helps and hindrances of individuals cancel each other, because each conditions the other) we shall be all the readier to return to the position that divine love does not reveal itself unequivocally except where it shows a generally protective and fostering care of what is highest and most specific in man, namely, his God-consciousness. And this, to Christian eyes, seems everywhere outside the sphere of redemption to be in a depressed condition. Thus we again find ourselves in the sphere of the divine self-impartation. So that, even when we are only seeking to exhibit the divine love as beneficent and protective, we cannot as Christians afford to insist on anything less or lower than that impartation of God in Christ and the Holy Spirit whereby the God-consciousness is renewed and made perfect. For even though every form of the God-consciousness, however imperfect (indeed, even its latent presence as something merely longed for), ranks for us as a divine impartation to human nature, it yet is not such that we can rest in it. On the contrary, such a divine impartation viewed from whatever side appears merely as a transitional stage, to which belong only human states that are provisional and imperfect.

2. On the other hand, it is objected to our paragraph, for one thing, that it was not necessary to wait for redemption in order to

---

[1] Cf. § 85, 1.

perceive the divine love even in its character as a divine self-impartation, and for another that it is in the highest degree unsympathetic and ungrateful to find that love solely and exclusively in redemption. Now as regards the first point, people say that an impartation of God occurs in whatever in man can be taken as belonging to the image of God, therefore in reason with all its endowments—nay, in everything on which the original perfection of man is based, as well as in all those germs of spiritual development with which our nature is endowed. To this, it is granted, there certainly also belongs that God-consciousness which underlies piety ; but if we were on that account to bind up the knowledge of divine love with redemption alone, we should be attaching the highest worth of all to what is really less important. For, it is argued, the difference in God's dealings with creatures incapable of God-consciousness, and with such as develop this consciousness even in the feeblest and most imperfect way, is greater by far than that existing between His dealings with the latter and with those whom we call regenerate ; for obviously the difference between the content of the God-consciousness in the last two classes is far less than that between the first two. To this we may reply that in virtue of their capacity for the God-consciousness all men certainly are also objects of the divine love ; but the divine love does not realize itself in them simply as such ; rather, starting from the fear of God (which was, of course, the prevailing religious temper under the law) they at most get through to the negative consciousness that the Supreme Being is devoid of jealousy—which is still very far from being a recognition of the divine love. *That* only comes with the efficacious working of redemption, and it comes from Christ. As for those who still (this we can say in a true sense of the whole non-Christian world) hover between idolatry and godlessness, just in so far as they do not love God, He cannot love them. And thus here, too, we come back to the position that He loves them only as He sees them in Christ, just as it is only when they themselves are in Christ that they come to a knowledge of the divine love.

As regards the second point, it is urged that even if wherever self-consciousness as such includes God-consciousness, the love of God first comes out in redemption, yet elsewhere it reveals itself in much that is exactly the same outside Christianity as within, and pre-eminently in all the triumphs of human knowledge and mastery of Nature. But to this we reply that all human life is to be pervaded by the powers of redemption, and that it is only as so pervaded that it reaches perfection. So that no human good of any kind is conformed to the relevant divine will, except as it is thus brought into connexion with that predominance of the God-consciousness in our soul which we owe to Christ. On the other hand, nothing which does not represent the divine will can reveal the divine love. Our paragraph, therefore, has only to be taken in the sense made inevitable by what went before [1] to justify itself perfectly.

§ 167. *God is Love.*

1 John 4[16].

1. Already it has been stated repeatedly that in God there can be no distinction between essence and attributes, and that just for that reason the conception ' attribute ' is not particularly well fitted to set forth the Divine Essence. Still, this also implies that, in so far as anything true is predicated of God by means of what we posit as a divine attribute, what is thus truly predicated must also express the Divine Essence itself. On this account it must necessarily be possible to form similar propositions, affirming of Him all other attributes, if these as such have any claim to be posited at all. However, no such propositions occur in Scripture, nor has it ever been laid down in Church doctrine that God is eternity, or omnipotence, or the like. And while certainly we might venture to say that God is loving omnipotence or omnipotent love, yet we must admit that in the first of these forms as much as in the second love alone is made the equivalent of the being or essence of God. Hence it is in this exclusive form that our paragraph has to be established and justified, namely, that love alone and no other attribute can be equated thus with God. Only, it is understood that here also we wish to have nothing to do with any conception of God reached by way of speculation, but that what we have to show is merely why this attribute is thus distinguished from the others which we have come to affirm in the course of our argument.

2. To begin with, as regards the attributes which we arrived at in the first part of this work, they made then no claim to rank as such designations of the Divine Essence that they could be substituted for the name ' God.' [2] Even although we explain omnipotence as the attribute in virtue of which all finite things are through God as they are, while we certainly in that case posit the

---

[1] § 164.   [2] Cf. § 56, Postscript.

divine act in its entirety, it is without a motive, and therefore as an action wholly indeterminate in character ; and it can only be incorrectly, and under the influence of quantitative standards of measurement, that we name God omnipotence. The finite as such is not merely a manifold ; it is also something mutable, and is invariably given to us solely in impermanent states or stages of transition. So that the statement in question really conveys nothing but what the finite is through God, as willed and posited by Him ; and unless we pass out beyond the finite sphere we all the time remain uncertain as to the nature of the will of God which as such is implied in omnipotence. The same thing of course holds true of the other divine attributes treated of in the same context. We arrived at each of them by abstraction from the definite feeling-content of our God-consciousness ; hence, if we are not to project them in thought into the attributes yielded by reflection on this feeling-content (as happens in the formula that God is omnipotent or eternal love), but rather to take them strictly by themselves, we are bound to say that belief in God as almighty and eternal is nothing more than that shadow of faith which even devils may have.[1]

Nor are the two attributes (holiness and justice) discussed in our Second Part, under its second aspect, such as originally could stand as expressions of the Divine Essence. For we cannot say that God in Himself is justice or holiness ; for neither of these attributes can be conceived apart from a relation to evil as well as to the antithesis between evil and good. And neither the antithesis nor its solution has any existence for God, considered solely in Himself. Hence the action of these attributes separately from the others is exclusively limited to a certain sphere, and it is only when we cancel this separation and resolve them into those attributes which we are now discussing as the result of the second half of our exposition, that they are recognizable as divine attributes at all. So that what was formerly considered as the work of divine holiness and justice is now properly (even though it be more by way of preparation than of fulfilment) reckoned in as part of the work of redemption. Thus both of these attributes, like the others, merge for us in the divine love, this last viewed solely in its preparatory manifestations ; and the divine love is holy and just love inasmuch as essentially it begins with these preparatory stages ; in the same way it is almighty and eternal love. Love and wisdom alone, then, can claim to be not mere attributes but also expressions of the very essence of

[1] Jas. 2[19].

God, while yet we do not say God is wisdom precisely as we do God is love ; and the point is one which we can elucidate as follows, even before we deal with the conception of wisdom. If we look at the way in which we become aware of the two attributes respectively, it turns out that we have the sense of divine love directly in the consciousness of redemption, and as this is the basis on which all the rest of our God-consciousness is built up, it of course represents to us the essence of God. But the divine wisdom does not enter consciousness thus directly, but only as we extend our self-consciousness (as personal, but even more as racial consciousness) to cover the relation of all the elements of reality to each other. Indeed, since the two attributes cannot be conceived in separation from each other, and since love is not the perfection of wisdom but wisdom the perfection of love, it follows that love would not be implied in so absolute a degree if we thought God as wisdom, as wisdom would be if we thought Him as love. For where almighty love is, there must also absolute wisdom be.

SECOND DOCTRINE : THE DIVINE WISDOM

§ 168. *The divine wisdom is the principle which orders and determines the world for the divine self-imparting which is evinced in redemption.*

1. The special relationship, previously lacking,[1] which is required to justify our positing the divine wisdom as an attribute distinct from the divine omniscience, is found in this connexion of wisdom with the divine love. Yet it remains true that, no less definitely than was brought out in that earlier context, the divine omniscience indicates in God precisely the same as the divine wisdom does ; only that the timeless relation involved naturally has for us a twofold aspect, wisdom being the word that looks forward, omniscience the word that looks backward. Moreover, the latter is in the same relation to the divine love as the former ; all existence being posited in God simply as that which is mediated by His love. All this forms a supplement to what I have written elsewhere [2] for another discipline as to the relation between love and wisdom—in this respect, that the antecedent word is also directly the creative word. From the fact that we take the divine love as being also wisdom it follows, first of all, that we cannot

---

[1] Cf. § 55, p. 221.
[2] In my article on the scientific treatment of the conception of virtue see *Werke*.

possibly regard all finite being in its relation to our God-consciousness except as (whatever else be the meaning we give to the term
' world ') an absolutely harmonious divine work of art.   Even in
human affairs the primary work of wisdom is correctly and completely to outline the idea which the work of art is to embody, so
that actions proper are only traceable to wisdom in proportion as
both in the context of a man's life and in themselves they can be
regarded as works of art or parts thereof ; and he would be the
most perfect man all of whose plans for works or actions formed
a complete whole of self-communicative presentation.   Similarly,
the divine wisdom is nothing but the Supreme Being viewed as
engaged in this absolute (not compositely, but simply and originally, perfect) self-presentation and impartation.[1]   Only we must
think away all division between those two ; there is no distinction
between divine works and acts, nor is it the case that (as with us
men) impartation preponderates in acts, but presentation in works.
It is only for our minds that divine acts are primarily impartation
and then become presentation, and divine works the reverse.   The
sending of Christ, however, is for us primarily divine impartation,
and it is for this reason that the term ' impartation ' is put first.
The growth of our consciousness of the wisdom of God consists in
this, that His impartation in its temporal progress becomes for us
ever more and more a perfect presentation of the almighty love of
God.

Next, we must be on our guard lest we again falsify the conception we have reached, by introducing the contrast of end and
means.   The reason for caution lies in what has just been said.
Every human work of art is the more perfect, the more it conforms
to the idea that elements within it should not be distinguishable
as end and means, but are all reciprocally related as parts to the
whole ; whereas means remain external to it.   In a still higher
degree of perfection, this manifestly applies to a complete human
life.   How then could it be that divine wisdom did not exclude
the contrast of end and means even more completely ?   There is
nothing outside the world which could be used as means ; all
things within it, rather, are so ordered that viewed in connexion
with one another they each stand related as parts to the whole ;
while every particular in itself is so entirely both things—means and
end—that each of these categories is constantly abrogating itself
and passing over into the other.   So generally recognized is this

[1] Acts 17[24-28].

that no one imagines that in God, as distinct from wisdom (taken exclusively as meaning rightness of purpose) there is to be found sagacity as well, in the sense of perfectness in the choice and use of means. Yet it is common enough, and equally confusing, for people to include sagacity as an *additional* element in the idea of divine wisdom, and to interpret wisdom as meaning the divine perfectness alike in the fixing of ends and the determination of means. Means are never employed except where the agent has to have recourse to something not originated by himself. Nor can we easily conceive the determination of means otherwise than in the form of choice, which means reverting to that very mediate knowledge which we discarded. With this is in keeping also the fact that both the wisdom and the omniscience of God are each equivalent to the other and to the divine creativeness, and that we cannot set this equivalence aside without spoiling the conceptions themselves, and *vice versa*.

2. Our recognition of redemption as the real key to the understanding of the divine wisdom is itself the specifically Christian view of this subject. Our Christian consciousness, however expanded, cannot transcend that which stands in relation to us ; and all the divine ordering of the world within this sphere, if we would truly appropriate it, we can only interpret by reference to the revelation of God in Christ and the Holy Spirit. But this ought never to degenerate into an inquisitive search (unfriendly to scientific inquiry) with a view to discovering particular aids to the Kingdom of God in particular events ; for in such a case we should always be dealing merely with transition stages, of whose value for the whole we were utterly ignorant. But we shall do well to be on our guard against ascribing to divine wisdom the divine ordering of external and physical nature, as well as institutions for the all-round development of the human mind, in such a manner as to separate them from the sphere of redemption. Anything wholly out of touch with redemption, and not at the same time totally isolated from human life (a description which would not hold true of any part even of external nature), might just as easily be injurious to the progress of redemption, and in that case would not be pre-formed by the divine wisdom. How could we think we had fathomed the divine wisdom, if we had no better grasp of its manifestations than to suppose that, even if only occasionally, it could conflict with the highest interests of man ? Hence everything in the world, in proportion as it is attributed to divine wisdom, must also be related to the redemptive or

new-creating revelation of God. Thus the proper work of divine wisdom is precisely the spread of redemption ; or, to put it otherwise, it is on the one hand the mode and the order in which election is carried out, and the regeneration of individuals as well as of whole masses of humanity effected, and on the other hand the changing transformation of the Christian fellowship, as often as living Christian piety enters, or ought to enter, into combination with this or that new aspect of human experience. Hence every effort to penetrate those depths of the divine wisdom still hidden from us, is in itself to be approved. Nor does it cease to be praiseworthy though at times it tends to go too much into detail (for what may be regarded as detail in the sphere of divine grace is not too small to be considered an object of divine wisdom) ; it is censurable only when we obscure the absolute unity of divine wisdom by introducing the contrast of end and means.

§ 169. *Theorem.—The divine wisdom is the ground in virtue of which the world, as the scene of redemption, is also the absolute revelation of the Supreme Being, and is therefore good.*

1. This proposition, which we indicated at an earlier point [1] but can only now set forth, and which rather summarizes in sharper outline what has already been said than contains anything new, makes in essence the demand that we should not look for a larger divine impartation than has been effected in the human race by means of redemption through Christ. And in this sense it has to be tested first by two propositions, which we find at either end of this Second Part of our exposition. In the first place, sin invariably brings with it a diminution of the God-consciousness, and therefore of the divine impartation. Now if we suppose a real condition of purity or even of moral and spiritual perfection to have existed before sin (a condition which might or might not be interrupted by sin), our paragraph would compel us to suppose that if no fall had taken place, no redemption would have been necessary, which means that the impartation of the Divine Essence would have been less than is now the case, owing to the presence not only of sin but of redemption. In the second place, as long as the unregenerate live here in company with the pious, they too experience gleams of blessedness through the God-consciousness latent in them ; and these make their presence felt powerfully as preparatory workings of grace. Now if we suppose that all who had not thus attained

[1] See § 59, Postscript.

to regeneration would have to bear an eternity of unmitigated wretchedness in hell, our paragraph would compel us to assert that even so the sum-total of the divine impartation would be larger than if the regeneration of those also who in this life had not been brought so far, had remained a possibility after death.

2. These implications of our paragraph we must consider from yet another side. If Christ be placed at the summit, as the individual who was entirely pervaded by the God-consciousness and therefore taken up into full unity with the Highest, everywhere else there exists only an imperfect and unequal pervasion, which decreases steadily within the sphere of rational being throughout the various areas in which corporate life is being prepared for redemption, and in irrational and inanimate nature (if this be taken as having independent existence) wholly disappears. And yet, according to our paragraph, this limited and sporadic impartation of the Supreme Being is the whole outcome in which the divine wisdom exhausts itself and the divine love finds complete satisfaction. In that case, we cannot but be extremely doubtful whether the non-rational and non-conscious is to be taken as in itself an object of the divine love merely on the ground that we find it within the domain ordered by the divine wisdom ; or whether it is excluded even from the divine wisdom since it can have no part in the divine love. For the plea that reason needs all these different stages of subordinate being as a substructure for its own life, is always unsatisfying ; it means that here the divine wisdom is assumed to be conditioned. Hence we must add, that whatever in itself is insusceptible of divine impartation shall yet be brought into vital connexion with that in which such impartation can dwell. Thence it follows that so long as this vital connexion is not in operation all round, so long as the Spirit is not yet expressing and presenting itself somehow even in all that is non-rational, the divine wisdom cannot exhibit itself as everywhere present. But when through us the world is become fully ready for us, it will appear clearly that nothing can really *be* save as it is also an object of the divine love.

3. It is only thus, by relation to the divine love, that the divine attributes expounded in the First Part gain their full significance. The divine wisdom, as the unfolding of the divine love, conducts us here to the realm of Christian Ethics ; for we are now confronted with the task of more and more securing recognition for the world as a good world, as also of forming all things into an organ of the divine Spirit in harmony with the divine idea originally underlying

the world-order, thus bringing all into unity with the system of redemption.   The purpose of this is that in both respects we may attain to perfect living fellowship with Christ, both in so far as the Father has given Him power over all things and in so far as He ever shows Him greater works than those He already knows.   Hence the world can be viewed as a perfect revelation of divine wisdom only in proportion as the Holy Spirit makes itself felt through the Christian Church as the ultimate world-shaping power.

CONCLUSION

THE DIVINE TRINITY

§ 170. *All that is essential in this Second Aspect of the Second Part of our exposition is also posited in what is essential in the doctrine of the Trinity ; but this doctrine itself, as ecclesiastically framed, is not an immediate utterance concerning the Christian self-consciousness, but only a combination of several such utterances.*

Symb. Quic. : Fides autem catholica haec est, ut unum Deum in trinitate et trinitatem in unitate veneremur.—*Conf. Aug.* i. : 'Firstly we teach . . . according to the decree of the Nicene Council that there is one single Divine Essence . . . and yet in the same single Divine Essence there are three Persons, equal in power, equal in eternity, etc.'—*Exp. simpl.* iii. : Eundem nihilominus Deum . . . credimus . . . personis inseparabiliter et inconfuse esse distinctum, Patrem, Filium et Spiritum sanctum, etc.—*Conf. Gallic.* vi. : Scriptura nos docet, in illa singulari et simplice essentiâ divinâ subsistere tres personas, Patrem, Filium et Spiritum sanctum.—*Conf. Hung.* : Hunc unum et solum Deum tres in coelo testes Patrem, Filium et Sp. s. esse credimus : qui, licet tres sint subsistentibus suis proprietatibus et officiis dispensatoriis, tamen hi tres unum quoque sunt.

1. An essential element of our exposition in this Part has been the doctrine of the union of the Divine Essence with human nature, both in the personality of Christ and in the common Spirit of the Church ; [1] therewith the whole view of Christianity set forth in our Church teaching stands and falls. For unless the being of God in Christ is assumed, the idea of redemption could not be thus concentrated in His Person. And unless there were such a union also in the common Spirit of the Church, the Church could not thus be the Bearer and Perpetuator of the redemption through Christ. Now these exactly are the essential elements in the doctrine of the Trinity, which, it is clear, only established itself in defence of the position that in Christ there was present nothing less than the Divine Essence, which also indwells the Christian Church as its common Spirit, and that we take these expressions in no reduced or sheerly artificial sense, and know nothing of any special higher essences, subordinate deities (as it were) present in Christ and the

[1] Cf. § 94 and § 123.

Holy Spirit. The doctrine of the Trinity has no origin but this ;
and at first it had no other aim than to equate as definitely as
possible the Divine Essence considered as thus united to human
nature with the Divine Essence in itself. This is the less doubtful
that those Christian sects which interpret the doctrine of redemption
differently are also necessarily without the doctrine of the Trinity—
they have no point of belief to which it could be attached—which
could not possibly be the case if even in Catholic doctrine there
existed at least some other points than this to which the attachment could be made. It is equally clear from this why those
divergent sects which are chiefly distinguishable by their denial of
the Trinity are not thereby forced into still other divergences in the
doctrine of God and the divine attributes, as must have been the
case if the doctrine of the Trinity were rooted in a special view of
the nature of the Supreme Being as such. But on the other hand,
they *are* forced to set up a different theory of the Person of Christ,
and hence also of man's need for redemption and of the value of
redemption. In virtue of this connexion, we rightly regard the
doctrine of the Trinity, in so far as it is a deposit of these elements,
as the coping-stone of Christian doctrine, and this equating with
each other of the divine in each of these two unions, as also of both
with the Divine Essence in itself, as what is essential in the doctrine
of the Trinity.

2. But at this point we would call a halt ; we cannot attach the
same value to the further elaboration of the dogma, which alone
justifies the ordinary term. For the term ' Trinity ' is really based
on the fact that each of the two above-mentioned unions is traced
back to a separate distinction posited independently of such union,
and eternally, in the Supreme Being as such ; further, after the
member of this plurality destined to union with Jesus had been
designated by the name ' Son,' it was felt necessary to posit the
Father in accordance therewith as a special distinction. The
result was the familiar dualism—unity of Essence and trinity of
Persons. But the assumption of an eternal distinction in the
Supreme Being is not an utterance concerning the religious consciousness, for there it never could emerge. Who would venture to say
that the impression made by the divine in Christ obliges us to conceive such an eternal distinction as its basis ? Anyone who were
to find this task set us in the Johannine conception of the Logos, as
if that conception definitely included one element of the doctrine
of the Trinity and the completion of the doctrine were called for by

that simple fact, would be in so difficult a position that he could hardly maintain his ground. For one thing, it is in this very passage that Arianism sought a foothold ; and the exegesis of both sides in that controversy is so exposed to equal though opposite objections that we cannot help saying that if either of the two antagonistic views was in John's mind as fundamental to the passage, it must be confessed that he went to work to express it in a highly unsatis-factory and ineffective manner. On the other hand, if the Trinity had been in the Apostle's mind, his exposition would very easily have lent itself to a similar introduction of the Holy Spirit, whose name occurs so often in Christ's discourses as reported by John ; nor would he have lacked opportunity elsewhere to bring in this other member, and to speak of the place of the Spirit as that which was in the beginning with God and was God. Assuming, however, that John here declares of the divine united in Christ with human nature that it existed in God from all eternity in a distinct form, it does not follow by any means that this was meant in the sense of the doctrine of the Trinity, and that that doctrine is therefore the true and the only natural completion of the Johannine statements. For underlying the elaboration of the doctrine is not merely a desire to reproduce very exactly our Christian consciousness that the Divine Essence in both forms of union is the same, and also is equal to the being of God *per se* ; rather, it was only after the dis-tinction had been eternalized and made antecedent to the union that there arose a need to guard against the semblance of polytheism, and to secure that this, in a sense separated, being of God was none the less embraced within the unity of the Divine Essence. But of such a need there is in John no trace whatever, which means that he was not on the way to the doctrine of the Trinity as we have it.

3. Hence the second part of our paragraph must not be under-stood as meaning that the orthodox doctrine of the Trinity is to be regarded as an immediate or even a necessary combination of utterances concerning the Christian self-consciousness. On the contrary, the intermediate step has been taken of eternalizing, in separation, the being of God in itself, and the being of God which makes union with human nature possible. Now if this arose so definitely out of the utterances of Christ Himself and of the Apostles concerning Him that we had to accept it on their testimony, the doctrine of the Trinity in that case would be a fully elaborated doctrine of this type, and we should accept it as a combination of testimonies regarding a supersensible fact ; but it would no more

be a ' doctrine of faith ' in the really original and proper sense of that phrase than the doctrines of the resurrection and ascension of Christ ; [1] and it would resemble these last also in this respect that our faith in Christ and our living fellowship with Him would be the same although we had no knowledge of any such transcendent fact, or although the fact itself were different.   But the exegesis meant to establish the position just mentioned has never been able to entrench itself so strongly as to escape constant attacks upon it. Hence it is important to make the point that the main pivots of the ecclesiastical doctrine—the being of God in Christ and in the Christian Church—are independent of the doctrine of the Trinity.

Let it be supposed that we further elaborate our knowledge of this supersensible fact and—to avoid the idea that the said distinction within the Supreme Being led to nothing up to the beginning of the union—teach besides that both the Second and the Third Person in the Trinity were implicated even in the creation of the world, while the Second Person was also the subject thereafter of all the Old Testament theophanies, and it was from the Third Person that the whole prophetic movement of the Old Testament received its impulse.   Then these statements are still further removed from being utterances about our Christian consciousness.   And we can wait all the more calmly to see whether the exegetical results on which these expansions of the doctrine rest are any more fully confirmed by the latest work on the subject than has hitherto been the case.

Postscript.—If success ever had attended, or ever could attend, the attempt to exhibit or prove a trinity in God from general conceptions or *a priori* (an effort perhaps stimulated by Church doctrine, apart from which it would hardly occur to anyone, but yet without any relation to the facts of redemption or any appeal to Scripture), still such a doctrine of the Trinity even though worked out with much greater elaboration than the ecclesiastical doctrine (bound up as it is with the basal facts of Christianity) has ever obtained or ever could obtain, could find no place in a Christian Dogmatic.   Even although it kept strictly to the use of the same terms in denoting both the trinity and the unity as are employed in the ecclesiastical doctrine, we should firmly maintain that as a doctrine it was different.   For deductions of that kind, standing in no connexion with those basal facts, do not merely show it to be quite different from the other in origin ; on that very account they are of no sort of use in Christian doctrine.   Therefore we must

---

[1] Cf. § 99.

simply put them aside as ' philosophemes ' ; nor are we in any way called upon to submit them to criticism, whether they originate with ancient [1] or modern [2] Church teachers.

§ 171. *The ecclesiastical doctrine of the Trinity demands that we think of each of the three Persons as equal to the Divine Essence, and* vice versa, *and each of the three Persons as equal to the others. Yet we cannot do either the one or the other, but can only represent the Persons in a gradation, and thus either represent the unity of the Essence as less real than the three Persons, or* vice versa.

Symb. Quic. : Fides autem catholica haec est ut unum deum in trinitate, et trinitatem in unitate veneremur.—Patris, filii et spiritus sancti una est divinitas, aequalis gloria, aequalis maiestas.—Et in hac trinitate nihil prius aut posterius nihil maior aut minus, sed totae tres personae coaeternae sibi sunt et coaequales. . . . Neque confundentes personas neque separantes substantiam.—*Augs. Conf.* I. : ' That there is one Divine Essence, which is named and truly is God, and yet in this same one Divine Essence there are three Persons. . . . And by the word Person is understood not a part, not an attribute inhering in something else, but what subsists in itself (sed quod proprie subsistit), as the Fathers have used the word in this matter.'—*Conf. Belg.* viii. : . . . qui est unica essentia, in qua tres sunt personae incommunicabilibus proprietatibus ab aeterno revera ac reipsa distinctae.

1. There can be no doubt that from this assumption of eternal distinctions in the Divine Essence, there necessarily follows the implication of the double equality of the divine in all three Persons, and of the divine in each Person with the Supreme Being as a unity. If divinity or power and glory were less in all the three Persons together than in the Supreme Being conceived as a unity, the three Persons would not be in but under the Supreme Being. In that case, the divine in them would only improperly be called divine, and our living fellowship with Christ as well as our participation in the Holy Spirit would not be fellowship with God. The result would be the same if the divine in the Persons themselves were not the same, only the divine in (say) the Father being truly and properly divine, but the divine in Christ and the Holy Spirit unreal and subordinate. In that case our indwelling sense of need for redemption would necessarily take a different form of expression, if indeed as a hindrance to fellowship to God it would in any way be met by a redemption which did not bring us to fellowship with God. In short, everything most important in Christianity

---

[1] *E.g.* Anselm, *Monolog.* ep. 29–61.
[2] *E.g.* Daub, *Theolog.*, §§ 126, 127.

would be changed. On those assumptions, no other definition can be reached than that posited by the ecclesiastical doctrine, and the ever-renewed zeal shown in its defence is perfectly intelligible.

2. The cited credal passages undeniably assert, to begin with, that power and divinity is not less in any of the three Persons than in the other two ; and this obviously would be sufficient to bar out all inequalities, if it were not for the inconsistency which emerges as soon as side by side with this equality the attempt is made to perpetuate the method of distinguishing the Persons. For it is then necessary to make this equality a canon to be followed in setting forth the difference between the Persons, in the sense that no element implying an inequality of the kind described can be admitted. If, however, Father and Son are distinguished by the fact that the Father eternally begets, but is Himself unbegotten, while the Son is begotten from all eternity but not Himself begetting, then (although this eternal generation is as different as possible from any generation that is temporal or organic in character), the term itself, if it means anything at all, must at least indicate a relationship of dependence. Hence if power has dwelt in the Father from all eternity to beget the Son as a second divine Person, whereas in the Son no such power dwells, and no relationship of dependence in which the Father stands to Him can be adduced as a counterweight, undeniably the power of the Father is greater than that of the Son, and in addition the glory which the Begetter has with the Begotten must be greater than that which the Begotten has with the Begetter.

The same holds true of the Spirit, whether as in the Greek dogma He proceeds from the Father only, or, as the Latin Church teaches, from the Father and the Son. In the former case, the Son has a twofold incapacity as compared with the Father : He does not beget, nor does a Person proceed from Him. In the latter case the Spirit alone exhibits this twofold dependence—for ' procession ' too is a relation of dependence, though meant to be a different one from being begotten, in spite of the fact that no one has ever succeeded in making clear what the difference between the two is. In this case, however, the Son has one capacity in common with the Father which places Him above the Spirit, whereas in the former case the Spirit is equal to the Son. Whichever way we take it, then, the Father is superior to the other two Persons, and the only subject of controversy is whether these two are equal to each other, or one of them subordinate to the other. But if such distinctions are made, the equality of the Persons is lost.

3. Similarly, the position that the divinity in all the three Persons is the same with that of the one Divine Essence ought to be the rule which controls our ideas of the relationship between the trinity of the Persons and the unity of the Essence. But if we are to take along with this what has just been dealt with, namely, the position that the Persons are distinguished from each other by peculiar properties not predicable of the Divine Essence in itself, while the Divine Essence itself has existence only in these three Persons, but not outside or apart from them (whether as a fourth Person or impersonally), and even in them does not distribute different attributes to different Persons,[1] but resides in each Person whole and undivided, on such terms the desired equality cannot result. For such a relationship as is here asserted we have no closer analogy, on which to form our thought of it, than that of the conception of a species with the individual members it contains ; for the conception of a species is similarly present whole and undivided in its individuals, but nowhere outside them. It is true, this has always been a moot point ; some thinkers admit the analogy,[2] others reject it.[3] But if the relationship is not to be conceived as of this type, then, as even its opponents allow,[4] we really are not in a position to form any definite ideas on the subject, and hence can have no interest in it. If, on the other hand, we do adopt the analogy, no equality is possible between the unity and the trinity ; either more realistically we must make the unity superordinate as the essence common to all three, in which case the distinction of Persons appears subordinate and falls into the background, while the divine *monarchia* stands out ; or more nominalistically we must make the trinity superordinate, in which case the unity as being abstract falls into the background. Then what has immediate existence for our religious consciousness—namely, the

---

[1] Passages like the following : . . . filium eius (*sc.* patris) sapientiam . . . spiritum s. eiusdem virtutem potentiam et efficaciam (*Conf. Gallic.* vi.), even if credal, are too vague to be taken into account.

[2] Τὸ οὐσία φύσιν σημαίνει, τὸ δὲ ὑπόστασις ἰδιότητας (Greg. Naz., *Encom. Athan.*). Ὁν ἔχει λόγον τὸ κοινὸν πρὸς τὸ ἴδιον, τοῦτον ἔχει ἡ οὐσία πρὸς τὴν ὑπόστασιν (Basil, *Ep.* ccxiv.). Κατά γε τὴν τῶν πατέρων διδασκαλίαν, ἣν ἔχει διαφορὰν τὸ κοινὸν ὑπὲρ τὸ ἴδιον, ἢ τὸ γένος ὑπὲρ τὸ εἶδος ἢ τὸ ἄτομον, ταύτην ἡ οὐσία πρὸς τὴν ὑπόστασιν ἔχει (Theodoret, *Dial. I.* ed. Hal. iv. p. 7).

[3] Non itaque secundum genus et species ista dicimus. . . . Nec sic ergo Trinitatem dicimus tres personas unam essentiam tanquam ex una materia tria quaedam subsistant (Augustine, *de Trin.* vii. 11).

[4] . . . propter ineffabilem coniunctionem haec tria simul unus Deus (Augustine, *ibid.* 8).

divinity of the Holy Spirit and the divinity of Christ, as also the
relation of Christ as Son to the Father—comes to the front ; but
so, too, does the danger of falling into tritheism. Between these
two lines of thought (for we must always start either from the
unity or from the trinity) no genuinely middle course seems possible
which would not really be an approximation to one or the other.
But from our assumptions neither the subordination of the unity
to the trinity nor the converse follows ; hence as regards the distinctions existing in the Supreme Being from all eternity there is
nothing for it but either to accept one of the two courses indicated,
which conflicts with what the credal passages insist on, or, if we
shrink from what they insist on, to conclude that it is impossible
for us definitely to reach either point—the unity or the trinity ;
we remain hesitating between the two.[1] In these circumstances
the doctrine can do little to secure those two main points (which
alone are in question), or to place them in a clearer light.

4. It still remains to show how unity and trinity are related to
the divine causality (apprehended in our self-conscious feeling of
absolute dependence) alike in redemption and sanctification and
generally in creation and preservation. The divine causality must
not be divided between the Persons, however natural it might be to
say that the Father alone is Creator and Preserver, the Son alone
Redeemer, and the Spirit alone Sanctifier. And if it is to be kept
undivided, we reach here the same conclusion as before, either that
these causalities all belong to the one Divine Essence as such, and
to the Persons only in so far as they are in the Essence, but not in
so far as they are distinct from each other, or they belong to the
three Persons as such, and to the unity of the Essence only in so far
as it consists of the Persons. The former view failed to establish
itself, obviously because in it the trinity falls more into the background than was permitted by the ruling tendencies of the time ; [2]
for it may almost be said that the Persons have reality only in the
previously mentioned special acts. The Father is real, in so far as
He begets the Son from all eternity, but creation and preservation
would appertain solely to the unity of the Divine Essence. The
Son, it is true, would not be merely begotten, or the Spirit merely

---

[1] Οὐ φθάνω τὸ ἓν νοῆσαι καὶ τοῖς τρισὶ περιλάμπομαι. οὐ φθάνω τὰ τρία διελεῖν, καὶ
εἰς τὸ ἓν ἀναφέρομαι (Greg. Naz., l.c.).

[2] That the tendency of Church teaching tends to emphasize the Persons
rather than the unity of the Essence may be seen clearly enough from the
following words of the *Symb. Quic.*, 19 : Sicut singillatim unamquamque
personam et deum et dominum confiteri christianâ veritate *compellimur*, ita
tres deos aut dominos dicere catholica religione *prohibemur*.

breathed into being, for the former also became man and the latter
was also poured forth ; but the justifying divine activity would
not be that solely of the Son or the sanctifying divine activity that
of the Spirit ; both would belong to the unity of the Divine Essence.
Hence the second view came to be accepted universally, that the
whole divine causality belongs to the three Persons ; but the form
it took in ecclesiastical doctrine appears to suffer from a hidden
contradiction.   For if the divine causality belongs to the Persons
as such, it belongs to each of them in so far as distinct from the
others ; and hence the same causality is, in the first Person, that of
the Unbegotten, in the second that of the Begotten, and thus is in
each case triple, because issuing in each case from that which is
personally distinctive, though but one in effect ; much as Christ
executes the same thing with His two wills, the three Persons execute
the same thing each in its own way, and thus each by its own act.
This consistent scheme, however, failed to commend itself, obviously
because the divine unity is obscured in a wholly nominalistic way,
and almost nothing is left for it but to represent the equality of the
three in essence and will.   On the other hand, the accepted view
that those causalities do indeed belong to the three Persons as such,
but that each causality is one and the same in all three, and not a
peculiar causality in each, means that the causality is really traced
back, not to the Persons, but after all to the Divine Essence in its
unity.   Thus, once the eternal trinity in the unity is assumed, from
this angle we arrive simply at the same difficulty as before, of
choosing between the preponderance of the one and the subordination of the other, or *vice versa.*

5. If we now consider the manner in which this doctrine is
handled almost everywhere in dogmatic expositions, it becomes
still clearer to how slight an extent what is insisted on in general
formulæ may be given effect to in the developed statement.   In the
first place, the doctrine of the Essence and attributes of God is
treated apart from the trinity, God being considered in His unity.
Here, however, the particular attribute under consideration is not
shown within the unity, as triply divided or separated in a definite
way.   Instead, the doctrine of the Persons is later treated of by
itself, apart from any such connexion and without being prepared
for by the consciousness of the being of God in Christ. and in the
Christian Church.   It is so treated of, however, that when it is
shown that this or that attribute also belongs to the three Persons,
the proof is specially led only for the Son and the Spirit, while that

it belongs to the Father is usually held to be self-evident.   But if the equality of the Persons is asserted not merely as a formula but as an operative rule, such self-evidence must hold either of all three Persons or of none.   The pre-eminence given to the Father in this respect proves that He is after all conceived as standing in a different relation to the unity of the Essence ; so that those who feel it to be superfluous to prove that divine attributes and activities belong to the Father, while they insist on proof for the Son and the Spirit, are all of them far from being strict Trinitarians ; for they identify the Father with the unity of the Divine Essence, but not the Son or the Spirit.   This can be traced right back to the idea of Origen, that the Father is God absolutely, while Son and Spirit are God only by participation in the Divine Essence [1]—an idea which is positively rejected by orthodox Church teachers, but secretly underlies their whole procedure.

§ 172.   *We have the less reason to regard this doctrine as finally settled since it did not receive any fresh treatment when the Evangelical (Protestant) Church was set up ; and so there must still be in store for it a transformation which will go back to its very beginnings.*

1. If we reflect, on the one hand, that the formulæ now accepted in the doctrine of the Trinity originated at a time when Christendom was still being recruited by mass-conversion from heathendom, and consider how easily, when it became necessary to speak of a plurality or distinction in God, unconscious echoes of what is pagan could find their way in, it is not surprising that the descriptions of such plurality should from the start have been vacillating and liable to misconception, and such as were no longer suited to later times, when no further admixture of heathenism was to be feared.   Cautions could not but be attached to the use of such descriptions, to guard against aberrations on different sides ; but even so it is seldom that such cautions do not approximate to one extreme in seeking to guard against the other.   Also they must lose their value once the danger of misunderstanding to which they relate has disappeared, and in that case the sinister suggestion they contain of the opposite error will come out all the more emphatically.   If we take the original tendency of the doctrine, namely, to make clear that it is no hyperbolical expression of our consciousness of Christ and of the

---

[1] αὐτόθεος ὁ θεός ἐστι . . . πᾶν δὲ τὸ παρὰ τὸ αὐτόθεος μετοχῇ τῆς ἐκείνου θεότητος θεοποιούμενον κτλ. *Comm. in Joann.* (ed. R. iv. p. 50), where the connexion puts it beyond doubt that αὐτόθεος is the Father.   Cf. *de princ.* i. vol. i. p. 62.

common Spirit of the Church to assert that God is in both, the first task of the doctrine is clearly this—to define this peculiar being of God in that which is other, in its relation both to the being of God in Himself and to the being of God in relation to the world in general. And obviously there is no prospect of ever so accomplishing this task that a formula adequate for all time could be constructed, and every departure therefrom repudiated as unchristian. We have only to do with the God-consciousness given in our self-consciousness along with our consciousness of the world ; hence we have no formula for the being of God in Himself as distinct from the being of God in the world, and should have to borrow any such formula from speculation, and so prove ourselves disloyal to the character of the discipline at which we are working. Further, if we feel that our dogmatic expressions for the relation of God to the world inevitably suffer in every case from faults of anthropomorphism, how could we suppose that we should have more success with the more intricate task of distinguishing the peculiar being of God in Christ as an individual, and in the Christian Church as an historical whole, from the omnipotent presence of God in the world in general, of which these are parts ? Rather we shall have to put up with the fact that the problem can only be solved approximately, and that formulæ which have antagonistic points of departure must always remain opposed in tendency ; for interest in the problem is bound always to spring up afresh.

2. This being so, it might seem very surprising that while so many other problems of later origin have been solved in a tolerably satisfactory way, precisely this one, so comprehensive in character, has remained so long stationary at the very unsatisfactory point to which it was brought at (so to say) the first rush. But the fact is, those later questions—particularly that of the Person of Christ and of the gracious operations of the Spirit—dealt with the same subject on the side next to the direct interests of faith ; and the Trinitarian definitions proper (all the more that they were made fundamental in the discussions just referred to) had to remain as they had already come to be, in spite of the undeniable fact that impassioned polemical zeal—so prone to error—had had only too large a share in their construction. But if the doctrine of the Trinity is not even yet free from vacillations as indicated above between equality and subordination on the one hand, and on the other between Tritheism and such a Unitarianism as must obscure all over again what was felt to be of the very first importance, namely, the eternal

distinctness of the Persons, we ought not to feel too much surprise
that anti-trinitarian opinions should ever and again emerge and
should occasionally gain ground ; nor ought we to be precipitate
in condemnation. It is here as with the doctrine of God in general :
many not merely profess to be but actually think they are opposed
to every belief in God, when in fact they are simply repelled by
ordinary presentations of the subject, but have by no means parted
with all those spiritual affections which spring from the God-consciousness. Similarly, it is natural that people who cannot reconcile
themselves to the difficulties and imperfections that cling to the
formulæ current in Trinitarian doctrine should say that they re-
pudiate everything connected with it, whereas in point of fact their
piety is by no means lacking in the specifically Christian stamp.
This is the case often enough at the present moment not only in
the Unitarian societies of England and America, but also among
the scattered opponents of the doctrine of the Trinity in our own
country. That circumstance supplies a further reason why we
should strive to secure freedom for a thoroughgoing criticism of the
doctrine in its older form, so as to prepare the way for, and introduce,
a reconstruction of it corresponding to the present condition of
other related doctrines.

3. The position assigned to the doctrine of the Trinity in the
present work is perhaps at all events a preliminary step towards
this goal. One who is a believer in the ecclesiastical sense of that
word can scarcely arm himself with the equanimity needful alike
for an impartial criticism of the old procedure and for a new construction, until he has become convinced that it is possible for our
faith in the divine present in Christ and in the Christian communion
to find fit theological expression, even before anything has been
heard of those more exact definitions which go to form the doctrine
of the Trinity. But this independence of mind can never attain to
clearness so long as that doctrine is dealt with before the chief points
of faith just mentioned ; for that arrangement of topics only too
easily leads to an impression (utterly contradicted by the history
of the Church) that acceptance of the doctrine of the Trinity is the
necessary precondition of faith in redemption and in the founding
of the Kingdom of God by means of the divine in Christ and in the
Holy Spirit. Not to speak of the fact that the theological character
of the entire presentation is distorted, and that neither the criticism
nor the points of attachment needed for the new construction can
be placed on a right foundation if the doctrine in question (which

is not directly a statement about our Christian consciousness at all) is set up as a fundamental doctrine, and therefore, of course, arrived at in a speculative way. The same speculative tone then comes to be imported into the doctrine of the Redeemer and of the Holy Spirit, as being dependent on the doctrine of the Trinity ; and thus the door is opened wide to the influx of speculative elements.

We ought not, however, to rest satisfied with this preliminary step ; we must at least give some indications of what yet remains to do. And on the present state of the question we may base, I think, the following reflections. The first unsolved difficulty lies in the relation of the unity of the Essence to the trinity of the Persons ; and here everything depends on the original and eternal existence of distinctions within the Divine Essence. Hence it would first be necessary to inquire whether this idea is so clearly and definitely present in passages of the New Testament that we are bound to regard it as a self-descriptive utterance of Christ and of the divine Spirit that guided the thinking of the Apostles. Of this there can scarcely be a better test than to ask whether these passages could not also be explained by the Sabellian view set up in opposition to our ecclesiastical interpretation. If this question must be answered in the negative, nothing is left but to try whether the ecclesiastical doctrine could not, without injury to the essential presuppositions mentioned above, be stated in formulæ which should not contradict the Biblical passages and yet should avoid the rocks on which the ecclesiastical presentation comes to grief. If, on the other hand, the question can be answered affirmatively, so that it is no longer possible to hold that the ecclesiastical doctrine, even if not purely exegetical in origin, can at least be sustained by purely exegetical proof, then the Athanasian hypothesis is simply on a par with the Sabellian ; and the question must be raised whether the latter cannot render us equal service, without involving us in equally insoluble difficulties. In other words, the question is whether formulæ cannot be devised which, without asserting eternal distinctions in the Supreme Being, are yet equally capable of exhibiting in their truth both unions of the Essence with human nature. Only, no mutability must thereby be ascribed to the Supreme Being ; and although the activities of the Supreme Being in effecting the unions are represented as taking place in time, this must be done no otherwise than we do it everywhere else ; for we cannot conceive the divine causality otherwise than as decree in its eternity, while yet we cannot represent its fulfilment otherwise than as in

time.   The second difficulty suggested by the ecclesiastical doctrine
was this, that the designation of the First Person as Father, as well
as the relations of the First Person to the other two Persons, seems
rather to set forth the relation of the Persons to the unity of the
Essence than to be consistent with the equality of the three Persons.
Here the question really comes to be, whether it was right at the
outset to give the name ' Son of God ' solely to the divine in Christ,
and to relate the term ' Father ' to one of the distinctions in the
Divine Essence and not rather to the unity of the Divine Essence as
such.   If it transpires that by ' Son of God ' Scripture always and
exclusively means the whole Christ Himself, and recognizes no difference between ' God,' as denoting the Supreme Being, and ' the Father
of our Lord Jesus Christ,' but uses the latter name in exactly the
same sense as the former, we should then have to try whether a
similar question might not be raised with regard to the Holy Spirit,
with a similar answer, leading to such forms of statement as would
solve our second difficulty.   If the results of both problems combined in one, a new construction could easily be arrived at ; if
otherwise, we should have to seek new solutions, as we could, of
the remaining differences.   This is of itself a sufficient explanation
why we are here unable to go beyond these indications in such
a way as to complete the whole task.

INDEXES

A. SUBJECTS

Dogmatic propositions, 78 ff. ; two-fold value of, 83 ff. ; collocation of, 85 ff. ; three forms of, 125 f., 140 f., 265 ff., 369.

Dogmatics, definition of, 3 ff. ; forms of, 88 ; as a science, 88 ff. ; method of, 94 ff. ; system of, 112 ff. ; language and arrangement of, 118 ff. ; contents of, 136 ; sources of, 137.

Doing, or action, 7 ff.

Eastern Church, 78, 101.

Ebionism, 99 ff., 396, 398.

Election, 533 ff., 536 ff. ; grounds of, 551 f.

Error, removal of, 691 f.

Eschatology, 703 ff.

Essence, in doctrine of Trinity, 395.

Eternity, of God, 201 ff.

Ethics, 3 f. ; Christian, 111, 516, 584 f.

Evangelical Church, see Protestantism.

Evil, 184 ff. ; and sin, 243 f., 320 ff., 434 ; doctrine of, 315 ff. ; as punishment, 317 ff., 347 ff. ; and divine causality, 338 ff.

Exaltation, of Christ, 473 ff.

Exegesis, 92 f.

Faith, 10 ; in Jesus, 68 ff., 483.

Fall, the, 292 ff.

Falling away, 513 f.

Feeling, 6 ff., and passim.

Fellowship, essential to religion, 26 ff. ; varieties of, 31 ff. ; in the Church, 525 f., 561 ff. ; with Christ, 651 ff.

Flesh, the, 272 ff.

Foreknowledge, 552 ff.

Fore-ordination, see Predestination.

Forgiveness, of sins, 496 ff., 515 ff., 651 ff.

Freedom, 14 ff., 132 f., 189 ff., 334 ; in God, 216 f. ; human, and divine foreknowledge, 227 f.

Free will, 293.

God, the Whence of our existence, 16 ff. ; eternity of, 201 ff. ; holiness of, 341 ff., 731 ; infinity of, 230 f. ; justice of, 345 ff., 731 ; love of, 726 ff. ; mercy of, 353 f. ; omnipotence of, 201 ff., 211 ff., 730 f. ; omnipresence of, 202 f., 206 ff. ; omniscience of, 202 f., 219 ff. ; unchangeability of, 206 ; unity of, 229 f. ; will of, 216 ff. ; wrath of, 350 ; see also Divine Attributes and Trinity.

God-consciousness, 17, 47, 55, and passim.

Godlessness, 54 f., 135 f.

Good-pleasure, of God, 555 ff.

Good Works, 517 ff. ; reward of, 521 f.

Government, divine, 117 f., 531, 723 ff.

Government, secular, 470 ff.

Grace, 262 ff., and passim.

Greek philosophy, 62.

Hardening, 311 f.

Heathenism, 60 f., 100.

Heresy, 95 ff.

Heterodoxy, 110.

High Priest, Christ as, 451 ff., 659.

Holiness, of God, 341 ff., 731.

Holy Scripture, 75 f. ; as test of doctrine, 112 ff., 588, 591 ff., 606 ff.

Holy Spirit, 490 f. ; communication of, 533 ff., 560 ff. ; in the New Testament, 562 f. ; and Christ's departure, 565 ff. ; as a common Spirit, 569 ff., 612 ; all believers share in, 574 ff. ; and Scripture, 597 ff. ; in Trinity, 738 ff. ; sin against, 310 f.

Human nature, 63 f.

Humiliation, of Christ, 473 ff.

Idol-worship, 34 ff., 135.

Immensity, of God, 210 f.

Immortality, of Christ, 416, 700 f. ; of Christians, 542 ff., 698 ff. ; conditional, 545, 701.

Impersonality, of Christ's human nature, 402 f.

Independence, of God, 218 f.

Individual, 47.

Infallibility, of the Church, 687 ff.

Infinity, of God, 230 f.

Inspiration, 75 f. ; of Scripture, 597 ff.

Intermediate State, 711 f.

Judaism, 37, 43 f., 49, 60 ff., 100, 115, 133, 157, 321, 387.

Judgment, final, 417 ff., 713 ff.

Justice, of God, 345 ff., 731.

Justification, 478 ff., 496 ff.

Keys, power of, 590, 660 ff.

King, Christ as, 466 ff., 660 ff.

Knowing, or knowledge, 7 ff. ; God's, 219 ff. ; His mediate, 224 ff.

Law, the, 76, 522 f., 608 ff. ; Christ's fulfilment of, 451 ff. ; in the Church, 660 f.

Lord's Supper, 638 ff. ; divergent

B. AUTHORS AND SOURCES

C. SCRIPTURE REFERENCES

harper ⚜ torchbooks

(Selected Titles)

I

II